The Economics of Safety and Physical Risk

M. W. JONES-LEE

Basil Blackwell

Copyright © M. W. Jones-Lee 1989

First published 1989

Basil Blackwell Ltd
108 Cowley Road, Oxford, OX4 1JF, UK

Basil Blackwell Inc.
432 Park Avenue South, Suite 1503
New York, NY 10016, USA

British Library Cataloguing in Publication Data

Jones-Lee, M. W. (Michael Whittaker) *1944–*
   The economics of safety and physical risk
   1. Risks
   I. Title
   363.1
   ISBN 0–631–14766–7

Library of Congress Cataloging in Publication Data

Jones-Lee, M. W.
   The economics of safety and physical risk.

   Bibliography: p.
   Includes index.
   1. Risk – Great Britain – Decision making.   2. Safety
   regulations – Great Britain – Decision making.
   3. Safety regulations – Great Britain – Cost effectiveness.
   I. Title.
   HB615.J68   1988   658.4   88–19270
   ISBN 0–631–14766–7

Typeset in 10 on 11 pt Times
by Graphicraft Typesetters Ltd., Hong Kong
Printed in Great Britain by Bookcraft Ltd., Bath, Avon

The Economics of Safety and Physical Risk

Contents

Figures

viii *List of Figures*

Tables

Preface

The past two decades have seen a substantial increase in the general level of concern with matters related to safety and physical risk. The anti-smoking lobby, dietary care, drink-driving campaigns, the nuclear power debate and so on – few of which had much of a profile in the fifties or sixties – are very much part of the public consciousness of the eighties.

One could speculate endlessly about why late twentieth-century man appears to be so much more preoccupied with risk than were earlier generations, but two explanations – both related to advancing medical and technological knowledge – suggest themselves. First, we are now very much more sensitive to our expanding individual and collective capacity for self-inflicted harm. Second, we are increasingly confident that, at a cost, it is within our power to limit the extent of damage from man-made and other causes.

Parallel to this growing awareness of our exposure to, and ability to control, risk there has been a healthy increase in appreciation of the fact that public sector budgets are not limitless and that hard choices must be made in the allocation of scarce resources.

In view of these developing strands of consciousness and concern, it is hardly surprising that during the past 20 years there has been a burgeoning in the literature related to the economics of safety. In part, the purpose of this book is to give an up-to-date account of the various issues that have been addressed in this literature and to provide a summary of the main conclusions that have emerged. This is the primary task of Chapters 1 and 2.

By contrast, Chapters 3 and 4 present new theoretical and empirical results concerning the economics of safety. To a substantial degree, these results are mutually reinforcing and further strengthen the author's conviction that safety is seriously undervalued – and hence *underprovided* – by public sector agencies in the UK and elsewhere.

In parallel with the developments that have occurred in the economic analysis of safety, there have also been significant advances in psychology and decision theory. Not surprisingly, the three disciplines have tended to address rather different aspects of the problem: nonetheless, one can reasonably entertain the expectation that they will, by and large, have produced complementary bodies of analysis. Accordingly, Chapter 5 summarizes the key contributions from psychology and decision theory and explores their relationship with, and implications for, the approach adopted by economists.

Over the years, the author's interest in the economics of safety has resulted in fairly extensive contact with various public sector or related bodies both in the UK and abroad. This has thrown up a number of intriguing problems in applied economics, some of which are discussed in Chapter 6, along with tentative solutions.

Finally, in Chapter 7, the main conclusions of the book are drawn together, speculations are offered concerning some of the key outstanding questions and the outline of an agenda for further research is suggested.

While parts of this book are, of necessity, somewhat technical, I have tried to ensure that the central ideas will be accessible to the intelligent layman. Admittedly, the material in Chapter 3 may, at first glance, appear somewhat daunting to the non-specialist. Nonetheless, the results derived in section 3.4, in particular, turn out to have significant policy implications. Thus, even if the reader is disinclined to follow the logic of the argument in Chapter 3 in finest detail, a brief perusal of its main results will, I believe, prove to be a worthwhile undertaking. Otherwise, a knowledge of ordinary-level mathematics should adequately equip the reader to cope with the bulk of the analysis presented elsewhere in the book.

It is now almost 20 years since my interest in the economics of safety was first stimulated while I was a graduate student at the University of York. Since then I have benefited from the comments and suggestions of many people, particularly colleagues at York, St Andrews and Newcastle. Rather than risk unintended omission, I shall not attempt to draw up a comprehensive list but I am, nonetheless, grateful to all those who have contributed to the development of my thinking on this subject. I also thank my secretary, Suzanne Craft, for the patience and skill that she has shown in typing this and many earlier drafts. Finally, I should say that writing this book has afforded me considerable pleasure: I hope that the reader will be similarly rewarded.

M. W. Jones-Lee
University of Newcastle upon Tyne

1

Safety in Public Sector Decision Making

The terms 'safety' and 'risk' are at the same time commonplace, evocative and somewhat obscure. As a result, it is hardly surprising that each of these terms has come to be used in a variety of subtly different ways, both in everyday language and in more technical discussion.[1] It would therefore seem appropriate to begin by explaining precisely what is to be meant by 'safety' and 'physical risk' in the present context. It is also important to be clear from the outset about the sense in which the argument that follows will attempt to provide an 'economic' analysis of these phenomena.

In this book 'safety' refers exclusively to the safety of human life and constitutes the degree of protection from – or more accurately, attenuation of – physical risk. The latter is, in turn, the extent of an individual's exposure to the possibility or chance of death or injury during a specified period of time. In much of what follows, physical risk will be described in terms of one or another kind of *probability*, in which case safety and physical risk became straightforward obverses of one another in that the former denotes the probability of surviving a forthcoming period (or avoiding a particular kind of injury during it) while the latter is the probability of dying during the period (or incurring the injury).[2]

Turning to the question of how economics comes to feature centrally in a discussion of safety and physical risk, it is essential to appreciate that improved levels of safety can normally be achieved only at the cost of a curtailment in some of the other desirable ways in which a society might make use of its scarce resources. Crudely put, the more a society spends on safety, the less will be available for, say, education, housing and the arts, or, in the last analysis, the manufacture of television sets and the brewing of pints of beer. Given that – other things being equal – most people prefer lower rather than higher levels of exposure to the risk of death or injury, it follows that the individual or social choice of an optimal level of safety in any particular context has a significant *economic* dimension in that it is a decision concerning the appropriate trade-off, or balance, between competing uses of scarce resources.

The following examples help to illustrate the form that this trade-off might take.

1   Research in transport engineering suggests that installation of over-head lighting on all stretches of motorway in the UK could be expected to reduce personal injury accident rates by more than 10%. The resource costs of installing such lighting, however, would be substantial – currently in the region of £20,000 per kilometre on a six-lane dual-carriageway – and would therefore entail a significant reduction in expenditure on some of the other investment projects that might be funded by the transport budget, such as the construction of new ringroads or motorways. To what extent would the installation of overhead lighting be justified?

2   Estimates of the adverse health effects of different doses of ionizing radiation have been derived from studies of various groups exposed to such radiation. Although experts are not in universal agreement about the precise nature of these effects, it appears that, even at very low doses, more exposure to radiation means more risk of contracting cancer or passing on genetic defects. At the same time, additional protective de-vices – designed to reduce or mitigate the effects of radiation – could be installed in nuclear power plants or in diagnostic radiotherapy units, *but at a cost*. Given that this additional cost would ultimately be reflected in, say, higher electricity prices or reduced health service facilities, is the introduction of these additional protective devices warranted?

3   Before the UK Committee on the Safety of Medicines will recom-mend that a new drug may be licensed for general use, it currently requires the drug to be tested on a relatively small sample of patients. While these tests can clearly be expected to detect the more prevalent adverse effects of a new drug, they are much less likely to detect effects that tend to occur only in a small proportion of cases. One way round this problem would be to conduct an extensive 'post-marketing surveillance' of any new drug during the period immediately following its introduction to general use. Such a surveillance, however, would involve considerable cost, a substantial proportion of which would undoubtedly fall upon the National Health Service. Would the increased likelihood of detecting any harmful effects of new drugs justify this additional cost?

4   In many developing countries road accidents have reached alarming proportions during recent years and have become a source of consider-able concern to aid agencies, politicians and transportation planners. There is little doubt that this toll of death, injury and damage could be reduced, but again only at a significant cost to societies that are in some cases already seriously impoverished.

These are just a few of the ways in which countries at all stages of economic development face the economic problem of choosing between safety and other desirable ways of utilizing scarce resources. This book is about such choices. It does not purport to provide clear-cut and unequi-vocal answers to the many difficult questions involved, but is instead an attempt to lay bare and shed light upon the central issues. While the questions considered are in many cases uncomfortable and the way in which they are addressed may seem to some people to be callous and distasteful, it remains the author's firm conviction that they are questions of such importance that a humane society simply cannot afford to set them aside or to leave their resolution to chance.

1.1 Possible Procedures for Taking Account of Safety Effects in Public Sector Allocative Decision Making

In decisions involving risk to human life it is tempting to suppose that one should always be guided by the old maxim, 'safety first'. Matters are not quite so straightforward, however. Certainly, if the risk of death or injury to the children in a primary school could be significantly reduced at the cost of installing one or two fire-resistant doors, then few of us would have much doubt that the cost would be worth incurring. But suppose, instead, that the safety improvement was very small (say a one in a million reduction in the annual risk of death), applied to only a few people (e.g. the half dozen victims of a very rare disease) and would be so costly that, if undertaken, it would preclude or delay the installation of equipment vital to the relief of suffering on the part of many hundreds of people. It is then not at all obvious that the safety improvement should be undertaken.

How might a humane decision maker in the public sector sensibly approach the problem of resource allocation and project appraisal when variations in safety are involved? On the assumption that he has access to reasonably reliable estimates of the safety effects of the various projects under consideration,[3] one can identify six broad avenues of approach that the decision maker might reasonably adopt. In particular, he could:

1 Ignore the estimates on the grounds that safety effects are, for one reason or another, incommensurable with the other costs and benefits of public sector projects.

2 Rely upon informal judgement in weighing safety effects against other costs and benefits.

3 Use safety standards or targets. This would involve the prespecification of 'acceptable' levels of risk in various contexts. Projects that failed to meet the safety standards would be rejected out of hand and those that met the standards would then be accepted or rejected on the basis of their other costs and benefits.

4 Use cost-effectiveness analysis. Basically, cost-effectiveness analysis seeks to maximize the extent of achievement of a given goal or objective (such as safety improvement) within a predetermined budget or, equivalently, to minimize the cost of achieving a particular goal.

5 Define and estimate monetary values of safety improvement and costs of risk so that safety effects can be incorporated directly into

standard procedures of economic appraisal, such as cost–benefit analysis or social welfare maximization.

6   Employ a decision analysis approach. Essentially, this involves the identification of the decision maker's main objectives and priorities and the subsequent estimation of the structure and parameters of a so-called 'multi-attribute utility function' for the decision maker. The primary purpose of this approach is not so much to turn decision making into a formulaic mechanical procedure as to facilitate decisions concerning complex issues by providing the decision maker with an ordered structure and framework within which to assemble and analyse a wide diversity of information.

In subsequent sections, each of these six approaches will be considered and evaluated in greater detail.

1.2   The 'No Analysis' Approach

While it cannot be denied that safety effects are inherently different in kind from many of the other benefits and costs of the typical public sector project, it is also incontrovertibly the case – as noted in the introductory section of this chapter – that safety competes with other desirable goals in the allocation of a society's scarce resources. Given this fact, it is a central contention of the argument developed in this book that safety effects *cannot* be ignored if anything remotely resembling an effective and equitable allocation of resources is to be achieved. It is as true of safety effects as of any of the other potential consequences of public sector projects that if they are ignored in the course of project appraisal then, to the extent that these effects are beneficial, they will tend to be *under*-provided, and, if harmful, *over*-provided. Thus, however awkward and uncomfortable it may be to take account of safety effects, it is essential that some attempt should be made to do so. This assertion would be qualified only if randomness in the allocation of resources was held to be desirable per se, or if the resource cost of analysing safety effects was itself prohibitive in relation to their potential impact.

1.3   Informal Judgement

Prima facie, reliance upon the informal judgement of the project planner or relevant politician in decisions that affect individual safety has much to commend it. Clearly this approach avoids the pitfalls of simply ignoring safety effects while at the same time avoiding the difficult and contentious problems of devising more formal methods of evaluation. In general it has the appeal of civilized circumspection in the face of complex moral issues. This seems to be the kind of consideration John Broome (one of the most vigorous critics of the approach advocated later in this book) had in mind when he wrote:

Table 1.1 Costs and benefits of two mutually exclusive projects

	Capital cost	*Expected reduction in fatalities*	*Other benefits*
Project A	£500,000	2	£550,000
Project B	£500,000	5	£250,000

They [decisions concerning safety] are normally made, like other hard decisions, by a political process. My alternative is to continue in that way and try to improve the process. When the questions are ones that have no unique right answer, as I believe these are, it is the process we must concentrate on, not its conclusion. Above all, we need to keep vividly in the decision-makers' imaginations just what they are deciding about: people's lives. If they come to think they have a neat and correct way to reduce lives to money and lump them in with other goods, then they will be hiding from themselves the real difficulty of their responsibilities. (Broome, 1983b, p. 13)

The most obvious objection to reliance upon informal judgement in the assessment of safety effects is that the process of reasoning that underpins the judgement is typically not open to scrutiny and critical evaluation, so that there is normally no way of detecting and reversing suspect judgements. Furthermore, reliance upon informal judgement will almost certainly lead to inconsistency in the treatment of safety effects both between different decision makers and on the part of a given decision maker in relation to different projects. This problem of inconsistency can best be illustrated by reference to the concept of an 'implicit value of safety', or, more graphically, an 'implicit value of life'. In order to introduce this concept suppose that a decision maker must choose one of two mutually exclusive projects, which for simplicity we take to have identical capital costs but which differ in their anticipated effects upon safety and other benefits. In particular, suppose that costs and benefits are as specified in table 1.1. A decision maker who chooses project A instead of project B reveals an 'implicit value of life' of less than £100,000 in that, by rejecting B in favour of A, he implicitly reveals that he does not regard the additional three lives saved under B as being 'worth' the loss of £300,000 in other benefits relative to A. Conversely, selection of project B would reveal an implicit value of life of *at least* £100,000.

By examining past decisions for and against projects with potential safety effects it is therefore possible to place upper and lower bounds on implicit values of life. Other things being equal, consistency of past decisions requires that these implicit values should have a broadly similar order of magnitude.[4] However, evidence from both the UK and the USA indicates widely divergent implicit values of life from past decisions affecting safety. For example, in the UK implicit values range from less than £1,000 per life (from a decision not to legislate for the child-proofing of drug containers) to more than £20,000,000 per life (from high-rise apartment safety standards). One obvious implication of this sort of inconsistency is that a straightforward transference of resources from high-rise apartment safety to child-proofing of drug containers would, on balance, save lives at no additional resource cost overall. Empirical evidence therefore tends to confirm the a priori expectation that leaving the evaluation of safety effects to informal judgement is likely to lead to inconsistency and consequent inefficiency[5] in the allocation of scarce resources.

While dealing with the concept of implicit values of life and safety, it is also worth remarking that *any* decision for or against a project with potential safety effects necessarily places an upper or lower bound on the relevant implicit value. Thus those who, for whatever reason, object to the idea of placing explicit values on life and safety must nonetheless face the fact that in this sort of decision making some sort of implied valuation is literally unavoidable.

1.4   Safety Standards

Like reliance upon informal judgement, the use of safety standards seems at first sight to be a simple and straightforward way of taking account of effects on physical risk in public sector decision making. Unfortunately, safety standards suffer from two very serious deficiencies. First, their use begs the vitally important question of the criteria by which the standards are to be set in the first place (just how safe is 'safe'?). Second, there is the related problem that rigid adherence to such standards allows no account to be taken of the *cost* of meeting them. Once again this is likely to lead to serious inconsistencies between implicit values of life and safety in different contexts and hence inefficiency in the allocation of scarce resources. To see how, consider the following simple example.[6] Suppose that the government of a small country is reviewing its policy concerning safety on inter-urban public transport. The country's two major cities are linked by parallel train and bus services with annual passenger loadings of 10 million and 5 million passenger-km respectively. Currently, the annual fatality rate for the railway is 1 death per 10^6 passenger-km while that for the bus service is 4 deaths per 10^6 passenger-km. The annualized cost of reducing each of these accident rates to various levels has been estimated to be as in table 1.2.

In the event, the government decides to impose a uniform safety standard of 0.8 fatalities per 10^6 passenger-km on each of the two modes, bringing train fatalities down to 8 p.a. and bus fatalities down to 4 p.a. at an aggregate annualized cost of £1,000,000 (i.e. £40,000 for the railway plus £960,000 for the buses).

If we now consider the value of avoidance of one fatality implied by the situation on the railways, we discover that this must be less than £25,000 because the government is apparently unwilling to spend an additional £25,000 p.a. to reduce the annual railway fatalities from eight to seven. By contrast, the implicit value of avoidance of one fatality on the buses

Table 1.2   The cost of reducing fatalities on two transport modes

Railway route			Bus route		
Fatality rate per 10⁶ pass.-km	*No. of fatalities p.a.*	*Annualized cost (£000)*	*Fatality rate per 10⁶ pass.-km*	*No. of fatalities p.a.*	*Annualized cost (£000)*
1.0	10	—	4.0	20	—
0.9	9	15	3.0	15	80
0.8	8	40	2.0	10	250
0.7	7	65	1.4	7	420
0.6	6	100	1.2	6	600
0.5	5	200	1.0	5	780
0.4	4	400	0.8	4	960
0.3	3	700	0.6	3	1,150

lies between £180,000 (the additional annualized cost of reducing bus fatalities from five to four) and £190,000 (the additional cost of reducing bus fatalities from four to three).

Clearly, then, the imposition of a uniform safety standard involves a serious inconsistency of valuation. Suppose, however, that the government could be persuaded to abandon its uniform safety standard and simply transfer £360,000 of its annual safety budget from buses to trains, thereby effectively equating the implicit value of life on the two modes at approximately £200,000. Certainly, the accident rate on the buses would rise from 0.8 to 1.2 fatalities per 10^6 passenger-km but the train rate would fall from 0.8 to 0.4, implying a reduction in the overall transport fatalities from 12 to 10 p.a.

The government's insistence upon the use of a safety standard and the consequent inconsistency in the implicit value of life can therefore be viewed as effectively costing the country two lives per annum. One objection to this line of reasoning is that equalizing the implicit value of life would result in a situation that was *unfair* to bus passengers in that they would be exposed to a higher fatality rate than users of the railway. However, it is not at all clear that fairness in this context is synonymous with equalization of fatality rates. Given that people are, by and large, free to choose which of the two modes to travel on, it would seem more plausible to argue that fairness requires that, at the margin, the resources devoted to avoiding one fatality should be equalized on the two modes (i.e. that the implicit value of life should be the same for each mode). All things considered, the use of safety standards would therefore seem likely to lead to an allocation of scarce resources that is not only inefficient (in the sense that it does not minimize the number of fatalities for a given overall expenditure on safety) but is also inequitable.

Finally, it seems natural in a section dealing with safety standards to consider the closely related concept of an 'acceptable' level of risk. While

Table 1.3   Costs and benefits of two mutually exclusive projects

	Capital cost (£)	Expected number of serious injuries avoided	Present value of other benefits (£)
Project A	1,000,000	1	999,999
Project B	1,000,000	10	999,980

some writers use the term in a careful and qualified (though I believe potentially misleading) way,[7] others have implied that there will exist levels of risk (or, more accurately, *increments* in risk) that are sufficiently small as not to warrant concern and hence are 'acceptable'. In this sense, acceptability is absolute: increments in risk below a certain level are acceptable; those above are not. But of course if risk is undesirable per se, then no rational individual would willingly accept an increment in risk, however small, unless there were some corresponding benefit. The central question is then how large the offsetting benefit needs to be to compensate for a given increment in risk, so that the whole issue of acceptability of risk becomes equivalent to the kind of approach discussed in section 1.6.

1.5   Cost-effectiveness Analysis

Basically, cost-effectiveness analysis seeks to maximize the extent of achievement of a given beneficial goal within a predetermined budget or, equivalently, to minimize the expenditure required to achieve a prespecified goal. In particular, and in marked contrast with cost–*benefit* analysis, no attempt is made to place a *monetary value* upon the beneficial goal. Clearly, then, this kind of analysis would be appropriate if (a) a decision maker's overall safety budget was predetermined and (b) the sole effect of the various projects under consideration was to improve levels of safety. What cost-effectiveness will *not* do is to give any indication of the appropriate size of the safety budget; nor will it resolve the problem of project selection whenever different projects provide more than one kind of beneficial effect with the mix of benefits differing between projects. In such circumstances one requires some common unit in which to aggregate the various benefits and this is precisely what cost-effectiveness analysis cannot do. As an example of the way in which the latter difficulty might manifest itself, consider a situation in which a budget of £1,000,000 must be expended on one of two mutually exclusive projects, each of which precisely exhausts the budget but which would have the mixes of safety effects and other benefits shown in table 1.3.

Given that the budget is predetermined, it might seem that the appropriate way to proceed is by comparing the *net cost* (capital cost minus other benefits) per serious injury avoided for each of the two projects. For project A this would be £1 while for project B it would be £2. Scheme A would therefore seem to be the more cost-effective. Does this mean that project A should be adopted? Anyone who is tempted to answer in the affirmative should simply note that rejection of project B in favour of A would be tantamount to treating the additional nine serious injuries avoided under B as being not worth the loss of £19 of other benefits – a conclusion that most people would surely find unacceptable.

In fact, it appears that what is required in a decision such as this is some means of aggregating safety effects with other benefits in order to arrive at an overall benefit figure for each project so that a direct comparison can be undertaken. One very obvious and direct way of doing this would be to confront squarely and explicitly the question of how to define and estimate monetary values of safety improvement and costs of increased risk. While it is not surprising that this is the kind of approach that has tended to appeal to economists, it is almost inevitable that in matters as sensitive as life, death and injury there should be no immediately obvious and universally acceptable way of defining and measuring monetary costs and values, so that in consequence a variety of different methods have been proposed. These various approaches to the costing of risk and valuation of safety are described in section 1.6 and the objections that have been raised in connection with them are summarized.

1.6   The Explicit Costing of Risk and Valuation of Safety

The idea that there is no unique, objective measure of cost or value may at first seem strange, especially to anyone accustomed to identifying these concepts with prices in a market economy. However, it is plainly the case that the appropriate definition of the 'cost' or 'value' of anything depends crucially upon the perspective from which cost or value is being assessed. In particular, the appropriate definition of cost or value in any context will ultimately be determined by the *objectives* being pursued by whoever is concerned with the cost or value. Thus, for example, the cost of constructing a factory in a given location may well be one thing to the firm that will own and operate the factory and quite another viewed from the wider perspective of society as a whole, including those who live in the vicinity of the factory and who will be adversely affected by its emission of smoke, noise and other pollutants.

In the case of costs of risk and values of safety, two broad sets of objectives can be identified as underpinning the various costing and valuation procedures that have been proposed, namely national output maximization objectives and social welfare maximization objectives. Roughly speaking, output maximization is concerned exclusively with maximization of one or other index of an economy's overall output and therefore tends to focus upon matters affecting national income accounts, whereas social welfare maximization represents a more circumspect attempt to capture and aggregate all effects upon the well-being of individual members of society, whether or not these effects are reflected in conventional measures of national income. Thus, to put matters somewhat crudely, the value of a safety improvement viewed from the perspective of a decision maker concerned solely with output maximization would reflect only the improvement's tendency to increase current and future levels of output, whereas for someone concerned primarily with social welfare maximization the value would derive principally from the fact that safety improvement reduces the probability of inherently undesirable events such as death or injury, rather than from its tendency to increase output.

1.6.1   Output-based Definitions

The output-based concept that has been most commonly employed in the safety field is the so-called 'gross output' or 'human capital' definition in which the major component of the cost of a fatality is treated as the discounted present value of the victim's future output (or income) extinguished as a result of his or her premature demise. Allowances are typically made for non-marketed output (such as housewives' services) and for various 'direct' economic costs such as damage, medical costs and so on. The value of preventing a fatality is correspondingly treated as the cost avoided. To give an idea of the sort of orders of magnitude that emerge under this definition, for developed economies such costs and values are typically in the region of £100,000–£200,000 in 1987 prices. The obvious objection to this way of defining cost and value in the present context is precisely that it focuses exclusively upon output effects and takes no account of the fact that most people value safety principally for its own sake rather than for its capacity to preserve current and future levels of national output. In short, people value safety mainly because of their aversion to death and injury per se rather than because of their concern to preserve productive resources and maintain future levels of gross national product. In an attempt to meet this criticism some advocates of the gross output approach have recommended the addition of a more or less arbitrary[8] allowance for the 'pain, grief and suffering' of victims and their dependents, relatives and friends. However, the fact that the allowance is effectively arbitrary largely vitiates this attempt to rescue the gross output approach.

A now largely discredited variant of the output-based approach is that in which the discounted present value of the victim's future consumption is subtracted from discounted future output to arrive at a so-called 'net output' figure. The net output approach thus provides a measure of the narrow, purely economic impact of the death or injury of an individual on the rest of society. The objection to the net output approach is, fairly obviously, that it will treat the death of anyone past retirement age as a negative cost (i.e. as a benefit) to the rest of society – a conclusion that is understandably repugnant to the majority of people.

1.6.2 Social Welfare Definitions

Turning to costing and valuation procedures based upon the social welfare maximization objective, two separate but related strands of thought can be identified. Basically, the question is whether one approaches the definition of values of safety and costs of risk from the essentially pragmatic perspective of conventional social cost–benefit analysis or within the somewhat more elegant but arcane context of maximization of a so-called 'social welfare function'. As it happens, the prescriptions of cost–benefit analysis are precisely those that would emerge from maximization of a social welfare function in a particular special case,[9] so that it is no surprise that the two approaches lead to broadly similar conclusions concerning the definition of values of safety and costs of risk.

The underlying prescriptive premise of conventional social cost–benefit analysis is that public sector allocative decisions should reflect, as far as possible, the preferences and wishes of those who will be affected by the decisions. This immediately raises the question of how such preferences and wishes are to be 'measured', for want of a better term. One possibility would be to proceed on the traditional democratic principle of 'one person, one vote'. However, quite apart from the fact that this would be an administratively extremely cumbersome and costly way to settle particular allocative or investment decisions in the public sector, according each person one vote in the allocative decision-making process would fail to take account of differences in people's *strength* of preference for one as opposed to another use of society's scarce resources. Plainly, what is needed is a variant of the 'one person, one vote' principle which will reflect the strength of individual preferences, bearing in mind the constraints imposed by the overall scarcity of resources. To this end, social cost–benefit analysis effectively replaces the question 'Would you vote in favour of undertaking investment scheme X rather than scheme Y?' by the question 'How much would you personally be willing to pay to have scheme X undertaken rather than scheme Y?'. The answer to this question, if truthfully given, will clearly be an indication of the individual's strength of preference for scheme X relative to scheme Y, conditioned by considerations of resource scarcity via his or her income constraint.

The most obvious objection to this procedure is that it replaces the principle of 'one person, one vote' with that of 'one pound, one vote' and, as such, inevitably gives the rich more votes in the allocative decision-making process than the poor. There are, broadly speaking, three ways in which advocates of cost–benefit analysis have responded to this criticism.

1 If one takes the view that income and wealth are optimally distributed, then it is quite appropriate that those with a greater command over resources should have a potentially more significant impact on the way they are allocated.

2 If, by contrast, one takes the view that income and wealth are *not* optimally distributed, then the appropriate way to effect a

redistribution is not by tampering with the results of cost–benefit analysis (by, for example, deflating the willingness to pay of the rich and inflating that of the poor) but, rather, by direct redistributional measures using taxes and transfers.

3   Because redistributional taxes and transfers are politically infeasible, individual willingness to pay should indeed be deflated or inflated using appropriate 'distributional weights' which, for those of more egalitarian persuasion, will clearly tend to be inversely related to income or wealth.

Whichever of these stances is adopted, the important point to appreciate is that the fundamental input to cost–benefit analysis is, in all cases, *individual willingness to pay*. A conventional analysis will simply aggregate this over all affected individuals and treat the result as the total 'benefit' of a project,[10] whereas an analysis with explicit distributional weights will clearly employ a weighted aggregate.

What does all this entail for the valuation of safety and costing of risk? Quite simply, it means that if values of safety and costs of risk are to be used in cost–benefit analysis – whether of the conventional or 'distributionally weighted' variety – then what is required in the first instance is information concerning individual willingness to pay for safety improvement, or requirement of compensation for increased risk. Often, though not always, the variations in safety – whether beneficial or harmful – will be quite small. Though more will be said on this question later, suppose for the time being that these variations in risk can be described in terms of changes in probability. To focus matters, consider changes in the probability of death during a forthcoming period and in addition (though, again, more will be said about this later) suppose that death is a 'homogeneous' event (i.e. at this stage we will not distinguish between various ways of dying). Denoting changes in the probability of death during a forthcoming period for each of n individuals owing to a particular investment project by δp_i ($i = 1, \ldots, n$) and their marginal rates of substitution of wealth for probability of death[11] by m_i ($i = 1, \ldots, n$), the aggregate willingness to pay (or required compensation) V will for δp_i small be well approximated by:[12]

$$V = -\sum_i m_i \delta p_i. \tag{1.1}$$

Now consider the case in which, for all i,

$$\delta p_i = -\frac{1}{n} \tag{1.2}$$

so that in particular $\Sigma_i \delta p_i = -1$.

In this case all individuals are afforded an equal improvement in safety which reduces the expected number of lives lost during the forthcoming period by precisely one. Such a safety improvement is said to involve the avoidance of one 'statistical death' or the saving of one 'statistical life'. Substituting from equation (1.2) into (1.1) it then follows that for the purposes of a conventional cost–benefit analysis the value of saving one statistical life (or, more succinctly, the 'value of statistical life') is given by

$$V = \frac{1}{n}\sum_i m_i \qquad (1.3)$$

i.e. by the arithmetic mean of m_i taken over the affected population.[13]

It might be objected that this argument depends crucially on the condition embodied in (1.2). However, it turns out that it is a straightforward matter to generalize the analysis to accommodate *unequal* variations in individual risk. For example, it follows from the definition of covariance[14] that

$$\text{cov}(m_i, \delta p_i) = \frac{1}{n}\sum_i m_i \delta p_i - \frac{1}{n^2}\sum_i m_i \sum_i \delta p_i. \qquad (1.4)$$

Hence, if we again consider the saving of one statistical life, so that $\Sigma \delta p_i = -1$, though the δp_i are not necessarily equal, then from (1.1) and (1.4)

$$V = \frac{1}{n}\sum_i m_i - n\,\text{cov}(m_i, \delta p_i). \qquad (1.5)$$

Thus, V again depends upon the arithmetic mean of m_i but now also contains a term reflecting the way in which δp_i varies with m_i across the affected population. In fact, it seems likely that for most safety improvements δp_i and m_i will be uncorrelated[15] so that the expression for V simplifies to precisely that given in (1.3).

Having examined the implications of the precepts of conventional social cost–benefit analysis for the definition of values of safety and costs of risk, let us now turn to the closely related but somewhat more general perspective of maximization of a utilitarian social welfare function. A great deal has been written about social welfare functions,[16] but the basic idea is to make 'social' choices (i.e. choices affecting more than one person in society) in such a way as to maximize an index of social welfare, W, where the latter depends only upon the well-being of the individuals that make up society. As such, social welfare maximization is clearly based upon the utilitarian tradition of 'consequentialism', whereby alternative courses of action are judged exclusively by their consequences (rather than by, say, the way that they measure up to other ethical precepts such as the desirability of protecting rights, telling the truth and so on). A further sense in which social welfare maximization is characteristically utilitarian is that consequences are assessed solely in terms of individual well-being or 'welfare' (this has been referred to as 'welfarism' (Sen and Williams, 1982, pp. 3–4)). As well as its inherent consequentialist and welfarist character, social welfare maximization is usually taken to embody three further features. First, it is normally (though not invariably[17]) held that individuals are the best judges of their own well-being so that the individual welfare indices ω_i are identified with one or another real-valued utility representation u_i of individual preferences.[18] In addition, writing $W = f(u_1, u_2, \ldots, u_n)$, it is normally taken that $\partial f/\partial u_i > 0$ $(i = 1, \ldots, n)$.[19] This is often referred to as the 'Paretian' value judgement[20] and is tantamount to the prescription that if one person prefers arrangement A to arrangement B and no-one prefers B to A then A is to be recommended. Finally, it is often, though again not always, assumed that it is appropriate to treat f as linear in individual utilities with, in particular,

$$W = \sum_i a_i u_i \qquad a_i > 0 \; (i = 1, \ldots, n). \tag{1.6}$$

In fact, Harsanyi (1955) has shown that provided individual and social choices under certainty and uncertainty obey a limited number of apparently quite appealing conditions and if (somewhat less plausibly) individual and social probability judgements coincide, then the social welfare function *necessarily* takes the form shown in (1.6) with the u_i being individual cardinal Von Neumann–Morgenstern utilities (Von Neumann and Morgenstern, 1947).

Furthermore, given Harsanyi's postulates, social choices under uncertainty will be taken so as to maximize the mathematical expectation[21] of W, which, given (1.6), is equivalent to maximizing $\Sigma_i a_i \mathrm{E} u_i$ where $\mathrm{E} u_i$ denotes the mathematical expectation of utility for the ith individual.[22]

What, then, would maximization of a social welfare function of the type specified in (1.6) imply for the definition of values of safety and costs of risk? Consider first a highly simplified situation in which individual expected utility can be written as[23]

$$\mathrm{E} u_i = (1 - p_i) u_i(w_i) \tag{1.7}$$

where p_i is the probability of death during the forthcoming period for the ith individual and w_i is his wealth. Suppose in addition that p_i depends upon public expenditure on safety, s, and that this expenditure is financed by individual lump-sum taxes t_i. Choice of an optimal level of s and taxes t_i $(i = 1, \ldots, n)$ can then be written as the following constrained social welfare maximization problem:

$$\max_{s, t_i} \sum_i a_i (1 - p_i) u_i (w_i - t_i) \text{ subject to } s = \sum_i t_i.$$

A little algebraic manipulation of the first-order conditions for a constrained maximum yields the following result:

$$c = \frac{1}{n} \sum_i m_i - nc \, \mathrm{cov}\left(m_i, \frac{\partial p_i}{\partial s}\right) \tag{1.8}$$

where

$$c = -\left(\sum_i \frac{\partial p_i}{\partial s}\right)^{-1}$$

and can therefore be interpreted as the marginal social cost of saving one statistical life and

$$m_i = \frac{u_i}{(1 - p_i)du_i/dw_i}$$

is, as above, the ith individual's marginal rate of substitution of wealth for probability of death in the context of the simplified expected utility model given in (1.7). Thus, to the extent that a social optimum requires that the marginal social cost of saving one statistical life should be equated with the marginal value of doing so, the result given in (1.8) indicates that the value of statistical life, at the margin, is given by

$$V = \frac{1}{n}\sum_i m_i - nc \ \text{cov}\left(m_i, \frac{\partial p_i}{\partial s}\right). \qquad (1.9)$$

Clearly then, in this case constrained social welfare maximization leads to an expression for the value of statistical life that is very similar to that given by the cost–benefit analysis approach and is indeed identical to it if m_i and $\partial p_i/\partial s$ are uncorrelated across individuals.[24]

Bergstrom and Dehez and Drèze have developed similar analyses to that just outlined but with more sophisticated models including insurance, annuities and a bequest motive.[25] In both cases, however, it was implicitly assumed that public expenditure on safety could be financed by lump-sum taxes so that the results derived were, as in (1.8), essentially 'first-best' solutions. In order to get some understanding for what a 'second-best' solution might look like, consider the case in which the social welfare function and individual expected utility are as specified in (1.6) and (1.7) but public expenditure on safety is financed by a proportional tax on wealth so that the constrained social welfare maximization problem becomes

$$\max_{s,t}\sum_i a_i(1-p_i)u_i[w_i(1-t)] \text{ subject to } s = t\sum_i w_i.$$

In this case the first-order conditions for a constrained maximum indicate that, provided that a_iu_i and $\partial p_i/\partial s$ are uncorrelated across individuals, then

$$c = \frac{\overline{a_iu_i}}{\overline{a_ib_i(1-p_i)du_i/dw_i}} \qquad (1.10)$$

where c is, as above, the marginal cost of saving one statistical life, bars denote population means and $b_i = w_i/\bar{w}_i$. Now it will be recalled that, for the expected utility model given in (1.7), the ith individual's marginal rate of substitution of wealth for probability of death, m_i, is given by

$$\frac{u_i}{(1-p_i)du_i/dw_i}.$$

Thus the second-best solution given in (1.10) requires that the value of statistical life be defined, not by the population mean of m_i (as in the first-best case), but rather in terms of the ratio of weighted averages of the numerator and denominator of m_i. For illustrative purposes, consider the highly simplified case in which all individuals have the same utility of wealth function,[26] $u_i(w_i) = w_i^{0.1}$, all individuals face a probability of death during the forthcoming year of 0.001 and the distribution of wealth is such that there are equal numbers of people with levels of wealth, including discounted lifetime labour income, of £50,000, £100,000 and £150,000 respectively. It then turns out that the first-best value of statistical life is £1,001,001 while the second-best value is £1,001,033 with equal distributional weights a_i and £1,001,116 with weights inversely proportional to wealth. This suggests that the distinction between the first- and second-best definitions may not be as significant as might initially have appeared to be the case. If this is so, then it would seem that whether one approaches the problem from the perspective of conventional social cost–benefit analysis or from that of maximizing a utilitarian social welfare function, under a wide range of conditions the value of statistical life is given by the population mean (or possibly by a *weighted* average) of individual marginal rates of substitution of wealth for probability of death. Not surprisingly, this has come to be known as the 'willingness-to-pay' definition. This result should of course be qualified (a) to the extent that people are concerned for others' safety (when it would appear to be necessary to augment the value of statistical life by an appropriate premium to reflect this concern[27]) and (b) to the extent that people have differential degrees of aversion to the prospect of different ways of dying (when it would, strictly speaking, be necessary to distinguish between, say, the value of statistical life for transport risks and the value for risks due to nuclear power generation and so on. Such distinction would not, of course, affect the underlying principles of the argument developed in this section).

Finally, as noted earlier, safety improvements will tend to reduce direct economic costs – such as damage, police and medical costs – as well as losses of net output. To the extent that such effects are not reflected in individual willingness to pay for safety (and there is evidence that they are not – see Chapter 4, section 4.3) then, strictly speaking, an allowance for these effects should be added to the value of statistical life. However, the magnitude of such an allowance will normally be very small indeed by comparison with typical estimates of mean m_i.

1.6.3 Criticisms of the Willingness-to-pay Approach

Let us now turn to some of the criticisms that have been levelled against the willingness-to-pay definition of the value of statistical life.

Some of the most penetrating criticisms of the willingness-to-pay approach have been developed by John Broome in a series of articles and publications (1978a, 1978b, 1982, 1983a, 1983b, 1985). Though Broome's arguments have by no means led to the wholesale rejection of the willingness-to-pay approach (apart from anything else he has so far offered no concrete workable alternative) he has caused at least some advocates of the approach to examine its rationale somewhat more closely than they might otherwise have done and to appreciate its more significant limitations and deficiencies. The following is a summary of Broome's principal objections.

1   The identification of an individual's interests with his preferences and more significantly his *choices* is particularly suspect in the case of decisions affecting the safety of his life. (Many people choose to smoke but is it thereby legitimate to conclude that it is in their best interests to do so?)

2   People may be rather poor judges of the nature and extent of the physical risks that they face, so that again their preferences and choices in relation to such risks may be seriously defective as indicators of what is in their best interests. (How many people have a clear idea of the numerical magnitude of the risk of death from, say, domestic fires and can therefore be regarded as having made rational, fully informed decisions concerning domestic fire prevention and detection?)

3   Even if they have access to identical 'full' information concerning a particular source of physical risk, different people may nonetheless quite legitimately form quite different subjective probability judgements concerning these risks – witness the substantial disagreements between experts concerning the risks associated with nuclear power generation. Such differences will render it virtually impossible for a government to guarantee that it will always take decisions concerning safety that are both democratic (in the sense that the decisions reflect individual preferences and wishes) and consistent (in the sense that they constitute rational decisions in relation to a *given* set of well-formed probability judgements).[28]

4   The definition of the value of statistical life within the context of cost–benefit analysis essentially involves the application of the Kaldor–Hicks hypothetical compensation test[29] to *ex ante* variations in risk. However, in the event, these variations in risk will result in one or another *ex post* outcome involving the saving or loss of a particular number of lives. Broome argues that if compensation tests are to be used at all in this kind of analysis then they should be applied to these various possible *ex post* outcomes rather than to *ex ante* variations in risk. For example, suppose that if a particular project is adopted then 10^6 people will each be exposed to independent incremental risks of death of 10^{-6} during the coming year. Under the willingness-to-pay approach one would ask about the *ex ante* compensation that each individual would require in order to be induced to accept the incremental risk of death. To the extent that the compensation required by each individual was finite then so too would be the aggregate compensation and hence the project might well be recommended if its beneficial effects were sufficiently extensive. Under Broome's proposal one would proceed in a rather different way. One would, in fact, recognize that the actual number of deaths caused by the

project would be given by a Poisson distribution with mean one and then apply the compensation test to each of the $10^6 + 1$ possible *ex post* outcomes – no deaths (with probability approximately 0.3679), one death (with probability approximately 0.3679), two deaths (with probability approximately 0.1839) and so on. However, as Broome notes, the compensation test will then resoundingly reject the project under each of the outcomes involving additional deaths (simply because for most people no sum, however large, could possibly compensate for the certainty of death) regardless of the other possibly highly beneficial consequences of the project.

5 In view of the particular difficulties associated with the compensation test in the context (and indeed because of its more general limitations[30]) Broome has proposed that it may be more appropriate to approach the definition of values of safety and costs of risk from the perspective of maximization of a utilitarian social welfare function. In fact, as already noted, this leads to a definition of the value of statistical life that is very similar, if not identical, to that implied by the compensation test. One might therefore suppose that this would satisfy Broome that the willingness-to-pay approach is ultimately well founded. However, Broome remains sceptical for a variety of reasons. Inter alia, these include a concern that in some cases (as in the second-best analysis considered above) it will be necessary to specify and employ distributional weights and that the conditions on individual preferences and probability judgements required to justify social welfare maximands of the type that lead to results such as (1.8) or (1.10) are somewhat unlikely to be fulfilled in practice.

6 A further aspect of the willingness-to-pay approach that concerns Broome is the proposal by some advocates of the approach[31] to use individual willingness to pay or requirement of compensation, not only as a basis for defining values and costs of variations in safety involving marginal changes in individual risk, but also in the definition of values and costs for 'large' changes in risk. To the extent that individual willingness to pay is an increasing, strictly concave function of the size of the risk reduction (and requirement of compensation a correspondingly increasing, strictly convex function of the size of the increase in risk) then the value of one statistical life will vary with the size of the population at risk. Thus, for example, under the willingness-to-pay approach the cost associated with the exposure of 1,000 people to incremental individual risks of death of 10^{-3} each over the coming year will be larger than the cost associated with exposing 10^6 people to incremental individual risks of 10^{-6} each, in spite of the fact that the expected loss of life is identical in the two cases. Broome considers the even more extreme case in which it is known for certain that one life will be lost, but not whose. Suppose that in option A it is known only that the life will be lost from a group of 1,000 people while under option B it may be any one of 10^6 people. Again, ignoring people's concern for others' safety, the willingness-to-pay approach would associate a higher cost with option A. Broome argues that

if a government were, on these grounds, to favour option B then it would be violating the 'sure thing' principle (and would hence be choosing 'incoherently'[32]) in that it is a sure thing that under either option one life will be lost, so that, setting aside considerations of differential valuations of different people's lives, a coherent government ought to be indifferent between the two options. In short, Broome argues that coherence of government decision making requires that, however the value of statistical life is, in fact, defined, it should be independent of the size of the population at risk (and hence of the magnitude of the variations in individual risk).

7   Broome's most recent objection to the willingness-to-pay approach is that, with the exception of Arthur (1981), all work in this area has ignored the impact of variations in safety on the size and composition of future population. More specifically, variations in a particular person's probability of death will also affect the probability that the person's potential, but as yet unborn, progeny will eventually come into being. Broome argues that any satisfactory procedure for valuing life or safety must recognize and allow for such effects and the willingness-to-pay approach plainly makes no explicit attempt to do so. Broome clearly regards the uncertainty that is, in reality, associated with future population effects as a severely complicating factor. Because of this, he focuses on the stylized problem of comparing two situations that differ in a deterministic way with respect to the size and composition of future population, regarding a satisfactory answer to this problem as a prerequisite for developing an acceptable procedure for dealing with the 'realistic' case. Unfortunately, Broome concludes that recent work by philosophers has failed to provide a satisfactory answer, even to the stylized problem (Parfit, 1984). He is also sceptical of the procedure employed in Arthur (1981) as a means of taking account of population effects.

As far as Broome's worries about the relationship between individual preferences and interests and the quality of individual perceptions of risk are concerned, there can be no doubt that most of us from time to time behave with an indefensible disregard for our own or others' safety and few of us would claim to have a particularly accurate notion of fatality and morbidity rates by various causes. Nonetheless, given adequate information concerning the likely consequences of decisions affecting safety, the majority of people would, I suspect, prefer that such decisions should reflect their own 'true' preferences and attitudes to risk (i.e. the preferences and attitudes that they would arrive at on careful reflection rather than in the heat of a rapidly made and possibly fickle decision). It would therefore seem appropriate to deal with Broome's first two criticisms by requiring that public sector decisions affecting safety should be taken in such a way as to reflect these well-informed and carefully thought out preferences.[33]

The possibility that a difference in subjective probabilities may bring democracy into conflict with consistency in government decision making is both intriguing and not a little disturbing. However, the preconditions for this sort of conflict – illustrated in note 31 – appear to be a marked divergence in subjective probabilities allied to a substantial difference between the way in which competing decisions benefit or harm affected individuals, and such a combination of divergences will almost certainly be the rare exception.

As has already been noted, Broome's objections to the willingness-to-pay approach based upon the limitations of the hypothetical compensation test are, to a large degree, answered by analyses such as those developed in Bergstrom (1982) and Dehez and Drèze (1982) which show that very similar results are obtained by constrained maximization of a social welfare function. Certainly, one encounters problems over the specification of distributional weights and divergences in subjective perceptions of risk, but the former problem is not special to the analysis of risk and the latter is probably best dealt with along the lines proposed in relation to poorly informed preferences.

Broome's next objection to the willingness-to-pay approach, namely that its use in the analysis of safety effects involving non-marginal changes in individual risk may result in violation of the 'sure thing' principle, is one of the most worrying and – like the potential impact of a difference in subjective probabilities discussed above – serves the very valuable function of highlighting what is probably the most fundamental difference between Broome and advocates of the willingness-to-pay approach. In particular, it is clear that under certain circumstances the dictates of coherence and consistency in government decision making will inevitably conflict with considerations of democracy (widely construed to include a requirement that government decisions should take account of individual wishes and attitudes to risk). In such conflicts, Broome appears to favour coherence whereas for advocates of the willingness-to-pay approach democracy is of primary importance. However, it should be noted that the conditions which generate this sort of conflict in the case of non-marginal changes in risk are rather special, involving as they do the *certain* saving or loss of as yet unidentified life. Thus, as with the potential problem associated with divergent subjective probabilities, one suspects that this difficulty will only rarely be encountered.

The argument that the willingness-to-pay approach largely fails to take account of effects on the size and composition of future population applies, it seems, not only to decisions affecting the safety of life, but also to virtually all individual and social choices. For example, Dr X's decision to move from York to Newcastle will almost certainly affect how his children will be educated, what careers they will pursue, whom they will meet and marry and hence who will and will not exist in a hundred years' time. Similarly, the present British Government's education policy plainly affects who does and does not enter higher education, hence who meets and marries whom and so who will and will not exist in the year 2588. To take a more extreme example – and with due deference to historians who may have a more accurate record of the true course of events – it is entirely possible that Christopher Columbus's mother met his father as a result of her decision to buy a loaf of bread at the local baker's shop, thereby unwittingly affecting the entire course of human history. Were Dr X, the British Government and (the future) Mrs Columbus all wrong to ignore the further-flung potential consequences of their decisions, as I am sure they all did? I very much doubt it. I think that, if confronted with 'Broome's dilemma' at the time of their respective decisions, they would all have argued that they had no more reason for supposing that the more remote and further-flung consequences of their decisions would be beneficial than that they would be harmful, so that the best they could do was to *ignore* such effects. The long and short of all this is that, far from simplifying the problem by abstracting from uncertainty, Broome massively adds to its difficulty by supposing that one might know the inherently unknowable and thereby finds himself stuck, as it were, without a reverse gear at the end of a blind-alley.

In addition to the points made by Broome, a number of other objections have been raised against the willingness-to-pay approach. Representative of these are the contributions of Zeckhauser (1975), Atiyah (1982), Keeney (1982), Linnerooth (1982) and Fischer (1979). While Zeckhauser does not argue for the wholesale rejection of the willingness-to-pay approach, he does advocate care and circumspection in its use and suggests that it be viewed as just one of possibly many aids to social decision making in the area of physical risk. In particular, Zeckhauser argues that individual willingness to pay for improved survival probability cannot be regarded as the definitive determinant of policy choices for a variety of reasons. In the first place, even if aggregate willingness to pay for a safety improvement exceeds the cost of effecting the improvement, it may nonetheless be impossible to arrange a structure of taxes and transfers such that everyone gains. A related point concerns the *process* by which such decisions are made. Zeckhauser argues that the way in which government decisions concerning safety are actually made may be every bit as important to affected individuals as the numerical magnitude of the money–risk trade-offs involved in the decisions. Other difficulties perceived by Zeckhauser include the effects of anxiety, the manner in which the interests of future generations are to be weighed in decisions having long-term effects on safety and the pervasive problem of how to take account of inequalities in the distribution of income.

Atiyah views the problem from an essentially legal perspective. His first objection to the willingness-to-pay approach is less one of principle than of practice and concerns the very high estimates of the value of statistical life produced by some recent studies.[34] In particular, Atiyah argues that unless court awards in cases involving death or injury are set at levels comparable with values of statistical life used in public sector allocative decisions then serious inconsistencies may emerge between private and public sector safety standards especially if, as seems probable, private sector safety decisions are influenced by the magnitude of prospective court awards in cases of alleged negligence. Atiyah seriously doubts the equity and feasibility, at least in the UK context, of setting court awards at the levels of the value of statistical life implied by some willingness-to-pay studies.

A second point that concerns Atiyah is the extent to which individuals may legitimately be supposed to have taken account of potential legal compensation for the negligence of others in making decisions concerning risky activities or, indeed, to have made such decisions in anything like a well-informed and reasoned manner.

Keeney's objections to the willingness-to-pay approach arise from the difficulty of obtaining reliable empirical estimates and from his view (similar to that expressed by Zeckhauser) that individual willingness to pay for safety – conditioned as it is by the funds available to the individual at risk – may have little relevance for the decision making of a public sector body whose budget constraint need bear little relation to the wealth of individuals who are affected by its decisions. In consequence, Keeney proposes that the problem be viewed, not from the perspective of affected individuals, but directly from that of decision makers within the public sector body concerned. To this end, Keeney proposes the use of a multi-attribute 'organizational utility function' as a means of summarizing the value judgements of the relevant decision makers. The nature and properties of such a function are explored briefly in section 1.7 and at greater length in Chapter 5.

Linnerooth's criticisms of the willingness-to-pay approach focus upon a variant of the ubiquitous problem of trading off equity and efficiency in public sector allocative decisions. If, as theory predicts (and empirical evidence confirms), willingness to pay is an increasing, strictly concave function of incremental survival probability (and, by corollary, required compensation an increasing, strictly convex function of incremental physical risk) then, as noted above, under the willingness-to-pay approach the cost (aggregate required compensation) of exposing a small number of people to relatively large incremental individual risks of death will exceed the cost of exposing a larger number of people to smaller risks even when expected lives lost are identical in both cases. It follows that it would be perfectly possibly for scheme A – involving large incremental risks for a few people – to be regarded as worse than scheme B – involving smaller increments for more people – in spite of the fact that the expected number of lives lost under A was fewer than that under B. In this case 'efficiency' (minimizing the expected number of lives lost) would be sacrificed in favour of 'equity' (avoiding large incremental risks for a few people) though it should be stressed that this concept of efficiency is somewhat narrower than that of economic (or 'Paretian') efficiency.[35]

A related, but not identical, problem that concerns Linnerooth arises from the influence of the existing level of an individual's survival probability on his willingness to pay. As shown by Jones-Lee (1976) and Dehez and Drèze (1982), under certain circumstances m_i will be larger the higher an individual's current exposure to physical risk. This is essentially because willingness to pay varies inversely with marginal expected lifetime utility of wealth and the latter is in turn an increasing function of survival probability. The most extreme example of this kind of phenomenon is the person who has been diagnosed as terminally ill and is, in consequence, willing to spend very large sums on possible cures with very low probabilities of success.

Thus, if social decisions concerning safety expenditure are based upon individual willingness to pay, then there will be a tendency for resources to be directed towards safety improvements for people currently facing high levels of physical risk, *at the expense of expected lives saved overall*, so that the willingness-to-pay approach again tends to favour equity in the trade-off with efficiency. While Linnerooth expresses some sympathy for pursuit of the equity objective per se, she doubts the appropriateness of allowing the trade-off between equity and efficiency to be resolved by considerations of individual willingness to pay alone.

Finally, while not objecting to the conceptual basis of the willingness-to-pay approach, Fischer expresses serious doubts about the reliability of empirical estimates of individual willingness to pay for risk reduction. Fischer's reservations derive principally from various empirical findings in cognitive psychology, the most significant of which are (a) that under certain circumstances people experience difficulty with, and mishandle, probability concepts (see, for example, Kahneman *et al.*, 1982) especially with small probabilities and (b) that people's capacity for storing the information needed to make 'rational' choices in complex decision problems is strictly limited (see Miller, 1956). Fischer argues that, in view of these problems, any attempt to obtain reliable empirical estimates of willingness to pay for risk reduction is almost certainly doomed to failure, especially when the probabilities concerned are very small, as is usually the case.

While accepting that the psychological evidence referred to does give some cause for concern, especially in relation to attempts to estimate marginal rates of substitution from actual choices, in the author's view this evidence is far less worrying in the case of estimation based on *hypothetical* choices – such as those described in Chapter 4 – particularly if the choices and probabilities concerned are carefully and clearly explained.

1.6.4   *Other Approaches to the Explicit Costing of Risk and Valuation of Safety*

In addition to the explicit costing and valuation procedures so far considered, at least four other methods have been proposed for defining and estimating costs of risk and values of safety. While each of the proposed methods has a superficial appeal, it transpires on closer examination that all are seriously deficient whether viewed from the narrow perspective of national output maximization or in the wider context of maximization of social welfare. The four methods are as follows:

1   The 'life insurance' method, in which the cost of death or injury (and the value of their avoidance) is directly related to the sums for which people typically insure their lives or limbs.

2   The 'court award' method, in which the sums awarded by the courts in damages for death or injury are treated either as indicative of an individual's loss of future output[36] or as some more nebulous reflection of the cost that society associates with death or injury.[37]

3   The 'implicit public sector valuation' method, in which the values of life and safety implicitly reflected in *past* public sector decisions (as discussed in section 1.3) are treated as indicative of the appropriate level at which to set explicit costs and values for *future* decisions.

4   The 'valuation of life in terms of value of time' method, in which the value of remaining life expectancy for an individual is defined as the aggregate value of time for the individual over his remaining life expectancy.

As a means of approximating a 'gross output' value of safety or cost of risk (appropriate to the national output maximization objective) the life insurance method would be satisfactory only if people tended to hold life insurance in an amount that fully covered their human capital or held injury insurance in an amount that would reflect the output loss due to injury. This seems highly improbable to say the least. In fact, it seems altogether more likely that those who hold life insurance will do so in such a way as to cover the expected financial requirements of their dependants so that if such cover is an approximation to anything it is 'net' rather than 'gross' output. Having said this, it must be admitted that in the case of injury insurance it is conceivable that the typical cover might give a rough indication of anticipated gross output losses. However, by no stretch of the imagination could any kind of insurance cover be held to reflect an individual's willingness to pay for his own safety or that of those he cares for (which, it will be recalled, is the appropriate basis for defining costs and values relevant to the social welfare maximization objective). Individuals who place very high values on their own safety might quite rationally hold no life insurance whatsoever (e.g. the bachelor with no relatives or dependants). Equally, people who place little or no value on their own continued survival, per se, may hold quite large amounts of life insurance (e.g. the potential suicide who is nonetheless concerned to ensure the continued financial well-being of his family and dependants). All in all then, the sums for which people typically insure their lives or limbs would seem to give little if any guide to the appropriate level at which to set the gross output or willingness-to-pay based costs of risk or values of safety. Nor, for that matter, do they appear to be relevant to any other conceivably sensible way of defining such costs and values.

Turning to court awards, the position is somewhat more complicated.

Essentially, the potential relevance of court awards for the estimation of either output- or social-welfare-based costs of risk and values of safety depends upon the underlying legal principles that can be held to determine whether or not a particular plaintiff is entitled to damages in any given case and, if so, in what amount. As Atiyah points out:

> most lawyers see the primary function of awards of damages for injury and fatal accidents, as compensatory alone. Indeed, in the UK it has for many years been emphatically stated by judges that the functions of the civil law are not penal or deterrent. English judges do not seem to regard damage awards as incentives to greater safety, perhaps partly because the great majority of damage awards are paid for by insurance companies, and English lawyers are sceptical of the extent to which the incentive effect of the law still operates when this is the case. In other countries it may be that the courts do not adopt quite the same extreme posture that English judges do. Even in other commonwealth countries (which usually follow English legal traditions) it would, I think, be found that there is a greater willingness to believe that damage awards have a minor or subsidiary role as deterrents, and this is certainly true also of the US. But even in these countries no lawyers would doubt that the primary purpose of damage awards is compensatory. (Atiyah, 1982, p. 188)

Given this state of affairs, the central question therefore concerns the way in which the courts in different countries construe the term 'compensation'. In fact, interpretations appear to vary quite widely. In the case of fatal injuries, for example, in the UK the dependants of the deceased can expect to recover damages for wrongful death only in an amount reflecting their share of the income that the deceased would have earned had he or she survived, and not for any 'subjective' losses such as grief and suffering. In the USA, by contrast, compensating awards for subjective losses to surviving dependants can be very large indeed. For non-fatal injuries, however, the English courts *will* make awards for subjective losses but only to the injured party and again in an amount typically substantially less than in comparable cases in the USA.

As in the case of life insurance, it would therefore seem that, in the UK at least, court awards for wrongful death might give some indication of the appropriate level of 'net output' based costs and values but are essentially irrelevant to the gross output or willingness-to-pay definitions. For non-fatal injuries in the UK, and in all cases in the USA, the presence of apparently more or less arbitrary awards for 'subjective' losses, varying substantially in magnitude between the two countries, renders the relevance of such awards to any definition of cost or value essentially undecidable. Only if one argues (as indeed some have[38]), that such awards are a true reflection of the cost that 'society' associates with death or injury would there seem to be any justification for treating the awards as indicative of the appropriate level at which to set costs of risk or values of safety. Such an argument seems somewhat tenuous, to say the least.

The objection to the 'implicit public sector valuation approach' is fairly obvious. Quite apart from the huge variation in implicit public sector values already noted,[39] it is clearly no answer to the question 'How ought public sector bodies to define and measure costs of risk and values of safety in future allocative decisions?' to advocate that one should simply employ the costs and values implicit in past decisions. In fact, such a procedure would be legitimate only if one were convinced that past decisions had been based on appropriately defined costs and values, and few of us would, one suspects, carry such a conviction, especially in view of the wide disparities evident in implicit public sector values.

The valuation of life in terms of value of time method can similarly be disposed of fairly briefly. Values of leisure time, for example, are essentially *relative* valuations – willingness to pay to do as one pleases with a marginal hour of time rather than spend it travelling on a bus or a train or whatever. Multiplying such a value by remaining hours of life expectancy therefore gives no indication whatsoever of either an individual's gross output or his marginal rate of substitution of wealth for physical risk. Indeed, to the extent that a value of leisure time is a marginal value, it is rather hard to imagine what interpretation to give to its product with remaining life expectancy – it could hardly be construed as an individual's willingness to pay to do as he pleases for the rest of his life rather than spend it travelling! Turning to values of working time, these are usually based upon gross of tax wages rates and can therefore be viewed as indicative of an individual's marginal productivity. Multiplying such a value by the remaining expectation of *working* hours would therefore give an approximation[40] to an individual's gross output. However, multiplying by remaining life expectancy would clearly substantially overestimate gross output and would certainly give no indication whatsoever of an individual's willingness to pay for safety.

1.7 The Decision Analysis Approach

The decision analysis approach to the evaluation of projects that have expected effects on the safety of life has been most fully developed in a sequence of papers by Keeney (1980a, 1980b, 1982). While the approach will be discussed in some detail in Chapter 5, it seems appropriate at this stage to provide a brief summary of its main features. Basically, the idea is first to identify the key consequences of potential accidents or disasters (e.g. number of lives lost, number of non-fatal injuries, percentage reduction in gross national product etc.) and then to define a Von Neumann–Morgenstern utility function whose arguments are the relevant consequences. This multi-attribute 'organizational' utility function is construed as being essentially that of the relevant decision maker (or decision-making group) and therefore ultimately reflects the value judgements of the decision maker concerning trade-offs between different consequences and choices between different probability distributions of particular consequences.[41] In the second and third papers Keeney's primary purpose is to demonstrate the inherent incompatibility of three fundamental value judgements that most people would probably wish the organizational utility function to reflect, namely (a) the desirability of minimizing expected loss of life, (b) the desirability of an equitable distribution of risk of loss of life amongst members of the population and (c) the desirability of avoiding catastrophes (i.e. the loss of large numbers of lives). Keeney shows that the first value judgement entails linearity of the utility function in number of lives lost, the second strict convexity and the third strict concavity – plainly mutually incompatible requirements. In his first paper the objective is more closely oriented to outlining a procedure by which the organizational utility function could, in principle, actually be estimated for a particular decision maker.

Taken at face value, Keeney's organizational utility function would seem to represent a potentially effective alternative to the estimation and use of explicit costs of accidents and values of accident prevention. Certainly its use would avoid the problems of inconsistency and inefficiency that beset some of the other approaches to the evaluation of preventive measures. Unfortunately this approach suffers from certain essentially practical limitations. In the first place it seems rather unlikely that the majority of decision makers would be willing to conduct the kind of thought experiments that are required in order to estimate parameters of the utility function (or at least would be unwilling to regard the results of such experiments as a conclusive and immutable representation of their views on safety etc.). Second, even if the estimation problem could be overcome, it seems improbable that decision makers would then be willing to allow decisions to be determined solely with reference to the mathematical expectation of the estimated utility function, effectively relinquishing their active decision-making role. Thirdly, there is nothing inherent in Keeney's approach that suggests to the decision maker how or by what criteria he *ought* to trade off life savings against other consequences such as avoidance of material damage etc., though he certainly has to make up his mind about such trade-offs before the organizational utility function can be estimated. In other words Keeney's approach begs precisely the question that lies at the heart of the explicit costing and valuation approach and simply returns the question unanswered (and indeed unilluminated) to the decision maker.[42]

Nonetheless, the decision analysis approach does have certain advantages as an aid to organizing thought about explicit costs of accidents and values of accident prevention, especially when one is dealing with the possible loss of large numbers of lives. An aspect of Keeney's analysis that is particularly useful in this respect is his concept of a 'disutility (strictly, the *negative* utility) of lives lost function' (see especially Keeney, 1980a) and his demonstration that the 'shape' of such a function (specifically, its linearity, concavity or convexity) has direct implications for the *relative* evaluation of loss of 'statistical' life (the exposure of a number of individuals to independent risks of death), the loss of 'anonymous' life (the certain loss of life of as yet unidentified individuals) and 'catastrophes' (typically, low probabilities of the loss of large numbers of lives). For example, suppose that the cost of the loss of one statistical life – say the exposure of 10^4 people to independent incremental probabilities of death of 10^{-4} each – has been estimated on a willingness-to-pay basis. Will it then be appropriate to treat the incremental probability of 10^{-4} of a catastrophe involving the loss of 10^4 lives as having the same cost? (Notice that both cases involve identical *expected* loss of life, i.e. *one*.) It turns out that the matter can be unambiguously resolved by reference to the form of Keeney's disutility of lives lost function. In fact, only if this function is linear will it be appropriate to treat the catastrophe risk as equivalent to the loss of one statistical life: if the function is decreasing and concave then the cost of the catastrophe risk will be larger and if the function is decreasing and convex it will be smaller. Furthermore, if the disutility of lives lost function is fully specified then it would be possible to determine the number of lives lost, 10^x, such that the incremental probability 10^{-4} of a catastrophe involving 10^x deaths would generate precisely the same expected disutility (for the decision maker) as the exposure of 10^4 people to independent incremental risks of death of 10^{-4} each. Specifically, denoting the disutility of the loss of i lives by $u(i)$, x would be given by the solution to

$$10^{-4}u(10^x) + (1 - 10^{-4})u(0) = \sum_{i=0}^{n} \binom{10^4}{i} 10^{-4i}(1 - 10^{-4})^{10^4 - i}u(i) \quad (1.11)$$

where $\binom{10^4}{i}$ denotes the number of different ways of selecting i people from 10^4 people.

It then follows that a catastrophe involving an expected loss of life equal to 10^{x-4} should be accorded precisely the same cost as the loss of one statistical life. The cost of a catastrophe involving an expected loss of life equal to one will therefore be given by approximately[43] 10^{4-x} *multiplied by* the cost of the loss of one statistical life.

It must be conceded that the argument just developed conflates the willingness-to-pay and decision analysis approaches and as such runs the risk of embodying conflicting and contradictory premises. However, this would be so only if individuals themselves took a distinctly different view from that of the decision maker concerning the relative undesirability of the loss of statistical life and the catastrophe risk. The underlying logic of the willingness-to-pay approach would then require that the cost of the catastrophe risk should reflect individuals' attitudes, whereas the decision analysis approach would focus upon the views of the decision maker. Nonetheless, it does seem possible that while individuals may find it relatively straightforward to think about their willingness to pay for their own safety and that of those they care for, they may also find it rather difficult to arrive at a clear conclusion concerning their relative aversion to the loss of statistical life and catastrophe risks and hence would prefer to leave such decisions to the political process. Under such circumstances the approach outlined above would appear to be logically consistent.

Finally, it should be noted that there is a certain similarity between Keeney's approach and the *ex post* approach to decisions involving risk advocated by John Broome. This is because under Keeney's approach the decision maker is required to associate a disutility with each possible adverse *ex post* outcome of a project (e.g. number of lives lost) and then to rank projects on the basis of the mathematical expectation of disutility. This has much in common with Broome's approach which requires that the decision maker should recognize that the exposure of 10^n people to independent incremental risks of 10^{-n} each will, in fact, involve $10^n + 1$ possible *ex post* outcomes and that each of these outcomes should be evaluated separately by the decision maker.

1.8 Summary and Concluding Comments

In this chapter it has been argued that many public sector decisions will require the selection of an appropriate trade-off or balance between individual safety and other desirable uses of scarce resources. In short, safety is generally not a 'free good' and the choice of an optimal level of safety in any context will typically involve a significant economic dimension. It follows that unless public sector decisions that affect safety are to be taken in a purely random and haphazard way, then it will be necessary to devise procedures by which estimated safety effects can be evaluated explicitly and systematically in the public sector decision-making process.

Six broad avenues of approach to such decisions have been identified. Of these approaches, four (namely, ignoring safety effects, relying upon informal judgement, using safety standards and using cost-effectiveness analysis) have each been shown to suffer from serious limitations that essentially derive from the failure of these approaches to provide a means of explicitly weighing safety effects against the other beneficial and harmful consequences of decisions. By contrast, the final two approaches considered in this chapter (the explicit costing of risk and valuation of safety and the decision analysis approach) do permit safety to be traded off directly against other beneficial and harmful effects.

In spite of the well-worn jest concerning economists' inability to reach accord on any topic related to their subject, it is perhaps somewhat surprising to the layman that there is not universal agreement amongst economists concerning the appropriate way in which to define costs of risk and values of safety. Of the various different definitions that have been proposed, only two appear to be capable of surviving serious scrutiny. These are the gross output and willingness-to-pay definitions. The gross output definition, under which costs of risk and values of safety are directly related to the losses of the future output of those who are killed or injured, would appear to be appropriate if the sole objective of public sector allocative decision making is the maintenance of current and future levels of gross national product. If, as seems more likely in a humane and civilized society, public sector decision makers are concerned with a somewhat wider conception of individual well-being and welfare, then it would seem appropriate to approach the definition of costs of risks and values of safety from the perspective of maximization of a social welfare function (basically, a device for aggregating indices of individual welfare) or on the basis of the related precepts of conventional social cost–benefit analysis. Under either approach one arrives at one or another version of the so-called willingness-to-pay definition in which the value of safety is intimately dependent upon individual marginal rates of substitution of wealth for physical risk.

In contrast with the willingness-to-pay approach, which is essentially an attempt to base costs of risk and values of safety on individual preferences, Keeney's decision analysis approach represents an attempt to identify explicitly the preferences and wishes of the relevant *decision maker*. As such, it does not tell the decision maker *how* to trade off safety against other benefits and costs but is rather intended as a structured framework of analysis which will assist the decision maker in identifying issues and thinking about them in an ordered and systematic way.

It has also been argued that as a means of bridging the gap between costs of risk and values of safety for situations in which fatalities, if they occur, will be few in number and corresponding costs and values for potential catastrophes involving the possible loss of large numbers of lives, a hybrid of the willingness-to-pay and decision analysis approaches may offer a possible solution. In particular it has been shown that, appropriately juxtaposed, the two approaches will permit the expression of the cost of a catastrophe risk involving the loss of 10^n lives with probability 10^{-n} as a multiple or fraction of the cost of exposing 10^n people to independent incremental risks of death of 10^{-n} each.

Lest the reader be left in any doubt on the matter, it is the author's firm conviction that for the kind of variations in risk most commonly encountered in public sector allocative decisions (typically involving small, effectively independent, changes in the probability of death or injury) the explicit costing of risk and valuation of safety, with costs and values defined according to the willingness-to-pay approach, offers by far the most promising line of attack. To be sure, Broome and others have exposed limitations and weaknesses in the approach but, again in the author's opinion, these are not fatal. Finally, although the decision analysis approach can hardly be regarded as a practically workable alternative to the willingness-to-pay approach, it does in principle provide a way of supplementing the latter so as to provide costs of risks and values of safety for the less common but nonetheless important and emotive case of catastrophe risks.

Notes

1 For example, in the physical context economists and decision theorists tend to treat 'risk' as being synonymous with the *probability* of an undesirable event, such as death or injury (see, for example, Schelling, 1968; Mishan, 1971; Jones-Lee, 1976; Blomquist, 1982; Keeney, 1982; and Broome, 1985). This also appears to be the sense in which the term is used by natural scientists and engineers in assessing the dangers of nuclear power generation and toxic chemicals (see Warner, 1981; International Commission on Radiological Protection, 1983, p. 3; and The Royal Society, 1983). By contrast, in the purely financial context, economists use the term 'risk' to describe the 'spread' of a probability distribution of gains and losses. Thus, for example, a situation in which one might gain or lose £10 with equal probabilities of 0.5 is described as being riskier than one in which one might gain or lose £5 with the same probabilities (see, for example, Tobin, 1958; or Machina, 1983). Psychologists, in turn, are inclined to view risk as a multidimensional concept having a variety of characteristics such as the extent to which risk is voluntary, controllable, known to science and so on (see, for example, Slovic *et al.*, 1981). Other uses of the term 'risk' include '. . . the expected number of lives lost, persons injured, damage to property and disruption of economic activity due to a particular natural phenomenon . . .' (Office of the United Nations Disaster Relief Coordinator, UNDRO, 1980). Finally, the public appears to use a variety of interpretations of the term (see Prescott-Clarke and Mostyn, 1982, pp. 9–10).

2 In some contexts it will be important to distinguish between the probabilities of death by different causes.

3 It must be conceded that this assumption begs a number of very difficult questions. Thus, while the safety effects associated with some kinds of activity can be fairly confidently predicted, there are many circumstances in which this is not the case. For example, there is considerable controversy concerning the health effects of low doses of ionizing radiation. However, the prediction of safety effects is essentially a matter for natural scientists, technologists and medical experts and clearly lies outside the scope of a book such as this. For a useful summary of some of the issues involved, see Warner (1981).

4 However, one can imagine exceptional circumstances – involving considerations overriding efficiency and consistency – that would warrant higher than average implicit values. For a discussion of such possibilities, see Linnerooth (1982).

5 An allocation of resources is said to be 'economically inefficient' if it would be possible, through some alternative allocation, to increase the extent of achievement of some desirable goal without detracting from that of any other.

6 This is a slightly modified version of an example given in Hills and Jones-Lee (1983).

7 For example, Fischoff *et al.* (1981) stress that the 'acceptability' of a risk is a relative rather than absolute concept and depends upon a careful weighing of the risks, costs and benefits of different options. However, even such qualified uses of the term remain potentially misleading in that they are so easily commuted by the casual reader into the naive use discussed below.

8 For example, the UK Department of Transport adds an allowance which was originally equal to the discounted present value of future consumption of an average (non-productive, e.g. retired) person, this being, it was argued, the

amount that society devotes to maintaining such people and is hence a reflection of the minimum value placed on their continued survival. This allowance was subjected to an essentially arbitrary increase of 50% following the report of the Leitch Committee (see Leitch, 1977) and represents about 28% of the Department of Transport's 1986 overall cost of a fatality.

9 In particular, that in which the marginal social utility of income is treated as being identical for all individuals.

10 Use of conventional cost–benefit analysis is therefore tantamount to application of the Kaldor–Hicks 'hypothetical compensation test' which effectively prescribes that if those who gain by adoption of a project do so to a sufficient degree to be able, if required, to compensate those who lose, then the project should be undertaken. Clearly if aggregate willingness to pay (the 'benefits' of the project) exceeds aggregate required compensation (the 'costs') then, *a fortiori*, the project passes the hypothetical compensation test. For a more detailed discussion of the hypothetical compensation test, see Sugden (1981), Chapter 7.

11 That is, the modulus (or absolute magnitude) of the rate at which the individual is willing to trade off wealth against probability of death, at the margin. Thus if an individual would be willing to pay £10 for a 10^{-5} reduction in probability then his marginal rate of substitution is (approximately) £10/10^{-5}, i.e. £1,000,000. This marginal rate of substitution will be given a more precise formal definition in later chapters. Notice also that the probabilities with which we are dealing here are essentially *subjective*, i.e. they are reflections of the individual's own perception of the risk that he or she faces. This has important implications for the empirical estimation of marginal rates of substitution – see Chapters 2 and 4.

12 Notice that in the case of a safety improvement δp_i will be *negative*, while for an increase in risk it will be positive. The minus sign in (1.1) therefore reflects the convention of treating willingness to pay for a safety improvement as positive and required compensation for an increase in risk as negative.

13 For simplicity, this argument has taken account only of individuals' concern for their own safety. If, as is almost certainly the case, most people are also concerned about, and hence willing to pay for, others' safety, then it will be necessary to augment the value of statistical life to reflect this additional willingness to pay. For a further discussion of this point see Chapter 2, sections 2.1.7 and 2.2.5. A further refinement of the argument would also take account of the 'direct' losses to the rest of society avoided by the saving of one statistical life (e.g. avoided police and medical costs and material damage as well as losses of net output). However, in numerical terms these are typically very small in relation to most empirical estimates of the mean of m_i.

14 Taken over n paired observations of x_i and y_i, the covariance of x_i and y_i, written $cov(x_i, y_i)$, is defined as

$$cov(x_i, y_i) \equiv \frac{1}{n} \sum_i \left(x_i - \frac{1}{n} \sum_i x_i \right) \left(y_i - \frac{1}{n} \sum_i y_i \right).$$

Thus the sign and size of covariance clearly reflects the extent to which x_i tends to be large when y_i is large and vice versa (although it should be noted that the size of covariance also depends upon the inherent variability of x_i and y_i).

15 The reason for this is quite simply that, whereas m_i is a reflection of an individual's preferences and attitudes, δp_i depends upon the nature of a

particular public sector investment or legislative decision so that *prima facie* there seems to be no reason why m_i and δp_i should be systematically related across individuals. However, it must be conceded that such a relationship is possible. Suppose, for example, that people with large values of m_i are inherently more cautious and therefore tend to experience smaller reductions in p_i as a result of road safety improvements (someone who would be inclined to slow down to 30 mph to take a dangerous bend will tend to enjoy a smaller reduction in risk if the bend is smoothed or eliminated than a more reckless person who would normally take it at 60 mph). Under such circumstances we would have $\text{cov}(m_i, \delta p_i) > 0$ – recall that $\delta p_i < 0$ for risk reductions – and V would hence be smaller than in the uncorrelated case. For a discussion of the possible magnitude of this sort of effect, see Chapter 4, note 27.

16 See, for example, Bergson (1938), Samuelson (1947) and Harsanyi (1955).

17 Obvious exceptions are cases of drug abuse and reckless, delinquent or criminal behaviour (though as an aside it is worth noting that the concepts of 'abuse', 'recklessness', 'delinquency' and 'criminality' may not be capable of satisfactory definition independently of the notion of individual 'well-being').

18 Essentially, a 'representation' is a means of conveying information about (or 'measuring') preferences. The weakest such representation, *ordinal* utility, conveys information only about the preference *ordering*, in that more preferred options are accorded higher numbers by the representation. More formally, such a representation is an isomorphism between the objects of preference and the binary relation 'preferred to' on the one hand and the real numbers together with the binary relative relation 'greater than' on the other. A stronger representation, *cardinal* utility, conveys further information about *strength* of preference.

19 Notice that cost–benefit analysis with distributional weights can be thought of as equivalent to the use of a social welfare function of this type, at least for small allocative adjustments. For example, suppose that u_i depends, inter alia, on wealth w_i and the probability p_i of death during the forthcoming period. Then consider a safety improvement that yields small variations δp_1, δp_2, ..., δp_n in individual probabilities of death. The change in social welfare, δW, will then be well approximated by

$$\delta W = \sum_i \frac{\partial W}{\partial u_i} \frac{\partial u_i}{\partial p_i} \delta p_i.$$

But,

$$\forall i, \quad \frac{\partial u_i}{\partial p_i} = -\frac{\partial u_i}{\partial w_i} m_i$$

where m_i is the ith individual's marginal rate of substitution of w_i for p_i. Hence

$$\delta W = -\sum_i \frac{\partial W}{\partial u_i} \frac{\partial u_i}{\partial w_i} m_i \, \delta p_i$$

which is simply the weighted sum of individual willingness to pay, $-m_i \delta p_i$, with weights equal to $(\partial W/\partial u_i)(\partial u_i/\partial w_i)$, i.e. weights that reflect the marginal social welfare of each individual's wealth. Thus the measurement of changes in social welfare by the weighted summation of individual willingness to pay, far from being an ad hoc, arbitrary and naive 'adding up' exercise (as some would claim), is, rather, a manifestation of one of the fundamental results of differential calculus, namely that a non-linear but well-behaved function can, at least locally, be well approximated by its linear tangent hyperplane. For alternative rationalizations for distributional weighting, see Chapter 4 and Le Grand (1984).

20 See, for example, Sugden (1981), Chapter 3.

21 That is, the *weighted average* of utility where the weights are the relevant probabilities.

22 Notice that this equivalence is crucially dependent upon the assumption of coincidence of individual and social probability judgements.

23 The expression for expected utility given in (1.7) is based upon the assumption that the utility index associated with the outcome of death is independent of wealth. In addition the utility function has been scaled so that this index is equal to zero.

24 Though it should be noted that whereas the m_i that appear in (1.3) and (1.5) are evaluated at existing levels of wealth and utility, those in (1.9) are evaluated at the overall social optimum.

25 See Bergstrom (1982) and Dehez and Drèze (1982). Amongst other things the existence of a bequest motive will mean that it is not appropriate to treat the utility of dying as constant, as in (1.7). In addition, the existence of life insurance and annuities means that m_i not only will reflect willingness to pay for improved survival prospects per se, but may also depend upon the extent to which increased life expectancy affects the terms of such contracts.

26 Notice that, since the utility of dying has been set equal to zero, this specification of $u_i(w_i)$ implies that survival with zero wealth is equivalent to death. This is a highly restrictive assumption which one would certainly not wish to form the basis for the development of a general theory and is made here solely for analytical simplicity in the context of an illustrative example. The exponent in the utility function has been chosen to ensure that the order of magnitude of mean m_i is similar to empirical estimates of the value of statistical life reported in Chapters 2 and 4.

27 However, Bergstrom (1982) has shown that the legitimacy (or otherwise) of adding such a premium depends crucially upon the *nature* of people's concern for others' safety. For a fuller discussion of this point and of the possible order of magnitude of the premium, see Chapter 2, sections 2.1 and 2.2.

28 For example, suppose that, were it known which of two states of the world, S_1 and S_2, would occur, then there would be no disagreement over the probabilities of death faced by two individuals A and B. Denote these (agreed) conditional probabilities by the ordered pair (p_A, p_B). Suppose in addition that the conditional probabilities of death for each of two alternative government decisions D_1 and D_2 are as follows:

	S_1	S_2
D_1	(0, 1)	(1, 0)
D_2	(0.9, 0)	(0, 0.9)

Finally, suppose that A and B have different subjective assessments of the probabilities of occurrence of each of the states of the world, A judging that the probability of S_1 is 0.6 while B judges it to be only 0.45. A and B will then *both* prefer D_1 to D_2, in that each will judge his own probability of dying under D_1 as being less than that under D_2. However, a government that values each of the individuals equally and obeys the axioms of rational choice under uncertainty will (whatever its judgement concerning the probabilities of S_1 and S_2) *necessarily* prefer D_2 to D_1 since, whichever state occurs, there will be one death for certain under D_1 but only a 0.9 probability of one death under D_2.

29 See note 10.

30 See, for example, Mishan (1969).

31 See Jones-Lee (1981), Jones-Lee and Poncelet (1982) and National Radiological Protection Board (1980).

32 In the parlance of choice theory, 'incoherence' involves the violation of one or some of the axioms of rational choice under uncertainty, such as those proposed by Savage (1954).

33 Harsanyi seems to have much the same sort of idea in mind when he argues that:

> All we have to do is to distinguish between a person's manifest preferences and his true preferences. His manifest preferences are his actual preferences as manifested by his observed behaviour, including preferences possibly based on erroneous factual beliefs or on careless logical analysis, or on strong emotions that at the moment greatly hinder rational choice. In contrast, a person's true preferences are the preferences he *would* have if he had all the relevant factual information, always reasoned with the greatest possible care, and were in a state of mind most conducive to rational choice .... In my opinion, social utility must be defined in terms of people's true preferences .... (Harsanyi, 1982, p. 55)

Similarly, Hare (1982) argues that when considering the desires of others one should attempt to establish '. . . what they would desire if they were fully informed and unconfused' and Mirrlees (1982) suggests that 'People sometimes have mistaken conceptions of their well-being. At least the conception must somehow be purified of obvious errors of foresight or memory.'

34 See Chapters 2 and 4.

35 See note 5.

36 This seems to be the underlying rationale for the approach adopted by Jones (1946).

37 See, for example, Abraham and Thedié (1960).

38 For example, Abraham and Thedié (1960).

39 See section 1.3, or Card and Mooney (1977) and Carlson (1963).

40 The result would not be exact to the extent that it would ignore factors such as discounting and productivity growth.

41 Implicit in the decision analysis approach is therefore the assumption that the decision maker's choices obey the axioms underpinning expected utility theory (i.e. are coherent).

42 In fact, one might even go so far as to argue that the question is actually *obfuscated* by the clutter of technical paraphernalia that is part and parcel of the approach.

43 This result is an approximation to the extent that the disutility of lives lost function is non-linear.

2

The Willingness-to-pay Approach: a Survey

In Chapter 1 it was argued that, in spite of its limitations, the willingness-to-pay approach appears to be the most effective means currently available for taking account of variations in safety in public sector allocative and legislative decisions. Not surprisingly, therefore, a considerable amount of theoretical and empirical research has been directed at this approach, particularly during the past decade. The purpose of this chapter is to provide a survey of some of the more significant results of this work.

2.1 Theoretical Developments

The theoretical analysis of individual willingness to pay for safety has been conducted predominantly, if not exclusively, within an expected utility maximization framework and therefore presupposes that individual decision making will, to an adequate approximation, display the kind of rationality or 'coherence' implicit in the Von Neumann–Morgenstern or Savage axioms, or variants thereof.[1] Broadly speaking, the models used fall into one of two categories. In the first of these, individual utility functions are defined on lifetime streams of consumption (and, in some cases, bequests) with physical risk reflected in uncertainty concerning the length of life. Examples of such analyses are those by Usher (1973), Conley (1976), Arthur (1981), Bergstrom (1982) and Shepard and Zeckhauser (1982). The alternative approach is to work with conditional utility of *wealth* functions whose properties vary over different possible states of the world during a forthcoming period or periods, physical risk being reflected in uncertainty as to which state of the world will occur. In the simplest version of this type of model there are just two conditional utility functions, $u_L(w_L)$ and $u_D(w_D)$, where u_L and u_D denote utility of wealth conditional, respectively, on survival or on death during a forthcoming period, w_L and w_D being the corresponding conditional levels of wealth. Under this approach, the properties of $u_D(w_D)$ reflect, inter alia, the individual's concern for the well-being of his or her surviving dependants.

Examples of this type of analysis are those of Drèze (1962), Jones-Lee (1974, 1976, 1980b), Cook and Graham (1977), Bailey (1978), Weinstein *et al.* (1980), Dehez and Drèze (1982), Fraser (1984) and Marshall (1984).

The conditional utility of wealth approach tends to make for ease of analysis and relative simplicity of mathematical expressions but is arguably based on less fundamental hypotheses concerning individual preferences and attitudes to risk than more sophisticated versions of the lifetime consumption approach. On the other hand, the lifetime consumption approach is typically based upon the assumption that the utility of a stream of consumption $(c_1, c_2, \ldots, c_T)$ can be expressed as an additive function of the 'period' utilities of consumption $u_t(c_t)$, i.e. that

$$u(c_1, c_2, \ldots, c_T) = \sum_{t=1}^{T} u_t(c_t)$$

and one of the problems with this formulation is that, because it focuses upon the utility of consumption, it is difficult to take account of the 'pure' utility of survival, per se.[2]

More specifically, the theoretical analysis of individual willingness to pay for safety has focused on a number of different issues, the most significant of which are the following:

1 The way in which marginal rates of substitution of wealth for probability of death vary with the existing level of risk, income, age and expenditure on life insurance.
2 The relationship between a typical individual's marginal rate of substitution and his human capital (i.e. his gross output).
3 Non-marginal variations and 'maximum acceptable' increments in physical risk.
4 Multiperiod variations in physical risk.
5 The optimal provision of safety within the context of social welfare maximization.
6 Safety, population effects and economic growth.
7 Benevolence and the value of other people's safety.
8 The value of statistical life before and after the occurrence of some life-threatening event such as a heart attack or kidney failure.
9 Consistency and the implications of non-uniform valuation of safety by different government departments.
10 The relationship between optimal expenditures on information concerning physical risk, risk reduction and compensation payments for increased risk, where the latter can vary across different states of the world.
11 Variations in different risks of death.
12 Compensating wage differentials and the value of statistical life.
13 The well-behavedness of the ranking of safety projects based on aggregate willingness to pay.
14 Willingness to pay for reduction in the probability of non-fatal illness or injury.

2.1.1   The Relationship between m_i, Current Risk, Life Insurance Expenditure, Income and Age

Apart from its intrinsic interest, information concerning these relationships has obvious relevance for an assessment of the way in which values of statistical life will vary between subgroups in society that differ in terms of current exposure to physical risk, income, age and so on. These questions have been addressed by a number of authors (see, for example, Cook and Graham, 1977; Bailey, 1978; Jones-Lee, 1978; Arthur, 1981; Dehez and Drèze, 1982; Linnerooth, 1982; Shepard and Zeckhauser, 1982; and Cropper and Sussman, 1985, 1987).

Both intuition and earlier analysis (see, for example, Raiffa, 1969; Jones-Lee, 1976; or Weinstein *et al.*, 1980) suggest that m_i will be an unambiguously increasing function of p_i, where (throughout this survey) the latter denotes the ith individual's probability of death for a forthcoming period. However, as Dehez and Drèze (1982) have shown, matters turn out to be rather less clear-cut and the relationship depends ultimately on the nature and terms of life insurance and annuity contracts available to the individual. Basically, the relationship between m_i and p_i hinges on two questions: (a) how is the expected marginal utility of wealth affected by variations in p_i, and (b) to what extent does m_i reflect willingness to pay for improved terms of life insurance and worsened terms of annuity contracts, as well as for improved survival prospects per se? If the individual does not hold life insurance or annuity contracts and the marginal utility of wealth conditional on survival exceeds the corresponding marginal utility conditional on death then, as suggested by intuition, m_i will increase with p_i, essentially because the expected marginal utility of wealth decreases with p_i. Clearly, the opposite is true, and m_i decreases with p_i, if the relationship between the conditional marginal utilities is reversed. If, by contrast, the individual *does* hold life insurance or annuity contracts but the terms of the latter do not vary with changes in p_i, then the outcome depends crucially upon whether or not the insurance and annuity contracts are initially actuarially fair. If such contracts are initially fair, then m_i is independent of p_i because, with optimal holdings of insurance or annuities, marginal utilities of wealth are equalized across survival and death states so that expected marginal utility is independent of p_i. Correspondingly, if insurance and annuities are less than (more than) fair then m_i decreases (increases) with p_i. Finally, consider the case in which the terms of insurance and annuity contracts vary with p_i so as, in particular, to maintain actuarial fairness. In this case one must take account not only of the tendency of insurance and annuities to equalize conditional marginal utilities, but also of the fact that a variation in p_i will affect the terms on which such contracts can be purchased, so that m_i will reflect an additional willingness to pay for these effects.[3] Dehez and Drèze show that under such circumstances m_i turns out somewhat counter-intuitively to be a non-increasing function of p_i.

Turning to the relationship between m_i and income or wealth, not surprisingly none of the theoretical work during the last decade has cast doubt upon the early-established proposition (see, for example, Jones-Lee, 1976) that safety is a normal good, so that m_i increases with y_i and w_i where the latter denote the ith individual's income and wealth respectively. However, some more recent analyses have shed rather more light upon the quantitative nature of this relationship for various different classes of underlying utility function. For example, Jones-Lee (1980b) considers an individual with an additive-separable utility function in wealth w_i (including discounted lifetime earnings) and time of death τ_i such that $U_i(w_i, \tau_i) = u_i(w_i) + \ell_i(\tau_i)$. Given perfect insurance and annuities markets, this individual will arrange for w_i to be independent of τ_i (i.e. will fully cover his human capital with life insurance) and m_i is given by

$$m_i = \frac{E\ell_i - \ell_i(1)}{(1 - p_i)u_i'(w_i)} \tag{2.1}$$

where $E\ell_i$ is the expectation of ℓ_i taken over all τ. Differentiating with respect to w_i and rearranging gives

$$\frac{\partial m_i}{\partial w_i} = \frac{-m_i}{w_i} \, w_i \, \frac{u''(w_i)}{u'(w_i)} \tag{2.2}$$

or, interpreting $-w_i u''(w_i)/u'(w_i)$ as the individual's Pratt–Arrow coefficient of relative risk aversion RR_i,

$$\frac{w_i}{m_i} \frac{\partial m_i}{\partial w_i} = RR_i. \tag{2.3}$$

That is, the elasticity of m_i with respect to w_i for this type of utility function is given simply by RR_i.

Shepard and Zeckhauser (1982) show that for an individual who maximizes the expectation of multiperiod utility of consumption, with constant relative risk aversion for the period utility of consumption function, m_i will be approximately *proportional* to discounted future earnings so that the elasticity referred to above is roughly equal to unity.

Finally, consider the manner in which m_i varies with age. The precise nature of the predicted relationship clearly depends on the detailed properties of underlying functions and other parameters of the models employed. However, under rather plausible assumptions concerning preferences (constant relative risk aversion for the period utility of consumption function) Shepard and Zeckhauser (1982) show that with no life insurance and annuity markets m_i will follow a pronounced 'inverted-U' life-cycle – peaking at about age 40 and falling by about 50% by age 60 – while with perfect markets the relationship is much flatter in early years of adulthood, although there is a marked decline thereafter. Arthur's (1981) analysis, developed within a rather different type of model that takes account of birth rates and population effects, predicts a steadily decreasing relationship, with m_i falling by roughly 50% between the ages of 20 and 50. More recently, Cropper and Sussman (1985, 1987) have extended Shepard and Zeckhauser's model to incorporate a head of household's concern for the consumption of his dependants, both while he is alive and following his death. Using the same sort of period utility of consumption function as Shepard and Zeckhauser, Cropper and Sussman show that for a married man with a wife and two children, under a wide range of conditions on the availability of actuarially fair life insurance and annuities, m_i declines substantially with age beyond early adulthood, falling to a level of, or close to, zero at about age 90.

2.1.2   The Relationship between m_i and Human Capital

It is natural to wonder whether values of safety improvement based on the willingness-to-pay definition would be numerically significantly different from corresponding values based on the lost output definition. Since values of statistical life are typically defined in terms of the population mean of the relevant marginal rates of substitution m_i, and since the gross output definition is tantamount to equating the value of an individual's life with his human capital h_i, the relationship between m_i and h_i for a particular individual is clearly of considerable interest.

Conley (1976), Jones-Lee (1980a), Bergstrom (1982), Dehez and Drèze (1982) and Shepard and Zeckhauser (1982) have each addressed this question from a theoretical point of view and have examined, in particular, the conditions under which m_i will exceed h_i. Although the precise conditions vary subtly from one analysis to another, reflecting detailed differences in the way the underlying models are set up, these analyses all strongly suggest that sufficient conditions for $m_i > h_i$ are very weak indeed and can be expected to be fulfilled in the vast majority of cases. These conditions are most easily summarized by considering a simple single-period model in which an individual who has access to actuarially fair life insurance and annuity contracts may either survive the period with probability $1 - p_i$ and consume an amount c_i, or die during the period with probability p_i. Given the two degrees of freedom associated with utility functions in this context, we may set the utility of dying at zero,[4] so that expected utility is given by $(1 - p_i)u_i(c_i)$ where $u_i(c_i)$ is the individual's utility of surviving and consuming c_i. It then turns out that

$$(\forall c_i \geqslant 0,\ u_i'(c_i) > 0,\ u_i''(c_i) < 0,\ u_i(0) \geqslant 0) \Rightarrow m_i > h_i \qquad (2.4)$$

and

$$(\forall c_i \geqslant 0,\ u_i'(c_i) > 0,\ u_i''(c_i) < 0,\ u_i(0) < 0) \Rightarrow$$
$$(\exists c_i^*\ c_i > c_i^* \Rightarrow m_i > h_i) \qquad (2.5)$$

The first of these results indicates that, provided that u_i is strictly increasing and concave, a sufficient condition for $m_i > h_i$ is that the individual should prefer survival with zero consumption to death. The second result indicates that if, as seems more plausible, there is some (presumably low) level of consumption below which death is preferable to survival, then there will nonetheless exist a level of consumption c_i^* above which $m_i > h_i$. Conley (1976) asserts without proof that c_i^* will be below the typical value of c_i. Bergstrom (1982) provides an interesting variant on the above conditions. At the current level of c_i and p_i define a constant k_i such that $c_i = k_i/(1 - p_i)$. Then

$$-\frac{d}{dp_i} (1 - p_i)u_i(\frac{k_i}{1 - p_i}) > 0 \Leftrightarrow m_i > h_i \qquad (2.6)$$

Thus, a necessary and sufficient condition for $m_i > h_i$ is that a change δp_i (< 0) in probability of death would more than compensate for a decrease

$$\frac{k_i}{1 - p_i} - \frac{k_i}{1 - p_i - \delta p_i}$$

$$= -\frac{c_i \, \delta p_i}{1 - p_i - \delta p_i} \ (\approx - c_i \, \delta p_i \text{ for } 1 - p_i - \delta p_i \approx 1) \qquad (2.7)$$

in consumption. In contrast with Conley's assertion, it seems altogether more plausible to suppose that Bergstrom's condition will be fulfilled for all but those in a state of abject poverty.

2.1.3 Maximum Acceptable Increments in Physical Risk

An individual's marginal rate of substitution of wealth for physical risk tells us only what the individual would be willing to pay, or would require in compensation, for 'small' variations in current-period probability of death from the existing level $\bar{p}_i$. If we consider, in particular, large *increases* in the probability of death during the current period then it seems clear that, for most people, required compensation will become unbounded well before this probability equals one. If the reader doubts this, then he should ask himself whether any sum, however large, would induce him to play one round of Russian roulette with three bullets in a six-chamber revolver. If the answer is 'no' then his compensation has become unbounded before his probability of death increases to $\bar{p}_i + \frac{1}{2}$. Suppose that required compensation becomes unbounded when probability of death increases to $\bar{p}_i + \Delta p_i^*$. It is then natural to refer to Δp_i^* as the ith individual's 'maximum acceptable increase in physical risk'. Properties of Δp_i^* and its relationship to, in particular, m_i have obvious potential relevance for the setting of safety standards in, for example, nuclear power generation and waste disposal or other activities involving non-marginal changes in physical risk.

The properties of Δp_i^* for the typical individual have been considered from a theoretical point of view by Jones-Lee (1980b, 1981) and Jones-Lee and Poncelet (1982). These analyses assume the maximization of the expectation of a utility function whose arguments are current wealth (including human capital) w_i and time of death τ_i. In general, it is shown that, provided that this utility function is well behaved and, in particular, is bounded above with respect to w_i for all τ_i, then there will exist an inverse proportionality relationship between m_i and Δp_i^* taking the particular form

$$m_i \Delta p_i^* RL_i = k_i \qquad (2.8)$$

where RL_i is a measure of financial risk aversion that reflects the win–loss probability ratio at which an individual would just be willing to undertake a small stake, large prize financial gamble.[5] In general the magnitude of k_i (> 0) depends upon the precise properties of the utility function, but in the particular case in which the function takes the separable form $U_i(w_i, \tau_i) = u_i(w_i) + \ell_i(\tau_i)$ it turns out that k_i is exactly equal to unity.

Given that separability of $U_i(w_i, \tau_i)$ implies that the individual will arrange for full coverage of human capital with actuarially fair life insurance, and given that this degree of cover may not be an unreasonable approximation for many middle-income individuals with occupational pensions and insured mortgages, it would not be particularly surprising if the approximate relationship

$$m_i \Delta p_i^* RL_i \approx 1 \qquad (2.9)$$

held for a substantial proportion of people. If it does, then it allows a number of interesting inferences to be drawn. For example, it has been shown (Jones-Lee, 1980b) that, with the arguments of relevant utility of wealth functions defined to include human capital, $RL_i \leqslant RR_i/w_i$ where RR_i is the Pratt–Arrow measure of relative risk aversion which has been estimated to take on values that are typically less than 10.[6] Even if we set $RR_i = 10$, equation (2.9) gives $m_i \geqslant w_i/10\Delta p_i^*$. Since it seems extremely unlikely that for most people Δp_i^* will be as large as 10^{-1} and it will probably be less than 10^{-2}, we can conclude with considerable confidence that, for anyone whose preferences and attitudes to risk are such that (2.9) holds as a good approximation, m_i will almost certainly exceed human capital and will probably do so by a factor of more than 10.

While the author had not succeeded in establishing a proof of the result conjectured in (2.9) for the general case at the time at which Jones-Lee (1980b, 1981) and Jones-Lee and Poncelet (1982) were published, it has since proved possible to show that this approximation is almost universally valid. The proof is presented in Chapter 3, section 3.4.

2.1.4   Multiperiod Variations in Physical Risk

Few public sector projects will affect safety for just one future period (e.g. the coming year); more typically, safety effects can be expected to extend over a number of periods. While Jones-Lee (1976) gives results concerning individual valuation of variations in life expectancy which have some relevance for the multiperiod risk change problem, the usefulness of these results is limited by the fact that a unit variation in life expectancy is consistent with an indefinitely large number of different ways of perturbing the mortality schedule. Clearly, a preliminary requirement for a more satisfactory analysis of multiperiod variations in physical risk is information concerning the properties of marginal rates of substitution of *current* wealth for survival probability during the tth future period, $t = 1, 2, \ldots$. Results concerning these marginal rates of substitution are derived by Usher (1973), Bergstrom (1982), Jones-Lee and Poncelet (1982) and Needleman (1982). Basically, these analyses show that the marginal rate of substitution m_{it} of current wealth for survival probability t periods hence (conditional on surviving the preceding $t - 1$ periods) depends crucially upon the contribution to expected lifetime utility of survival *past* the tth period. Since the latter can be expected to fall as t increases, there will therefore be a not surprising tendency for m_{it} to decrease with t.

Now consider a perturbation in the mortality schedule that entails variations δp_{i1}, δp_{i2}, $\ldots$, δp_{iT} in the conditional[7] survival probabilities in each of T future periods. Provided that the δp_{it} are small, then we can write the individual's compensating variation δv_i for this perturbation as

$$\delta v_i = -\sum_{i=1}^{T} m_{it} \delta p_{it}. \tag{2.10}$$

Clearly, δv_i depends, inter alia, on the nature of the mortality schedule and on the δp_{it}. Jones-Lee and Poncelet (1982) consider the highly simplified case in which all p_{it} are equal (i.e. time of death is geometrically distributed) and $\delta p_{i1} = \delta p_{i2} = \ldots = \delta p_i$ (i.e. a change in safety that varies the probability of surviving the tth period – conditional on surviving the preceding $t - 1$ periods – by an equal amount for each and every future period). $\lim_{\delta p_i \to 0} |\delta v_i / \delta p_i|$ then gives the individual's marginal rate of substitution, M_i, of current wealth for *multiperiod* physical risk. Denoting the individual's current remaining life expectancy by E_i, it turns out that $M_i / m_{i1} \lessgtr E_i$ as lifetime utility is an increasing convex, linear or concave function of length of life. (The proof of this result is reproduced in Chapter 3, section 3.5.) Since it seems likely that concavity of the latter function will be the norm, then M_i will typically be somewhat less than remaining life expectancy times m_{i1}. Empirical results given in Needleman (1982) tend to confirm this, implying a value of M_i / m_{i1} of roughly 8.

2.1.5 Constrained Social Welfare Maximization

The result that the value of statistical life is given by the population mean of m_i has typically been established within the framework of conventional social cost–benefit analysis (see, for example, Jones-Lee, 1976). Given the inherent limitations of the hypothetical compensation test that underpins cost–benefit analysis, there is clearly a case to be made for examining the question of the value of safety within the more general and robust context of maximization of a social welfare function subject to a resource constraint. Analyses of this type have been developed by Bergstrom (1982) and Dehez and Drèze (1982). In the latter paper, social welfare is a weighted sum of individual expected utilities (the weights reflecting particular interpersonal utility comparisons) and safety is publicly provided and is financed by taxes levied on individuals. Tax payments are 'lump-sum' in that they are allowed to vary from individual to individual and are not, in particular, related to income or wealth. Finally, it is assumed that the terms of life insurance contracts do not vary with changes in individual safety. Under these circumstances, constrained maximization of social welfare entails the condition

$$c = \frac{1}{n}\sum_i m_i - nc \, \text{cov}\left(m_i, \frac{\partial p_i}{\partial s}\right) \tag{2.11}$$

where c is the marginal cost of avoiding one additional statistical death and s is overall public expenditure on safety. Bergstrom obtains a similar result.

Thus if, as seems reasonable, it is assumed that m_i and $\partial p_i/\partial s$ are uncorrelated across individuals, then constrained welfare maximization requires that public expenditure on safety should be undertaken up to the point at which the marginal cost of avoiding one statistical death equals the population mean of m_i. This more general formulation of the problem therefore leads to precisely the same result as that derived within the framework of conventional social cost–benefit analysis. However, as Dehez and Drèze note, the assumption of lump-sum taxes plays a crucial role and leads to what is essentially a 'first-best' solution. For a discussion of the 'second-best' solution when safety is financed by a proportional tax on wealth, see Chapter 1, section 1.6, where it is shown that in the absence of correlation between weighted utility indices and $\partial p_i/\partial s$ the value of statistical life is given, not by the population mean of m_i, but by the ratio of weighted averages of the numerator and denominator of m_i ($i = 1, \ldots, n$).

2.1.6   Safety, Population Effects and Economic Growth

Clearly, variations in safety not only will affect the survival prospects of those already alive, but will also have longer-term implications for the growth of a society's future population and hence its overall economic growth. The only theoretical analysis so far developed that takes account of these effects is that of Arthur (1981). Arthur employs a neoclassical framework involving a constant-returns production function and constant age-specific mortality and fatality rates. In addition, the economy is assumed to be in a Solow-type steady state in which the growth rate of the economy equals the (constant) population growth rate and all per capita variables are constant. The consumption of those outside labour participation ages is supported by intergenerational transfers from those who are currently productive and consumption is patterned so that its discounted marginal utility is the same at all ages. Within this framework Arthur shows that the loss of social welfare due to a perturbation in the mortality schedule entailing the loss of one additional life at age t comprises the value of remaining expected years of life at age t, remaining expected labour years at age t and remaining expected reproduction minus expected future consumption. Arthur then generates illustrative numerical estimates of the consumption equivalent of this loss of social welfare for various values of t for the case in which the utility function displays constant elasticity of consumption. Essentially, it transpires (as noted above) that the consumption equivalent of the welfare loss decreases fairly rapidly with age.

2.1.7   Benevolence and the Value of Other People's Safety

The result that the value of statistical life is given by the population mean of m_i is based on the assumption that people are concerned solely for their own safety. In fact, many people are also concerned (and therefore presumably willing to pay) for improvements in the safety of others. It has therefore been argued that the value of statistical life should be augmented by a sum reflecting this additional willingness to pay (see particularly Jones-Lee, 1976; and Needleman, 1976). However, Bergstrom (1982) shows that, under certain circumstances, addition of such a component to the value of statistical life would be invalid. Essentially, the question turns on the nature of a person's concern for other people's welfare. Consider first the case in which this concern is specific to safety – so that while i would be willing to pay £x for a particular improvement in j's survival prospects, he would not be willing to accede to j's request to buy him £x-worth of champagne instead. Under these circumstances it would appear that the Jones-Lee–Needleman prescription is valid. However, if benevolence takes what Bergstrom describes as the 'pure' form of concern for other people's *utility* then the prescription turns out to be unwarranted. The argument goes somewhat as follows. As has already been demonstrated, under first-best conditions, equality between the marginal cost of avoiding one statistical death and the population mean of m_i is a necessary condition for ensuring that no-one's 'selfish' expected utility can be increased without reducing anyone else's. The latter is, in turn, a necessary condition for maximizing the utility of someone who displays 'pure' benevolence. It therefore follows that the value of statistical life for a society displaying 'pure' benevolence should be the *unaugmented* population mean of m_i. As Bergstrom observes, 'pure' benevolence requires that at the margin a person's concern for other people's safety will be precisely balanced by his concern for the reduction in their consumption that will be required to finance the extra safety. In the end, then, it would appear that the legitimacy (or otherwise) of augmenting the value of statistical life to reflect concern for other people's well-being depends on the precise form that this concern takes.

2.1.8   The Value of Statistical Life Before and After the Occurrence of a Life-threatening Event

One of the more difficult decisions faced by those responsible for expending limited medical care budgets concerns the appropriate balance to be struck between preventive and curative medicine. In making such decisions it would clearly be valuable to have some idea about how individuals themselves regard small reductions from initially low levels of risk in relation to large reductions from initially high levels where, in particular, the number of statistical lives saved is the same in both cases.

Thus, suppose that n people each face a probability p of contracting a disease which, if caught, would involve a conditional probability q of death. A completely effective *preventive measure* would therefore avoid npq statistical deaths. Now consider $m = np$ people who have, in fact, contracted the disease. A completely effective *cure* would then also avoid $mq = npq$ statistical deaths. How would the n people's aggregate willingness to pay V_1 for the preventive measure compare with the victims' aggregate willingness to pay V_2 for the cure after contracting the disease? The answer to this question, along with the relative costs of prevention and cure, is clearly of direct relevance to a decision concerning whether to devote scarce resources to the preventive measure or to its curative counterpart.

Weinstein *et al.* (1980) address precisely this kind of question using a variant of the model developed by Jones-Lee (1976) and show that, *ceteris paribus*, $V_2 > V_1$ if individuals are risk neutral or risk seeking with respect to wealth, while the relationship is indeterminate if they are risk averse. Clearly V_1 and V_2 are aggregate compensating variations (or 'buying prices') for safety improvement. Weinstein *et al.* also consider the corresponding equivalent variations (or 'selling prices') E_1 and E_2 and show that for risk-neutral or risk-averse individuals $E_2 > E_1$ whereas for risk-seeking individuals the relationship is indeterminate. On the basis of these results Weinstein *et al.* conclude that the victims' value of statistical life after the occurrence of a life-threatening event will generally exceed the value of statistical life for all those at risk before its occurrence.[8] However, one is bound to question the robustness of this conclusion, especially in view of the indeterminacy of the relationship between V_1 and V_2 for risk-averse individuals. In fact, it seems probable that for large values of q (the probability of death conditional on occurrence of the life-threatening event) V_2 would be less than V_1 for individuals who are risk averse. For example, consider the extreme case in which $p = 1/n$ and $q = 1$. V_1 is then n people's aggregate willingness to pay to avoid one statistical death, while V_2 is one person's willingness to pay to avoid the certainty of death. While most people would no doubt pay a very considerable sum to avoid certain death, the amount would be bounded above by a person's *ability* to pay which in turn presumably cannot exceed his or her human capital. The results discussed in section 2.1.2 then suggest that V_1 would substantially exceed V_2 under such circumstances.

2.1.9   Consistency in the Valuation of Safety

Suppose that a 'true' value of statistical life, V^*, could be established. Abstracting from the fact that such a value would probably vary between different causes of death, it is clear that a first-best allocation of the overall public sector budget would require that all government departments should employ V^* in evaluating projects that affect safety. Now suppose that a particular department (say department 1) is convinced that V^* is the 'true' value but that other departments do not share this conviction (either because they have different views about the appropriate way to define such a value or because they have doubts about the soundness of the empirical estimation procedure from which V^* was derived). What, then, is the appropriate second-best action for department 1? Should it, in particular, evaluate its own safety projects using V^* as the value of statistical life, or are there reasons why department 1 should employ some other value? These questions are considered by Dobbs (1985). Dobbs first emphasizes the distinction between the central government decision concerning the division of its overall public sector investment budget between different sectors or departments (e.g. health, transport, education) and the *departmental* cost–benefit analysis of individual projects and consequent development of a departmental investment programme. Dobbs then introduces a simple but illuminating model of individual departmental decision making in which the jth department's investment programme is characterized by just three features, namely total capital outlay K_j, lives saved X_j and other net-of-outlay benefits A_j. The range of investment opportunities open to the department is then taken to be summarized by a bivariate density function for project outlays, $k_j(a_j, x_j)$, where $a_j = A_j/K_j$, $x_j = X_j/K_j$ and

$$\int_\alpha^\beta \int_\eta^\epsilon k_j(a_j, x_j) \ dx_j \ da_j$$

gives the total capital cost of projects having safety 'returns' in the interval $[\eta, \epsilon]$ and other 'returns' in the interval $[\alpha, \beta]$.

Using this model, Dobbs then proceeds to show that it will be appropriate for department 1 to set the value of statistical life at V^* (the 'true' value) only if *either* the central government has full information concerning $k_j(a_j, x_j)$ for all j and agrees with department 1 that V^* is the true value of statistical life, *or* (a) the central government decision concerning the level of departmental budgets is independent of the performance of projects within departments and (b) departmental decision makers are concerned only with the performance of their own department's projects. Suppose, by contrast, that in allocating funds between departments central government is influenced by the rates of return reported to it by individual departments, favouring those that are able to report higher rates of return. Under these circumstances it follows that if department 1 uses V^* as the value of statistical life and V^* tends to exceed the values of statistical life used by other departments, then there will be an unwarranted bias in favour of department 1 and against other departments in the central government decision concerning departmental budgets. In this case the appropriate second-best policy would be for department 1 to use a value of statistical life somewhat lower than V^*. Alternatively, suppose that the central government decision concerning the level of departmental budgets is independent of the performance of projects within departments but that departmental decision makers are concerned with the overall performance of public sector projects rather than solely with their own department's projects. It is then clear that, even with disagreement about the appropriate value for statistical life, there are potential gains to decision makers from moving towards some compromise 'middle' value,[9] although, as Dobbs points out, the precise nature of the appropriate compromise will depend upon the extent of information concerning $k_j(a_j, x_j)$, $j = 1, \ldots, n$, available to decision makers in each of the n departments. Nonetheless, it again follows that it will generally not be appropriate for department 1 to use V^* as the value of statistical life.

2.1.10   Information and State-dependent Compensation

If a government is actually going to compensate individuals for increases in physical risk due to public sector projects, then it is natural to wonder what properties an optimal compensation structure would, in fact, possess. The answer to this question is clearly inextricably bound up with the nature of optimal safety expenditure by the government and also – to the extent that government and individual perceptions of risk differ – with optimal government expenditure on the dissemination of information concerning risk.

In order to shed light on this matter, Fraser (1984) considers a situation in which

1 the government actually does make compensation payments to individuals when it introduces projects that increase physical risk,
2 compensation payments can be state-dependent in the sense that the sum paid conditional on the occurrence of death or injury during a given period may differ from the sum paid conditional on non-occurrence,
3 the government's objective is to minimize expected compensation payments subject to the condition that individual expected utility 'with' a project that increases risk is no lower than that without it, and
4 individual and government assessments of the probability of death or injury are not necessarily equal and are endogenous in the sense that they are capable of being influenced by government expenditures on information and/or risk-reducing activities.

Within the context of a simple single-period model, and on fairly plausible assumptions about the properties of utility functions and risk perception functions, Fraser concludes that the government will tend to engage in more risk reduction expenditure, or less informational expenditure, with state-dependent compensation than with compensation that is state-independent. State-dependent compensation would therefore seem to have certain advantages over state-independent compensation in that it will lead the government to provide more of what it perceives to be beneficial for individuals, though to the extent that informational expenditures are lower, individuals themselves may not share the government's view.

2.1.11 Variations in Different Risks of Death

An implicit assumption in much of the theoretical literature on the value of life and safety is that the death of a particular individual during a given period can be treated as a single 'homogeneous' event. In reality, of course, people face a wide variety of different risks of death, e.g. from car accidents, heart disease and so on. Nonetheless, provided that (a) people are indifferent between various ways of dying, (b) the events of death by different causes are mutually exclusive and (c) variation in the risk of death by one cause does not affect the risks of death by other causes, then a situation in which the ith individual faces probabilities p_{ij} $(j = 1, \ldots, m)$ of death from m different causes will be equivalent to one in which he faces a single probability p_i of death with

$$p_i = \sum_{j=1}^{m} p_{ij}$$

and

$$V_j, \frac{\partial w_i}{\partial p_{ij}} = \frac{\partial w_i}{\partial p_i}. \tag{2.12}$$

Under these circumstances there will therefore be no ambiguity associated with the concept of the individual's marginal rate of substitution of wealth for survival probability. However, if *either* people are not indifferent between various ways of dying *or* the events of death by different causes are not mutually exclusive *or* variation in the risk of death by one cause affects the risks of death by other causes, then matters become more complicated.

Clearly, the nature of individual attitudes to death by different causes is an essentially empirical matter, so that one is unlikely to gain any significant insights from a priori theoretical analysis. However, such analysis can shed some light on the relationship between different causes of death. In particular, Sussman (1984) considers the case in which the events of death by different causes are independent (rather than mutually exclusive) while maintaining the assumptions that individuals are indifferent between different ways of dying and that variation in the risk of one cause of death does not affect the risks of death by other causes. In this case

$$p_i = 1 - \prod_{j=1}^{m} (1 - p_{ij})$$

so that in general

$$\frac{\partial w_i}{\partial p_{i1}} \neq \frac{\partial w_i}{\partial p_{i2}} \neq \ldots \neq \frac{\partial w_i}{\partial p_i}.$$ (2.13)

Thus in this case it is necessary, strictly speaking, to distinguish between the various different marginal rates of substitution of wealth for
risk of death and hence various different values of statistical life even
when individuals are indifferent between different ways of dying. However, it is clear that with all p_{ij} small (as will be the case for most people)
the distinction between mutually exclusive and independent causes of
death is of only limited significance with, in particular,

$$1 - \prod_{j=1}^{m}(1 - p_{ij}) \approx \sum_{j=1}^{m} p_{ij}$$ (2.14)

so that it is no surprise that Sussman finds that the differences between
the various $\partial w_i/\partial p_{ij}$ are less than 1% for typical orders of magnitude of
the p_{ij}.

2.1.12   *Compensating Wage Differentials and the Value of Statistical Life*

One of the more common approaches to estimating the value of statistical
life is based upon compensating wage differentials in labour markets.
Implicit in this approach is the assumption that, *ceteris paribus*, wage
rates will adjust to compensate for differences in risk between industries
and occupations. In a recent paper Marshall (1984) sets up a model
designed to highlight the nature of compensating wage differentials. In
particular, Marshall assumes that workers must (a) choose between a safe
and a risky industry, (b) have access to actuarially fair life insurance and
(c) have access to actuarially fair gambles in wealth. In this model, it
turns out that workers' choice of industry is ultimately dependent upon
the outcome of gambles in wealth in that 'losers' opt for the risky industry in order to augment their consumption claims with higher wage
rates while 'winners' are content to accept the lower wage rate in the safe
industry. Furthermore, it is a feature of equilibrium in this model that the
wage differential is not large enough to compensate for the difference in
risk so as to equalize expected utility between the two groups of workers.
Nonetheless, Marshall shows that, given the availability of fair gambles
and life insurance, the marginal rate of substitution of wealth for survival
probability is equalized between the two groups of workers and is in turn
equal to the wage differential divided by the difference in risk. Thus,
somewhat paradoxically, it turns out that the appropriateness of using the
latter as an exact measure of the value of statistical life appears not to
depend upon the fact that wage differentials compensate for risk so as
to equalize expected utility, but rather to be a result of the availability of
appropriate opportunities for financial gambles and life insurance. However, Marshall notes that, even in the absence of such opportunities, the
wage differential–risk difference ratio provides an approximation to the

required value of statistical life with the quality of the approximation depending upon, amongst other things, the size of the difference in risk.

2.1.13 The Well-behavedness of the Ranking of Safety Projects

The possibility that the hypothetical compensation test – effectively, the 'aggregate (unweighted) willingness-to-pay' criterion – may produce badly behaved rankings of projects is one of the best known results in welfare economics.[10] Given this possibility, it is natural (a) to expect that, under certain circumstances, the aggregate willingness-to-pay approach to the valuation of safety will produce badly-behaved rankings and (b) to ask under what circumstances rankings will definitely be well behaved.

Blackorby and Donaldson (1986) address precisely the latter question. Their results are, to say the least, stark and *prima facie* somewhat startling. Essentially, Blackorby and Donaldson show that if individuals are expected utility maximizers *and probabilities of death differ across individuals*, then the aggregate willingness-to-pay criterion, whether in weighted or unweighted form, will produce a well-behaved ranking of safety projects *if and only if* individual preferences satisfy one or other of two conditions, namely

1. life is strictly preferred to death even at zero consumption and individuals display constant degrees of financial risk proneness (in the Pratt–Arrow sense) or
2. individuals display constant risk aversion but death is preferred to life at all levels of consumption.

For the special case in which individual probabilities of death are equal, Blackorby and Donaldson show that the ranking of safety projects produced by the aggregate willingness-to-pay approach (weighted or unweighted) will be well behaved given expected utility maximization if and only if individual preferences satisfy one or other of conditions (1) or (2) above or a third condition, namely

3. for all individuals the expected utility associated with the (common) survival probability $\bar{\Pi}$ and consumption c_i ($i = 1, \ldots, n$) takes the form
   $$EU_i = \bar{\Pi} A_i c_i^r \quad (A_i, r > 0, i = 1, \ldots, n) \tag{2.15}$$
   so that all individuals display the same constant coefficient of relative financial risk aversion.

Since it is plainly almost inconceivable that any of conditions (1)–(3) would actually be fulfilled in practice, Blackorby and Donaldson's results effectively amount to an impossibility theorem with respect to the well-behavedness of the ranking of safety projects – at least for the case of expected utility maximization. However, as with all impossibility results, one is bound to wonder just how pervasive the (apparently inevitable) badly-behavedness of the ranking can be expected to be. Plainly, if only a fraction of a per cent of those projects actually assessed will be inconsistency ranked then things will probably not be too serious, whereas if the problem can be expected to be substantially more pervasive then one would have grounds for serious concern. In fact, Blackorby and Donaldson claim that 'it is very easy to produce examples of inconsistencies'. In order to illustrate this possibility they consider a case in which there are just two individuals, both of whom are expected utility maximizers whose utility of 'lifetime' consumption takes the form

$$u_i(c_i) = c_i \ (i = 1,2) \tag{2.16}$$

so that expected utility of lifetime consumption is given by

$$Eu_i = \pi_i c_i \ (i = 1,2) \tag{2.17}$$

where π_i denotes the ith individual's survival probability. Blackorby and Donaldson then consider an initial situation A in which

$$\pi_1 = 0.75, \ \pi_2 = 0.5, \ c_1 = 10{,}000 \text{ and } c_2 = 10{,}000 \tag{2.18}$$

and an alternative B involving an increase in risk to individual 1 and a gain in consumption to individual 2 such that

$$\pi_1 = 0.5, \ \pi_2 = 0.5, \ c_1 = 10{,}000 \text{ and } c_2 = 14{,}000. \tag{2.19}$$

Given that expected utility for both individuals is as specified in (2.17), the compensating variations for the change from A to B are −5,000 and 4,000 for individuals 1 and 2 respectively. The unweighted aggregate willingness-to-pay criterion therefore ranks A above B. However, the compensating variations for the move from B to A are 3,333 and −4,000 for individuals 1 and 2 respectively so that B is now ranked above A, thereby clearly violating the asymmetry condition. On the face of it, then, things look rather bad for the willingness-to-pay criterion. However, it should be noted that the increase in risk of death for individual 1 implied by the move from A to Be is massive by comparison with the size of variations typically encountered in public sector project appraisal (introduction of seat-belt legislation in the UK reduced the probability of fatal injury to car drivers and passengers by, at most, about 5×10^{-5} p.a.). Suppose, then, that we rework the Blackorby and Donaldson example with a variation in risk nearer to (but still, it should be noted, substantially larger than) the kind of change in risk that one might normally expect to encounter. In particular, suppose that for the initial situation A we have

$$\pi_1 = 0.999, \ \pi_2 = 0.998, \ c_1 = 10{,}000 \text{ and } c_2 = 10{,}000 \tag{2.20}$$

and for B

$$\pi_1 = 0.998, \ \pi_2 = 0.998, \ c_1 = 10{,}000 \text{ and } c_2 = 10{,}000 + x. \tag{2.21}$$

It then turns out that, given (2.17), the compensating variations for the move from A to B are -10.02 and x while those for the move from B to A are 10.01 and $-x$. Clearly, then, the aggregate willingness-to-pay criterion will produce an asymmetric ranking in this case if and only if

$$10.01 < x < 10.02. \qquad (2.22)$$

Thus, with variations in risk nearer to the order of magnitude normally encountered in public sector safety decisions, it appears that the possibility identified by Blackorby and Donaldson may well provide grounds for substantially less concern than might initially have seemed to be the case. In short, Blackorby and Donaldson's analysis, while indisputably interesting and elegant, should probably be viewed in much the same light as most other 'impossibility' results in welfare economics, i.e. as demonstrations of the impossibility of perfection but, for most practical purposes, as being of little serious consequence.

2.1.14 Non-fatal Injury and Illness

In the case of transport risks, in particular, it is the case that in sheer numerical terms the number of non-fatal injuries during any period of time far outweighs the number of fatalities. Similar comments apply to the relative number of cases of morbidity and mortality in the context of medical care. For these and other obvious reasons it is clearly important to explore the extent to which the willingness-to-pay approach – initially developed for the case of mortality risks – can be extended to cover variations in the risk of morbidity.

Those who have attempted to measure the cost of non-fatal injury and illness and the value of their avoidance have tended to do so either using an approach broadly equivalent to the gross output method of defining the cost of a fatality or by defining the value of a health or safety improvement in terms of the consequential savings in expenditures undertaken on preventive measures. It is therefore natural to ask how such costs and values would compare with a willingness-to-pay based 'value of avoidance of statistical morbidity' of equivalent severity. This is one of the questions addressed both theoretically and empirically by Berger *et al.* (1987). Essentially, Berger *et al.* work with utility of consumption functions conditional (a) upon avoidance of a particular injury or illness during a forthcoming period and (b) upon sustaining the injury or contracting the illness. The utility index associated with death during the period is arbitrarily set at zero so that no bequest motive is considered. Initially, the model is set up so that survival probability is less than one and dependent upon the health state of the individual, though subsequently the authors simplify the analysis and focus exclusively upon morbidity risks, setting survival probability at one. The probability of incurring the non-fatal injury or contracting the illness is taken to depend upon expenditures undertaken to prevent the injury or illness and an environmental 'shift' parameter. For the special case in which the possibility of death is ignored, it is shown that under plausible conditions willingness to pay for a beneficial marginal change in the environmental shift parameter will exceed (a) the impact of the change on output losses and (b) the impact of the change on preventive expenditures.

These results therefore complement the conclusion outlined in section 2.1.2 that under plausible conditions the value of statistical life will exceed the magnitude of costs or values defined in terms of lost output.

Finally, it is also important to establish how the magnitude of a willingness-to-pay based value of avoidance of statistical morbidity of given severity might be expected to compare with the value of statistical life for a particular way of dying. While a result concerning this relative magnitude is asserted without proof for a special case[11] in Jones-Lee *et al.* (1985), to the author's knowledge no other work has so far been undertaken on this subject. Accordingly, the issue is explicitly addressed in Chapter 3, section 3.7.

2.2   Empirical Estimates

Basically, two types of approach have been employed in the empirical estimation of individual marginal rates of substitution of wealth for physical risk – and hence values of statistical life. These have been described as the 'revealed-preference' (or 'implicit value') and 'questionnaire' (or 'contingent market') approaches.[12] Essentially, the revealed-preference approach involves the identification of situations in which people actually do explicitly or implicitly trade off wealth or income against the risk of death or injury. The most obvious source of such data is the labour market where, *ceteris paribus*, riskier jobs can be expected to carry clearly identifiable wage premia as compensation for risk. In fact, the majority of revealed-preference studies conducted to date have been of this type and are commonly referred to as 'compensating wage differential' or 'hedonic price' studies. Other kinds of revealed-preference study have been based upon data concerning the time–inconvenience–safety trade-offs involved in car seat-belt use, the fuel–time–safety trade-off involved in motorway speed decisions, house price–air pollution trade-offs, the purchase price and maintenance costs of domestic smoke detectors and the frequency of car tyre replacement.

In marked contrast with the revealed-preference studies, those based on the questionnaire approach involve asking a sample of individuals more or less directly about their willingness to pay – or required compensation – for various hypothetical changes in risk.

Clearly, the revealed-preference approach has the advantage of being based upon real rather than hypothetical choices. However, the compensating wage differential approach, in particular, has the major disadvantage that wage rates depend on many other factors besides risk, so that it is necessary to control for these factors in order to isolate the pure wealth–risk trade-off. This is typically done by regressing wage rates on various explanatory variables, including measures of risk. Clearly, the reliability of any estimate derived in this way depends (a) upon the quality of the regression analysis and the avoidance of, in particular, specification errors and omitted variables bias and (b) the nature and quality of workers' *perceptions* of job risks. (Thus, for example, if the value of statistical life is defined in terms of individual marginal rates of substitution of wealth for subjective probability of death, then it would clearly be inappropriate to base an empirical estimate of this value on wage premia for 'objectively' measured job risk if the latter diverged significantly from workers' perceptions of this risk.)

Another fairly obvious limitation of the revealed-preference approach is that it produces highly aggregated results – market equilibrium wage premia for risk – and is inherently incapable of generating estimates at the individual level.

While the questionnaire approach clearly suffers from the hypothetical nature of the trade-offs that it presents to subjects, it does avoid some of the major difficulties encountered in the revealed-preference studies. Thus, with appropriate design of the questionnaire, one can in principle go directly to the wealth-risk trade-off without the necessity to control for other variables as in the wage differential studies. Furthermore, the questionnaire approach facilitates direct investigation of the relationship between subjective and objective probabilities. Finally, and perhaps most significantly, the questionnaire approach yields estimates of *individual* valuation of safety, thereby allowing the researcher to make inferences about the way in which the latter varies with income, age, social class and so on. It is also a straightforward matter to compute values of statistical life with various distributional weighting schemes, an exercise that would, incidentally, be extremely difficult – if not impossible – under the revealed-preference approach.[13]

On balance, then, it seems that there are pros and cons associated with both the revealed-preference and questionnaire approaches. In the author's opinion, neither approach is inherently superior and, indeed, they are almost certainly best viewed as essentially complementary rather than competing estimation procedures.

2.2.1 Compensating Wage Differential Studies

In the elementary economic theory of labour markets, wage rates are supposed to adjust so as to ensure that firms' aggregate demand for labour of any particular type is exactly equal to workers' aggregate supply of that sort of labour (where firms' demand for labour reflects corporate objectives and production technology, while individual workers' willingness to supply labour depends upon income–leisure preferences and attitudes to work, per se).

At a somewhat more sophisticated level, a comprehensive description of any particular job requires specification of not only the wage rate and the tasks involved but also various other job characteristics such as working conditions, location and job risk. Clearly, just as in the elementary theory, different wage rates will call forth different aggregate demands and supplies for each type of labour, so in the more sophisticated analysis it will be the mix of job characteristics, including wage rates and job risk, that determines demand and supply and will, in an efficiently functioning market mechanism, adjust to clear markets for each type of labour. It follows that in full labour market equilibrium, each occupation will have its own particular equilibrium mix of job characteristics. However, it is also clear that, as one considers different occupations, *ceteris paribus*, jobs with higher risk will tend to command correspondingly higher wage rates. This is essentially because (a) firms will incur costs in improving job safety and so will offer lower wages for safer jobs (and vice versa) and (b) workers will require higher wage rates in order to be induced to accept increased job risk. In short, there will exist an equilibrium wage–risk function which is strictly increasing and has the property that workers located at any particular point on the function have marginal rates of substitution of wealth (or income) for risk that equal the slope of the function at that point, while firms located at the same point have marginal costs of risk reduction that also equal this slope. The essential and common purpose of the various compensating wage differential studies is to estimate this equilibrium wage–risk function, while controlling for the various other job characteristics and factors that are likely to be influential in determining the demand and supply of labour.

A full and comprehensive account of the various compensating wage differential studies that have been undertaken to date is clearly beyond the scope of this chapter. For the reader interested in a more detailed description and assessment of these studies, surveys by Smith (1979), Blomquist (1982) and especially Violette and Chestnut (1983) and Miller *et al.* (1984) are recommended. However, brief summaries of the key features and results of this work are presented below.

Thaler, R. and Rosen, S. (1973) This is one of the earliest and most widely quoted of the compensating wage differential studies. The risk data employed concerned probability of death for individuals in various particularly hazardous occupations and were obtained from the *1967 Occupation Study* by the US Society of Actuaries. Using these data, 'excess' risks over and above those that apply to the general population were computed for each of a number of different occupations using standard life tables. Finally, a sample of 907 individuals in the various hazardous occupations was selected from the *1967 Survey of Economic Opportunity*, which provided data concerning variables such as geographical location, family size, nature of industry, unionization, nature of occupation, age, education and weekly wage.

In all, Thaler and Rosen ran eight separate regressions, four in linear form with various different sets of explanatory variables, including interaction terms, and four in semilogarithmic form (i.e. with the natural logarithm of weekly wages as the dependent variable). The results of the regression analysis were mixed, with only one regression having a risk coefficient significant at the 5% level and two having a risk coefficient significant at about 10%. In addition, values of statistical life implied by these estimated risk coefficients ranged from \$96,000 to \$260,000 in the linear specifications and from $5,000 to $189,000 in the semilogarithmic cases, all in 1967 US dollars. In general, the lower estimates of the value of statistical life came from equations with interaction terms such as age × risk, married × risk and union × risk, which tended to be significant at the 5% level, suggesting that the risk measure employed by Thaler and Rosen may have reflected factors other than job risk. For example, the Society of Actuaries data reflect the risk of death from all causes for individuals in a given hazardous occupation and it is entirely possible that a part of this risk may have as much to do with the nature and lifestyle of individuals attracted to a particular occupation as with the occupation itself – Lipsey (1976) cites the example of bartenders whose overall risks may well reflect an inherent tendency to drink to excess, a tendency which would manifest itself even in very much safer occupations.

In spite of these limitations, Thaler and Rosen conclude that their results indicate a value of statistical life '. . . in the neighborhood of $200,000 1967 dollars'.

Smith, R. S. (1973, 1976)   The principal purpose of both these studies was to estimate the extent of an injury tax necessary to induce firms to improve job safety by various amounts. However, the studies do produce as significant by-products estimates of the equilibrium wage premia required at different levels of risk. The risk data used by Smith (1973) were 1966–7 US Bureau of Labor Statistics (BLS) injury rates, by industry, measured in injuries per million hours worked. While these data conflate risks of death and risks of injury, they were converted to separate estimates of risk of fatal injury, risk of permanent impairment and risk of temporary impairment using data on proportions of injuries in each category from the May 1967 *Current Population Survey* (CPS) (US Bureau of the Census) which also provided data on wage rates, unionization and other socioeconomic variables. The sample comprised over 3,000 white males. The 1976 study employed essentially the same model, but used updated data sources in the form of 1970 BLS injury rates and 1973 CPS data.

In the 1973 study Smith used two semilogarithmic specifications, one with and one without industry group dummies. In both cases the coefficient of the fatal risk variable was positive and significant at the 5% level, but matters were less clear-cut in the case of the non-fatal risk variables, which had the 'wrong' sign in the case of temporary impairments in the specification that excludes industry dummies and which were insignificant in the other specification. One possible interpretation of these results is that, while one can expect compensating wage differentials in the case of injuries that are, *ex post*, uncompensatable, the same may not be true of non-fatal injuries for which *ex post* compensation – in the form of insurance or workers' compensation – is possible. The values of statistical life implied by the coefficients of the fatal injury variables were $2,600,000 for the specification that includes industry dummies and $4,900,000 for that which does not. Both estimates are in US dollars in 1967 prices.

The 1976 study, designed in part to resolve the very substantial difference between the estimates of the value of statistical life from the 1973 study and those obtained by Thaler and Rosen, employed only data concerning workers in manufacturing industry so as to avoid biases from omitted variables – such as job disutility and strength of union – which may well have an effect in cases such as coal mining or construction. In addition, a separate regression was run for those workers in manufacturing who were paid on an hourly basis. Finally, in view of the results of Smith (1973) the coefficients of the non-fatal injury variables were constrained to be zero. The estimated coefficients of the fatal risk variables were again significant at the 5% level and implied values of statistical life of $1,600,000 for the full sample and $1,500,000 for the hourly workers subsample, both in 1973 US dollars.

Of the various estimates, Smith suggests that those reported in the 1976 study are probably more reliable.

Melinek, S. J. (1974)   This study did not employ regression analysis but proceeded on the basis of a very much more ad hoc argument related to International Labour Office (ILO) job evaluation procedures. In particular, in job evaluation studies the ILO awarded a maximum of 5 points to the most dangerous jobs in arriving at an overall job score whose maximum was itself 100 points. Using UK Central Statistical Office (CSO) data on deaths from industrial accidents in various occupations for 1971, Melinek estimated that the incremental annual risk of death per ILO point is 10^{-4}. In addition Melinek calculated the standard deviation of wages of males in full-time employment from 1971 CSO data and, on the assumption that ILO job scores are symmetrically distributed about a mean of 50, concluded that each ILO point is equivalent to an incremental wage of £20 p.a. Dividing this by the annual risk per ILO point yields a value of statistical life of £200,000 in 1971 prices.

Viscusi, W. K. (1978a)   This study is similar to, although in some ways rather more sophisticated than, that conducted by Smith. In particular, the same risk data source (BLS) was employed but this was supplemented by information on whether or not a worker perceived his job to be dangerous. Fatal and non-fatal risks were estimated by multiplying the total injury rate given in the BLS data by the relevant percentages of fatal and non-fatal injuries. In addition, Viscusi used data from the University of Michigan *1969–70 Survey of Working Conditions* which provides information on individual earnings and various job and personal characteristics not included in Smith's study, such as number of employees in the enterprise, whether the worker is supervised, whether the worker has decision-making discretion and so on. The sample size was 495.

Viscusi ran linear and semilogarithmic regressions on five separate specifications of the wage equation. Basically, the difference between these specifications lay in the nature of the risk variables employed. For example, in specification 1 only the industry death risk estimated from the BLS data was included. In specification 2 the non-fatal injury rate was also included, whereas in specification 3 this was replaced by a dummy for self-assessed danger. In specifications 4, 5 and 6 industry death risk was replaced by the product of industry death risk and the self-assessed danger dummy so that the risk level was non-zero only if the worker perceived it to be so. Estimated values of statistical life range from $600,000 to $1,770,000 with the majority in excess of $1,000,000, while values of avoidance of statistical injuries are between $5,500 and $9,500, all in 1969 US dollars.

Veljanovski, C. (1978) This was the first regression analysis of compensating wage differentials for the UK and, broadly speaking, was modelled on earlier US studies. The data for 53 manufacturing industries for 1971 were collected from various sources. The risk data, which gave reported accidents during 1971 per 100,000 workers at risk broken down into fatalities, severe injuries and other reported accidents, were obtained from the *UK Factory Inspectors' Annual Report 1974*. Wage and unionization data were obtained from *New Earnings Survey 1971*, while data concerning organization of work (e.g. shift work, payment-by-results etc.) were obtained from *New Earnings Survey 1971* and *New Earnings Survey 1973*. Other variables were obtained from the *Bureau of Labor Statistics Year Book 1971*, *Census of Production 1971* and *Digest of Incapacity Statistics 1969–70*. Three separate specifications of the regression relationship were estimated, namely linear, semilogarithmic and log–log. In all three cases the coefficients of the fatal accident variables were positive and significant at the 5% level, with implied values of statistical life in 1971 prices of £823,000, £807,000 and £1,118,000 respectively. The coefficients of the severe injury variables were also significant but of the 'wrong' sign, as in the Smith (1973) study. Veljanovksi suggests, as did Smith, that these results may reflect either the fact that the existence of accident insurance for non-fatal injuries may actually depress wage rates or that the findings may be a result of worker ignorance of the true risks of non-fatal injury.

Dillingham, A. E. (1979) This study employed risk data obtained from the New York Workmen's Compensation Board for injuries during 1970 together with employment data from the *1970 US Census*. Risk data were broken down into death rates and various rates for non-fatal injury. Various different regressions were run, all with the natural log of annual earnings as the dependent variable but with different specifications, some involving the inclusion of interaction variables such as fatal injuries multiplied by age, education, marital status and white/non-white. These regression analyses were conducted for two samples, the first comprising all males in full-time employment in New York State in 1970 and the second comprising only full-time males in blue collar occupations in manufacturing and construction in New York State.

The results of the regression analyses were very mixed, both in terms of the significance of estimated risk coefficients and in terms of the implied values of statistical life. For the sample of all males in full-time employment, the specification including risk interaction variables yielded no significant coefficients for the risk variables. However, when the interaction variables were omitted the coefficient of the fatal injury rate was significant and implied a value of statistical life of about $1,000,000 in 1970 prices. In fact, the value of statistical life implied by the estimated coefficients when all risk interaction variables were included was as low as $23,000 (an estimate based on the coefficients of all variables would be justified in spite of insignificance if it were held that there was a high degree of multicollinearity between these variables).

In the case of the smaller blue collar sample the coefficient of the fatality rate variable was significant in four of the five specifications, but the coefficients of the non-fatal injury variables were, with one exception, insignificant. As in other studies, the significant non-fatal injury coefficient was negative, providing further evidence of the tendency for workers' compensation to eliminate compensating wage differentials. Values of statistical life implied by the estimated coefficients in this sample ranged from $140,000 to $449,000 in 1970 prices.

Clearly the disparity between the regression results of the two samples is, *prima facie*, somewhat disturbing but Dillingham notes that the injury rates for white collar workers, who were included in the larger sample, are in fact lower than the corresponding rates for injuries in the home, so that it may be that there simply are no wage premia for risk associated with such jobs. Nonetheless, even the estimates for the blue collar sample are significantly lower than most of those obtained from other compensating wage differential studies.

Brown, C. (1980)   One of the most common criticisms of the studies surveyed so far is that the estimated risk coefficients may have been the subject of omitted-variables bias. In particular, if personal characteristics that tend to increase wage rates and are positively correlated with risk are omitted in the specification of the wage equation then estimates of the risk coefficients will be biased upwards, whereas negative correlation will produce the opposite effect. The purpose of Brown's study was to reduce such potential biases by including more comprehensive data on personal characteristics than had been employed in earlier studies.

In fact a variety of data sources were used, the main ones being *The National Longitudinal Survey Young Men's Sample* (which provided data on various personal characteristics including human capital investments, unionization, marital status and health problems for the years 1967–71 and 1973), the *Dictionary of Occupational Titles* file (which provided data on various job characteristics), the 1966 *Current Population Survey* and the *1967 Occupation Study by the US Society of Actuaries* (which gave data on the increase in the actuarial probability of death associated with hazardous occupations – all other occupations were assigned an incremental risk of zero). The sample size was 470.

Eight separate regressions were run, all with the natural logarithm of total compensation (including wage and non-wage components) as the dependent variable, but with different combinations of the explanatory variables. In four of these regressions 'individual-specific intercepts' were included to capture the effects of characteristics specific to individuals that do not change over time. In the remaining four regressions these intercepts were omitted and replaced with conventional time-invariant determinants of workers' wages in order to facilitate comparison with the results of other studies.

In the regressions that did not include individual-specific intercepts, the coefficients of the risk of death variable were statistically significant and equal to about three times the estimates obtained by Thaler and Rosen, implying a value of statistical life of roughly $600,000 in 1967 prices.[14] In the regressions that did include individual-specific intercepts, however, the coefficients of the risk variable were an order of magnitude smaller and statistically insignificant. While Brown offers various possible explanations for this and other disappointing results of his study, he acknowledges that none of these is particularly convincing, so that his analysis can be regarded as providing only partial support for the compensating wage differential hypothesis.

Needleman, L. (1980) This study, like Melinek's, did not employ regression analysis but focused instead upon the incremental risk and corresponding danger money paid for undertaking specific hazardous activities in the construction industry in the UK.

Data on the incremental risks of a fatal accident in various construction activities were obtained from the *Annual Reports of the Chief Inspector of Factories*, while data concerning 'condition money' (i.e. extra payments for work involving risk, discomfort or inconvenience) were obtained from a survey conducted by the UK National Board for Prices and Incomes during 1968.

The overall average value of statistical life for all construction workers was estimated by dividing the net of tax average hourly 'condition money' by the average hourly incremental risk of death in various hazardous construction activities, yielding a figure of about £22,000 in 1968 prices. Needleman suggests that this estimate is in the nature of an upper bound for two reasons. The first is that, in his view, workers probably overestimate the incremental risks from hazardous activities, so that dividing danger money by objective incremental risk will tend to overstate the relevant marginal rates of substitution (which, as noted in Chapter 1, should, strictly speaking, be defined in terms of subjective probabilities). Needleman's second reason for believing that his estimate should be treated as an upper bound is that 'condition money' represents compensation not only for incremental risk but also for discomfort and inconvenience.

Separate estimates of the value of statistical life for different occupations within construction were also obtained and were, in particular, roofing workers, £8,000; steel erectors, £17,000; and scaffolders, £46,000.

Noting that his estimates of the value of statistical life are very low by comparison with most others obtained prior to 1980, Needleman offers various explanations for this discrepancy. His first suggestion is that workers' perceptions of risks, particularly in industries other than their own, may be of insufficient quality to justify the assumptions underpinning those wage differential studies that are based on large numbers of industries or occupations, so that the estimates of the value of statistical life from these studies are inherently unreliable. A further factor that Needleman cites as detracting from the reliability of other studies is the lack of fineness of the risk data used, which typically consisted of risks by industry or occupation whereas one would ideally want a far finer breakdown within industries or occupations.

In the author's view neither of these explanations of the difference in magnitude between Needleman's estimate and those obtained in other studies is particularly persuasive. Specifically, the explanations give no reason for supposing that the estimated risk coefficients in the other studies will have been biased *upwards* and it is, of course, the case that the values of statistical life implied by these coefficients are generally substantially higher than Needleman's estimate. An altogether more plausible explanation for the discrepancy is that Needleman's study focuses upon an industry that happens to attract workers with atypically sanguine attitudes to risk and/or that the psychological phenomenon of 'cognitive dissonance' is at work. While this concept is discussed more fully in Chapter 5 its essential feature in the present context is that individuals, having opted for a particular course of action (e.g. employment in a hazardous occupation), tend to discount or minimize the potential adverse aspects of that action.

Olson, C. A. (1981)   This study employed US Bureau of Labor Statistics data on fatalities during 1973 together with data on earnings and other personal and occupational characteristics from the May 1973 *Current Population Survey*. As such, the data sources were similar to those used by R. S. Smith. However, Olson's study also involved data on non-fatal accidents from the US Department of Labor *Occupational Safety and Health Statistics: Concepts and Methods*, 1978. Another feature of Olson's study that distinguishes it from earlier exercises is the inclusion of a nonlinear fatal accident variable which allows, inter alia, for the possibility that the equilibrium wage–risk relationship is *concave*, reflecting the tendency for those with lower physical risk aversion to gravitate to more hazardous occupations.

Olson regressed the natural logarithm of weekly and hourly earnings in turn on various explanatory variables, including the non-linear risk variable (the square of annual probability of a fatal accident). Separate regressions were also run with interaction variables, including a risk × union dummy and a risk-squared × union dummy. In the regressions that excluded interaction variables the coefficients on the risk variables were significantly positive, while those on the risk-squared variable were significantly negative, confirming the hypothesis of an increasing, concave equilibrium wage–risk relationship. Evaluated at the means of all variables these coefficients implied a value of statistical life of about $3,300,000 in 1973 prices. For those at lowest risk in the sample (probability of fatal accident equal to about 1.5×10^{-5}) the implied value of statistical life was about $3,700,000, while for those at the highest risk (3×10^{-4}) the value was approximately $2,200,000.

In general, non-fatal accident variables had significantly positive coefficients in these regressions, in contrast with most earlier studies, indicating a value of avoidance of a statistical non-fatal accident of about $7,300 with a further $33 for each additional working day lost.

When the interaction variables were included, only those involving risk and unionization were significant. In particular, the risk $\times$ union dummy coefficient was positive, indicating that membership of a union raises the wage premium for risk. In these regressions the coefficient of the risk variable was significantly positive while that for risk-squared was insignificant. However, the risk-squared $\times$ union dummy interaction variable was significantly negative.

Because union membership appeared to have a significant effect on wage premia, separate regressions were run for union members and non-members. The values of statistical life implied by the estimated coefficients were about $8,000,000 in 1973 prices for union members and about $1,500,000 for non-members.

Finally, because the regressions excluding interaction terms produced values of statistical life so much larger than those obtained by R. S. Smith, in spite of the similarity between the data sets, Olson also ran these regressions without the risk-squared variable for comparison. In this case the estimated value of statistical life fell to a level very much closer to that obtained by Smith.

Marin, A. and Psacharopoulos, G. (1982) This is the most recent and most comprehensive compensating wage differential study so far carried out for the UK. The study was based upon data concerning risk, individual and job characteristics for a large number of different occupations ranging from managerial and professional to manual for male workers in the UK. Risk data were obtained from the UK Office of Population Censuses and Surveys 1978 *Occupational Mortality Decennial Supplement* and from unpublished tabulations provided by a member of the Office of Population Censuses and Surveys. Individual and occupational data were obtained from *General Household Survey 1975* individual data tapes.

One of the many novel and interesting features of this study is that it employs two alternative measures of risk. The first measure, referred to by the authors as GENRISK, reflects the excess risk of death for members of each occupational group over and above the risk faced by members of the general population of the same age and social class. Thus, this measure is similar to that employed by Thaler and Rosen and others and is subject to the criticism that the excess risk may include a component that is entirely independent of work-related risks. In consequence, Marin and Psacharopoulos used a second risk measure, ACCRISK, which was based upon the excess risk of a fatal accident *at work* in each occupation, over and above the 'average' risk of such an accident for workers as a whole, taking account of the age pattern of the group.

Regressions were run for the whole sample and for subsamples comprising managers and professionals, non-manual workers and finally, manual workers. In general, alternative specifications with and without a risk × union dummy interaction variable were employed.

In all cases the estimated risk coefficients were positive and significance tend to increase as one moves from the 'managerial' to the 'manual' end of the spectrum – at the manual end significance is substantial. Marin and Psacharopoulos argue that the relative lack of significance for managerial workers is hardly surprising in view of the fact that there is a low spread of risks in managerial jobs and that for most managers and professionals there is a zero or negative excess risk of accidental death at work. Values of statistical life implied by the significant estimated coefficients of the ACCRISK variable – strongly preferred on a priori grounds by the authors – range from about £650,000 in 1975 prices for manual workers to over £2,200,000 for non-manual workers with a value of roughly £650,000 for the sample as a whole (which included managers and professionals, who were not included in the non-manual subsample and whose estimated risk coefficient in a separate regression was insignificantly different from zero, probably because of the low level and spread of occupational risk within this group). In general, inclusion of the risk × union interaction variable tended to depress estimates somewhat, the figures referred to above being midpoint estimates obtained from the 'with' and 'without' interaction variable specifications. Based on the 'with' specification, for example, the whole-sample estimate of the value of statistical life was about £600,000, while that obtained when the interaction variable was omitted was over £680,000. Interestingly and in line with other studies that used overall death risk (rather than occupational accident risk) variables, values of statistical life based on the estimated coefficients of GENRISK are substantially smaller. Finally, subsidiary regressions were run (a) with a quadratic risk variable and (b) for a subsample comprising the top third of the jobs in terms of risk. In contrast with Olson's findings, the coefficient of the risk-squared variable tended to be insignificant. Furthermore the coefficient of the risk variable for the subsample of high risk jobs is not markedly different from that for the whole sample. These results therefore do not support the hypothesis of a concave equilibrium wage–risk relationship with less risk-averse workers gravitating to the most risky jobs.

Smith, V. K. (1983)   Smith's study has several novel features. In the first place his analysis attempts to explain differences in wage rates not only in terms of job characteristics, including risk, but also in terms of site characteristics (such as crime rate, air pollution, number of urban facilities – including museums and hospitals – unemployment and weather) on the hypothesis that households' choice of residential location will also be reflected in wage rates. Smith also adjusted wage rates for regional differences in the cost of living and included an industry index of exposure to carcinogenic materials. Finally, a variable reflecting the fraction of workers in each industry subject to collective bargaining agreements with provisions concerning health and safety issues was also included on the hypothesis that such workers would be better informed about risks.

The risk data, which did not distinguish between fatal and non-fatal risks, were obtained from the 1975 Bureau of Labor Statistics *Occupational Injuries and Illnesses in the United States by Industry*. The index of exposure to carcinogenic materials was obtained from Hickey and Kearney (1977), while personal occupational and locational data were obtained from the May 1978 *Current Population Survey*.

As in other studies, various specifications of the wage relationship were estimated, some including risk interaction variables and others not. In all cases the dependent variable was the real hourly wage rate adjusted for local cost of living. In almost all cases the coefficient of the risk variable was significantly positive and of broadly the same order of magnitude. However, inference of a value of statistical life from these estimates is complicated by the fact that the risk variable included fatal and non-fatal accidents. In order to derive a value of statistical life one must therefore make an assumption about the proportion of the wage premium that applies to fatal as opposed to non-fatal accidents. Olson's study indicated that about one-third of the premium relates to fatal accidents while Viscusi (1978b) estimates the proportion as being between a half and a little less than one-third. On this basis the value of statistical life implied by Smith's estimate of the premium from the specification without interaction terms would be in the region of $400,000–$700,000 in 1978 prices. However, it will be recalled that R. S. Smith's (1973) study suggested that, because of the existence of insurance or workers' compensation, there are no compensating wage differentials for non-fatal injuries so that the entire wage premium applies to fatalities. If this hypothesis is correct then V. K. Smith's estimates would yield a value of statistical life of about $1,400,000.

Arnould, R. J. and Nichols, L. M. (1983) This study represents an attempt to refine Thaler and Rosen's analysis by incorporating data on workers' compensation, payable by employers, on the hypothesis that, for reasons already explained, failure to take account of such compensation will tend to bias estimated wage premia for risk in a downward direction.[15]

The risk data source was the same as that employed by Thaler and Rosen (i.e. the US Society of Actuaries) which gives the fatality rates for various hazardous occupations. It was assumed that non-fatal injury rates were proportional to fatality rates. Other data were obtained from

Public Use Samples of Basic Records from the 1970 Census, US Department of Commerce, Bureau of the Census, and data concerning workers' compensation from Rosenblum, M., *Compendium of Workmen's Compensation*, National Committee on State Workmen's Compensation, Washington, DC, 1973.

Various regressions were run, but the authors report only those with weekly wages as the dependent variable. The risk coefficients were generally significant at the 5% level, though the coefficient of a risk-squared variable was not. With the effect of worker's compensation included, the implied value of statistical life was $223,000 in 1970 prices, and with the effect excluded, $200,000.

Weiss, P. et al. (1986)   To date, compensating wage differential studies have focused almost exclusively upon the US and UK labour markets. This study is unusual in that it is based upon data concerning the Austrian labour market. However, apart from this, the approach employed is basically standard.

Data concerning personal characteristics for 4,200 Austrian blue collar workers were obtained from the 1981 *Microcensus File* of the Austrian Central Bureau of Statistics, and data concerning job-related fatal accidents and all job-related accidents (fatal and non-fatal) by industry for the period 1977–84 were obtained from two Austrian insurance companies. Attention was focused upon blue collar workers, essentially because it was felt that in the case of white collar workers and civil servants, for example, there would exist no perceptible wage–risk relationship, while agricultural workers, although they face very high job-related risks, have abnormally low earnings levels, possibly as a result of non-pecuniary job satisfaction.

Two specifications of the regression relationship were employed. The first involved regression of the logarithm of monthly income on various characteristics, including a linear job risk variable, while the second included linear *and* quadratic risk variables. These regressions were run separately on data concerning fatal and 'all' risks (including non-fatal accidents).

In spite of the fact that job safety in Austria is closely regulated and monitored by a work inspectorate (so that it would not have been surprising to discover little evidence of wage–risk premia), the coefficients of all risk variables in the regressions were significant at the 5% level. A finding of some interest was that the coefficient of the quadratic risk variable was negative, suggesting that, as conjectured by Olson and others, there is a tendency for less risk-averse workers to gravitate to riskier occupations.

The value of statistical life implied by the regression based on fatal accident data and using a linear risk variable was Sch33,000,000 in 1981 prices while the specification that included a quadratic risk variable gave a value of Sch55,000,000. The authors clearly regard the latter as their preferred estimate since this was obtained essentially by computing a separate marginal rate of substitution of wealth for risk for each individual in the sample from the estimated regression relationship – a procedure that allows for the non-uniform distribution of individual valuation of safety within the sample.

2.2.2 Other Revealed-preference Studies

In addition to estimates produced by the compensating wage differential studies, willingness-to-pay based values of statistical life have also been derived from data concerning 'real' choices in a variety of situations. In some cases the wealth–risk trade-off is very direct so that implied values of statistical life can be computed in a straightforward manner. In others, choices can be expected to have been influenced by a variety of factors besides effects on wealth and risk so that, as in the case of the wage differential studies, it is necessary to use more or less sophisticated statistical techniques to control for these other influences. The summaries that follow illustrate the varying complexity of these studies.

Melinek, S. J. (1974) This study focuses upon the trade-off between safety, time and inconvenience involved in the decision concerning use or non-use of pedestrian subways. Data given in Road Research Laboratory (1963) indicate that pedestrians will typically use subways only if doing so takes no more than about 25% longer than crossing a road directly, and will use a pedestrian bridge only if this takes no longer than the direct crossing.

Ministry of Transport (1966) reports that the typical vertical ascent–descent distance involved in the use of a subway is 2.5 m while that for the use of a bridge is, at minimum, 5.5 m. Given that pedestrians are indifferent between bridge use and direct crossing when the time costs are identical, it follows that the inconvenience costs of a 5.5 m ascent–descent are equivalent to the cost of the incremental risk from the direct crossing. Melinek therefore concludes that the inconvenience cost of a 2.5 m ascent–descent in subway use is equal to roughly 2.5/5.5 times the cost of the risk that is thereby avoided.

Using this result, together with data concerning the horizontal walking distance involved in subway use (also given in Ministry of Transport, 1966) and a value of commuting time reported by Harrison and Quarmby (1970), Melinek derives an estimate of the overall incremental time and inconvenience costs that people appear to be willing to incur in order to use subways. This, together with an estimate of the consequent reduction in the risk of a fatal injury based on data reported in Road Research Laboratory (1963), yields a value of statistical life of £87,000 in 1972 prices.

Ghosh, D. et al. (1975) This study is based upon the premise that, whether viewed from a social or a private perspective, at the optimal motorway speed the marginal benefits of time savings due to increased speed will equal the marginal costs of fuel consumption and increased risk of death or injury. Given appropriately estimated fuel consumption–speed and risk–speed relationships it is then possible to derive a socially optimal motorway speed for particular social values of time and safety. Alternatively – and for our purposes, more significantly – given a particular *private* value of time one can derive an implied private value of safety on the assumption that current average motorway speeds are reflective of a private optimization process.

Using an estimate of the fuel consumption–speed relationship derived by the UK Transport and Road Research Laboratory and an estimate of the risk–speed relationship based on monthly UK data for the period January 1972 to March 1974, together with an assumed value of time of £1.00 per hour and price of petrol of £0.35 per gallon (broadly reflective of the UK hourly wage rate and price of petrol in 1973) the value of statistical life was estimated to be £94,000 in 1973 prices. Ghosh *et al.* also tested the sensitivity of their estimate to variations in the value of time and the price of petrol. In particular, it was found that with the value of time reduced to £0.65 the value of statistical life falls to zero and that with the price of petrol set at zero (or, equivalently, if the marginal fuel cost of extra speed is ignored) then the implied value of statistical life rises to over £250,000.[16]

Jones-Lee, M. W. (1977)   The essential idea of this study is that the probability of an injury accident caused by tyre failure (i.e. puncture or skid) is an increasing function of tyre wear. Motorists therefore face an implicit trade-off between wealth and safety in that, the more frequently tyres are replaced, the greater the discounted present value of expenditure on them. On the assumption that motorists will choose tyre replacement frequencies so as to equate their marginal rates of substitution of wealth for risk with the marginal rate of transformation implied by the trade-off referred to above, it should therefore be possible to make inferences about these rates of substitution from estimates of the rate of transformation.

Essentially, the marginal rate of transformation between wealth and risk was estimated by

1   computing the impact on discounted lifetime tyre expenditure of a small increase in the frequency of replacement,
2   estimating the impact on life expectancy of the same small increase in the frequency of replacement, and hence
3   deriving the implied marginal rate of transformation (and hence marginal rate of substitution) of wealth for life expectancy. From this it is possible, on admittedly rather strong assumptions, to derive a corresponding marginal rate of substitution of wealth for current-period probability of death.[17]

In order to make the analysis workable a number of rather strong simplifying assumptions were made. For example, the entire exercise focused upon a 'typical' motorist, aged 30, who chooses to change car tyres when 1 mm of tread depth remains and drives an annual mileage equal to the UK average.[18] Average tyre life was assumed to be 15,000 miles and the purchase price of a set of four tyres was taken to be £40 in 1976 prices. Since real rates of interest were zero or negative in the mid-seventies in the UK, the discount rate was set at zero in computing present values of lifetime expenditure on tyres.

Estimation of the impact of tyre replacement frequency on the probability of a tyre-failure-induced accident – and hence on life expectancy – was, to say the least, far from straightforward. First, time profiles of the risk of puncture or skid over the life-cycle of a set of tyres were estimated up to a scale factor from data reported in Grogan and Watson (1974) and French and Hofferberth (1967) respectively. Not surprisingly both kinds of risk were found to increase exponentially with tyre wear. From these estimated time profiles, a cyclical risk function was constructed showing the risk of puncture or skid rising exponentially over the life of the first set of tyres, falling discontinuously at the first tyre replacement, rising again exponentially, falling at the second replacement and so on. This cyclical function was then scaled so that its integral over the assumed driving life of the typical individual equalled the probability that he would eventually die in an accident caused by puncture or skid. In order to derive this probability it is necessary to have an estimate of the number of fatalities per annum that are a direct consequence of tyre failure. Data provided by the UK Transport and Road Research Laboratory suggested that between 1% and 13% of car occupant fatalities were caused by tyre failure. Accordingly, the scaling of the cyclical risk function was performed for a variety of values within this range.

Finally, in order to compute the impact of variation in frequency of tyre replacement on life expectancy, the cyclical risk function was 'blended' with a density function for time of death, obtained from standard mortality tables.

Not surprisingly, variation in the assumed values of the numerous parameters involved in the study produced a wide range of estimates of the value of statistical life. However, for the 'best-guess' range of parameter values, estimates of the value of statistical life were in the interval £200,000–£1,250,000 in 1976 prices, a range that is broadly consonant with the spread of values derived in other studies.

Blomquist, G. (1979) The basic idea of this analysis is that, in the absence of compulsory seat-belt legislation, the decision whether or not to wear motorcar seat-belts is essentially a trade-off between the safety effects of doing so and the time and inconvenience costs involved. In particular, given a free choice, an individual will elect to wear seat-belts only if the marginal value of the consequent safety improvement exceeds the marginal time and inconvenience costs. It follows that if the only costs were the time costs of putting on and taking off seat-belts and the only safety effect was a reduction in the probability of being killed in a car accident, then for anyone who was indifferent about whether or not to wear seat-belts, the marginal rate of substitution of wealth for risk would simply be given by the time costs divided by the corresponding probability reduction. However, things are not quite so simple. In the first place, for most people faced with a free choice, inconvenience is almost certainly a significant factor in the seat-belt use decision. Furthermore, it is plainly the case that seat-belt use affects not only the risk of death but also that of serious injury and disfigurement. Finally, most people will presumably be well inside (or outside) the margin of indifference as to whether or not to use seat-belts.

Blomquist's study attempts to take account of these various complicating factors through probit analysis. Essentially, this produces an estimate of an equation giving a standardized index $\hat{s}_i$ of seat-belt use as a linear function of various measurable personal and other characteristics likely to influence individual seat-belt use decisions. Under the hypothesis upon which probit analysis is based, the probability that the ith individual will wear seat-belts is then given by $\int_{-\infty}^{\hat{s}_i} n(x) \, dx$ where n is the standard normal density function and $\hat{s}_i$ is predicted for the ith individual from the estimated probit equation. It follows that the probability that individual i will use seat-belts is greater than, equal to or less than 0.5 as $\hat{s}_i \gtreqless 0$. Blomquist argues that $\hat{s}_i$ evaluated at the sample means of the various explanatory variables in the probit equation can be equated to the average net benefits of seat-belt use for the sample, appropriately normalized. Clearly, net benefits will consist of the value of reduction in mortality risk *plus* the value of reduction in risk of non-fatal injury *minus* the time costs of seat-belt use and inconvenience costs. The normalization is required to ensure that net benefits are expressed in the same units as the standardized index $\hat{s}_i$. Essentially, the normalization factor is obtained by comparing the effect of a unit variation in the wage rate (a) upon the standardized index $\hat{s}_i$ and (b) upon the monetary time costs of seat-belt use. It is clear, then, that given $\hat{s}_i$ evaluated at the sample means of the explanatory variables, the average value of reduction in risk of death can be expressed as a function of the value of reduction in non-fatal injury, time costs, inconvenience costs and the normalization factor. It would then be a short step to derive an estimate of the mean marginal rate of substitution of wealth for risk of death from the estimated average normalized value of reduction in mortality risk. However, the major stumbling block in such an exercise is the difficulty in obtaining a reliable estimate of the inconvenience cost of seat-belt use. Blomquist therefore proceeds by arguing that if time and inconvenience costs were zero then one would expect virtually everyone to wear seat-belts. With $\hat{s}_i = 2.326$, the probability of seat-belt use is 0.99, so that setting $\hat{s}_i$ at this level and time and inconvenience costs at zero one can obtain the lowest value of reduction in mortality risk – and hence value of statistical life – that would be consistent with effective universal use of seat-belts.

Data on seat-belt use and other personal characteristics were obtained from *A Panel Study of Income Dynamics 1968–1974* (Survey Research Center, 1972, 1973, 1974) which provides data on over 5,500 households in the USA over a seven-year period. Estimates of the effectiveness of seat-belt use in reducing mortality risks were obtained from various studies[19] and the estimate of the impact on non-fatal injury risks was based upon data obtained from the US National Safety Council, the US Department of Transportation and the Illinois Department of Transportation. The average cost of a non-fatal injury was a gross output based figure which included an arbitrary 'pain, grief and suffering' allowance and was obtained from the US Department of Transportation. Finally an estimate of the average time taken to put on, adjust and take off seat-belts was obtained from a simple time and motion study carried out by Blomquist himself.

Lower bounds to the value of statistical life, based on a number of alternative assumptions concerning the various parameters involved in the study, ranged from $250,000 to $820,000 in 1978 prices. Blomquist's preferred configuration of parameter values yields a lower bound to the value of statistical life of $368,000 in 1978 prices. Finally, Blomquist's study provides an estimate of 0.3 for the elasticity of the marginal rate of substitution of wealth for risk with respect to lifetime earnings.

Dardis, R. (1980) This study employed data concerning the purchase price of domestic smoke detectors – together with estimates of the effectiveness of such devices in reducing the probability of death or injury – to derive values of statistical life on the assumption that individual subjective perceptions of domestic fire risks can be approximated by historical relative frequencies. Clearly, for those who do purchase smoke detectors (13% of households in the USA in 1976) the estimated value of statistical life should be treated as a lower bound, while for those who do not, the reverse is the case. Furthermore, since it is impossible to determine the proportion of the purchase price that reflects willingness to pay for reduction in the risk of death as opposed to injury, it is necessary to base the estimate of the value of statistical life on more or less arbitrary assumptions about the relative valuation of reductions in mortality and morbidity risks.

The annualized cost of a smoke detector, including the cost of battery replacement, was estimated from Sears Roebuck price data for 1974–9 using alternative discount rates of 5% and 10%, on the assumption that the detectors have a life expectancy of ten years. Effectiveness in terms of risk reduction was estimated from the following: (a) data concerning the numbers of domestic fire deaths and injuries in the USA during 1976 contained in reports by the National Fire Protection Association, the National Fire Prevention and Control Administration and the US Consumer Product Safety Commission, together with an unpublished report by Barancik and Shapiro (1972); (b) data concerning the proportion of households owning smoke detectors; (c) estimates of the proportion of detectors that are operational at any particular time; (d) estimates of the proportions of domestic fires in which a detector would avoid death or injury.

Values of statistical life were then estimated under each of three different assumptions concerning the relative values of avoidance of statistical injury and statistical death, namely 0.5, 0.1 and zero. Furthermore, values were computed for each of the years 1974–9 given that (a) smoke detector prices declined systematically over this period as a result of technological change and (presumably) market penetration and (b) sales expanded. Using weights to reflect the relative importance of sales in each year, the minimum value of statistical life to households that purchased smoke detectors was estimated to range from $189,000 (with the value of avoidance of statistical injury equal to 50% of the value of statistical life and a discount rate of 5%) to $295,000 (with the value of avoidance of statistical injury set at zero and a discount rate of 10%). These values should presumably be treated as being in prices at somewhat past the midpoint of the period of the study (1974–9), given that sales increased over this period.

Portney, P. R. (1981)   Just as equilibrium wage rates can be taken to depend on a variety of personal and job characteristics, including risk, so equilibrium house prices can be expected to reflect a number of different housing and environmental characteristics, including mortality risk from local air pollution. Portney argues that the house price–mortality risk trade-off derived from this relationship can be interpreted '. . . as the additional amount people reveal themselves willing to pay in higher property values for dwellings that expose them to a lesser risk of death from illness related to air pollution'.

In order to estimate the equilibrium house price–mortality risk trade-off, Portney employed regression results concerning (a) the relationship between house prices and air quality reported by Spore (1972) and (b) the relationship between mortality risks and air quality reported by Gregor (1977). As it happens, both of these regression analyses employed data for the same geographical area (Allegheny County, Pennsylvania) and period (pre-1972). In fact, Gregor's regression analysis yields age- and sex-specific effects of variation in air quality on mortality risk and, using these results, Portney calculated the overall effect of air quality on the total household mortality risk to a 'typical' family comprising a 40-year-old couple with one child. On the assumption that '. . . the household values equally reductions in risk to each of its members . . .', Portney then combined this effect on total household risk with the estimated equilibrium house price–air quality effect to obtain a value of statistical life 'per household member' of about $142,000 in 1978 prices. Alternatively, one can think of Portney's estimate as the head of the household's average value of own and relatives' lives.

As Portney himself acknowledges, a major limitation of his study is that it fails to take account of the fact that air quality may be valued for its own sake, quite independently of its effects on mortality risk, so that attribution of the entire air quality–house price premium to risk reduction will bias the estimated value of statistical life in an upward direction.

Another fairly obvious source of bias in this study – again, acknowledged by Portney – is the quality of individual perception of the risk of death from air pollution. In fact, one suspects that risk–pollution relationships are very poorly understood by most people and, indeed, evidence reported by Lichtenstein *et al.* (1978) suggests that pollution risks will typically be severely underestimated. If this is so, then Portney's estimate will have been subject to a very substantial downward bias that counteracts, and probably outweighs, that described in the previous paragraph.

Ippolito, P. M. and Ippolito, R. A. (1984) The central premise of this paper appears to be that, on receipt of information concerning the health hazards of smoking, cigarette smokers will (a) reduce their demand for cigarettes of any given nicotine content and (b) switch from cigarettes of higher to lower nicotine content. Interpreting the demand shift as a compensating variation per unit cigarette consumption, Ippolito and Ippolito then divide this by the change in life expectancy per unit cigarette consumption to obtain what they call an 'annualized value of life-saving' but which, in the terminology employed in this book, is more appropriately regarded as a marginal rate of substitution of wealth for life expectancy.

In fact, the impact of health-hazard information was obtained by comparing the actual 1980 demand for cigarettes – based on widely publicized information about health hazards – with the 'counterfactual' projection to 1980 of earlier smoking patterns which were based on little, if any, information about risks. While the authors did take account of variations in tastes for nicotine content and differences in the reactions to risk information across the population, their primary estimates assume uniform beliefs – identical to the 'objective' data – concerning the impact of smoking on life expectancy. However, when the primary estimates were recomputed using survey data concerning the distribution of consumer beliefs concerning the health effects of smoking, the impact upon the mean value of safety was not dramatic, although it did increase somewhat.

The estimated 'annualized value of life-saving' was found to vary widely across the population and to be highly right-skewed, with a mean of between $5,142 and $16,008 per annum in 1980 prices – this range reflecting the 95% confidence intervals of the various estimates used to compute the 'annualized values'.

In order to render their estimates comparable with the results of other empirical studies, Ippolito and Ippolito multiply their mean 'annualized value of life-saving' by average male life expectancy (which is about 35 years) to obtain what they call a 'mean value of life-saving' in the range $179,970–$560,280 in 1980 prices. While this may, *prima facie*, seem to be a somewhat crude way in which to compute the value of statistical life, it is possible to show that under certain circumstances individual marginal rates of substitution of wealth for current-period probability of death can be well approximated by the marginal rate of substitution of wealth for life expectancy multiplied by life expectancy itself, so that there are some grounds for deriving a value of statistical life in the manner used by Ippolito and Ippolito. However, it should be noted (a) that the conditions under which this approximation is valid are somewhat stringent (see the discussion of Jones-Lee, 1976, in section 2.2.3 below) and (b) that unless the marginal rate of substitution of wealth for life expectancy is uncorrelated with life expectancy itself (and one doubts that this is so) then multiplying the mean of one by the mean of the other will produce a biased estimate of the mean of their product.[20] In fact, theoretical results and empirical evidence both suggest that individual valuation of safety will decline with age, at least beyond the middle years of life, so that the correlation referred to above will tend to be positive and Ippolito and Ippolito's estimates will consequently have been biased downwards.

Bearing in mind these caveats, the best estimates of Ippolito and Ippolito of the value of statistical life, based on all their estimates and sensitivity tests, fall in the range $300,000–$600,000 in 1980 prices.

2.2.3 Questionnaire Studies

Essentially, the questionnaire approach involves asking a sample of people more or less directly how much each would be willing to pay – or would require in compensation – for a (normally small) variation in physical risk of a given type. In principle, individual marginal rates of substitution can then be approximated[21] by dividing willingness-to-pay responses by the corresponding variations in probability.

In practice, however, things are rather less straightforward. In the first place there is the problem of ensuring that the questions are readily intelligible, believable, unambiguous and, so far as possible, involve choices of a type that are familiar to the respondent. For example, one must avoid the use of technical terms, such as 'statistically independent events' or 'conditional probabilities' as well as excessively complex scenarios. As far as believability is concerned, the chances that a respondent will treat a given willingness-to-pay question seriously will be greatly enhanced if the question posed involves a choice or decision such as the respondent might realistically expect to encounter in everyday life. Avoidance of ambiguity is, in turn, clearly essential if one is to derive reliable estimates from questionnaire responses. Finally, one is much more likely to elicit responses that are truly reflective of underlying preferences if the choices with which respondents are confronted are of a type that they have already actually experienced.

Even if the problems of intelligibility, believability, ambiguity and familiarity can be resolved, there remain three further difficulties. First, the way in which a given question is worded may substantially influence responses, and indeed there is evidence that such 'framing' effects can be quite dramatic. Thus, great care has to be taken in questionnaire design to ensure that there are no obvious biases of this type. The final two difficulties, however, are arguably the most serious for the questionnaire approach. These concern the possibility (a) tnat willingness-to-pay responses may be made either in a mendacious or random manner (subjects may seek deliberately to misrepresent their true preferences or may simply 'pull numbers out of the air') and/or (b) that the majority of people may be quite unable to comprehend probability concepts, so that responses to questions concerning willingness to pay for variations in the probability of death or injury are essentially meaningless. So far as possible, it is therefore important that any effective questionnaire exercise should embody built-in consistency checks to test for the more obvious manifestations of these phenomena. This said, it must be conceded that there is, ultimately, no way of being abolutely sure that the results of the studies summarized below have not been significantly influenced by mendacity, randomness or incomprehension. It is for this reason that, in the author's opinion, a judgement concerning the reliability of estimates of the value of statistical life generated by the questionnaire approach is best formed by considering these estimates collectively, and indeed in relation to results obtained under the revealed-preference approach.

Acton, J. P. (1973)   Acton's survey, which was part of a larger study of the costs and benefits of different measures to reduce the risk of death by heart attack in the USA, involved a variety of questions concerning willingness to pay for various programmes (such as a mobile cardiac ambulance unit) designed to reduce the probability of death should a heart attack occur. Three different samples were used. The first was a stratified random sample[22] of 36 respondents, 18 men and 18 women, drawn from three communities in the Boston area during 1970. Acton describes these communities as 'low income, working class', 'more affluent' and 'affluent'. For this sample the questionnaires were administered by interviewers, although it is not clear whether these were professionally trained. The second sample of 21 trade union leaders was drawn from a group attending a 13-week course at Harvard Business School. This sample was given a brief explanation of the nature and purpose of the questionnaire prior to private completion. The third sample of 36 was drawn from a group of senior executives attending an advanced management course, also at Harvard Business School. This sample was self-selected from 160 executives who were asked to complete the questionnaire privately and without prior discussion.

While Acton's study addresses a number of different issues, the most significant for present purposes concern

1   willingness to pay for a heart attack programme that is essentially in the nature of a public good, i.e. one that is expected to save a particular number of lives in the local community,
2   advice to a neighbour concerning the appropriate amount to pay for a programme which, should the neighbour suffer a heart attack, would reduce the risk that the attack would prove fatal and
3   own willingness to pay for a similar programme.

Table 2.1   Implied reductions in the probability of death

Initial probability of death	Final probability of death	Reduction in probability of death
4×10^{-3}	2×10^{-3}	2×10^{-3}
4×10^{-3}	3×10^{-3}	1×10^{-3}
2×10^{-2}	1×10^{-2}	1×10^{-2}
2×10^{-2}	1.5×10^{-2}	5×10^{-3}

In the public goods questions two different expected reductions in mortality were considered, namely the expected saving of 10 and 20 lives respectively in a community of 10,000 people. In the case of the 'advice' and 'own' willingness-to-pay questions, risk of heart attack and the reduction in risk of death conditional on heart attack were each varied across questions in such a way that the implied overall reductions in the probability of death during the coming year were as shown in table 2.1.

As far as mean responses are concerned, with one or two exceptions these varied across questions in a more or less consistent manner (i.e. in the way predicted by theory). Thus, for example, in the 'public goods' question, mean willingness to pay to avoid 20 deaths exceeded that for the avoidance of 10 deaths in all three samples by a factor of about 3/2. Furthermore, in both the 'advice' and 'own safety' questions, willingness to pay for a reduction in risk from a given base level increased with the size of the reduction.

Intuitively, one might expect that larger reductions in risk from higher base levels would tend to elicit larger willingness to pay than smaller reductions from lower levels. While mean responses on the whole displayed this sort of pattern, individual responses were, in this respect, more varied and were clearly regarded by Acton as being somewhat anomalous. However, more recent theoretical work suggests that these results may constitute less serious grounds for concern. In particular, results summarized in section 2.1.1 indicate that while willingness to pay for a 2×10^{-3} reduction in annual probability of death from a base level of 4×10^{-3} should exceed that for a 1×10^{-3} reduction from the same base, nothing concrete can be said, a priori, about how such responses should relate to those for reductions from a different base (such as 2×10^{-2}). Acton appears to have hypothesized that willingness to pay would depend *only* upon the size of the risk reduction and, in particular, would be independent of the initial level of risk. Thus, in spite of the fact that two of his 'own' willingness-to-pay questions relate to a base risk of 4×10^{-3} and two to a base of 2×10^{-2}, Acton clearly expected that the responses to all four questions would lie on a *single* increasing concave curve when plotted against the size of the risk reduction and, not surprisingly, he was disappointed in this expectation.

Regression analysis of the willingness-to-pay responses indicated that those factors that one might have expected to be the principal determinants of individual valuation of safety were, in fact, capable of explaining only a relatively small proportion of the overall variation in willingness to pay across individuals. In the main, coefficients of income and wealth variables were insignificant at the 5% level, while dummy variables for concern about heart disease, awareness of the heart attack ambulance programme, the respondent's own state of health and headship of household tended to be significant.

Although values of statistical life implied by the responses to Acton's survey vary across different questions and samples, they are on the whole very low in relation to estimates generated by the revealed-preference approach. In particular, responses to the 'public goods' questions (involving the saving of a specified number of lives in a community of 10,000) imply values ranging from $16,500 to $43,000, while responses to the 'advice' questions imply values ranging from $12,100 to $47,000, and responses to the 'own' safety questions imply values ranging from $7,400 to $43,000, all in 1970 prices.[23] Of all the estimates, Acton believed that most respondents '. . . thought rather carefully about the [own safety] question that implies a value of $28,000 per expected life saved . . .' – this was the question involving a 2×10^{-3} reduction in the probability of death from a base of 4×10^{-3}.

Melinek, S. J. et al. (1973)   This study, described by its authors as '. . . only an experiment . . ., intended to test the feasibility of the approach . . .' asked questions about both people's perception of risk and their willingness to pay to reduce risk. The sample appears to have been self-selected and non-random and comprised 873 people attending Open Days at the UK Fire Research Station, Borehamwood, in 1972. Questionnaires were completed by the respondents themselves, presumably without the assistance of an interviewer.

The perception questions included such tasks as placing various activities in order of risk, comparing various risks with that of being killed or injured if caught in a domestic fire, and estimating the proportion of fatal domestic fires in which there is more than one death. The results of these questions suggest that while people are, in the main, reasonably accurate in their ranking of risks, their perceptions of the numerical magnitude of these risks are not so accurate compared with historical frequencies.

The questionnaire contained three different questions concerning valuation of safety. However, one of these involved a trade-off between time and safety and the responses will not be reported here, save to note that as part of the question respondents were required to estimate the incremental risk of death when overtaking on a road with two-way traffic. Responses tended to confirm the earlier observation that most people are poor at estimating risks in numerical terms: the mean perceived risk was 1.4×10^{-4} and the median 8×10^{-6} whereas the 'actual' risk, based on historical frequencies, is 1.4×10^{-8}.

The two monetary valuation questions concerned (a) willingness to pay for a domestic smoke detector which, it was asserted, would reduce by 90% the existing annual risk of death in a domestic fire of 1 in 80,000 per person, and (b) willingness to pay for hypothetical 'safe' cigarettes. In the case of the smoke detector question it was assumed that responses reflected willingness to pay for own safety as well as that of other members of the household and, accordingly, an average willingness to pay 'per person at risk' was computed. This, together with the risk reduction given in the question, implied a value of statistical life of £55,000 in 1972 prices. Interestingly, however, responses were highly right-skewed with a value of statistical life of only £20,000 implied by the median response.[24]

Finally, the value of statistical life implied by the mean response to the 'safe' cigarettes question was £17,200, again in 1972 prices.

Unfortunately, no questions concerning age, income etc. were asked, so that it was not possible to attempt to explain variations in willingness to pay by means of regression analysis.

Jones-Lee, M. W. (1976)   This study, like the one just discussed, was not intended as a definitive exercise in the estimation of values of safety, but rather as an example of the way in which one might proceed to obtain empirical estimates and as a means of exploring the feasibility of the questionnaire approach and the possible order of magnitude of the results that it might be expected to produce. The study also included an extensive discussion of the scientific status of questionnaire-based exercises in this context.

Basically, the questionnaire contained just two types of valuation question, each involving various increases and decreases in risk from a given base level. The first type of question concerned willingness to pay or required compensation (in the form of maximum acceptable increases or minimum acceptable reductions in an air fare) for variations in air travel safety from a base of 4×10^{-6} per flight. The second type of question asked about the premia or discounts on a standard house purchase price that would just induce the respondent to live in areas with varying levels of environmental pollution when the sole effect of the latter was to increase or decrease life expectancy by specified amounts.

The sample was small, self-selected and non-random, comprising 31 academics, researchers and public sector employees, and the survey, conducted by postal questionnaire, was carried out early in 1975. The majority of respondents provided answers that seemed, *prima facie*, to meet minimal conditions of consistency. For the air safety questions the implied value of statistical life was £3,100,000 for a 'one-off' air journey involving self-only (as opposed to self plus family) and £2,500,000 for a journey that would have to be undertaken weekly for a year, again on a self-only basis. All values are in 1975 prices. Distributions of responses were bi-modal and right-skewed so that median responses were some 10%–25% below means.

Responses to the questions concerned with environmental pollution implied marginal rates of substitution of wealth for life expectancy of

£900 per year for self-only and £1,790 per year for self plus family. While it is tempting to suppose that values of statistical life could be inferred directly from these estimates of willingness to pay for increased life expectancy, there are two reasons why this is not so. In the first place, the questions concerning environmental pollution were worded in such a way as to imply that the variation in life expectancy would reflect *simultaneous* variations in the probability of death for each of a number of future years, whereas inference of a value of statistical life, as defined in Chapter 1, would require that we consider a variation in life expectancy due to a *ceteris paribus* change in the probability of death for the coming year only. The only circumstance in which this difficulty would disappear seems to be that in which individuals value a unit increase in life expectancy *independently* of the pattern of age-specific probabilities of death that produce that increase. One could then infer willingness to pay for a *ceteris paribus* reduction in the probability of death for the coming year from willingness to pay for increased life expectancy, since it is easy to show that, with p_1 small, $\partial \mu / \partial p_1 \approx \mu$, where μ denotes life expectancy and p_1 denotes the probability of death during the forthcoming year.[25] Even if this condition were fulfilled, however, there would remain a further difficulty, namely that the smallest increase in life expectancy referred to in the study was one year. Now, in order to produce such an increase, the *ceteris paribus* reduction in p_1, given that $\partial \mu / \partial p_1 \approx \mu$, would have to be approximately equal to $1/\mu$ which, being many multiples of most people's current level of p_1, would simply not be feasible!

Maclean, A. D. (1979) It is surprising that this study has not been more widely discussed in the literature, since it represents an extremely thorough attempt to assess the workability of the questionnaire approach as a means of arriving at reasonably reliable estimates of individual valuation of safety.

The questionnaire contained a number of different questions which can be categorized, broadly speaking, as follows:

1 Questions designed to elicit subjects' numerical estimates of various risks, including risk of death in a domestic fire, risk of death in a hotel fire, risk of death in a road accident and risk of death by electrocution.

2 Questions designed to elicit subjects' estimates of the percentage reduction in each of the above risks afforded by various safety devices such as domestic smoke detectors and safety tyres.

3 Questions designed to establish respondents' willingness to pay for the various devices referred to above. In the case of fire safety, questions involving both private and public provision were included.

4 In-depth questions designed to check on the quality of respondents' understanding of the probabilistic concept of risk, to check as far as possible on the veracity of valuation responses, and to explore the general nature of attitudes to safety. These questions were put to

a subsample of those who had answered the earlier categories of question.

The quota sample of 325 respondents, designed to be representative of the overall population in terms of age, sex and socioeconomic group, was drawn from the London area. Interviews were carried out in the respondents' own homes by members of Research Surveys of Great Britain Ltd during 1978 and 1979. This professional survey organization had also refined the questionnaire following extensive piloting by the author. Interviews lasted between 30 minutes and one hour.

The questionnaire design included many novel features, but one in particular deserves special mention, namely the procedure for conveying information about probabilistic risks. Briefly, three risks (being struck by lightning, being killed as a motorcyclist and being killed as a pedestrian) were described in terms of the number of deaths per year in a group the size of the population of a large town such as Birmingham (which happened, at the time of the study, to have about a million inhabitants). This information was supplemented by a pictorial display using a 'thermometer chart'. In all subsequent questions concerning risks, respondents were asked to express their answers in similar terms and, if they so chose, to do so using the pictorial display. The in-depth questions suggested that respondents were comfortable with and understood the concept of risk explained in this way. In addition, Maclean notes that:

> The ease with which most people were able to express their estimates of the levels of risk helped to dispel any preconceptions of difficulties in dealing with small probabilities. (Maclean, 1979, p. 10)

The results of the survey are many and varied but the following seem to be the most significant for present purposes.

1　Respondents appeared in the main to be able to comprehend the concepts involved in the questions and were willing to provide apparently consistent answers.
2　Respondents' perceptions of the rank ordering of various risks accorded well with the 'objective' ordering based on relative frequencies. However, subjective perceptions of the numerical magnitude of these risks varied widely.
3　Roughly 50% of respondents were provided with 'objective' risk data after they had supplied their own subjective estimates but before answering the valuation questions. However, no significant difference was found between the valuation responses of these respondents and the remainder of the sample. This finding was confirmed by responses to the in-depth questions which indicated that subjective 'feelings' for a level of risk were not influenced by information concerning the 'objective' level.
4　Responses to valuation questions produced a wide variety of estimates of the value of statistical life. However, while there are doubts about the procedure employed to arrive at some of these

estimates,[26] it appears that the value of statistical life based on willingness to pay for domestic fire safety was correctly computed and this was estimated to be £1,400,000 in 1979 prices.

5   While it would appear that there were no significant relationships between valuation responses and sex or social class, some questions did produce a significantly decreasing relationship with age.

Frankel, M. (1979)   This study, like Maclean's, has many interesting features and produces a number of useful insights. The questions concerned willingness to pay for air safety and willingness to pay, or requirement of compensation, for variations in life expectancy.

The sample of 169 was made up of academics (72%) and middle-rank executives attending a Master of Business Administration programme (28%). As such, the scenarios with which respondents were confronted, as well as the nature of the sample, were very similar to those in Jones-Lee (1976).

The first of two air safety questions asked about willingness to pay to eliminate a risk of 1.5×10^{-6} of a fatal accident on a single flight. The mean response was $18.33 and the median $4.45, implying values of statistical life of $12,000,000 and $3,000,000 respectively, both in 1979 prices. For this question, 23% of respondents indicated that they would be willing to pay nothing for the safety improvement and 12% reported a willingness to pay $100 or more. Asked to rank the risk of 1.5×10^{-6} on a scale from 1 ('negligible') to 6 ('very high'), 74% of respondents reported that they regarded the risk as 'neligible'.

A second air safety question asked about willingness to pay to eliminate a risk of 1×10^{-3} on a single flight. In this case the median response was $50.37 (no mean is reported), implying a value of statistical life of $50,000. For this question, over 50% of respondents regarded the risk as 'high' or 'very high'.

The questions dealing with variations in life expectancy asked about willingness to pay for one-year and five-year increases in life expectancy, willingness to pay for a *certain* increase in length of life by one year, and finally requirement of compensation for the loss of one year and five years of life expectancy. The responses to all these questions varied very widely indeed, with over 30% of the sample indicating unwillingness to pay anything for the various increases in life expectancy and a substantial proportion (15%–30%) reporting a willingness to pay of over $5,000. The mean willingness to pay for a one-year increase in life expectancy was just over $1,000 (which is broadly comparable with the result for a similar question reported in Jones-Lee, 1976), although it should be noted that the median response was a mere $5.33. Not surprisingly, willingness to pay for the certain extra year of life was substantially higher, with a mean of over $1,800 and a median of $500. Compensation required for the one-year loss of life expectancy was also very substantial, only 3% of the sample indicating that they would require nothing and 26% stating that over $100,000 would be needed. In this case the mean response was $45,000 and the median $30,000. In general, the questions involving five-year variations in life expectancy elicited responses that moved in the 'right' direction in relation to their one-year counterparts. As was noted in the section reporting the results of Jones-Lee (1976), it seems inappropriate to attempt to derive values of statistical life from the responses to the questions involving variations in life expectancy.

Undoubtedly, the two most significant features of the results of Frankel's study are the enormous disparity between the values of statistical life implied by the responses to the two air safety questions and the large proportion of the sample reporting unwillingness to pay anything for an increase in life expectancy (44% for the one-year increase and 33% in the five-year case). As far as the disparity between the values of statistical life are concerned, this could be taken as evidence of the inherent unreliability of the questionnaire approach in general and one has to admit that these results do provide cause for some anxiety on this score. It should be borne in mind, however, that the risk reductions involved in the air safety questions were, respectively, very small and very large indeed. In the case of the very small reduction, any estimate of the value of statistical life based on stated willingness to pay for such a reduction will be extremely sensitive to even small variations in the amount concerned (in particular, with a risk reduction of 1.5×10^{-6}, a $1 variation in the mean response will produce a $666,667 change in the value of statistical life). If one adds to this the fact that the typical response to this question involved a very small amount of money relative to the respondent's income – so that reported willingness to pay may not have been particularly carefully thought out – then it would seem reasonable to conclude that one should not expect very reliable estimates of the value of statistical life from questions involving such small changes in risk. For rather different reasons, estimates derived from questions involving very large risk reductions are also likely to be of doubtful reliability. For example, a risk reduction of 1×10^{-3} represents a very substantial proportion of the annual risk of death faced by most people and one suspects that many respondents would find it difficult to imagine that such a large reduction could actually be 'delivered' unless there were, in addition to any sum paid for the reduction, very substantial costs of discomfort or inconvenience – as in the case of giving up smoking or undergoing radiation treatment or chemotherapy for cancer.[27] In other words, a situation in which one might actually be able to purchase, say, a 25% or even 50% improvement in one's survival prospects for the coming year *without incurring substantial discomfort or inconvenience costs* is so far outside most people's experience that, again, responses to questions involving such large changes should probably *not* be taken too seriously. The long and short of all this is that Frankel's results, rather than pointing out a fundamental flaw in the questionnaire approach, are probably better viewed as highlighting the importance of posing questions that are believable, relate to familiar situations, and involve choices or decisions that respondents will 'take seriously'.

The zero responses to the increased life expectancy questions are,

The Willingness-to-pay Approach: a Survey 83

prima facie, more puzzling and disturbing. Frankel offers various possible explanations for these results. For example, he suggests that a proportion of people may believe that '. . . their life spans, though unknown, are essentially predetermined by spiritual or mechanistic forces . . .'. Another effect that Frankel conjectures may have been at work is '. . . the belief that one's longevity is a very chancy thing, and that an expected year more or less doesn't count for much'. Finally, Frankel notes that, in written comments, several respondents referred to their concern about the possibility of poor health during any period of extended longevity.

Whatever the reasons for zero valuations, one is tempted to suppose that the attitudes to risk that give rise to such valuations lie outside the scope of the analysis developed in this book. However, this view is almost certainly mistaken. If, on careful reflection and given 'adequate' information, a person genuinely elects to place a value of zero on a particular effect, then any decision criterion that purports to take account of individual preferences (as does the willingness-to-pay approach) should reflect that person's valuation, even though it is zero and even though, as an independent observer, one regards the valuation as eccentric. Only if the valuation appears to be based on false information, or faulty information processing, or some form of misrepresentation of preferences, would it seem justifiable to consider setting the valuation aside in the process of 'aggregation' of individual preferences.

Jones-Lee, M. W. et al. (1985)[28]   This study, which was designed to shed light on a range of issues concerning individual perception and valuation of transport safety, is discussed in detail in Chapter 4 and so will be reviewed only very briefly here.

The study involved a number of questions concerning willingness to pay, or requirement of compensation, for various kinds of safety effect (including changes in own safety, other people's safety, effects that were in the nature of private goods, those that were publicly provided and so on). However, the results that are most directly comparable with those of the other empirical studies reviewed so far were the responses to questions concerning (a) willingness to pay for a car safety feature that would provide various specified reductions in the annual probability of death in a car accident and (b) willingness to pay, or requirement of compensation, for variations in coach safety on a foreign trip. In these questions variations in risk were expressed in multiples of 1 in 100,000, respondents having been told that the annual risk of death in a car accident in the UK for a car driver is, on average, about 10 in 100,000. In addition, all statements about risk were accompanied by a visual display in which the appropriate number of squares had been 'blacked out' on a sheet of graph paper containing 100,000 squares.

The study was commissioned by the UK Department of Transport, following a one-year feasibility exercise,[29] and was carried out by National Opinion Polls Ltd (NOP) using a questionnaire designed and piloted by the authors and further piloted and refined by NOP. The three-stage stratified random sample was drawn from 93 parliamentary constituencies in England, Scotland and Wales and produced 1103 full and 47 partial interviews. The response rate was 67% and interviews, conducted by professional interviewers, took an average of 45 minutes to complete. A follow-up survey of 210 of the respondents to the main study was conducted to test for the temporal consistency of responses.

The main findings of the study were as follows.

1   A substantial majority of respondents were willing and able to provide answers to the various questions put to them.

2   While a proportion of respondents gave apparently inconsistent answers to some of the questions and experienced difficulty with the concepts involved, it was the authors' opinion that the balance of the evidence from the survey supported the view that the quality of perception of transport risks, ability to process probability information and the veracity of responses were, on the whole, sufficient to justify the inference of at least broad orders of magnitude of the value of statistical life for transport risks.

3   The values of statistical life implied by mean responses to the car and coach safety questions referred to above (with a few suspect outlying responses removed) ranged from £1,200,000 to £2,200,000 in 1982 prices, while values based on median responses ranged from £500,000 to £1,200,000. Given these results, the authors argue for a value of statistical life for 'self-only' transport risks of *at least* £500,000, with a value closer to £750,000 warranted by consideration of median responses and about £1,500,000 by (trimmed) means.

4   Regression analysis indicated that individual valuation of safety is significantly affected by income and age, with the coefficient of a linear income variable implying an income elasticity of the marginal rate of substitution of wealth for risk of death of about 0.3, and the coefficients of linear and quadratic age variables implying that the marginal rate of substitution follows a clear 'inverted-U' life-cycle.

5   Under the willingness-to-pay definition, the value of avoidance of a serious injury (where seriousness was construed in terms specified by the respondent) was at least one-hundredth of the value of statistical life.

Smith, V. K. and Desvousges, W. H. (1987)   While the results of this study do not permit the inference of unambiguous values of statistical life, they do bear directly upon the properties of the individual valuation function $v(p_t)$ discussed in Chapter 3 or, more accurately, upon the *multiperiod counterpart* to this function. In addition, Smith and Desvousges' results have some features that are strikingly similar to the (as yet unpublished) results of various pilot-scale studies recently conducted by the UK Health and Safety Executive. It therefore seems appropriate to include a brief summary of the main findings of the study of Smith and Desvousges in this survey.

Smith and Desvousges' principal purpose was to test various 'standard' hypotheses concerning the relationship between individual willingness to pay and the size and nature of the risk reduction concerned. For example, simpler theoretical models predict that willingness to pay will be an increasing, strictly concave function of reduction in the probability of death during a forthcoming period and also that willingness to pay for a given reduction in this probability will be an increasing function of its initial level (see, for example, Jones-Lee, 1976; or Weinstein *et al.*, 1980).[30] Another implication of standard theory is that the amount that an individual would be willing to pay to reduce the probability of death during a forthcoming period from p_a to p_b (with $p_b < p_a$) will be identical to the sum he would pay to prevent the probability rising from p_b to p_a, other things equal. Finally, since their main interest was in risks from hazardous wastes, Smith and Desvousges wished to examine the extent to which standard hypotheses – which typically apply to variations in the *annual* risk of death – stand up in situations in which risks vary over a very much more protracted period. In fact, Smith and Desvousges considered variations in the probability that hazardous wastes would cause premature death within a 30-year period. (It is essentially for this reason that one cannot derive unambiguous estimates of the value of statistical life from their results.)

The survey and questionnaire design were relatively sophisticated and involved extensive pre-testing, in-depth discussion with members of the public, practice sessions for interviewers and so on. The stratified cluster sample of about 700 was drawn from the Boston area and produced over 600 fully completed interviews. The sample was randomly partitioned into eight subsets (referred to as 'design points'), while combinations of base risk and risk reduction (or increase) were varied across design points in order to test the hypotheses described above.

All statements about risk were presented in the form of a risk R of being exposed to hazardous waste during the 30-year time horizon and a separate conditional risk q of death from the exposure. This ensured that the separate risks R and q were, in most cases, large enough to be representable in a 'pie-chart' visual display that accompanied the questions.

In essence, the main findings of the survey were as follows.

1   As in other questionnaire studies, the vast majority of respondents were willing and able to answer the questions asked of them.

2   Within each design point, mean willingness to pay was – as predicted by theory – an increasing function of the size of risk reduction from a *given* base risk. However, while in some cases the function was concave, in others the evidence was consistent with linearity or even convexity.

3   Far from increasing with the level of base risk, mean willingness to pay for a given risk reduction showed a marked tendency to *fall*. In addition, and somewhat more disturbingly, design points with larger risk reductions did not appear to elicit correspondingly higher mean or median willingness to pay.

4   The mean willingness to pay to reduce risks from p_a to p_b (with $p_b < p_a$) was uniformly larger than mean willingness to pay to avoid an increase from p_b to p_a.

5   When the non-zero willingness-to-pay responses, divided by the corresponding variation in risk, were regressed on various explanatory variables with a semilogarithmic specification, consistently significant income coefficients were obtained. These coefficients imply income elasticities of between 0.18 and 0.24 which, it will be recalled, are very similar to the estimates reported by Blomquist (1979) and Jones-Lee *et al.* (1985).

The findings of this study are therefore, to say the least, mixed, in relation both to conventional wisdom and to the results of other empirical studies. The authors offer various possible explanations for the major discrepancies, including the fact that their study dealt with risks that are relatively poorly understood, involve the possibility of painful, lingering death and were explicitly described in the study as applying over a protracted period. In addition, they suggest that various of the phenomena identified by work in experimental psychology – such as 'anchoring' and subjective overestimation of low 'objective' probabilities – may go some way towards explaining the more puzzling relationships between responses from different design points.

In fact, Smith and Desvousges' results taken as a whole probably represent somewhat less serious cause for concern than might at first appear to be the case. In the first place, while simpler and more restrictive theoretical analyses certainly do predict strict concavity of the willingness to pay versus risk reduction relationship, there are grounds for expecting that this relationship may well be approximately linear or even, in some cases, locally convex, as noted in Chapter 3. Furthermore Dehez and Drèze (1982) have shown that quite plausible assumptions concerning the properties of life insurance and annuity contracts – typically ignored in the simpler models – can produce predictions about the relationship between willingness to pay and base levels of risk that are entirely consistent with Smith and Desvousges' findings.

Nonetheless, it must be admitted that two aspects of the results of this study defy explanation in terms of the conventional conceptual apparatus of economic analysis. These concern the facts that, as one moves from one design point to another, larger reductions in risk do not appear to elicit larger willingness to pay and that mean willingness to pay for a given risk reduction significantly exceeds mean willingness to pay to avoid the corresponding increase in risk. In order to make sense of these results one probably has to appeal to the ideas of cognitive psychology (such as anchoring and framing) rather than economics. If Smith and Desvousges' study does no more than help to remove one more piece of the artificial disciplinary boundary that separates economics and psychology then it will have served a very useful purpose.

2.2.4 Other Questionnaire Studies

Various other studies have used the questionnaire approach to investigate individual attitudes to and valuation of physical risk. However, ambiguities in the wording of the willingness-to-pay questions in these studies were, unfortunately, such as to render inference of unambiguous estimates of the value of statistical life virtually impossible. For example, Mulligan (1977) conducted a survey of willingness to pay for reduction in risks of a nuclear plant accident in which respondents were asked about the premia on their monthly energy (e.g. electricity) bills that they would accept in order to effect various reductions in their own and their children's risks of being killed or injured in a nuclear accident. However, the questionnaire did not specify the period with respect to which the risk reduction applied. 'Sensible' interpretations clearly range from a month to a lifetime, leaving implied values of statistical life indeterminate up to a factor of several hundreds. In addition, Mulligan's willingness-to-pay questions almost all contain a leading prompt. For example, 'What is the largest increase on your monthly energy bill that you would pay to cause this change, about $5? (Would you be willing to pay more, less, nothing?)' The objections to this procedure need no rehearsal.

In another questionnaire-based exercise, Brown and Green (1981) asked a small sample of car-owning students about their preferences over combinations of petrol price and car safety. Given information about respondents' petrol consumption, it should then have been possible to estimate the typical order of magnitude of the marginal rate of substitution of wealth for risk using, for example, the sort of technique employed in the estimation of values of leisure time.[31] However, Brown and Green apparently made no attempt to determine levels of petrol consumption and, in addition, presented risks as relative magnitudes of the chances of occurrence of an unspecified 'harmful event', which could presumably lie anywhere on a spectrum from a minor accident to fatal injury. Inference of a value of statistical life from Brown and Green's results is therefore effectively impossible.

Finally, Prescott-Clarke (1982), in an otherwise excellent study of public attitudes to various kinds of risk, asked questions about required wage premia for increased job risk and willingness to pay to eliminate all risks from nuclear power plants. However, in the case of job risks, these were described in terms of the occurrence of a 'serious accident' while the concept of 'all risks' associated with nuclear power seems equally nebulous. Once again, therefore, inference of unambiguous values of statistical life seems to be impossible.

2.2.5 Willingness to Pay for Other People's Safety

The studies summarized in sections 2.2.2 and 2.2.3 were principally concerned with individuals' valuation of their *own* safety. However, it is plainly the case that many people are also concerned about (and therefore willing to pay for improvements in) the safety of others, especially family and friends. To the extent that the safety effects of public sector projects apply to individuals *and* to those they care for, there is therefore a case to be made for augmenting values of statistical life to reflect this additional willingness to pay for other people's safety.[32]

Using US data concerning the proportions of parents, siblings and children refusing to donate kidneys to, respectively, children, siblings and parents,[33] Needleman (1976) estimated the relevant 'coefficients of concern' – essentially, marginal rates of substitution of own survival probability for that of another person. On the basis of these estimates, together with informed guesses about the magnitude of corresponding coefficients for more distant relatives and data concerning the impact of transplants on donors' and recipients' life expectancy,[34] Needleman estimated the 'relatives' valuation ratio' – essentially, the aggregate willingness to pay for *j*'s safety on the part of *j*'s relatives as a proportion of *j*'s own willingness to pay – to be about 45% for a group having the same age and sex distribution as the population of Great Britain. This suggests that values of statistical life defined to include people's willingness to pay for others' safety would be at least 1.45 times the values reported in sections 2.2.1–2.2.3.[35] Notice that since Needleman's estimate of the 'relatives' valuation ratio' is based upon data concerning refusal rates in actual, rather than hypothetical, transplant decisions, it should be regarded as falling within the category of revealed-preference estimates.

As part of the questionnaire-based study described briefly in section 2.2.3 and in more detail in Chapter 4, Jones-Lee *et al.* (1985) asked about willingness to pay for own and passengers' car safety as well as own safety alone. A comparison of the responses to the two sets of questions permits the inference of drivers' marginal rates of substitution of own wealth for risk to an 'average' passenger (typically, one assumes, a close relative or friend). In 1982 prices, the mean of these marginal rates of substitution was £500,000. This suggests that for 'everyday' risks, such as those encountered in transport, values of statistical life defined to include willingness to pay for others', as well as own, safety will be at least £500,000 greater than values based on willingness to pay for 'own' safety alone. Since the latter were estimated to be about £1,500,000 in the Jones-Lee *et al.* study, this premium is broadly consistent with Needleman's result. Having said this, however, it should be noted that the median marginal rate of substitution of own wealth for risk to an average passenger was *zero*, which, it must be conceded, is a rather disturbing result.[36]

2.3   Summary and Concluding Comments

The theoretical analysis of individual willingness to pay for safety would appear to have its origins in Jacques Drèze's seminal but, paradoxically, infrequently acknowledged paper in the *Revue Française de Recherche Opérationelle*. The body of analysis that has since developed provides us with a number of insights into the way in which a 'rational'[37] economic agent might be expected to behave. Thus, given relatively plausible restrictions on preferences and attitudes to physical and financial risk, theory predicts that for most people safety will be a normal good and that individual valuation of safety will tend to follow an 'inverted-U' life-cycle, or will, at least beyond some point, decline with age. More surprisingly, theoretical analysis indicates that an individual's marginal rate of substitution of wealth for risk need not necessarily be an increasing function of the level of risk to which the individual is initially exposed.

Theory also suggests that individual marginal rates of substitution of wealth for risk – and hence values of statistical life – will typically exceed measures of human capital, probably by many multiples. In addition, we have reasonable grounds for conjecturing that there may exist simple and potentially powerful relationships between these marginal rates of substitution and maximum acceptable increase in physical risk (i.e. increases that individuals would not accept 'at any price') and, indeed, results proved in Chapter 3 confirm that this conjecture is well founded. Furthermore, we know something of the relative magnitude of valuations of single-period and multiperiod variations in risk. And so on.

Arguably, the major weakness of this body of analysis is that it is almost universally based upon expected utility theory and it has to be conceded that experimental evidence is casting increasing doubt upon the empirical robustness of the axioms from which that theory is derived.[38] While a case in defence of expected utility theory is developed at some length in Chapter 3, it is worth remarking that results reported in section 3.8 suggest that the key qualitative conclusions of the theoretical analysis of individual valuation of safety may be largely unaffected if expected utility theory is replaced by one of the alternative theories of choice under uncertainty proposed to accommodate the experimental evidence referred to above.

An even more Draconian objection to the sort of theoretical work surveyed in this chapter is that individual perceptions of and attitudes towards physical risk may not, on the whole, display even the minimal degrees of consistency and stability typically presupposed by economists.[39] Indeed, it has been suggested that, in the context of physical risk, perceptions may be so fuzzy and attitudes so fickle as to vitiate the results of any analysis based on the assumption of well-defined and clearly held preferences. Chapter 5 examines this objection in more detail.

Turning to the empirical estimation of values of statistical life, it has to be admitted that, as in so many other areas of economic analysis, the addition of empirical flesh to theoretical bones is far from straightforward and empirical work in this field has certainly produced estimates that lack the precision and reliability one would ideally wish for. However, this difficulty is almost certainly endemic to the study of human behaviour and one should not be surprised to encounter it in fairly acute form in a context as complex, contentious and emotive as this.

In fact, reactions to the plethora of empirical estimates summarized in section 2.2 appear to fall into one of two categories. Sceptics take the view that the variation in these estimates raises such serious doubts about their individual and collective reliability as to render them virtually worthless as a source of information about the 'true' magnitude of marginal rates of substitution and hence values of statistical life. This appears to be the position currently adopted by the UK Department of Transport (1987, p. 7), although it should be said that at the time of going to press there are encouraging signs that the Department may be in the process of reviewing this position.

Alternatively, one can set about the difficult (and, admittedly, somewhat speculative) task of trying to identify the reasons for the large differences in the empirical estimates – and of evaluating their relative reliability – so as to be able to make an informed judgement about the appropriate order of magnitude of values of statistical life for use in public sector decision making. It is the author's firm conviction that this more positive approach to the evidence is markedly preferable on philosophical, scientific and practical grounds. This conviction is reinforced by the fact that those government agencies (both in the UK and elsewhere) that have explicitly or implicitly rejected the willingness-to-pay estimates have thereby been driven to a position in which decisions concerning the allocation of resources to safety improvement are either based on procedures that are demonstrably flawed (for reasons detailed in Chapter 1) or employ the 'gross output' definition of the cost of risk and the value of safety, which is by now almost universally regarded as being seriously deficient.

Before proceeding to compare and evaluate the different empirical estimates of willingness-to-pay based values of statistical life, it is clearly desirable that they should all be converted to a common currency and year. Accordingly, table 2.2 summarizes the results of the various revealed-preference studies, with all values converted to pounds sterling, in March 1987 prices, and rounded to the nearest £10,000, while table 2.3 summarizes the questionnaire results.[40] The reader should be warned that, while many individual studies produced a variety of estimates, with one or two exceptions these have been distilled into a single 'representative' figure for each study, either by taking the particular author's preferred estimate or by a straightforward process of averaging. The only case in which this was not done was for Frankel (1979) in which the estimates differed by more than an order of magnitude.

The first thing to notice about the figures summarized in tables 2.2 and 2.3 is that, in spite of the fact that the estimates have been converted to a common currency and year, there remain considerable differences between them. In fact, the various estimates can usefully be thought of as falling within one of four broad intervals, namely less than £250,000, between £250,000 and £500,000, between £500,000 and £1,000,000, and more than £1,000,000. The numbers and percentages of the estimates in each of these intervals are given in table 2.4.

Taken at face value, therefore, the empirical evidence summarized in

Table 2.2 Revealed-preference estimates of the value of statistical life (£-sterling, 1987)[a]

Author(s)	Nature of study	Estimated value of statistical life
Thaler and Rosen (1973)	Compensating wage differentials (USA)	420,000
Smith, R. S. (1973)	Compensating wage differentials (USA)	7,950,000
Melinek (1974)	Compensating wage differentials (UK)	990,000
Melinek (1974)	Time–inconvenience–safety trade-off in use of pedestrian subways (UK)	400,000
Ghosh et al. (1975)	Motorway time–fuel–safety trade-off (UK)	400,000
Smith, R. S. (1976)	Compensating wage differentials (USA)	2,470,000
Jones-Lee (1977)	Wealth–safety trade-off involved in frequency of tyre replacement (UK)	1,830,000
Viscusi (1978a)	Compensating wage differentials (USA)	2,590,000
Veljanovksi (1978)	Compensating wage differentials (UK)	4,550,000
Dillingham (1979)	Compensating wage differentials (USA)[b]	400,000
Blomquist (1979)	Time–inconvenience–safety trade-off in use of car seat-belts (USA)	400,000
Brown (1980)	Compensating wage differentials (USA)[c]	1,270,000
Dardis (1980)	Purchases of domestic smoke detectors (USA)	280,000
Needleman (1980)	Compensating wage differentials (UK)	130,000
Olson (1981)	Compensating wage differentials (USA)[d]	5,260,000
Portney (1981)	House price–air pollution trade-off (USA)	150,000
Marin and Psacharopoulos (1982)	Compensating wage differentials (UK)	1,910,000
Smith, V. K. (1983)	Compensating wage differentials (USA)	600,000

Table 2.2 (Continued)

Author(s)	Nature of study	Estimated value of statistical life
Arnould and Nichols (1983)	Compensating wage differentials (USA)	410,000
Ippolito and Ippolito (1984)	Cigarette smokers' responses to health-hazard information (USA)	390,000
Weiss *et al.* (1986)	Compensating wage differentials (Austria)	3,250,000
	Mean	1,720,000
	Median	600,000

[a] With the exception of Jones-Lee (1977), Dardis (1980) and Portney (1981), all estimates are for 'self-only' risks and do not include an allowance for willingness to pay for others', as well as own, safety. Portney's estimate is based on the aggregate risk of death from pollution-induced disease to all members of a household together with the assumption that all household members' safety is valued equally. This can therefore be viewed as an average value of own and relatives' lives. To the extent that the risks in the Jones-Lee and Dardis studies applied to all the occupants of a motorcar or household, then the estimates from these studies will presumably reflect an additional willingness to pay for other people's safety. These studies will therefore, if anything, tend to overestimate the value of statistical life for 'self-only' risks.
[b] Estimate given is for the blue collar sample only.
[c] Estimate given is for regression *excluding* individual-specific intercepts.
[d] Estimate given is for regression *excluding* risk interaction variables.

Table 2.3 Questionnaire estimates of the value of statistical life (£-sterling, 1987)[a]

Author(s)	Nature of study	Estimated value of statistical life[b]
Acton (1973)	Small non-random[c] sample survey ($n = 93$) of willingness to pay for heart attack ambulance (USA)	50,000
Melinek *et al.* (1973)	Non-random sample survey ($n = 873$) of willingness to pay for domestic fire safety (UK)	250,000

Table 2.3 (Continued)

Author(s)	Nature of study	Estimated value of statistical life[b]
Melinek *et al.* (1973)	Non-random sample survey (n = 873) of willingness to pay for hypothetical 'safe' cigarettes (UK)	80,000
Jones-Lee (1976)	Small, non-random sample survey (n = 31) of willingness to pay for airline safety (UK)	8,250,000
Maclean (1979)	Quota sample survey (n = 325) of willingness to pay for domestic fire safety (UK)	2,480,000
Frankel (1979)	Small, non-random sample survey (n = 169) of willingness to pay for elimination of small airline risk (USA)[d]	11,700,000
Frankel (1979)	Small, non-random sample survey (n = 169) of willingness to pay for elimination of large airline risk (USA)[e]	50,000
Jones-Lee *et al.* (1985)	Large, random sample survey (n = 1,150) of willingness to pay for transport safety (UK)	1,860,000
	Mean	3,090,000
	Median	1,060,000

[a] At the time of going to press I am awaiting details of a questionnaire study of which I have only recently become aware, namely Landefeld (1979). I understand that this study, which was conducted in the USA, involved questions concerning willingness to pay to reduce cancer deaths and produced a value of statistical life that converts to about £1,600,000 in pounds sterling, 1987.

[b] With the exception of Melinek *et al.* (1973) and Maclean (1979) all estimates are for 'self-only' risks and do not include an allowance for willingness to pay for others', as well as own, safety. The Melinek *et al.* figure was based on each respondent's willingness to pay for domestic fire safety, divided by the average number of people per household. Crudely speaking, this should therefore be regarded as an average value of own and relatives' lives. By contrast, the Maclean estimate did not involve normalization by household occupancy and so, like the Jones-Lee and Dardis estimates in table 2.2, reflects *aggregate* valuation of own and relatives' safety.

[c] While Acton describes one of his subsamples as 'random', in the strict sense of the term it was not. See note 22.

[d] Specifically, a risk of 1.5×10^{-6} of a fatal accident on a single flight. Note that, while Frankel reported values of statistical life based on *median* willingness-to-pay responses, the values given here were derived from *mean* responses estimated from reported frequency distributions. This explains the apparent discrepancy between these figures and values reported by Jones-Lee (1987d) which were based on median responses.

[e] Specifically, a risk of 1×10^{-3} of a fatal accident on a single flight.

Table 2.4   Numbers and percentages of all estimates of the value of statistical life in various intervals

	Number	Percentage
Less than £250,000	5	17.3
Between £250,000 and £500,000	9	31.0
Between £500,000 and £1,000,000	2	6.9
More than £1,000,000	13	44.8

tables 2.2–2.4 seems to suggest that, if a 'true' value of statistical life exists, then it is very unlikely to be much less than £500,000 in 1987 prices and may, indeed, be well in excess of £1,000,000. However, these conclusions should be qualified by two considerations. In the first place, as was remarked earlier in this chapter, individual marginal rates of substitution – and hence values of statistical life – will almost certainly differ from one cause of death to another, so that it may not be appropriate to attempt to extract a single figure from a set of estimates obtained from studies related to different causes. Second, it is clear that some of the estimates in tables 2.2 and 2.3 deserve to be regarded as being inherently more reliable than others. To take the author's own work, for example, it is plainly the case that by virtually all the relevant criteria (e.g. sample size, quality of survey design, intelligibility of questions, existence of built-in consistency checks and so on) the Jones-Lee et al. (1985) study is markedly superior to its 1976 predecessor. Given this, it is clearly important to apply some sort of weighting scheme to reflect differences in quality and reliability before attempting to derive any kind of point estimate from the various results.

As far as variation in the value of statistical life with different causes of death is concerned, one would certainly expect the extent of aversion to risks from, say, nuclear power – and hence the value of statistical life for such risks – to be significantly greater than for more familiar and better understood risks, such as those encountered in transport or in the non-nuclear workplace (and results reported in Chapters 4 and 5 tend to confirm this expectation). However, if one sets aside the more controversial, emotive and poorly understood sources of risk, there seem to be good grounds for expecting that values of statistical life would show at least a broad correspondence across different causes of death. If this conjecture is correct, then it seems to be quite legitimate, at least as a first approximation, to seek a single, summary value of statistical life for all commonplace 'everyday' risks of quick and (one assumes) painless death. Almost without exception, the risks to which the estimates in tables 2.2 and 2.3 relate appear to fall within this category.

Assessment of the relative reliability of the different estimates is clearly a highly judgemental matter, but there do seem to be some rather obvious sources of bias that can be attributed to particular studies or types of study. For example, in their excellent review, Violette and Chestnut (1983) suggest that the compensating wage differential studies, as a group, probably suffer from four major potential sources of bias, namely (a) the quality of workers' perceptions of job-related risks, (b) workers' attitudes and aversion to job-related risks, (c) the extent to which wage–risk premia reflect risks of non-fatal as well as fatal injury and (d) the omitted-variables problem. Of these, Violette and Chestnut argue that the first two factors will tend to bias estimated values of statistical life in a downward direction, while the third and fourth will have the opposite effect. In particular, workers who underestimate risk will tend to gravitate to more dangerous jobs and vice versa, so that actual wage differentials will be smaller than they would be if perceptions were 'correct'.[41] Furthermore, if workers in the occupations that formed the basis for these studies were atypically sanguine about physical risk compared with the overall population, then again one would expect values of safety based on their required wage premia to be biased downwards. While Violette and Chestnut's comments applied exclusively to the US studies, this point would seem to apply with particular force to Needleman's (1980) study which, it will be recalled, focused upon construction workers. By contrast, if wage premia reflect compensation for risks of non-fatal as well as fatal accidents, then the bias in treating premia as exclusively for the latter is clearly in the upward direction. Finally, to the extent that wage premia are, in fact, paid in compensation for factors that are additional to job risk but are both positively correlated with risk *and* omitted from the specification of wage equations, then again the consequent bias in estimated values of statistical life will be unambiguously upward.

Another limitation of the US compensating wage differential studies identified by Violette and Chestnut concerns the quality of the risk data sets employed in these studies. In general, these either broke down risks insufficiently finely (as in the case of the BLS data) or focused on more hazardous occupations and failed adequately to distinguish between job-related and other risks (as with the Society of Actuaries data set). In this sense, the Marin and Psacharopoulos (1982) study, based on a fairly fine occupational classification covering a wide range of occupations and using the job-specific ACCRISK concept, must be judged markedly superior. It is also worth remarking that when Marin and Psacharopoulos employed the conceptually inferior GENRISK measure (which, like the Society of Actuaries data, conflated work-related and other risks), the estimated value of statistical life fell substantially, paralleling the tendency for those US studies based on BLS data (which focused exclusively on work-related risks) to produce much larger estimates than studies that used the Society of Actuaries data.

As far as the other revealed-preference studies are concerned, with the exception of Dardis (1980), these all involved relatively complex or indirect trade-offs and the extraction of estimated values of statistical life required a number of rather restrictive, not to say precarious, assumptions.

Table 2.5   Numbers and percentages of the more reliable estimates of the value of statistical life in various intervals

	Number	Percentage
Less than £250,000	1	6.3
Between £250,000 and £500,000	4	25.0
Between £500,000 and £1,000,000	1	6.3
More than £1,000,000	10	62.4

These estimates should therefore probably be treated with some caution.

Of all the empirical studies, however, undoubtedly the most controversial are those based upon the questionnaire approach. In the first place, most of these studies employed relatively small, non-random samples. Second, questions posed were of very variable quality when judged by the criteria adduced in section 2.2.3. Third, there was little, if any, attempt to probe respondents in order to shed light upon the underlying rationale for responses. Finally, by their very nature, such studies produce estimates that are questionable, if only because they are derived from responses to hypothetical questions rather than from observations of real choices.

In the author's view, the studies that are least vulnerable to these criticisms are those of Acton (1973), Maclean (1979) and Jones-Lee *et al.* (1985). Though modesty inhibits expression of the judgement, the last of these would seem to deserve the most serious attention, if only because of the relative sophistication of the sampling procedure employed and because the questions related to familiar kinds of risk and involved fairly straightforward scenarios. Inevitably, also, this study was able to benefit from many of the lessons learned in earlier surveys of this type.

All things considered, then, the more reliable estimates are probably those given by the compensating wage differential studies (with the possible exceptions of those by Melinek and Needleman) together with Dardis's study and the questionnaire surveys of Acton, Maclean and Jones-Lee *et al.* Focusing upon these estimates, their mean and median are, respectively, £2,230,000 and £1,890,000, while the numbers and percentages of the estimates in the various intervals are given in table 2.5.

Finally, if one is to attempt to identify a subset of the *most* reliable estimates, then the following would seem to be serious candidates for inclusion in this category:

1   Estimates derived from those compensating wage differential studies for the USA that employed BLS data since these, in contrast with the studies using Society of Actuaries data, concerned work-related rather than general risks.

2   The Dillingham (1979) compensating wage differential estimate for the USA, which also used work-related risk data.

3   The compensating wage differential estimates given by Veljanovski

Table 2.6 Numbers and percentages of the most reliable estimates of the value of statistical life in various intervals

	Number	Percentage
Less than £250,000	0	0.0
Between £250,000 and £500,000	2	18.2
Between £500,000 and £1,000,000	1	9.1
More than £1,000,000	8	72.7

(1978) and Marin and Psacharopoulos (1982) for the UK and by Weiss *et al.* (1986) for Austria, all of which were based upon data concerning accidents at work.

4 The Dardis (1980) revealed-preference estimate based on smoke detector purchases, which involves a simple and direct wealth–risk trade-off.

5 The Jones-Lee *et al.* (1985) questionnaire estimate which was based upon a large, random sample survey involving questions concerning familiar, everyday risks.

The mean and median of the most reliable estimates are, respectively, £2,830,000 and £2,470,000, while the numbers and percentages of these estimates in the various intervals are given in table 2.6.

The results given in tables 2.5 and 2.6 therefore indicate that, if anything, an attempt to weight the different estimates for relative reliability is likely to reinforce substantially the earlier conclusions concerning the appropriate magnitude of the value of statistical life for 'everyday' risks, such as those encountered in transport or in the workplace. Indeed, given the empirical evidence assembled to date, together with the theoretical results summarized in sections 2.1.2 and 2.1.3, it is very difficult to resist the conclusions that (a) the value of statistical life for more commonplace risks almost certainly exceeds £250,000, (b) it is highly probable that the value is at least £500,000 and (c) a respectable case can be made for a value of over £1,000,000.

The last of these conclusions seems all the more persuasive when one bears in mind that the two most recent and comprehensive empirical studies for the UK (namely those of Marin and Psacharopoulos, 1982; and Jones-Lee *et al.*, 1985) both produce estimates in the region of £1,900,000 in 1987 prices in spite of the fact that one study used the revealed-preference approach while the other was based on the questionnaire method. Furthermore, these two estimates are for 'self-only' risks and include no allowances for the 'direct' economic effects of safety improvement, such as avoided police and medical costs as well as losses of net output. If values of statistical life are augmented to reflect concern for other people's safety as well as direct economic effects, then figures in excess of £2,000,000 in 1987 prices could well be warranted. Lest the reader should be tempted to regard this as being an outrageously large number, it should be borne in mind that, given the willingness-to-pay definition of the value of statistical life, use of such a figure in the transport context would be tantamount to assuming that motorists would, on average, be willing to pay about £20 per annum for a 10% reduction in the risk of being killed in a car accident.[42] That, surely, is not *so* outrageous.

Notes

1 See Von Neumann and Morgenstern (1947), Savage (1954), or Drèze (1987).
2 One might be tempted to suppose that, with the utility index of not surviving arbitrarily set equal to zero, the pure utility of survival from period $t - 1$ to period t would be given by $u_t(0)$. However, one must recognize the possibility that, for some people, very low levels of consumption may be viewed as being 'as bad as or worse than death', so that $u_t(0)$ would in fact be *zero or even negative*, thereby rendering the interpretation of $u_t(0)$ as the pure utility of survival uncomfortable to say the least. Bergstrom (1982) very neatly resolves this difficulty by defining the utility of a stream of consumption as

$$u(c_1, c_2, \ldots, c_T) = f(T) + \sum_{t=1}^{T} u_t(c_t)$$

f being an increasing function of T. Under this specification, $f(T)$ clearly reflects the pure utility of survival. For a rather different perspective on the pure utility of survival problem, see Linnerooth (1979).
3 However, it should be noted that those who have considered the case in which the terms of insurance and annuity contracts vary with changes in risk have done so on the implicit assumption that the terms of *all* contracts, including those already held by the individual, will vary so as to maintain actuarial fairness – see, for example, Cook and Graham (1977) or Dehez and Drèze (1982). In fact, if the terms of insurance and annuity contracts are to vary at all with changes in individual risk, then it seems altogether more plausible to assume that only *new* contracts will be affected and in this case it turns out that the marginal rate of substitution of wealth for physical risk is *identical* with that which applies in the case of invariance of the terms of insurance and annuity contracts. For a fuller discussion of this point, see Chapter 3, note 19.
4 It might be supposed that the utility of dying would be minus infinity. However, utility functions of the type under consideration are, of necessity, bounded both above and below (see, for example, Arrow, 1971, pp. 63–9). It should also be noted that setting the utility of dying equal to zero necessarily makes this utility independent of wealth, which in turn rules out the possibility that the individual may be concerned for the well-being of surviving dependants. It is in this sense that we are dealing with a highly simplified model.
5 Specifically, RL_i is defined as $u'_i(w_i)/[u_i^* - u_i(w_i)]$ where u_i is the utility of wealth and u_i^* denotes $\sup[u_i(w_i)]$.
6 See, for example, Friend and Blume (1975) and Drèze (1981).
7 p_{it} is the probability of surviving the tth period conditional upon having survived the preceding $t - 1$ periods.
8 Weinstein *et al.* refer to the former as the value of statistical life *ex ante* the event and the latter as the value *ex post*. I have avoided the use of this

terminology in view of the possibility of confusion with the rather different and more common usage in this context discussed in Chapter 1, section 1.6.

9 For a development of this kind of argument see, for example, Sugden and Williams (1978), pp. 187–90.

10 Let R denote the binary relation of 'being ranked above'. The well-behavedness of R is then tantamount to the requirement that R is *transitive* (so that for all projects A, B and C, ARB and $BRC \Rightarrow ARC$) and *asymmetric* (so that for all projects A and B, $ARB \Rightarrow \sim BRA$). For a lucid explanation of the way in which the hypothetical compensation test may violate these conditions see, for example, Mishan (1969). The reader may be puzzled by the possibility that a criterion which is equivalent to the adoption of any project that increases social welfare for a particular specification of the social welfare function (see Chapter 1, note 19, might produce a badly behaved ranking of projects. The reason is essentially that the equivalence between the aggregate willingness-to-pay criterion and increasing social welfare applies only to *marginal* adjustments.

11 In particular, the case in which the events of 'illness' and 'death' during a forthcoming period are treated as being mutually exclusive. However, it is shown in Chapter 3 that the result derived for this case also applies when these events are treated as independent.

12 While some authors (e.g. Blomquist, 1982) apply the 'contingent market' or 'contingent valuation' terminology to all cases involving any kind of direct questioning concerning individual willingness to pay or required compensation, others, such as Cummings *et al.* (1986), appear to want to reserve the term 'contingent valuation method' for procedures of questioning that conform to a particular type of structure, including the use of iterative bidding to elicit individual willingness to pay (see Cummings *et al.*, 1986, p. 15). In this respect, what is referred to in this book as the 'questionnaire approach' is closer to Blomquist's more eclectic use of the 'contingent valuation' concept.

13 Ideally, the computation of distributionally weighted values of statistical life requires observations of *individual* marginal rates of substitution and income. While it would be possible to arrive at estimates on the basis of marginal rates of substitution broken down by different income bands, to the best of the author's knowledge revealed-preference studies have so far produced estimates of marginal rates of substitution only for very coarse breakdowns such as managerial and professional, non-manual and manual.

14 Ambiguity over the appropriate price level arises because of the protracted period (1967–73) to which some of the data relate.

15 Dorsey and Walzer (1983) have also attempted to take account of the effect of workers' compensation on wage differentials for risk by including data on the rates payable by employers for workers' compensation liability insurance – broken down by industry and state in the USA – in a regression analysis using CPS and BLS data. However, their results are very mixed in terms of sign and significance of both the compensation and fatal risk coefficients. In connection with the latter, it is worth noting that Hammermesh (1977) also failed to find consistent evidence of compensating wage differential effects, though he used a 0–1 dummy to reflect the classification of jobs as 'safe' or 'dangerous' (self-reported by workers themselves) rather than a continuous risk variable.

16 The second of these estimates is reported in an earlier version of the paper. Notice that since it is being assumed that, at the current average motorway speed, the marginal benefits of time savings due to increased speed equal the

marginal cost of fuel consumption plus the marginal cost of risk, the latter will clearly be an *increasing* function of the value of time and a *decreasing* function of the price of petrol.

17 In particular, it is necessary to assume that individuals are indifferent between the different patterns of variation in age-specific probabilities of death that produce a given variation in life expectancy – see section 2.2.3 for a more detailed discussion of this point. Notice that since the variation in life expectancy involved in this study was very small, the objection to the use of non-marginal variations developed in section 2.2.3 does not apply.

18 About 10,000 miles p.a.

19 These included Levine and Campbell (1971), Campbell *et al.* (1974) and Council and Hunter (1974).

20 I am grateful to Ian Dobbs for drawing this point to my attention.

21 This is an approximation in the sense that a ratio of finite changes is being used to estimate a derivative. To the extent that willingness to pay is an increasing, concave function of risk reduction and required compensation an increasing, convex function of increased risk, the approximation will yield an underestimate for risk reductions and an overestimate for increases in risk.

22 Though Acton describes his sample as 'random', it cannot strictly speaking be regarded as such since it was drawn from three communities in the Boston area – presumably not selected at random – and did not therefore give all individuals in the USA (or, for that matter, the Boston area) an equal probability of selection.

23 While Acton is specific about the year during which the Boston area survey was conducted (1970), I have been unable to find an explicit reference to the dates of the other two exercises. However, it seems reasonable to assume that they took place round about 1970.

24 That is, the value of statistical life that would be obtained if everyone had a marginal rate of substitution of wealth for risk equal to that implied by the median response.

25 See, for example, Jones-Lee (1976), p. 142.

26 Thus, for example, Maclean defines the value of statistical life – which he refers to as a 'standardized value' – as $c_i/p_ir_ik_i$ where c_i is '. . . the average value attributed to the risk reduction . . .', r_i is '. . . the fractional reduction in risk . . .', k_i is '. . . the proportion of the year for which the [safety] improvement is offered . . .' and p_i is the '. . . initial level of risk . . . measured over a period k_i . . .'. If Maclean's definition of p_i is taken literally, then it is clearly inappropriate to include k_i in the denominator of the expression for the value of statistical life, since the risk reduction for which c_i is the average value is p_ir_i rather than $p_ir_ik_i$. In fact, Maclean's expression is correct only if one interprets p_i as the *annual* risk from the source concerned and it is not clear whether – in spite of the way he defines p_i – Maclean proceeded on the basis of that interpretation. It follows that for all questions that involved risk reductions over periods other than one year, there are serious doubts about the values of statistical life reported by Maclean.

27 Notice that this argument is not symmetrical with respect to large *increases* in risk, in that one can readily think of many ways in which it would be a straightforward matter to worsen substantially one's survival prospects for the coming year without incurring any significant costs of discomfort or inconvenience.

28 A preliminary account of the results of this study is presented in Jones-Lee *et al.* (1983, 1987).

29 For a summary of the results of the feasibility study, see Hammerton *et al.* (1982a).
30 However, also see the qualifying remarks in section 2.1.1 and Chapter 3, section 3.3.
31 See, for example, Harrison and Quarmby (1972).
32 Though it should be recalled that Bergstrom has provided persuasive reasons why values of statistical life should *not* be augmented in this way if people's concern for others' well-being is 'pure' in the sense that it is not focused upon specific 'goods' such as safety. An alternative argument for excluding altruistic preferences from any calculus of social choice – essentially on the grounds that inclusion would involve 'double counting' – is developed by Broome (1978a).
33 These data were apparently obtained from a variety of sources, including Calne (1967), Rapaport (1973), Lesourd *et al.* (1968) and Woodruff (1966).
34 These data are reported by Bergan (1973), Hamburger and Crosnier (1968), National Institute of Allergy and Infectious Diseases (1972) and Klarman *et al.* (1973).
35 The extent to which this figure would be further augmented by inclusion of the willingness to pay of those outside an individual's immediate circle of relatives, friends and acquaintances remains an open question.
36 *Prima facie*, this result appears to reflect indifference concerning passengers' safety on the part of most car drivers. Alternatively it could be taken to cast serious doubt upon the reliability of the responses from which it was derived.
37 That is, an individual whose preferences and choices meet certain minimal consistency conditions such as those that most of us would presumably wish our well-thought-out preferences and choices to exhibit.
38 See, for example, Kahneman and Tversky (1979).
39 See, for example, Fischer (1979) or Brown and Green (1981).
40 All conversions were performed using consumer price indices and exchange rates from *International Financial Statistics*.
41 Citing experimental evidence reported in Lichtenstein *et al.* (1978), Blomquist (1982) argues that virtually all revealed-preference estimates will have been biased downwards by misperceptions of risk. In particular, since people show a systematic tendency to underestimate the kinds of risk involved in these studies, they will presumably also underestimate the magnitude of the risk reductions afforded by given devices or arrangements, and as a result estimated values of statistical life will be lower than they would be if perceptions had been correct. In the light of Lichtenstein *et al.*'s results Blomquist proposes that compensating wage differential estimates should be increased by 23.5% to correct for misperception biases, values implied by motorway speeds and seat-belt use by 63.4%, values derived from domestic smoke detectors by over 100% and, finally, values obtained from willingness to pay to reduce the risk of lung cancer and house price–air pollution trade-offs by a massive 770%.
42 The risk of being killed in a car accident is currently about 10^{-4} p.a. for the 'average' motorist.

3

The Theoretical Analysis of Individual Valuation of Safety: Some New Results

While there are those who have expressed a measure of impatience with the kind of theoretical analysis surveyed in Chapter 2, section 2.1 (on the grounds that we need 'hard' empirical estimates of individual valuation of safety rather than a priori, qualitative generalizations[1]), it is the author's view that such analysis is potentially valuable in at least three respects.

1 Theoretical analysis provides an explanation for some of the initially puzzling features of the results of empirical work, as well as suggesting, in advance of such work, what sort of patterns and regularities to look for. For example, the theoretical prediction that willingness to pay will be an increasing, strictly concave function of incremental survival probability (and required compensation a correspondingly increasing, strictly *convex* function of incremental physical risk) serves to explain some apparently peculiar asymmetries between individual willingness to pay for safety improvement and requirement of compensation for increased risk that have emerged from various empirical studies.[2]

2 Theoretical analysis provides a useful framework for ordering thought about policy issues. For example, theoretical predictions concerning the nature of the relationship between willingness to pay and age, income or current exposure to risk are valuable in informing policy decisions about priorities concerning safety improvements that affect different subgroups in society to different degrees.

3 Theoretical analysis provides a very powerful adjunct to, and check upon, empirical estimates of individual willingness to pay. This is particularly so in the case of theoretical results concerning the relationship between a typical individual's willingness to pay and other more readily quantifiable aspects of his attitudes to physical and financial risk.

Of course it is clear that, for a theoretical analysis of individual willingness to pay for safety to be at all effective in any of these respects, it is essential that the assumptions upon which the theory is based should take the form of plausible generalizations concerning individual preferences and attitudes to risk that can be expected to be true for 'most people, most of the time'. The purpose of this chapter is to develop a theoretical analysis that not only would appear to satisfy this condition but is at the same time sufficiently manageable to permit the derivation of a large number of rather interesting results which are, in some cases, both unexpected and surprisingly concrete.[3]

More specifically, the objective of the analysis in this chapter is to shed light upon the general properties of the relationship between individual willingness to pay (or required compensation) v on the one hand and the subjective probability p_t of death during the tth future period on the other. As earlier chapters have indicated, the value of statistical life for 'small' individual risk changes will depend intimately upon the magnitude of individual marginal rates of substitution of wealth for physical risk, i.e. upon the modulus of the derivative of $v(p_t)$ evaluated at $\bar{p}_t$ (the existing level of p_t). This derivative is therefore one of the principal focuses of concern in early sections of this chapter. However, a number of other properties of $v(p_t)$ are also considered. In particular, section 3.4 shows that for most people $v(p_t)$ will embody a remarkably simple and therefore potentially very powerful 'inverse proportionality' relationship between (a) an individual's marginal rate of substitution of wealth for physical risk, (b) his maximum acceptable increase in physical risk and (c) a particular measure of his attitude to *financial* risk. To the extent that it is fairly easy to place bounds upon the magnitudes of (b) and (c), this result offers a very direct means of delineating the order of magnitude of the marginal rate of substitution.

Section 3.5 explores the relationship between willingness to pay and 'multiperiod' variations in physical risk (i.e. safety effects that involve changes in the subjective probability of death during more than one future period). Section 3.6 shows that, for a particular but not entirely implausible special case, it is possible to specify the *entire* function $v(p_t)$ given $\bar{p}_t$ and just *two* properties of an individual's attitudes to physical and financial risk, namely the maximum acceptable increase in p_t and the individual's Pratt–Arrow coefficient of relative risk aversion. Section 3.7 then considers individual valuation of variations in the risk of *non-fatal injury* or illness.

Sections 3.1–3.7 assume that individuals behave as expected utility maximizers. However, there is growing evidence that, under certain circumstances, individuals will systematically violate the axioms of expected utility theory and, as a result, a number of alternative theories of individual choice under uncertainty have been proposed to accommodate such evidence. Section 3.8 therefore examines the implications of basing the analysis of individual valuation of safety upon some of these alternative theories of choice.

3.1   The Model

The fundamental assumption of the main body of analysis developed in this chapter is that an individual's preference ordering over joint subjective probability distributions of wealth w (defined to include discounted lifetime labour income or 'human capital') and time of death τ (measured from the present)[4] can be represented by the mathematical expectation of a cardinal Von Neumann–Morgenstern utility function $U : R^{2+} \rightarrow R$, assigning real-valued utility indices to each wealth–time of death pair (w,τ).[5] In addition, it is assumed that

1　U is at least twice-differentiable with respect to both arguments (this assumption implies that there are no discontinuous 'jumps' in the rate at which the individual is willing to trade off wealth for safety),

2　$\forall w, \tau, \dfrac{\partial U}{\partial w} > 0$ and $\dfrac{\partial U}{\partial \tau} > 0$

　(i.e. the individual prefers more wealth to less and prefers to die later rather than sooner, *ceteris paribus*),

3　$\forall w, \dfrac{\partial^2 U}{\partial w^2} < 0$

　(i.e. the individual is financially risk averse in the conventional sense), and

4　$U(w,\tau)$ is bounded above and below for each value of τ. Denoting $\sup_w[U(w,\tau)]$ by $U^*(\tau)$, it will also be assumed that $\tau_2 > \tau_1 \Rightarrow U^*(\tau_2) > U^*(\tau_1)$. (Amongst other things, the first part of this assumption ensures that the individual is immune to versions of the celebrated St Petersburg paradox.)

Given the existence of the utility function, assumptions (1)–(4) would indeed seem to place only relatively weak and rather plausible restrictions on its properties. However, the assumption concerning existence per se is not as innocuous as might initially appear to be the case. The first temptation – to which the author certainly succumbed (Jones-Lee, 1980a, b) – is to regard U as an indirect 'utility of wealth and time of death' function corresponding to a 'utility of lifetime consumption and bequest' function of the type proposed by Yaari (1965). According to this way of looking at things, given a level of wealth w and a time of death τ, there will exist an optimal lifetime consumption and bequest plan for the individual so that $U(w,\tau)$ can be viewed quite simply as the utility associated with this optimal plan.

However, in order to be valid, this interpretation of U would require that all uncertainty concerning w and τ was resolved sufficiently soon for the individual to be *able* to contemplate carrying out the optimal lifetime consumption and bequest plan associated with specific values of w and τ. In reality, of course, uncertainty concerning τ is not resolved until the time of the individual's death, so that one cannot associate a unique optimal lifetime consumption and bequest plan with each (w,τ) pair; indeed, one needs to be able to specify the *entire* joint distribution of w and τ before the optimal plan can be determined.[6] In view of this, it is probably preferable to abandon any attempt to give U an interpretation in terms of the utility of lifetime consumption and bequests and instead to assume that w and τ are *themselves* the principal focus of concern for an individual in choices affecting safety with, in addition, preferences over joint subjective probability distributions of w and τ being such as to imply that the individual behaves as an expected utility maximizer in such choices. As such, this assumption begs two rather substantial questions: (a) is it in fact reasonable to regard w and τ as the main objects of concern for an individual in decisions affecting safety and, if so, (b) is it legitimate to assume that preferences over joint distributions of w and τ are, in the main, such as to entail expected utility maximization? The assumption that individuals tend to focus directly on w and τ rather than upon the consumption streams that they will sustain, though perhaps somewhat unconventional, may nonetheless square rather well with the way most people actually do think and behave. If in doubt, the reader is invited to recall his or her most recent major economic decision and ask whether that was more significantly influenced by considerations of current and future real income prospects or by well-articulated lifetime consumption plans. It may well be the case that for most people consumption is the end object of economic activity, but the majority of us probably find it easier to assess the economic consequences of important decisions by reference to effects upon indices of generalized purchasing power (i.e. real income or wealth) rather than by detailed consideration of current and future consumption plans. Nonetheless, even if people do, in the first instance, tend to focus upon wealth and survival prospects, there remains the rather deep question of whether attitudes to physical and financial risk – in the form of preferences over subjective probability distributions of w and τ – can be taken to satisfy axioms of the type entailing expected utility maximization. In spite of the growing body of evidence suggesting that many people can be induced, under particular sets of circumstances, to make choices involving systematic violation of such axioms,[7] it remains the author's firm conviction that, as a simple summary description of the way most people tend, on the whole, to make choices under uncertainty, the Von Neumann–Morgenstern or Savage axioms retain a powerful appeal. In the first place, the predictions of theories based on such axioms have stood up well to empirical tests in a wide variety of contexts.[8] Secondly, the kind of choices in which people have been found to exhibit systematic violation of the axioms tend to be rather special and indeed, one might be forgiven for suggesting, somewhat contrived. For example, a version of the celebrated Allais paradox involves the following pairwise choices:[9]

A: 50% chance to win a three-week tour of England, France and Italy   versus   B: A one-week tour of England with certainty

C: 5% chance to win a three-week tour of England, France and Italy   versus   D: 10% chance to win a one-week tour of England

Faced with these choices, many people will express a preference for B over A and also for C over D, thereby violating the axioms underpinning expected utility theory.[10] Quite apart from the fact that some people, having made such choices, can be persuaded that they have simply 'made a mistake',[11] it should also be stressed that, whereas the probabilities in A and B are large, those in C and D are relatively small, so that the expression of a preference for B over A and C over D might be viewed as being somewhat akin to succumbing to an optical illusion.[12] It could therefore be argued that paradoxes of this type pose no more of a threat to expected utility theory *as a summary description of general tendencies in choice under uncertainty* than do the standard optical illusions to the proposition that most people have, on the whole, quite acute powers of visual perception.

A third point in favour of expected utility theory is that no alternative theory of individual choice under uncertainty so far proposed is clearly superior on all, or even a majority of, the criteria by which such theories might be judged. For example, Kahneman and Tversky's 'prospect theory', while admittedly offering an explanation for some of the commonly observed choice patterns that are inconsistent with expected utility theory, suffers from a rather disturbing arbitrariness in the specification of its 'value' function and the discontinuities of its 'weighting' function also have some rather unfortunate implications.[13] Similarly, 'regret' theories of the type proposed by Loomes and Sugden (1982) or Bell (1982) also appear to accommodate many of the paradoxes of observed choices but can so far only be satisfactorily applied (positively or normatively) to pairwise choices.

Finally, it is worth noting that the bulk of the evidence against expected utility maximization involves choices concerning financial rather than phyical risk. While it cannot be denied that appropriately framed choices might reproduce 'paradoxical' results in the physical as well as the financial context, it is also possible that the presence of consequences such as 'survival' and 'death' in such choices would, to paraphrase Dr Johnson, serve to concentrate the mind wonderfully.

Thus, if one is required to make simple yet general summary statements concerning the way most people tend to choose under conditions of uncertainty, it is the author's opinion that the axioms underpinning expected utility theory remain the most plausible currently available from an explanatory and predictive point of view and the most persuasive when considered from a normative perspective. Nonetheless, as already noted, a later section in this chapter will examine the implications of replacing the expected utility maximization hypothesis with alternative hypotheses – proposed to accommodate phenomena such as the Allais paradox – in the current context. To the extent that these alternatives appear to entail few substantial modifications to the results derived in the main body of this chapter, what follows can probably fairly lay claim to capturing the essential features of the behaviour of 'most people, most of the time'. Alternatively, the analysis below might simply be regarded as a summary

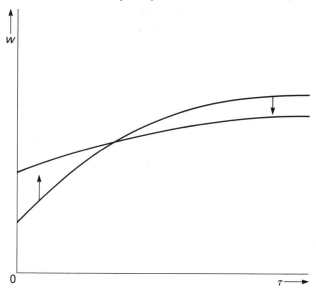

Figure 3.1   Wealth (including human capital) as a function of time of death.

of the way in which an idealized 'rational model' would value variations in physical risk. Under this way of looking at things, the results of the analysis will be irrelevant only if one rejects expected utility theory from both a positive *and* a normative point of view – and there can surely be few who would go as far as that.

3.2   Optimal Expenditure on Life Insurance and Annuities

Given that w has been defined to include discounted lifetime labour income, it follows that in the absence of opportunities to purchase life insurance or annuities w will in general be an increasing function of τ, at least up to the value of τ corresponding to an individual's retirement age. From the point of view of the present analysis, the principal impact of the existence of opportunities to purchase life insurance or annuities is that such opportunities allow the individual to alter the way in which w varies with τ. For example, the net present value of a whole-life insurance policy – which pays the sum assured at the time of an individual's death – is a decreasing function of the length of time for which the insured person survives. The current purchase of such a policy would therefore shift the graph of w as a function of τ in the manner shown in figure 3.1.

The current purchase of an annuity would clearly have the opposite effect. In general, given access to a sufficiently wide range of actuarially fair insurance and annuity contracts, the individual will effectively be able to choose any relationship between w and τ provided that it satisfies the condition that the mathematical expectation of w with insurance is equal to the mathematical expectation without it. The individual's decision concerning the optimal purchase of life insurance and/or annuities can therefore be written as

$$\max_{w} \int_0^T U(w,\tau)\bar{\rho}(\tau) \, d\tau \text{ subject to } \int_0^T w\bar{\rho}(\tau) \, d\tau = \text{constant}$$

where T is the longest time for which the individual could conceivably survive and $\bar{\rho}(\tau)$ is the individual's current (subjective) probability density function for τ.[14]

As such, this is a standard calculus of variations problem with an *isoperimetric* constraint for which a necessary condition for an interior[15] extremum is

$$\frac{d}{d\tau} \frac{\partial U}{\partial w} = 0. \tag{3.1}$$

Thus, with optimal current and planned holdings of actuarially fair life insurance and annuities, w will vary with τ in such a way as to ensure that the marginal utility of wealth is independent of τ. Furthermore, from the chain rule

$$\frac{d}{d\tau} \frac{\partial U}{\partial w} = \frac{\partial^2 U}{\partial w^2} \frac{dw}{d\tau} + \frac{\partial^2 U}{\partial \tau \partial w} \tag{3.2}$$

so that, from (3.1) and (3.2),

$$\frac{dw}{d\tau} = -\frac{\partial^2 U/\partial \tau \partial w}{\partial^2 U/\partial w^2}. \tag{3.3}$$

Hence, from (3.3), with $\partial^2 U/\partial w^2 < 0$,

$$\frac{\partial^2 U}{\partial \tau \partial w} \gtreqless 0 \Leftrightarrow \frac{dw}{d\tau} \gtreqless 0. \tag{3.4}$$

Thus, the question of whether w is an increasing or decreasing function of τ following the optimal current and planned purchase of insurance or annuities depends entirely on the sign of the cross-partial of U. For most people it seems probable that the latter will be positive, so that with optimal insurance w will typically be a strictly increasing function of τ.

Now suppose that the individual's survival prospects are affected by some public sector project so that $\bar{\rho}(\tau)$ changes to $\rho(\tau)$. While insurance companies might be expected to react to a major change in an individual's health status by altering the terms on which they offer life insurance or annuities, it seems unlikely that they would respond in such a way to the safety effects of a public sector project, at least in the short-term. If this were so, then insurance would cease to be actuarially fair and the individual's decision problem would become

$$\max_{w} \int_0^T U(w,\tau)\rho(\tau)\ \mathrm{d}\tau \text{ subject to } \int_0^T w\bar{\rho}(\tau)\ \mathrm{d}\tau = \text{constant.}$$

For this problem, the necessary condition for an interior extremum is

$$\frac{\mathrm{d}}{\mathrm{d}\tau}\left(\frac{\partial U}{\partial w}\frac{\rho(\tau)}{\bar{\rho}(\tau)}\right) = 0. \tag{3.5}$$

Thus, in contrast with the case in which insurance is actuarially fair, $\partial U/\partial w$ will not now be independent of τ but will instead vary in inverse proportion to the ratio $\rho(\tau)/\bar{\rho}(\tau)$ with, in particular, $\partial U/\partial w$ being larger for those values of τ for which $\rho(\tau) < \bar{\rho}(\tau)$, and vice versa. The intuition behind this result is actually quite straightforward. Suppose that the probability of early death rises for some particular individual. We shall then have $\rho(\tau) > \bar{\rho}(\tau)$ for τ small and $\rho(\tau) < \bar{\rho}(\tau)$ for larger values of τ. If, however, the terms on which life insurance is made available to the individual remain unaltered, then he will naturally tend to respond by increasing his current cover, thereby increasing w (and hence reducing $\partial U/\partial w$) for τ small and decreasing w (and hence increasing $\partial U/\partial w$) for τ large.

3.3 Willingness to Pay and Required Compensation

Having considered the way in which the existence of opportunities to purchase life insurance and annuities affects the relationship between w and τ, let us now turn to the central question of this chapter, namely individual willingness to pay for safety improvement and requirement of compensation for increased risk.

Suppose – as in the previous section – that a public sector project, if undertaken, will cause the individual's subjective probability density function for time of death to change from $\bar{\rho}(\tau)$ to $\rho(\tau)$. If, as assumed, the individual behaves as an expected utility maximizer, then the maximum sum v that he would be willing to pay for a desirable perturbation (or the minimum sum he would accept in compensation for an undesirable perturbation) will be given by the solution to

$$\max_{v,w} v \text{ subject to } EU(w-v,\tau) = \bar{E}U(\bar{w},\tau) \text{ and } \bar{E}w = \bar{E}\bar{w}$$

where E and $\bar{E}$ denote mathematical expectations with respect to $\rho(\tau)$ and $\bar{\rho}(\tau)$ respectively and $\bar{w}$ denotes the optimal (time-dependent) values of w corresponding to $\bar{\rho}(\tau)$. The requirement that $\bar{E}w = \bar{E}\bar{w}$ reflects the invariance of the terms on which (initially actuarially fair) life insurance and annuities can be purchased. To simplify the analysis it will be convenient at this stage to split the interval $[0,T]$ into T periods, each short relative to $[0,T]$. There will then be little error in writing[16]

$$\text{E}U(w-v,\tau) = [U(w_1-v,1)p_1] + [U(w_2-v,2)(1-p_1)p_2] + \ldots \quad (3.6)$$

$$\bar{\text{E}}U(\bar{w},\tau) = [U(\bar{w}_1,1)\bar{p}_1] + [U(\bar{w}_2,2)(1-\bar{p}_1)\bar{p}_2] + \ldots \quad (3.7)$$

$$\bar{\text{E}}w = w_1\bar{p}_1 + w_2(1-\bar{p}_1)\bar{p}_2 + \ldots \quad (3.8)$$

$$\bar{\text{E}}\bar{w} = \bar{w}_1\bar{p}_1 + \bar{w}_2(1-\bar{p}_1)\bar{p}_2 + \ldots \quad (3.9)$$

where p_t ($t = 1, \ldots, T$) denotes the probability of death during period t conditional upon survival through the preceding $t - 1$ periods, $\bar{p}_t$ ($t = 1, \ldots, T$) denotes the initial value of p_t, w_t denotes w conditional on death during period t and $\bar{w}_t$ denotes the initial (optimal) value of w_t.

In order to establish necessary conditions for maximizing v subject to the expected utility and expected wealth constraints, consider the Lagrangean

$$L = v + \lambda\{[U(w_1-v,1)p_1] + [U(w_2-v,2)(1-p_1)p_2] + \ldots - \bar{\text{E}}U(\bar{w},\tau)\}$$
$$+ \mu(w_1\bar{p}_1 + w_2(1-\bar{p}_1)\bar{p}_2 + \ldots - \bar{\text{E}}\bar{w}) \quad (3.10)$$

where λ and μ are Lagrange multipliers. Necessary conditions for a constrained maximum of v then include[17]

$$\frac{\partial L}{\partial v} = 1 - \lambda \text{E}U_t' = 0 \quad (3.11)$$

$$\left.\begin{array}{l} \dfrac{\partial L}{\partial w_1} = \lambda U_1'p_1 + \mu\bar{p}_1 = 0 \\[2pt] \vdots \\[2pt] \dfrac{\partial L}{\partial w_T} = \lambda U_T'(1-p_1)(1-p_2) \ldots p_T + \mu(1-\bar{p}_1)(1-\bar{p}_2) \ldots \bar{p}_T = 0 \end{array}\right\} (3.12)$$

where U_t' denotes $\partial U(w_t,t)/\partial w_t$ and $\text{E}U_t'$ denotes the expectation of U_t'.

Second-order conditions for a constrained maximum of v are fulfilled as a result of the assumed strict concavity of U in w.[18] Summing over (3.12) gives

$$\lambda \text{E}U_t' = -\mu \quad (3.13)$$

so that from (3.11) and (3.13), $\mu = -1$ and

$$U'_t = \frac{(1-\bar{p}_1)(1-\bar{p}_2) \ldots \bar{p}_t}{\lambda(1-p_1)(1-p_2) \ldots p_t} \quad (t = 1, \ldots, T) \quad (3.14)$$

which is the discrete-time counterpart to (3.5).

Now consider a variation in safety that affects only the current-period probability of death, i.e.

$$(\bar{p}_1, \bar{p}_2, \ldots, \bar{p}_T) \to (p_1, \bar{p}_2, \ldots, \bar{p}_T).$$

While it is possible to derive an expression for $\partial v/\partial p_1$ using the envelope theorem, it is somewhat more illuminating to proceed directly by differentiating through the expected utility equality constraint. Thus, setting $p_t = \bar{p}_t$ ($t = 2, \ldots, T$) in (3.6) and differentiating through the constraint $\text{E}U(w - v,\tau) = \bar{\text{E}}U(\bar{w},\tau)$ with respect to p_1 gives

$$\frac{U(w_1-v,1) - \mathrm{E}U(w-v,\tau)}{1-p_1} - \mathrm{E}U_t' \frac{\partial v}{\partial p_1} + \mathrm{E}\left(U_t' \frac{\partial w_t}{\partial p_1}\right) = 0 \qquad (3.15)$$

where $\mathrm{E}(U_t' \, \partial w_t/\partial p_1)$ denotes the expectation of $U_t' \, \partial w_t/\partial p_1$ and $\partial w_t/\partial p_1$ is the rate of change of w_t with respect to p_1 owing to adjustments in the optimal holdings of life insurance or annuities. Multiplying through the first equation in (3.12) by $\partial w_1/\partial p_1$, the second by $\partial w_2/\partial p_1$ etc., setting $\mu = -1$ and summing over all equations gives

$$\mathrm{E}\left(U_t' \frac{\partial w_t}{\partial p_1}\right) = \frac{1}{\lambda} \, \bar{\mathrm{E}} \, \frac{\partial w_t}{\partial p_1}. \qquad (3.16)$$

Furthermore, differentiating through the constraint $\bar{\mathrm{E}}w = \bar{\mathrm{E}}\bar{w}$ with respect to p_1 gives

$$\bar{\mathrm{E}} \, \frac{\partial w_t}{\partial p_1} = 0 \qquad (3.17)$$

so that from (3.15), (3.16) and (3.17)

$$\frac{\partial v}{\partial p_1} = \frac{U(w_1-v,1) - \mathrm{E}U(w-v,\tau)}{(1-p_1)\mathrm{E}U_t'}. \qquad (3.18)$$

The individual's *marginal rate of substitution* m_1 of wealth for current-period probability of death, evaluated at the current level of the latter, is simply $-(\partial v/\partial p_1)_{\bar{p}_1}$. When $p_1 = \bar{p}_1$ it is necessarily the case that $v = 0$ and in addition, from (3.12), $U_1' = U_2' = \ldots = U_T'$. It therefore follows that[19]

$$m_1 = \frac{\bar{\mathrm{E}}U(\bar{w},\tau) - U(\bar{w}_1,1)}{(1-\bar{p}_1)U'} \qquad (3.19)$$

where U' denotes the common value of U_t'.

Now it seems reasonable to assume that for the vast majority of people the solution to the constrained maximization of v will satisfy

$$U(w_1-v,1) < U(w_2-v,2) < \ldots < U(w_T-v,T) \qquad (3.20)$$

i.e. we shall ignore the possibility that the individual plans to purchase life insurance in such an amount as to render death in period t preferable to death in period $t + 1$. From (3.18), (3.19) and (3.20) it follows that, given $U_t' > 0$,

$$\frac{\partial v}{\partial p_1} < 0 \quad \text{and} \quad m_1 > 0. \qquad (3.21)$$

In addition, it will be assumed that it will typically be the case that no sum, however large, could compensate for an increase in physical risk entailing $p_1 = 1$. Thus

$$\bar{\mathrm{E}}U(\bar{w},\tau) > U^*(1) \qquad (3.22)$$

In view of (3.22) it is clear that there will exist some 'maximum

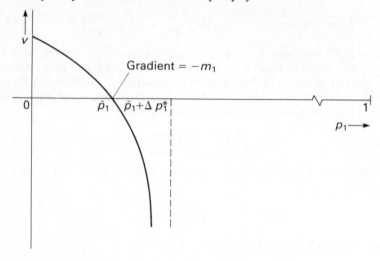

Figure 3.2 v as a function of p_1.

acceptable' value of p_1 (or more accurately, though somewhat less graph-ically, a least upper bound to compensatable levels of p_1) in the sense that $v \to -\infty$ as p_1 approaches this value. In what follows it will be con-venient to denote this value of p_1 by $\bar{p}_1 + \Delta p_1^*$ (so that Δp_1^* is the maximum acceptable *increase* in first-period probability of death). Letting $(\bar{p}_1, \bar{p}_2, \ldots, \bar{p}_T) \to (\bar{p}_1 + \Delta p_1^*, \bar{p}_2, \ldots, \bar{p}_T)$ and $v \to -\infty$ in the constraint $EU(w-v,\tau) = \bar{E}U(\bar{w},\tau)$ and rearranging gives

$$\Delta p_1^* = \frac{(1-\bar{p}_1)[\bar{E}U^*(\tau) - \bar{E}U(\bar{w},\tau)]}{\bar{E}U^*(\tau) - U^*(1)} \tag{3.23}$$

where $\bar{E}U^*(\tau)$ is the expectation of $U^*(\tau)$ with respect to $\bar{\rho}(\tau)$. Hence, from (3.22) and (3.23),

$$p_1 + \Delta p_1^* < 1. \tag{3.24}$$

In view of (3.21) and (3.24) it would therefore seem that the relation-ship between v and p_1 would be of the general form shown in figure 3.2.

While it is indeed possible to show that v is a strictly decreasing, concave function of p_1 for more restrictive models of willingness to pay for safety,[20] it somewhat surprisingly turns out that the assumptions made so far are not sufficient to guarantee that the function is everywhere strictly concave. Basically, the possibility of local convexity arises from the fact that, given the assumption concerning the terms on which life insurance is made available, it is possible that w_1 rises so rapidly with p_1 – at least over some initial interval – that the difference between $EU(w-v,\tau)$ and $U(w_1-v,1)$ falls faster than $(1-p_1)EU_t'$ over this interval. However, in order for this to happen it would be necessary for the individual to effect a very considerable increase in his first-period life insurance cover in response to an increase in p_1. In fact most people seem to have something in the nature of a 'target' level of life insurance cover that they do not adjust significantly in response to variations in physical risk, so that the kind of effect described above will probably be relatively rare. In what follows it will therefore be assumed that $v(p)$ is everywhere strictly concave, though it should be stressed that strict concavity is not essential to the remainder of the argument in this chapter which depends, basically, *only* upon the properties of $v(p)$ reflected in (3.19), (3.21), (3.23) and (3.24).

Turning now to a *ceteris paribus* variation in p_t, by a process of reasoning analogous to that developed above it can be shown that

$$\frac{\partial v}{\partial p_t} = \frac{E_t U(w-v,\tau) - EU(w-v,\tau)}{(1-p_t)EU_t'} \tag{3.25}$$

where $E_t U(w-v,\tau)$ denotes the expectation of $U(w-v,\tau)$ with respect to the vector of conditional probabilities $(\bar{p}_1, \bar{p}_2, \ldots, \bar{p}_{t-1}, 1)$ with w_1, $w_2, \ldots, w_t$ taking on identical values to those in $EU(w-v,\tau)$. Thus, it is clear that $E_t U(w-v,\tau)$ is the value to which $EU(w-v,\tau)$ would fall if the probability of survival to $\tau > t$ went to zero, with everything else held constant. It is therefore natural to regard $E_t U(w-v,\tau)$ as 'truncated lifetime expected utility'. It then follows that the individual's marginal rate of substitution m_t of wealth for p_t (evaluated at the current level of the latter) is given by

$$m_t = \frac{\bar{E}U(\bar{w},\tau) - E_t U(\bar{w},\tau)}{(1-\bar{p}_t)U'}. \tag{3.26}$$

Now it is clearly possible that for some people there exists a value of t for which $E_t U^*(\tau) > \bar{E}U(\bar{w},\tau)$. For such an individual there would exist a finite sum that would compensate for the perturbation $\bar{p}_t \to p_t = 1$. However, this 'Faustian' case will almost certainly be the exception, at least for smaller values of t, and in what follows we shall therefore concentrate on the case in which $E_t U^*(\tau) < \bar{E}U(\bar{w},\tau)$ so that no sum, however large, would compensate for $\bar{p}_t \to p_t = 1$. In such cases there will exist a maximum acceptable increase Δp_t^* in p_t. Letting $(\bar{p}_1, \bar{p}_2, \ldots,$ $\bar{p}_t, \ldots, \bar{p}_T) \to (\bar{p}_1, \bar{p}_2, \ldots, \bar{p}_t + \Delta p_t^*, \ldots, \bar{p}_T)$ and $v \to -\infty$ in the constraint $EU(w-v,\tau) = \bar{E}U(\bar{w},\tau)$ and rearranging gives

$$\Delta p_t^* = \frac{(1-\bar{p}_t)[\bar{E}U^*(\tau) - \bar{E}U(\bar{w},\tau)]}{\bar{E}U^*(\tau) - E_t U^*(\tau)} \tag{3.27}$$

where $E_t U^*(\tau)$ denotes the truncated lifetime expectation of $U^*(\tau)$, i.e. the expectation with respect to $(\bar{p}_1, \bar{p}_2, \ldots, \bar{p}_{t-1}, 1)$.

3.4 The Relationship between m_t and Δp_t^*: an (Almost) General Approximation Theorem

Intuitively, it seems plausible that there will exist some sort of inverse relationship between m_1 and Δp_1^*, i.e. the larger an individual's marginal rate of substitution of wealth for probability of death in the current period, the smaller will be his maximum acceptable increase in that probability. In Jones-Lee (1980b) it was shown that for the case in which U takes the additive-separable form $U(w,\tau) = u(w) + \ell(\tau)$, m_1 and Δp_1^* are, in fact, inversely *proportional* to each other, the coefficient of proportionality being interpretable as a measure of *financial* risk aversion. Specifically, let U take the additive-separable form in the expressions for m_1 and Δp_1^* given in (3.19) and (3.23). It then follows that[21]

$$m_1 \Delta p_1^* \left[\frac{u'(\bar{w})}{u^* - u(\bar{w})} \right] = 1 \tag{3.28}$$

where $u'(w)$ and u^* denote, respectively, the first derivative and supremum of the component utility of wealth function $u(w)$. Now consider the expression in brackets on the left-hand side of (3.28). It is a straight-forward matter to show that if an individual with separable U is offered the opportunity to undertake a financial gamble with small stake x and a net-of-stake prize y, sufficiently large that $u(\bar{w} + y) \approx u^*$, then the win probability π that will just induce him to participate will satisfy

$$\frac{\pi}{1 - \pi} \approx x \left[\frac{u'(\bar{w})}{u^* - u(\bar{w})} \right]. \tag{3.29}$$

It is therefore natural to interpret the expression in brackets in (3.28) as a measure of the individual's attitudes to small stake–large payoff financial gambles. This expression was referred to by Jones-Lee (1980b) as the *coefficient of asymptotic risk aversion* and denoted by RL[22] so that, maintaining that notation, (3.28) can be written more succinctly as

$$m_1 \Delta p_1^* \text{RL} = 1. \tag{3.30}$$

   This, it must be conceded, is a result of remarkable simplicity and elegance. However, thus far the result has been established only for the rather restricted case in which U is separable. Nonetheless, one is tempted to conjecture that such a relationship might hold, at least as an approximation, in a wider class of cases and if this were true then a number of potentially very important policy implications would follow.[23] For example, it seems likely (and it would, in principle, be a straight-forward matter to confirm empirically) that for most people the maximum acceptable increase in the probability of death during the coming year would not be as large as 10^{-2}. Equally, if we consider a financial gamble having, say, a £1 stake and a £1,000,000 payoff then one would expect that most people could be induced to participate in the gamble if the chances of winning were as high as 1 in 5,000. It therefore seems reasonable to suppose that for the vast majority of people $\Delta p_1^* < 10^{-2}$ and, given the interpretation of RL implied by (3.29), that with w measured in pounds sterling RL $< 2 \times 10^{-4}$. Thus, provided that it could be shown that a relationship such as (3.30) applied in general and not merely to the case in which U is separable, then one could conclude with some confidence that m_1 will typically exceed £500,000 – a result that would lend considerable support to the empirical results reported in Chapters 2 and 4.

A second potentially significant implication of a generalized version of (3.30) would concern the relationship between values of statistical life (or costs of fatalities) and legally (or conventionally) imposed safety standards. Such a standard normally has the property that any project or activity that violates the standard will be rejected out of hand *however beneficial the project or activity might be in other respects*. As such, safety standards can be viewed as public sector decision-making counterparts to individual 'maximum acceptable' increases Δp_1^* in physical risk. Indeed, from a utilitarian point of view there is a case to be made for setting safety standards so as to reflect typical orders of magnitude of Δp_1^*. If, in addition, one defines values of statistical life in terms of the population mean of m_1, then a generalization of (3.30) would provide a simple and direct consistency check on proposed values of statistical life and safety standards. For example, the National Radiological Protection Board (NRPB) has proposed costs per collective dose of ionizing radiation and a maximum acceptable dose per capita (Clark *et al.*, 1981; National Radiological Protection Board, 1986) that imply, respectively, a value of statistical life of about £150,000 and a maximum acceptable increase in annual risk of death of about 10^{-4} for members of the general public. However, given a relationship such as (3.30), consistency between these magnitudes would require that RL ≈ 0.07 which, recalling the interpretation of RL, is an absurdly high value for most people. In fact, the clear implication of a relationship like (3.30) is that the NRPB's value of statistical life is far too low and/or its maximum acceptable dose per capita is far too small.

However, these conclusions concerning the magnitude of m_1 and the consistency of the NRPB's recommendations are, perforce, in the nature of speculations until it can be demonstrated that the relationship $m_1\Delta p_1^*\text{RL} = 1$ applies, at least as a good approximation, to a far wider class of cases than those in which U is separable. The purpose of the remainder of this section is to provide such a demonstration and, indeed, to show that a counterpart to (3.30) will apply also to $t = 2, 3$ etc.

In order to show that the approximation $m_1\Delta p_1^*$ RL ≈ 1 has very wide applicability, notice first of all that, as shown by Jones-Lee (1980b), with $p_1 = \bar{p}_1, p_2 = \bar{p}_2$ etc. the appropriate definition of RL for non-separable forms of U is given by

$$\text{RL} \equiv \frac{U'}{\bar{\text{E}}U^*(\tau) - \bar{\text{E}}U(\bar{w},\tau)}. \tag{3.31}$$

(In particular, this definition sustains the interpretation of RL in terms of the critical win–loss probability ratio in the small stake–large payoff financial gamble.) It then follows from (3.19), (3.23) and (3.31) that in the general case

$$m_1\Delta p_1^*\text{RL} = \frac{\bar{\text{E}}U(\bar{w},\tau) - U(\bar{w}_1,1)}{\bar{\text{E}}U^*(\tau) - U^*(1)}. \tag{3.32}$$

Clearly, it is possible that the expression on the right-hand side of (3.32) could be substantially less than unity and if this were so then the basis for the sort of argument developed above concerning a lower bound on m_1 would collapse. However, with $\bar{w}_1$ finite, by definition $U^*(1) > U(\bar{w}_1,1)$, so that

$$\frac{\bar{E}U(\bar{w},\tau) - U(\bar{w}_1,1)}{\bar{E}U^*(\tau) - U^*(1)} > \frac{\bar{E}U(\bar{w},\tau) - U^*(1)}{\bar{E}U^*(\tau) - U^*(1)}. \tag{3.33}$$

Furthermore, from (3.23),

$$\frac{\bar{E}U(\bar{w},\tau) - U^*(1)}{\bar{E}U^*(\tau) - U^*(1)} = 1 - \frac{\Delta p_1^*}{1-\bar{p}_1} \tag{3.34}$$

so that from (3.32), (3.33) and (3.34)

$$m_1 \Delta p_1^* \text{RL} > 1 - \frac{\Delta p_1^*}{1-\bar{p}_1}. \tag{3.35}$$

Since, for those below the age of 60, $\bar{p}_1$ is typically substantially less than 10^{-2} and, as argued above, Δp_1^* will probably not exceed 10^{-2}, (3.35) indicates that for most people $m_1 \Delta p_1^* \text{RL}$ will normally be greater than 0.98. This result in itself carries us a considerable way towards confirming our earlier speculations concerning a lower bound on m_1 and the consistency of the NRPB's recommendations. However, one can go somewhat further. To see how, notice first that the expression on the right-hand side of (3.32) can be written as

$$\frac{\bar{E}U(\bar{w},\tau) - U(\bar{w}_1,1)}{\bar{E}U^*(\tau) - U^*(1)}$$

$$\equiv \frac{[\bar{E}U(\bar{w},\tau) - U^*(1)] + [U^*(1) - U(\bar{w}_1,1)]}{[\bar{E}U^*(\tau) - \bar{E}U(\bar{w},\tau)] + [\bar{E}U(\bar{w},\tau) - U^*(1)]}. \tag{3.36}$$

However, with slight rearrangement, (3.23) gives

$$\frac{\bar{E}U(\bar{w},\tau) - U^*(1)}{\bar{E}U^*(\tau) - \bar{E}U(\bar{w},\tau)} = \frac{1 - \bar{p}_1 - \Delta p_1^*}{\Delta p_1^*}. \tag{3.37}$$

In order to simplify (3.36) still further it therefore remains only to establish the relationship between $U^*(1)-U(\bar{w}_1,1)$ and *either* $\bar{E}U(\bar{w},\tau) - U^*(1)$ *or* $\bar{E}U^*(\tau) - \bar{E}U(\bar{w},\tau)$. In fact, it turns out to be possible to express the second of these relationships in a rather simple and quite concrete way if we consider an individual's preferences over the following two options:

Under option A you will receive a very large increase in wealth if you survive the current period but your estate will receive no increase if you die during the current period.[24]

Under option B your estate will receive a very large increase in wealth if you die during the current period but you will receive no increase if you survive the current period.

(Your existing wealth $\bar{E}\bar{w}$ will be unaffected by the choice of option and you will not be permitted to adjust life insurance or annuity holdings in response to your choice of option.)[25]

Clearly, holding the conditional probabilities of death in the second and subsequent period constant at $\bar{p}_2$, $\bar{p}_3$ etc., the expected utility of each option will depend upon p_1. Denoting the expected utility for option A by $EU_A(p_1)$ and that for option B by $EU_B(p_1)$ we shall have

$$EU_A(p_1) = U(\bar{w}_1,1)p_1 + U^*(2)(1-p_1)\bar{p}_2 + \\ U^*(3)(1-p_1)(1-\bar{p}_2)\bar{p}_3 + \ldots \qquad (3.38)$$

and

$$EU_B(p_1) = U^*(1)p_1 + U(\bar{w}_2,2)(1-p_1)\bar{p}_2 + \\ U(\bar{w}_3,3)(1-p_1)(1-\bar{p}_2)\bar{p}_3 + \ldots \qquad (3.39)$$

Now with $\bar{w}_t$ finite, $U^*(t) > U(\bar{w}_t,t)$, so that from (3.38) and (3.39) $EU_A(0) > EU_B(0)$ and $EU_A(1) < EU_B(1)$. In addition, $EU_A(p_1)$ and $EU_B(p_1)$ are both continuous, linear functions of p_1 so that there must exist a unique $0 < \hat{p}_1 < 1$ such that the individual is indifferent between option A and option B. From (3.38) and (3.39) $\hat{p}_1$ will satisfy

$$U(\bar{w}_1,1)\hat{p}_1 + U^*(2)(1-\hat{p}_1)\bar{p}_2 + U^*(3)(1-\hat{p}_1)(1-\bar{p}_2)\bar{p}_3 + \ldots \\ = U^*(1)\hat{p}_1 + U(\bar{w}_2,2)(1-\hat{p}_1)\bar{p}_2 + U(\bar{w}_3,3)(1-\hat{p}_1)(1-\bar{p}_2)\bar{p}_3 + \ldots \quad (3.40)$$

which, on rearranging and simplifying, gives

$$\frac{\bar{E}U^*(\tau) - U^*(1)\bar{p}_1}{1 - \bar{p}_1} - \frac{\bar{E}U(\bar{w},\tau) - U(\bar{w}_1,1)\bar{p}_1}{1 - \bar{p}_1} \\ = \frac{\hat{p}_1}{1 - \hat{p}_1}[U^*(1) - U(\bar{w}_1,1)] \qquad (3.41)$$

and hence

$$\frac{U^*(1) - U(\bar{w}_1,1)}{\bar{E}U^*(\tau) - \bar{E}U(\bar{w},\tau)} = \frac{1 - \hat{p}_1}{\hat{p}_1 + \bar{p}_1 - 2\hat{p}_1\bar{p}_1}. \qquad (3.42)$$

Thus, substituting from (3.36), (3.37) and (3.42) into (3.32) and rearranging gives

$$m_1\Delta p_1^* \mathrm{RL} = 1 + \frac{(1-2\hat{p}_1)\Delta p_1^*}{\hat{p}_1 + \bar{p}_1 - 2\hat{p}_1\bar{p}_1}. \qquad (3.43)$$

Notice first that since $\bar{p}_1 > 0$ and $\hat{p}_1 < 1$ we must have $\hat{p}_1 + \bar{p}_1 - 2\hat{p}_1\bar{p}_1$ $(= \hat{p}_1(1-\bar{p}_1) + \bar{p}_1(1-\hat{p}_1)) > 0$ so that $m_1\Delta p_1\mathrm{RL} \gtreqless 1$ as $\hat{p}_1 \lesseqgtr 0.5$. This together with (3.30) suggests that $\hat{p}_1 = 0.5$ corresponds to the case in which U is additive-separable, and letting U take the separable form in (3.40) does indeed yield $\hat{p}_1 = 0.5$, confirming that this is so.

At a more general level, it seems clear that $\hat{p}_1$ will be smaller the greater an individual's concern for the well-being of surviving dependants in the event of his death during the current period, and vice versa. Now it

Table 3.1 $m_1 \Delta p_1^* \text{RL}$ for $\bar{p}_1 = 0.000,5$

$\hat{p}_1$	Δp_1^*			
	0.000,1	*0.001*	*0.01*	*0.1*
0.000,1	1.166,660	2.666,611	17.666,077	167.661,072
0.001	1.066,577	1.665,776	7.657,771	67.577,667
0.01	1.009,341	1.093,422	1.934,223	10.342,231
0.1	1.000,795	1.007,967	1.079,680	1.796,812
0.2	1.000,299	1.002,995	1.029,955	1.299,550
0.3	1.000,133	1.001,332	1.013,324	1.133,244
0.4	1.000,050	1.000,500	1.004,997	1.049,987
0.5	1.000,000	1.000,000	1.000,000	1.000,000
0.6	0.999,967	0.999,667	0.996,666	0.966,661
0.7	0.999,943	0.999,428	0.994,284	0.942,841
0.8	0.999,925	0.999,250	0.992,497	0.924,972
0.9	0.999,911	0.999,111	0.991,107	0.911,071
0.99	0.999,901	0.999,010	0.990,096	0.900,961
0.999	0.999,900	0.999,000	0.990,005	0.900,050

has already been noted that an individual for whom U takes the additive-separable form will arrange to hold life insurance in such an amount as to ensure that his human capital is fully covered (in the sense that w_t is *independent* of t). This in itself almost certainly represents an above-average degree of cover and hence concern for dependants' well-being. Given that additive-separability of U entails $\hat{p}_1 = 0.5$ it would therefore seem that $\hat{p}_1$ would typically be somewhat larger than 0.5. If this were so, then recalling the lower bound given in (3.35)[26] we could write

$$1 - \frac{\Delta p_1^*}{1 - \bar{p}_1} \leqslant m_1 \Delta p_1^* \text{RL} \leqslant 1 \tag{3.44}$$

so that with $\bar{p}_1 < 10^{-2}$ and $\Delta p_1^* < 10^{-2}$ it would indeed appear to follow that $m_1 \Delta p_1^* \text{RL}$ is approximately equal to unity.

However, in the interests of generality it would also seem appropriate to consider those cases in which $\hat{p}_1 < 0.5$. Tables 3.1–3.3 therefore give values of $m_1 \Delta p_1^* \text{RL}$ for various values of $\hat{p}_1$ and Δp_1^* for each of $\bar{p}_1 = 0.000,5$, 0.001 and 0.01 (these being the approximate 'objective' annual probabilities of death for UK residents aged 20, 35 and 60 respectively). Finally, since the expression on the right-hand side of (3.43) is an unambiguously decreasing function of $\hat{p}_1$ and since $0 < \hat{p}_1 < 1$, it follows that $m_1 \Delta p_1^* \text{RL}$ *cannot* exceed $1 + \Delta p_1^*/\bar{p}_1$ (the value given by setting $\hat{p}_1 = 0$ in (3.43)).

From tables 3.1–3.3 it is clear that $m_1 \Delta p_1^* \text{RL}$ is significantly greater than unity only if Δp_1^* is larger than $\bar{p}_1$ *and* $\hat{p}_1$ is smaller than $\bar{p}_1$. Such a case would seem to involve a combination of (a) a relative lack of concern

Table 3.2 $m_1\Delta p_1^*$RL for $\bar{p}_1 = 0.001$

$\hat{p}_1$	Δp_1^*			
	0.000,1	*0.001*	*0.01*	*0.1*
0.000,1	1.090,906	1.909,073	10.090,742	91.907,364
0.001	1.049,950	1.499,498	5.994,994	50.949,905
0.01	1.008,924	1.089,252	1.892,531	9.925,316
0.1	1.000,793	1.007,936	1.079,364	1.793,650
0.2	1.000,299	1.002,990	1.029,909	1.299,102
0.3	1.000,133	1.001,331	1.013,314	1.133,155
0.4	1.000,050	1.000,500	1.004,996	1.049,974
0.5	1.000,000	1.000,000	1.000,000	1.000,000
0.6	0.999,967	0.999,667	0.996,666	0.966,656
0.7	0.999,943	0.999,428	0.994,282	0.942,824
0.8	0.999,925	0.999,249	0.992,494	0.924,944
0.9	0.999,911	0.999,110	0.991,103	0.911,032
0.99	0.999,901	0.999,009	0.990,091	0.900,912
0.999	0.999,900	0.999,000	0.990,000	0.900,000

Table 3.3 $m_1\Delta p_1^*$RL for $\bar{p}_1 = 0.01$

$\hat{p}_1$	Δp_1^*			
	0.000,1	*0.001*	*0.01*	*0.1*
0.000,1	1.009,900	1.099,010	1.990,096	10.900,966
0.001	1.009,089	1.090,891	1.908,924	10.089,248
0.01	1.004,949	1.049,494	1.494,948	5.949,492
0.1	1.000,740	1.007,407	1.074,073	1.740,740
0.2	1.000,291	1.002,913	1.029,125	1.291,261
0.3	1.000,132	1.001,315	1.013,157	1.131,578
0.4	1.000,050	1.000,497	1.004,974	1.049,750
0.5	1.000,000	1.000,000	1.000,000	1.000,000
0.6	0.999,967	0.999,665	0.996,655	0.966,555
0.7	0.999,943	0.999,425	0.994,253	0.942,529
0.8	0.999,924	0.999,244	0.992,443	0.924,433
0.9	0.999,910	0.999,103	0.991,031	0.910,314
0.99	0.999,900	0.999,000	0.990,002	0.900,020
0.999	0.999,899	0.998,991	0.989,909	0.899,092

for own safety, (b) a relative lack of concern to augment own and dependants' consumption prospects conditional on own survival and (c) a *very high* degree of concern for the material well-being of surviving dependants conditional on own death. Tables 3.1–3.3 also emphasize the fact that unless $\bar{p}_1$, Δp_1^* and $\hat{p}_1$ are *all* very large, then $m_1\Delta p_1^*$RL will not be markedly less than unity. Cases in which $\bar{p}_1$, p_1^* and $\hat{p}_1$ are all large are, of course, those in which the individual is at high risk, relatively unconcerned for own safety and relatively unconcerned with the well-being of surviving dependants. Since neither this sort of case nor the one considered previously would seem to be other than rare exceptions, we can therefore conclude with considerable confidence that for the vast majority of individuals

$$m_1 \Delta p_1^* \text{RL} \approx 1 \qquad (3.45)$$

confirming our earlier conjecture and the consequent speculations concerning a lower bound on m_1 and the consistency of the NRPB's recommendations. In addition, (3.45) has very direct implications for the way in which m_1 varies with wealth. For example, it is clear from (3.7) and (3.9) that for given $\bar{p}_1$, $\bar{p}_2$ etc. $\bar{\text{E}}U(\bar{w},\tau)$ is an unambiguously increasing function of $\bar{\text{E}}\bar{w}$. From (3.23) it then follows that Δp_1^* is a strictly decreasing function of $\bar{\text{E}}\bar{w}$ with, in particular, $\Delta p_1^* \to 0$ as $\bar{\text{E}}\bar{w} \to \infty$. Furthermore, as already noted, on the usual assumption that the Pratt–Arrow measure of absolute risk aversion RA is positive and decreasing with wealth, RL will also be a strictly decreasing function of wealth. From (3.45) it is therefore clear that m_1 will tend to *increase* with wealth.

So far, the discussion in this section has been exclusively concerned with the relationship between m_1, Δp_1^* and RL. Let us now turn to the relationship between m_t, Δp_t^* and RL for those cases in which Δp_t^* is well defined. From (3.26), (3.27) and (3.31) it follows that

$$m_t \Delta p_t^* \text{RL} = \frac{\bar{\text{E}}U(\bar{w},\tau) - \text{E}_t U(\bar{w},\tau)}{\bar{\text{E}}U^*(\tau) - \text{E}_t U^*(\tau)}. \qquad (3.46)$$

Once again, it is clear that if U is additive-separable then the right-hand side of (3.46) is exactly equal to unity. It also follows from (3.27) and (3.46) that

$$m_t \Delta p_t^* \text{RL} > 1 - \frac{\Delta p_t^*}{1 - \bar{p}_t}. \qquad (3.47)$$

So far, then, the relationship between m_t, Δp_t^* and RL for $t > 1$ precisely parallels that for $t = 1$. However, the generalization of the argument that led to (3.43) is, as it turns out, rather complicated so that only the case of $t = 2$ will be considered in detail. The argument for $t = 3$, 4 etc. is broadly similar, however.

First notice that with $t = 2$ the right-hand side of (3.46) can be written as

$$\frac{\bar{\text{E}}U(\bar{w},\tau) - \text{E}_2 U(\bar{w},\tau)}{\bar{\text{E}}U^*(\tau) - \text{E}_2 U^*(\tau)}$$

$$\equiv \frac{[\bar{\text{E}}U(\bar{w},\tau) - \text{E}_2 U^*(\tau)] + [\text{E}_2 U^*(\tau) - \text{E}_2 U(\bar{w},\tau)]}{[\bar{\text{E}}U^*(\tau) - \bar{\text{E}}U(\bar{w},\tau)] + [\bar{\text{E}}U(\bar{w},\tau) - \text{E}_2 U^*(\tau)]}. \qquad (3.48)$$

Setting $t = 2$ in (3.27) and rearranging gives

$$\frac{\bar{E}U(\bar{w},\tau) - E_2U^*(\tau)}{\bar{E}U^*(\tau) - \bar{E}U(\bar{w},\tau)} = \frac{1 - \bar{p}_2 - \Delta p_2^*}{\Delta p_2^*}. \tag{3.49}$$

In order to simplify the right-hand side of (3.48) it will therefore be sufficient to establish the relationship between $E_2U^*(\tau) - E_2U(\bar{w},\tau)$ and $\bar{E}U^*(\tau) - \bar{E}U(\bar{w},\tau)$. Consider the choice between the following two modified versions of options A and B referred to above.

> *Under option A'* you will receive a very large increase in wealth if you survive periods 1 and 2 but your estate will receive no increase if you die during either of these periods.

> *Under option B'* your estate will receive a very large increase in wealth if you die during periods 1 or 2 but you will receive no increase if you survive these two periods.

(The same conditions on existing wealth and life insurance or annuity holdings apply as in options A and B.)

Denoting the level of p_2 at which the individual is indifferent between options A' and B' by $\hat{p}_2$ we can then write[27]

$$U(\bar{w}_1,1)\bar{p}_1 + U(\bar{w}_2,2)(1-\bar{p}_1)\hat{p}_2 + U^*(3)(1-\bar{p}_1)(1-\hat{p}_2)\bar{p}_3 + \dots$$
$$= U^*(1)\bar{p}_1 + U^*(2)(1-\bar{p}_1)\hat{p}_2 + U(\bar{w}_3,3)(1-\bar{p}_1)(1-\hat{p}_2)\bar{p}_3 + \dots. \tag{3.50}$$

Dividing both sides of (3.50) by $1-\hat{p}_2$, collecting terms and rearranging gives

$$\frac{\bar{E}U^*(\tau)}{1-\hat{p}_2} - 2\bar{p}_1U_1^*(1) - \frac{\hat{p}_2 + \bar{p}_2 - 2\hat{p}_2\bar{p}_2}{(1-\bar{p}_2)(1-\hat{p}_2)} E_2^*U(\tau)$$
$$= \frac{\bar{E}U(\bar{w},\tau)}{1-\bar{p}_2} - 2\bar{p}_1U(\bar{w}_1,1) - \frac{\hat{p}_2 + \bar{p}_2 - 2\hat{p}_2\bar{p}_2}{(1-\bar{p}_2)(1-\hat{p}_2)} E_2U(\bar{w},\tau) \tag{3.51}$$

so that

$$E_2U^*(\tau) - E_2U(\bar{w},\tau) \tag{3.52}$$
$$= \frac{1-\hat{p}_2}{\hat{p}_2 + \bar{p}_2 - 2\hat{p}_2\bar{p}_2}\{[\bar{E}U^*(\tau)-\bar{E}U(\bar{w},\tau)] - 2\bar{p}_1(1-\bar{p}_2)[U^*(1)-U(\bar{w}_1, 1)]\}$$

and hence from (3.42) and (3.52)

$$\frac{E_2U^*(\tau) - E_2U(\bar{w},\tau)}{\bar{E}U^*(\tau) - \bar{E}U(\bar{w},\tau)} \tag{3.53}$$
$$= \frac{1-\hat{p}_2}{\hat{p}_2 + \bar{p}_2 - 2\hat{p}_2\bar{p}_2}\left(1 - \frac{2\bar{p}_1(1-\bar{p}_2)(1-\hat{p}_1)}{\hat{p}_1 + \bar{p}_1 - 2\hat{p}_1\bar{p}_1}\right)$$

Notice that with $\bar{w}$ finite the assumed properties of U entail $\bar{E}U^*(\tau) > \bar{E}U(\bar{w},\tau)$ and $E_2U^*(\tau) > E_2U(\bar{w},\tau)$. From (3.53) it therefore follows that, since $0 < \hat{p}_1, \hat{p}_2, \bar{p}_1, \bar{p}_2 < 1$,

$$1 - \frac{2\bar{p}_1(1-\bar{p}_2)(1-\hat{p}_1)}{\hat{p}_1 + \bar{p}_1 - 2\hat{p}_1\bar{p}_1} > 0 \tag{3.54}$$

or

$$\hat{p}_1 > \frac{\bar{p}_1(1-2\bar{p}_2)}{1 - 2\bar{p}_1\bar{p}_2}. \tag{3.55}$$

Amongst other things, this rather unexpected restriction on $\hat{p}_1$ has the fortunate implication that some of the more extreme values of $m_1\Delta p_1^*\mathrm{RL}$ given in tables 3.1–3.3 are ruled out.

If we now substitute from (3.48), (3.49) and (3.53) into (3.46), bearing in mind the restriction on $\hat{p}_1$ given in (3.55), we get

$$m_2\Delta p_2^*\mathrm{RL} = \frac{\dfrac{1 - \bar{p}_2 - \Delta p_2^*}{\Delta p_2^*} + \dfrac{1 - \hat{p}_2}{\hat{p}_2 + \bar{p}_2 - 2\hat{p}_2\bar{p}_2}\left(1 - \dfrac{2\bar{p}_1(1-\bar{p}_2)(1-\hat{p}_1)}{\hat{p}_1 + \bar{p}_1 - 2\hat{p}_1\bar{p}_1}\right)}{1 + \dfrac{1 - \bar{p}_2 - \Delta p_2^*}{\Delta p_2^*}}. \tag{3.56}$$

It must be conceded that the right-hand side of (3.56) is an expression whose properties are, to say the least, not immediately obvious to inspection. However, it will be recalled that additive-separability of U implies that $m_2 \Delta p_2^* \mathrm{RL} = 1$ so that a rough and ready check on (3.56) can be conducted by substituting the values of $\hat{p}_1$ and $\hat{p}_2$ entailed by separability of U. It will be recalled that separability gives $\hat{p}_1 = 1/2$ and from (3.50) it is also clear that separability implies $\hat{p}_2 = (1-2\hat{p}_1)/2(1-\hat{p}_1)$. The faint-hearted will be reassured by the fact that substituting these values for $\hat{p}_1$ and $\hat{p}_2$ into the right-hand side of (3.56) does indeed give $m_2\Delta p_2^*\mathrm{RL}=1$.

Further insights into the way in which the expression on the right-hand side of (3.56) varies with its arguments are probably best gained by straightforward computation. For simplicity, and because it seems unlikely that $\bar{p}_2$ and $\hat{p}_2$ will differ significantly from $\bar{p}_1$ and $\hat{p}_2$ respectively, tables 3.4–3.6 therefore give values of $m_2\Delta p_2^*\mathrm{RL}$ for various values of $\hat{p}_1$, $\hat{p}_2$, $\bar{p}_1$, $\bar{p}_2$ and Δp_2^* with, in particular, $\hat{p}_2$ set equal to $\hat{p}_1$ and $\bar{p}_2$ set equal to $\bar{p}_1$. Notice that the restriction in (3.55) then requires that

$$\hat{p}_1 > \bar{p}_1 \frac{1 - 2\bar{p}_1}{1 - 2p_1^2}.$$

Tables 3.4–3.6 therefore indicate that the relationship between m_2 and Δp_2^* is very similar to that which exists between m_1 and Δp_1^* and that for most people we shall have

$$m_2 \Delta p_2^* \mathrm{RL} \approx 1. \tag{3.57}$$

In addition, differentiation of the expression on the right-hand side of (3.56) with respect to $\hat{p}_1$ and $\hat{p}_2$ indicates that for $\bar{p}_1 < 0.5$ the expression will be an increasing, concave function of $\hat{p}_1$ for any given value of $\hat{p}_2$ and that for $\bar{p}_2 < 0.5$ it will be a decreasing, convex function of $\hat{p}_2$ for any given value of $\hat{p}_1$. Furthermore, setting $\hat{p}_2 = 1$, the expression simplifies to $1 - \Delta p_2^*/(1-\bar{p}_2)$ as it also does when $\hat{p}_1$ is set at the lower bound specified in (3.55). Also, by a similar argument to that which led to the

Table 3.4 $m_2 \Delta p_2^* \text{RL}$ for $\bar{p}_2 = \bar{p}_1 = 0.000,5$

$\hat{p}_2 = \hat{p}_1$	Δp_2^*			
	0.000,1	0.001	0.01	0.1
0,000,5	0.999,950	0.999,500	0.994,997	0.949,975
0.001,0	1.022,162	1.221,628	3.216,290	23.162,888
0.005,0	1.014,737	1.147,376	2.473,760	15.737,597
0.010,0	1.008,451	1.084,515	1.845,155	9.451,550
0.050,0	1.001,748	1.017,485	1.174,848	2.748,483
0.100,0	1.000,789	1.007,887	1.078,877	1.788,776
1.150,0	1.000,462	1.004,623	1.046,238	1.462,383
0.200,0	1.000,298	1.002,979	1.029,795	1.297,955
0.300,0	1.000,133	1.001,327	1.013,269	1.132,700
0.400,0	1.000,050	1.000,497	1.004,975	1.049,762
0.500,0	0.999,999	0.999,999	0.999,990	0.999,900
0.600,0	0.999,967	0.999,666	0.996,662	0.966,617
0.700,0	0.999,943	0.999,428	0.994,282	0.942,822
0.800,0	0.999,925	0.999,250	0.992,496	0.924,966
0.900,0	0.999,911	0.999,111	0.991,107	0.911,070
0.990,0	0.999,901	0.999,010	0.990,096	0.900,961
0.999,0	0.999,900	0.999,000	0.990,005	0.900,050

Table 3.5 $m_2 \Delta p_2^* \text{RL}$ for $\bar{p}_2 = \bar{p}_1 = 0.001$

$\hat{p}_2 = \hat{p}_1$	Δp_2^*			
	0.000,1	0.001	0.01	0.1
0.001,0	0.999,950	0.999,499	0.994,995	0.949,950
0.005,0	1.011,008	1.110,089	2.100,902	12.009,017
0.010,0	1.007,298	1.072,993	1.729,940	8.299,406
0.050,0	1.001,698	1.016,985	1.169,849	2.698,503
0.100,0	1.000,777	1.007,776	1.077,770	1.777,706
0.150,0	1.000,458	1.004,580	1.045,813	1.458,136
0.200,0	1.000,296	1.002,958	1.029,592	1.295,921
0.300,0	1.000,132	1.001,320	1.013,206	1.132,070
0.400,0	1.000,049	1.000,495	1.004,952	1.049,525
0.500,0	0.999,999	0.999,998	0.999,980	0.999,800
0.600,0	0.999,967	0.999,666	0.996,657	0.966,567
0.700,0	0.999,943	0.999,428	0.994,278	0.942,788
0.800,0	0.999,925	0.999,249	0.992,493	0.924,931
0.900,0	0.999,911	0.999,110	0.991,103	0.911,029
0.990,0	0.999,901	0.999,009	0.990,091	0.900,912
0.999,0	0.999,900	0.999,000	0.990,000	0.900,000

Table 3.6 $m_2\Delta p_2^* \text{RL}$ for $\bar{p}_2 = \bar{p}_1 = 0.01$

$\hat{p}_2 = \hat{p}_1$	Δp_2^*			
	0.000,1	*0.001*	*0.01*	*0.1*
0.010,0	0.999,949	0.999,495	0.994,949	0.949,495
0.050,0	1.001,006	1.010,069	1.100,689	2.006,893
0.100,0	1.000,602	1.006,018	1.060,184	1.601,851
0.150,0	1.000,387	1.003,872	1.038,723	1.387,236
0.200,0	1.000,260	1.002,610	1.026,110	1.261,099
0.300,0	1.000,120	1.001,209	1.012,097	1.120,975
0.400,0	1.000,045	1.000,452	1.004,529	1.045,296
0.500,0	0.999,998	0.999,980	0.999,800	0.998,000
0.600,0	0.999,966	0.999,657	0.996,566	0.965,660
0.700,0	0.999,942	0.999,422	0.994,216	0.942,157
0.800,0	0.999,924	0.999,243	0.992,431	0.924,306
0.900,0	0.999,910	0.999,103	0.991,029	0.910,289
0.990,0	0.999,900	0.999,000	0.990,002	0.900,020
0.999,0	0.999,899	0.998,991	0.989,909	0.899,092

conclusion that $m_1\Delta p_1^* \text{RL}$ cannot exceed $1 + \Delta p_1^*/\bar{p}_1$, setting $\hat{p}_1 = 1$ and $\hat{p}_2 = 0$ in (3.56) indicates that $m_2\Delta p_2^* \text{RL}$ cannot exceed $1 + \Delta p_2^*/\bar{p}_2$. These properties, together with the results in tables 3.4–3.6, indicate that the graph of $m_2\Delta p_2^* \text{RL}$ as a function of $\hat{p}_1$ and $\hat{p}_2$ will take the general form shown in figure 3.3, given $\bar{p}_1, \bar{p}_2 < 0.5$, a restriction which it seems reasonable to suppose will apply to the vast majority of cases.

Finally, direct computation of the expressions for $m_3\Delta p_3^* \text{RL}$ and $m_4\Delta p_4^* \text{RL}$ strongly suggests that these products will both also be approximately equal to unity in most cases, so that at least for modest values of t the relationship

$$m_t\Delta p_t^* \text{RL} \approx 1 \qquad (3.58)$$

would appear to hold for the majority of individuals.

3.5   Multiperiod Variations in Physical Risk

Up to this point, the discussion in this chapter has been exclusively concerned with willingness to pay (or required compensation) for perturbations in $\bar{p}(\tau)$ that take the form of variations in the probability of death during a single period, conditional on survival of preceding periods. However, it is clear that in many cases, public sector investment projects or legislative intervention will affect safety over a *number* of future periods. This section therefore considers individual willingness to pay for *multiperiod* variations in physical risk.[28]

Given that the events of death by various different causes during any

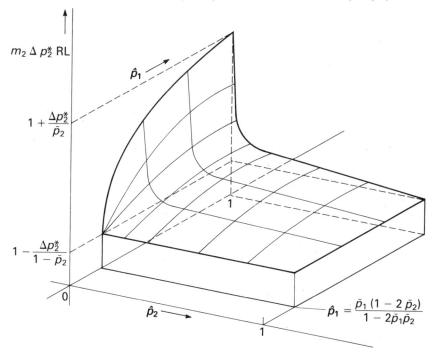

Figure 3.3 $m_2\Delta p_2^* \text{RL}$ as a function of $\hat{p}_1$ and $\hat{p}_2$.

period t are to all intents and purposes mutually exclusive,[29] the conditional probability of death, p_t, will be the *sum* of the probabilities for each of these different causes. Furthermore, it seems likely that any given public sector project will affect the probability of death by some particular cause by an *equal amount* for each of a number of future periods. This being the case, it therefore seems natural to focus upon multiperiod variations in physical risk that change all p_t over some interval of future periods by *equal* absolute amounts. Let us begin by considering a very simple case, namely that in which τ is geometrically distributed with $p_1 = p_2 = p_3 = \ldots = p$. While this distribution clearly fails to reflect the fact that for most people p_t is an increasing function of t, it is probably a reasonable approximation, at least for smaller values of t.

With τ geometrically distributed it follows that

$$EU(w-v,\tau) = [U(w_1-v,1)p] + [U(w_2-v,2)(1-p)p] + \ldots \quad (3.59)$$

and

$$\bar{E}U(\bar{w},\tau) = [U(\bar{w}_1,1)\bar{p}] + [U(\bar{w}_2,2)(1-\bar{p})\bar{p}] + \ldots \quad (3.60)$$

where $\bar{p}$ is the initial (pre-perturbation) value of p.

Differentiating through the constraint $EU(w-v,\tau) = \bar{E}U(\bar{w},\tau)$ with respect to p then gives

$$\frac{EU}{p} - U(w_2-v,2)p - 2U(w_3-v,3)(1-p)p -$$
$$\ldots - EU_t'\frac{\partial v}{\partial p} + E\left(U_t'\frac{\partial w_t}{\partial p}\right) = 0. \tag{3.61}$$

By an argument similar to that developed in section 3.3, $E(U_t' \, \partial w_t/\partial p) = 0$. Eliminating this term from (3.61) and multiplying through by $1-p$ we then get

$$EU\frac{(1-p)}{p} - U(w_2-v,2)(1-p)p -$$
$$2U(w_3-v,3)(1-p)^2p - \ldots - (1-p)EU_t'\frac{\partial v}{\partial p} = 0 \tag{3.62}$$

or

$$\frac{EU}{p} - EU - U(w_2-v,2)(1-p)p -$$
$$2U(w_3,3)(1-p)^2p - \ldots - (1-p)EU_t'\frac{\partial v}{\partial p} = 0 \tag{3.63}$$

or

$$\frac{EU}{p} - U(w_1-v,1)p - 2U(w_2-v,2)(1-p)p -$$
$$3U(w_3-v)(1-p)^2p - \ldots - (1-p)EU_t'\frac{\partial v}{\partial p} = 0 \tag{3.64}$$

and hence

$$\frac{\partial v}{\partial p} = \frac{EU/p - E(\tau U)}{(1-p)EU_t'}. \tag{3.65}$$

But, for τ geometrically distributed, $E\tau = 1/p$, so that finally

$$\frac{\partial v}{\partial p} = -\frac{\text{cov}(\tau,U)}{(1-p)EU_t'} \tag{3.66}$$

where $\text{cov}(\tau,U)$ is the covariance between τ and $U(w_t-v,\tau)$ with $\tau = t$.

The individual's marginal rate of substitution M of wealth for p evaluated at the initial value of the latter (the marginal rate of substitution of wealth for 'multiperiod' risk) is therefore given by

$$M = \frac{\overline{\text{cov}}(\tau,U)}{(1-\bar{p})U'} \tag{3.67}$$

where $\overline{\text{cov}}(\tau,U)$ is the covariance between τ and $U(\bar{w}_t,\tau)$ with $\tau = t$. From (3.19) and (3.67) it follows that

$$\frac{M}{m_1} = \frac{\overline{\text{cov}}(\tau,U)}{\bar{E}U(\bar{w},\tau) - U(\bar{w}_1,1)}. \tag{3.68}$$

In section 3.3 it was argued that with optimal insurance $U(w_1-v,1) < U(w_2-v,2) < \ldots$ so that $\text{cov}(\tau,U)$, and $\overline{\text{cov}}(\tau,U)$ in particular, will be positive. In order to say more about $\overline{\text{cov}}(\tau,U)$ it would be necessary to place further restrictions on the relationship between $U(\bar{w}_1,1)$, $U(\bar{w}_2,2)$ etc. and the assumptions made so far concerning U do not allow us to do so. Nonetheless, it seems intuitively plausible to suppose that $U(\bar{w}_t,\tau)$ will be a strictly *concave* function of τ. To see why, suppose that an individual is required to maintain his existing degree of life insurance cover etc. but is offered a perturbation in $\bar{\rho}(\tau)$ that (a) keeps life expectancy constant but (b) increases the variance of τ. To the extent that most people would presumably be averse to such a perturbation, then it is clear by the usual argument concerning risk aversion and concavity of utility functions that $U(\bar{w}_t, \tau)$ will typically be a strictly concave function of τ. For analytical simplicity, consider first the limiting case of concavity, with $U(\bar{w}_t,\tau) = f(\tau)$ where f is an increasing *linear* function of τ. Equation (3.68) can then be written as

$$\frac{M}{m_1} = \frac{\overline{\text{cov}}(\tau,f)}{\bar{\text{E}}f - f(1)} \tag{3.69}$$

which, given the linearity of f, simplifies to

$$\frac{M}{m_1} = \frac{\overline{\text{var}}(\tau)}{\bar{\text{E}}\tau - 1} \tag{3.70}$$

where $\bar{\text{E}}\tau$ and $\overline{\text{var}}(\tau)$ denote initial life expectancy and the variance of τ, respectively.

But for τ geometrically distributed, we have $\bar{\text{E}}\tau = 1/\bar{p}$ and $\text{var}(\tau) = (1-\bar{p})/\bar{p}^2$ so that (3.70) simplifies to

$$\frac{M}{m_1} = \bar{\text{E}}\tau. \tag{3.71}$$

Thus, with τ geometrically distributed and $U(\bar{w}_t,\tau)$ a linear function of τ, we get the remarkably simple but intuitively plausible result that the marginal rate of substitution of wealth for multiperiod risk is simply life expectancy times the marginal rate of substitution of wealth for current period risk.

Now consider the case in which $U(\bar{w}_t,\tau) = g(\tau)$ where g is an increasing, *strictly* concave function of τ. We shall then have

$$\frac{M}{m_1} = \frac{\overline{\text{cov}}(\tau,g)}{\bar{\text{E}}g - g(1)}. \tag{3.72}$$

Given the two degrees of freedom associated with U it is possible to scale g and the linear function f of the preceding discussion so that $g(1) = f(1)$ and $\bar{\text{E}}g = \bar{\text{E}}f$. It then follows that there will be some value of τ, say $\hat{\tau}$, such that

$$\tau \lesseqgtr \hat{\tau} \Rightarrow g(\tau) \gtreqless f(\tau) \tag{3.73}$$

and hence, given the equality of $\bar{E}g$ and $\bar{E}f$,

$$\sum_{\tau < \hat{\tau}} [g(\tau) - f(\tau)] \bar{p}(1-\bar{p})^{\tau-1} = \sum_{\tau > \hat{\tau}} [f(\tau) - g(\tau)] \bar{p}(1-\bar{p})^{\tau-1}. \qquad (3.74)$$

Thus, since τ is non-negative,

$$\sum_{\tau < \hat{\tau}} \tau[g(\tau) - f(\tau)] \bar{p}(1-\bar{p})^{\tau-1} < \sum_{\tau > \hat{\tau}} \tau[f(\tau) - g(\tau)] \bar{p}(1-\bar{p})^{\tau-1} \qquad (3.75)$$

so that

$$\bar{E}(\tau g) < \bar{E}(\tau f). \qquad (3.76)$$

Given that f and g have been scaled so that $g(1) = f(1)$ and $\bar{E}g = \bar{E}f$ it follows from (3.76) that

$$\frac{\bar{E}(\tau g) - \bar{E}g\bar{E}\tau}{\bar{E}g - g(1)} < \frac{\bar{E}(\tau f) - \bar{E}f\bar{E}\tau}{\bar{E}f - f(1)} \qquad (3.77)$$

and hence

$$\frac{\overline{\text{cov}}(\tau g)}{\bar{E}g - g(1)} < \frac{\overline{\text{cov}}(\tau f)}{\bar{E}f - f(1)}. \qquad (3.78)$$

In view of (3.71) and (3.78) it is therefore clear that with $U(\bar{w}_t, \tau)$ an increasing and strictly concave function of τ, the ratio M/m_1 will be *less than* $\bar{E}\tau$.[30]

3.6   Some Further Implications of Additive-separability

While earlier sections have established a number of qualitative results concerning key features of the relationship between v and p_t for the general case, it is clear that a fuller specification of the properties of this relationship would normally require very much more detailed information concerning an individual's preferences and attitudes to risk than is contained in the assumptions made so far.[31] However, there is at least one not entirely uninteresting special case in which it is possible (a) to reach rather strong conclusions concerning the behaviour of the function $v(p_t)$ for $p_t < \bar{p}_t$ (i.e. for risk *reductions*), given *only* information concerning the relative magnitudes of RA versus RL and Δp_t^* versus $\bar{p}_t$[32] and (b) to generate a *complete specification* of $v(p_t)$ on the basis of information concerning $\bar{w}$, $\bar{p}_t$, Δp_t^* and a limited number of properties of an individual's attitudes to purely financial risk.

The special case that allows these insights is, in fact, that in which (a) the utility function U takes the additive-separable form[33] $U(w,\tau) = u(w) + \ell(\tau)$, and (b) variations in w_t due to changes in life insurance and annuity holdings following a perturbation in $\rho(\tau)$ are of second order of smallness compared with variations in v. Apart from the economy of information required to reach strong conclusions concerning the properties of $v(p_t)$ when U takes the additive-separable form, there is a further reason for focusing upon what might at first seem to be too special a case to warrant detailed investigation. In section 3.4 it was established that although the equality $m_t \Delta p_t^* \text{ RL} = 1$ is exact only under particular circumstances, including those in which U is additive-separable,[34] the relationship nonetheless represents a close approximation in the vast majority of (non-separable) cases. It follows that if we consider two individuals i and j, the former having a non-separable and the latter a separable utility function, and who also share the same values of $\bar{p}_t$, Δp_t^* and RL, then their functions $v(p_t)$ will effectively coincide in a neighbourhood of $\bar{p}_t$ *and* will also have identical asymptotes as $p_t \rightarrow \bar{p}_t + \Delta p_t^*$. It would therefore seem not unreasonable to suppose that the properties of $v(p_t)$ implied by separability of U will at least serve to give a broad indication of the properties of this function in the general case. In this section we shall therefore proceed to establish the properties of $v(p_t)$ implied by separability of U.

In section 3.4 it was noted that in the separable case, at the initial level of risk, $\bar{w}_1 = \bar{w}_2 = \ldots = \bar{w}_T = \bar{w}$. If subsequent variations in $\rho(\tau)$ produce negligible variations in $\bar{w}_1$, $\bar{w}_2$ etc. then the constraint $EU(w-v,\tau) = \bar{E}U(\bar{w},\tau)$ can be written as

$$u(\bar{w}-v) + E\ell = u(\bar{w}) + \bar{E}\ell \tag{3.79}$$

where, as before, $E\ell$ and $\bar{E}\ell$ denote the expectations of $\ell(\tau)$ with respect to $\rho(\tau)$ and $\bar{\rho}(\tau)$ respectively. Now, setting $p_1 = \bar{p}_1$, $p_2 = \bar{p}_2$, $\ldots$, $p_{t-1} = \bar{p}_{t-1}$, $p_{t+1}, = \bar{p}_{t+1}$ etc., differentiating through (3.79) with respect to p_t and rearranging gives

$$v'(p_t) = -\frac{\bar{E}\ell - E_t\ell}{(1-\bar{p}_t)u'(\bar{w}-v)} \tag{3.80}$$

where $v'(p_t)$ denotes $\partial v/\partial p_t$ and $E_t\ell$ denotes $E\ell$ with $p_1 = \bar{p}_1, p_2 = \bar{p}_2$, $\ldots$, $p_{t-1} = \bar{p}_{t-1}$ and $p_t = 1$ (i.e. what was referred to in section 3.3 as a truncated lifetime expectation of $\ell(\tau)$).

Now, assuming that v is at least three-times differentiable with respect to p_1 then, recalling that $v(\bar{p}_1) = 0$, we can use Taylor's theorem to write

$$v(p_t) = (p_t-\bar{p}_t)v'(\bar{p}_t) + \frac{(p_t-\bar{p}_t)^2}{2}v''(\bar{p}_t) + \frac{(p_t-\bar{p}_t)^3}{6} v'''(\check{p}_t) \tag{3.81}$$

where $v''(.)$ and $v'''(.)$ denote the second and third partial derivatives of v with respect to p_t and $\check{p}_t$ is in the open interval $(p_t,\bar{p}_t)$.

But from (3.80)

$$v''(p_t) = \left[\frac{\bar{E}\ell - E_t\ell}{(1-\bar{p}_t)u'(\bar{w}-v)}\right]^2\frac{u''(\bar{w}-v)}{u'(\bar{w}-v)} \tag{3.82}$$

$$= -[v'(p_t)]^2\text{RA} \tag{3.83}$$

where RA is the Pratt–Arrow measure of absolute risk aversion evaluated at $\bar{w} - v$.

Furthermore, differentiating through (3.83) with respect to p_t gives

$$v'''(p_t) = -2v'(p_t)v''(p_t)\text{RA} + [v'(p_t)]^3 \frac{d\text{RA}}{dw} \qquad (3.84)$$

so that from (3.83) and (3.84)

$$v'''(p_t) = [v'(p_t)]^3\left(2\text{RA}^2 + \frac{d\text{RA}}{dw}\right). \qquad (3.85)$$

Clearly, given that $\forall w$, $u'(w) > 0$, it follows from (3.80) that $v'(p_t)$ is *negative*. However, the sign of $v'''(p_t)$ is strictly indeterminate if, as is usually assumed, RA is a decreasing function of wealth. Nonetheless, there are strong grounds for supposing that dRA/dw will normally be small enough for us to ignore its effect and treat $\partial^3 v/\partial p_1{}^3$ as negative. Thus, for example, consider the exponential and homogeneous forms of $u(w)$, $u(w) = -\alpha e^{-\beta w}$ and $u(w) = -\gamma w^{-\eta}$ ($\alpha,\beta,\gamma,\eta > 0$).[35] These forms of $u(w)$ in a sense represent limiting cases in the class of utility functions having the desirable 'decreasing absolute/increasing relative risk aversion' properties (the exponential utility function has constant absolute and increasing relative risk aversion, while the homogeneous form exhibits decreasing absolute and constant relative risk aversion).[36] In the exponential case dRA/dw is exactly zero. In the homogeneous case we have $\text{RA} = (\eta+1)/w$ and $d\text{RA}/dw = -(\eta+1)/w^2$ so that the term $2\text{RA}^2 + d\text{RA}/dw$ in (3.85) becomes $(\eta+1)(2\eta+1)/w^2$ which is unambiguously positive. It would therefore seem appropriate to treat $v'''(p_t) < 0$ as the 'normal' case so that from (3.81)

$$p_t < \bar{p}_t \Rightarrow [v(p_t) > (p_t-\bar{p}_t)v'(\bar{p}_t) + \frac{(p_t-\bar{p}_t)^2}{2}\,v''(\bar{p}_t)]. \qquad (3.86)$$

But, given $v''(p_t) < 0$, it must also be the case that

$$p_t < \bar{p}_t \Rightarrow [v(p_t) < (p_t-\bar{p}_t)v'(\bar{p}_t)]. \qquad (3.87)$$

Thus from (3.46), (3.83), (3.86) and (3.87)

$$p_t < \bar{p}_t \Rightarrow \left[(p_t-\bar{p}_t)v'(\bar{p}_t) > v(p_t) > \right.$$
$$\left.(p_t-\bar{p}_t)v'(\bar{p}_t)\left(1 + \frac{p_t - \bar{p}_t}{2\Delta p_t^*}\frac{\text{RA}}{\text{RL}}\right)\right]. \qquad (3.88)$$

Clearly, then, the error in treating $v(p_t)$ as linear for $p_t < \bar{p}_t$ with, in particular, $v = -m_t(p_t-\bar{p}_t)$ depends on the size of the term $[(p_t-\bar{p}_t)/2\Delta p_t^*]\,\text{RA}/\text{RL}$. While it is generally true that, with u well behaved, RA $\geqslant$ RL (see Jones-Lee, 1980b), it is again instructive to consider the exponential and homogeneous forms of $u(w)$. In the exponential case we have $\text{RA} = \text{RL}$, while in the homogeneous case $\text{RA}/\text{RL} = (\eta+1)/\eta$. However, studies by Friend and Blume (1975) and Drèze (1981) suggest that RR, the Pratt–Arrow measure of *relative* risk aversion (= $\eta + 1$ in this case) is typically between 2 and 10 so that there is probably little error in treating RA $\approx$ RL as the 'typical' case. Thus if, for example,

$\Delta p_t^* \geq 2\bar{p}_t$ (and with the objective counterpart to $\bar{p}_t$ being about 10^{-3} for the coming year for an individual aged 20–40, this does not seem unduly restrictive) then the error in treating $v(p_t)$ as linear over the entire interval $[0, \bar{p}_t]$ would be at most about 25% and substantially less than this if we restricted attention to, say, the interval $[\bar{p}_t/2, \bar{p}_t]$. While this argument admittedly lacks the robustness and generality of the earlier result concerning the relationship between m_t, Δp_t^* and RL, it would nonetheless seem legitimate to treat approximate linearity of $v(p_t)$ for $p_t < \bar{p}_t$ as the norm rather than the exception.[37]

To see how one can go still further in the specification of $v(p_t)$ in the separable case, set $p_1 = \bar{p}_1, p_2 = \bar{p}_2, \ldots, p_{t-1} = \bar{p}_{t-1}, p_{t+1} = \bar{p}_{t+1}$ etc. in (3.79). A little rearrangement then gives

$$u(\bar{w}-v) - u(\bar{w}) = \frac{p_t - \bar{p}_t}{1 - \bar{p}_t} (\bar{E}\ell - E_t\ell) \qquad (3.89)$$

where, as above, $E_t\ell$ denotes the truncated lifetime expectation of $\ell(\tau)$.

But from (3.27), when U takes the separable form it follows that

$$\bar{E}\ell - E_t(\ell) = \frac{1 - \bar{p}_t}{\Delta p_t^*} [u^* - u(\bar{w})] \qquad (3.90)$$

where u^* denotes sup $[u(w)]$. Hence from (3.89) and (3.90)

$$u(\bar{w}-v) - u(\bar{w}) = \frac{p_t - \bar{p}_t}{\Delta p_t^*} [u^* - u(\bar{w})] \qquad (3.91)$$

or, setting $u^* = 0$, as we may do given the two degrees of freedom associated with U,

$$\frac{u(\bar{w}-v)}{u(\bar{w})} = 1 - \frac{p_t - \bar{p}_t}{\Delta p_t^*}. \qquad (3.92)$$

Clearly, then, specification of $\bar{p}_t$, Δp_t^* and the parameters of the component utility of wealth function $u(w)$ will allow us to derive the precise relationship between v and p_t over its entire domain of definition. In what follows we shall again focus upon the exponential and homogeneous forms of $u(w)$ given that these are, as already noted, 'limiting cases' of the commonly hypothesized 'decreasing absolute, and increasing relative, risk aversion'.

When the utility of wealth function takes the exponential form[38] $u(w) = -\alpha e^{-\beta w}$ ($\alpha, \beta > 0$), equation (3.92) gives

$$e^{\beta v} = 1 - \frac{p_t - \bar{p}_t}{\Delta p_t^*}. \qquad (3.93)$$

Furthermore, for the exponential class of utility functions, $\beta = RR/\bar{w}$ (where RR is the Pratt–Arrow measure of relative risk aversion), so that from (3.93)

$$v = \frac{\bar{w}}{\text{RR}} \ln\left(1 - \frac{p_t - \bar{p}_t}{\Delta p_t^*}\right). \tag{3.94}$$

In the homogeneous case[39] $u(w) = -\gamma w^{-\eta}$ (γ, $\eta > 0$), equation (3.92) reduces to

$$\left(1 - \frac{v}{\bar{w}}\right)^{-\eta} = 1 - \frac{p_t - \bar{p}_t}{\Delta p_t^*}. \tag{3.95}$$

In this case $\eta = \text{RR} - 1$ so that (3.95) gives

$$v = \bar{w}\left[1 - \left(1 - \frac{p_t - \bar{p}_t}{\Delta p_t^*}\right)^{1/(1-\text{RR})}\right]. \tag{3.96}$$

For illustrative purposes, v has been computed for various values of p_t with $\bar{p}_t$ set equal to 10^{-3} and $\bar{w}$ equal to £100,000 since these are, respectively, the (approximate) 'objective' probability of death during the coming year in the UK for an individual aged 20–40 and the (approximate) present value of current UK average earnings over 35 years, discounted at 10%. Given the range of values for RR suggested in the studies referred to above, RR has been given values of 2, 5 and 10. Finally, for an individual with $\bar{p}_t = 10^{-3}$, it would be surprising if Δp_t^* exceeded 10^{-1} or were less than 10^{-4}, so that Δp_t^* has been set at 10^{-4}, 10^{-3}, 10^{-2} and 10^{-1}.

The graphs of v as a function of p_t for a selection of the consequent combinations of RR and Δp_t^* are shown in figure 3.4 for the exponential form of u and in figure 3.5 for the homogeneous form. These graphs exhibit a number of interesting features. In the first place, the relationship between v and p_t clearly displays the general properties summarized in figure 3.2 above. Second, with the exception of the case in which RR = 2 and $\Delta p_1^* = 10^{-4}$, the relationship implied by the exponential specification of u is remarkably similar to that generated by the homogeneous form, suggesting that, for given values of RR, $\bar{p}_t$ and Δp_t^*, the function $v(p_t)$ may be rather robust with respect to variations in other utility function parameters. Third, unless $\Delta p_t^* > 10^{-2}$, then m_t (the modulus of the gradient of $v(p_t)$ and $p_t = \bar{p}_t$) exceeds £1,000,000. Finally, for $\Delta p_t^* > 10^{-3}$, $v(p_t)$ is approximately linear for $p_t < \bar{p}_t$, reflecting the theoretical result established earlier in this section for the separable form of $U(w,\tau)$. This suggests that, for risk reductions, the approximation $v \approx -m\delta p_t$ may be valid for *all* δp_t, thereby legitimating the definition of values of statistical life in terms of m_t for non-marginal as well as marginal reductions in risk. All these conclusions are, of course, subject to the caveats entered above concerning the extent to which the separable form of $U(w,\tau)$ can be treated as being representative of the general case.

3.7   The Value of Variations in the Risk of Non-fatal Injury or Illness

Hitherto, the analysis in this chapter has been exclusively concerned with variations in the risk of fatality. Nonetheless, it is tempting to suppose

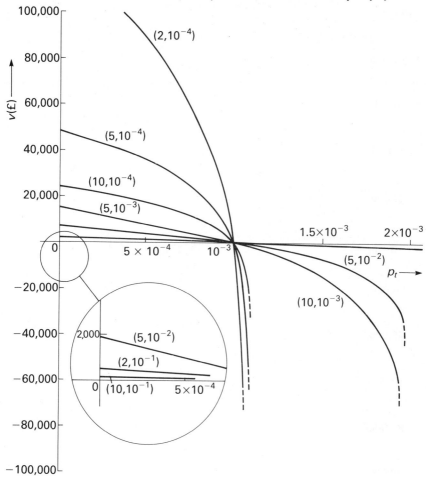

Figure 3.4 v as a function of p_t for exponential $u(w)$.

that much of what has been said would also apply, *mutatis mutandis*, to variations in the risk of non-fatal injury or illness. However, while this would certainly seem to be true in the case of marginal rates of substitution of wealth for risk, it seems somewhat unlikely that there would exist counterparts to the maximum acceptable increases in risk, Δp_t^*, for other than the most severe and disabling forms of injury or illness. Thus, it would not appear to be possible to place bounds on the order of magnitude of marginal rates of substitution of wealth for risk of morbidity (as opposed to mortality) by appeal to an approximation such as $m_t \Delta p_t^* RL \approx 1$ (or, for that matter, using the kind of argument developed by Conley or Bergstrom[40]). It might therefore seem that in the case of risk of

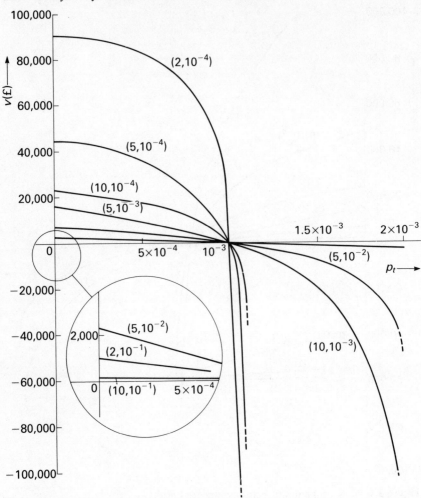

Figure 3.5 v as a function of p_t for homogeneous $u(w)$.

morbidity, theoretical analysis would have relatively little to tell us and that a direct empirical approach would be called for. However, it transpires that theoretical analysis affords at least one rather nice result concerning the relative magnitude of marginal rates of substitution of wealth for risks of morbidity, m_I, on the one hand and mortality, m_D, on the other. Such a result has obvious potential significance either as a check upon direct empirical estimates of these magnitudes or, alternatively, as a means of delineating the magnitude of m_I in terms of estimates of m_D.

While it would be possible to develop a full multiperiod counterpart to the analysis of section 3.3 together with various forms of insurance possibilities (including life, medical and what is referred to in the UK as 'permanent health' insurance[41]), for simplicity this section will employ a simple single-period model in which the individual may either survive the period in good health, die during the period with probability p, or suffer some specific injury or illness during the period with probability r, the respective conditional utility of wealth functions being denoted by $L(w)$, $D(w)$, and $I(w)$.

Clearly, there is a wide variety of potential interrelationships between the events of injury and/or illness and death during a forthcoming period. In particular, the occurrence of some kinds of injury or illness will increase the probability of death by particular causes, while other forms of injury or illness will tend to reduce the probability of death by some causes (e.g. persons who are bedridden are necessarily protected from the possibility of death in a car accident during the period of their confinement). For simplicity, however, it will be assumed in what follows that the events of injury and/or illness and death are *independent*, though it should be noted that, as it happens, the key result of the analysis below can also be shown to hold for the case in which these events are mutually exclusive (the argument is analogous to the one developed here).

Assuming that the individual behaves as an expected utility maximizer, the compensating variation v for a perturbation in the probabilities of death or injury and/or illness from $(\bar{p},\bar{r}) \to (p,r)$ will satisfy

$$(1-p)(1-r)L(\bar{w}-v) + pD(\bar{w}-v) + (1-p)rI(\bar{w}-v) \quad (3.97)$$
$$= (1-\bar{p})(1-\bar{r})L(\bar{w}) + \bar{p}D(\bar{w}) + (1-\bar{p})\bar{r}I(\bar{w})$$

where $\bar{w}$ denotes the individual's initial level of wealth. Differentiating through (3.97) with respect to p and then setting $p = \bar{p}$, $r = \bar{r}$ and $v = 0$ gives

$$m_D = \frac{(1-\bar{r})\bar{L} - \bar{D} + \bar{r}\bar{I}}{(1-\bar{p})(1-\bar{r})\bar{L}' + \bar{p}\bar{D}' + (1-\bar{p})\bar{r}\bar{I}'} \quad (3.98)$$

where $\bar{L}$, $\bar{L}'$ etc. denote $L(w)$, $L'(w)$ etc. evaluated at $w = \bar{w}$. Similarly, differentiating through (3.97) with respect to r and then setting $r = \bar{r}$, $p = \bar{p}$ and $v = 0$ gives

$$m_I = \frac{(1-\bar{p})(\bar{L}-\bar{I})}{(1-\bar{p})(1-\bar{r})\bar{L}' + \bar{p}\bar{D}' + (1-\bar{p})\bar{r}\bar{I}'}. \quad (3.99)$$

From (3.98) and (3.99) it then follows that

$$\frac{m_D}{m_I} = \frac{(1-\bar{r})\bar{L} - \bar{D} + \bar{r}\bar{I}}{(1-\bar{p})(\bar{L}-\bar{I})}. \quad (3.100)$$

Now suppose that the individual is indifferent between a change δp in the probability of death and a change δr in the probability of injury and/or illness. Given that the individual is an expected utility maximizer, δp and δr will then satisfy

$$(1-\bar{p}-\delta p)(1-\bar{r})\bar{L} + (\bar{p}+\delta p)\bar{D} + (1-\bar{p}-\delta p)\bar{r}\bar{I} \qquad (3.101)$$
$$= (1-\bar{p})(1-\bar{r}-\delta r)\bar{L} + \bar{p}\bar{D} + (1-\bar{p})(\bar{r}+\delta r)\bar{I}$$

so that

$$\frac{\delta r}{\delta p} = \frac{(1-\bar{r})\bar{L} - \bar{D} + \bar{r}\bar{I}}{(1-\bar{p})(\bar{L}-\bar{I})}. \qquad (3.102)$$

Notice that (3.102) holds for *all* variations δp and δr – whether small or large, positive or negative – provided that the individual is indifferent between these variations. In then follows from (3.100) and (3.102) that

$$\frac{m_D}{m_I} = \frac{\delta r}{\delta p}. \qquad (3.103)$$

Thus, if one could establish the order of magnitude of $\delta r/\delta p$ by, for example, direct enquiry, then it would be possible to make inferences about m_I for any particular form of injury or illness from (3.103) given an empirical estimate of m_D. Equally, (3.103) could be used as a direct check upon independent empirical estimates of m_D and m_I.

3.8   Some Implications of Alternative Theories of Choice under Uncertainty

In section 3.1 it was noted that recent experimental work has exposed systematic violation of the axioms of expected utility theory. While I have argued that these violations need not be viewed as fatal for expected utility theory, particularly in the present context, it seems appropriate to explore the way in which the theoretical analysis of individual valuation of safety might be affected if expected utility theory is replaced by some of the alternative theories of choice under uncertainty that have been proposed in response to the experimental results referred to above. In particular, this section examines two of the apparently more promising alternatives to expected utility theory, namely the prospect theory of Kahneman and Tversky (1979) and Chew and MacCrimmon's ratio-form theory (Chew and MacCrimmon, 1979; Machina, 1983; Sugden, 1986). Regret theory (Loomes and Sugden, 1982; Bell, 1982) and disappointment theory (Bell, 1985), which also show some promise as alternatives to expected utility theory, will not be considered, simply because these theories are based upon potential psychological responses to the resolution of uncertainty that for obvious reasons would appear to have no part to play in the analysis of physical – as opposed to financial – risk, at least when the former is the risk of *fatality*.[42]

3.8.1   *Prospect Theory*

Prospect theory assumes that, in making decisions under uncertainty, individuals begin by simplifying complex risky prospects in an 'editing' process in which, for example, consequences that are common to a pair of options are discarded in any comparison between them. Edited prospects

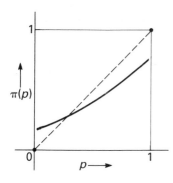

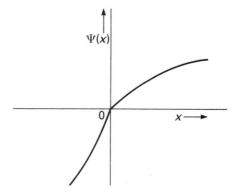

Figure 3.6 $\pi(p)$ as a function of p.   **Figure 3.7** $\Psi(x)$ as a function of x.

are then evaluated on the basis of a decision-weighted 'value' function, where the decision weights are functions of probabilities but do not themselves obey the axioms of probability theory, and the value function is defined on *variations* in wealth (or any other desideratum) from its current level. In addition, the value function is assumed to have a singularity at the current level of wealth and to be concave for increases from that level and convex for decreases.

In particular, denoting the decision weight associated with an objective (or stated[43]) probability p by $\pi(p)$ and the value function for a variation x in wealth by $\psi(x)$,[44] Kahneman and Tversky hypothesize that $\pi(p)$ and $\psi(x)$ will exhibit the general properties shown in figures 3.6 and 3.7 (which are effectively reproduced from Kahneman and Tversky (1979)). Notice that $\pi(p)$ is assumed to be discontinuous at $p = 0$ and $p = 1$ with, in particular, $\pi(0) = 0$ and $\pi(1) = 1$.

In applying prospect theory to the analysis of individual valuation of safety, it seems appropriate to make the following assumptions.

1 It is in the nature of the choices considered in this context that there is little, if any, scope for editing.

2 Given that we will, in the main, be dealing with relatively small variations in already small probabilities, then in line with the assumptions reflected in figure 3.6 it seems legitimate to treat $\pi(p)$ as linear over the range of probabilities considered with, in addition, $\pi'(p) < 1$.

3 To the extent that in prospect theory $\pi(p)$ is a subjective decision weight associated with an objective or stated probability, it appears to be necessary to interpret p as being, in some sense, 'objective'. Accordingly, in contrast with previous sections, p will be interpreted as some sort of 'expert's assessment' of risk, rather than as an individual's subjective probability. Alternatively p might be thought of as a probability *quoted* to the individual in a process of direct enquiry about his valuation of safety (as in the case of the questionnaire studies described in Chapters 2 and 4).

4   The counterpart to the utility function $U(w,\tau)$ employed in previous sections will be a value function $\psi(x,\tau)$. In line with the assumptions implicit in figure 3.7 we shall take it that

$$x > 0 \Rightarrow \frac{\partial\psi}{\partial x} > 0, \frac{\partial^2\psi}{\partial x^2} < 0$$

and

$$x < 0 \Rightarrow \frac{\partial\psi}{\partial x} > 0, \frac{\partial^2\psi}{\partial x^2} > 0$$

and

$$x = 0 \Rightarrow \frac{\partial\psi}{\partial x} + < \frac{\partial\psi}{\partial x} -$$

where $\partial\psi/\partial x+$ and $\partial\psi/\partial x-$ denote right and left derivatives respectively.

5   $\forall\tau, \dfrac{\partial\psi}{\partial\tau} > 0$.

6   $\psi(x,\tau)$ is bounded above and below for each value of τ. Denoting $\sup_x[\psi(x,\tau)]$ by $\psi^*(\tau)$ it will also be assumed that $\tau_2 > \tau_1 \Rightarrow \psi^*(\tau_2) > \psi^*(\tau_1)$.

7   Individuals seek to maximize $\varepsilon\psi(x,\tau)$ where

$$\varepsilon\psi(x,\tau) = \psi(x_1,1)\pi(p_1) + \psi(x_2,2)\pi[(1-p_1)p_2]$$
$$+ \psi(x_3,3)\pi[(1-p_1)(1-p_2)p_3] + \ldots$$

i.e. $\varepsilon\psi(x,\tau)$ is the *weighted average* of $\psi(x,\tau)$ with the $\pi(p)$ as weights.

The compensating variation v for a perturbation in the vector of conditional probabilities of death $(\bar{p}_1,\bar{p}_2,\ldots,\bar{p}_T)$ will then be given by the solution to

$$\max_{v,\delta w} v \text{ subject to } \varepsilon\psi(\delta w - v,\tau) = \bar{\varepsilon}\psi(0,\tau) \text{ and } \bar{E}\delta w = 0$$

where E is the expectations operator and δw are variations in (time-dependent) values of w resulting from changes in optimal holdings of life insurance. Given that $\pi(p)$ is being treated as linear in p, it follows by a process of reasoning broadly similar to that employed in section 3.3 that, provided that $|\delta w| < |v|$,[45]

$$m_{1-} = \left[\frac{\bar{E}\psi(0,\tau) - \psi(0,1)}{(1-\bar{p}_1)\bar{\varepsilon}\psi'_{t-}}\right]\pi'(p)$$

and

$$m_{1+} = \left[\frac{\bar{E}\psi(0,\tau) - \psi(0,1)}{(1-\bar{p}_1)\bar{\varepsilon}\psi'_{t+}}\right]\pi'(p)$$

(3.104)

where m_{1-} denotes the marginal rate of substitution of wealth for *reductions* in the current-period 'objective' (or stated) probability of death, m_{1+} is the corresponding marginal rate of substitution for increases, $\bar{E}$, as before, denotes an expectation with respect to $\bar{p}_1$, $\bar{p}_2$ etc., $\bar{\varepsilon}$ denotes a weighted average with $\pi(\bar{p}_1)$, $\pi[(1-\bar{p}_1)\bar{p}_2]$ etc. as weights, $\bar{\varepsilon}\psi'_{t-}$ denotes the weighted average of $\partial\psi/\partial x$ — evaluated at $x = 0^{46}$ and $\bar{\varepsilon}\psi'_{t+}$ is the corresponding weighted average of $\partial\psi/\partial x+$. The presence of E operators in (3.104) is a direct consequence of the assumed linearity of $\pi(p)$ in p. Notice that from (3.104), given the assumed properties of $\psi(x,\tau)$, $m_{1-} < m_{1+}$ so that in the context of prospect theory it is necessary to distinguish between values of statistical life for decreases and increases in risk. It also follows that Δp_1^* (the maximum acceptable increase in p_1) is given by

$$\Delta p_1^* = \frac{\bar{\varepsilon}\psi^*(\tau) - \bar{\varepsilon}\psi(0,\tau)}{\bar{E}\psi^*(\tau) - \psi^*(1)} \frac{1 - \bar{p}_1}{\pi'(p)} \qquad (3.105)$$

where, again, the presence of the E operator is a result of the assumed linearity of $\pi(p)$ in p. Finally, it would seem natural to define RL as

$$\text{RL} \equiv \frac{\bar{\varepsilon}\psi'_{t-}}{\bar{\varepsilon}\psi^*(\tau) - \bar{\varepsilon}\psi(0,\tau)}. \qquad (3.106)$$

Substitution from (3.104), (3.105) and (3.106) then gives

$$m_{1-} \Delta p_1^* \text{ RL} = \frac{\bar{E}\psi(0,\tau) - \psi(0,1)}{\bar{E}\psi^*(\tau) - \psi^*(1)}. \qquad (3.107)$$

However, defining RL as in (3.106) renders its interpretation in terms of the critical win–loss probability ratio in a small stake–large payoff financial gamble somewhat problematic, and it will be recalled that this interpretation was an essential component of the argument concerning a lower bound on m_1. Specifically, denote the objective (or quoted) probability that will just induce an individual to undertake such a gamble by q. If the individual's choices conform to the assumptions of prospect theory then, denoting the small stake by x, we shall have

$$\bar{\varepsilon}\psi(0,\tau) = \{\psi^*(1)\pi(qp_1) + \psi^*(2)\pi[q(1-p_1)p_2] + \dots\} \qquad (3.108)$$
$$+ \psi(-x,1)\pi[(1-q)p_1] + \dots.$$

But with $\pi(p)$ linear we can write $\pi(qp_1) = \pi(p_1) - \pi'(p)p_1 + \pi'(p)qp_1$ etc. and, with x small, $\psi(-x,1) \approx \psi(0,1) - x\psi'_{t-}$ etc. so that, with a little algebraic manipulation, (3.108) gives

$$\frac{q}{1-q} \approx \frac{x\bar{\varepsilon}\psi'_{t-} + \pi'(p)\,\bar{E}\psi^*(\tau) - \bar{\varepsilon}\psi^*(\tau)}{\bar{\varepsilon}\psi^*(\tau) - \pi'(p)\bar{E}\psi(0,\tau) + \pi'(p)x\bar{E}\psi'_{t-} - x\bar{\varepsilon}\psi'_{t-}}. \qquad (3.109)$$

Thus, defining RL as in (3.106), it is clear that $q/(1-q)$ will *not* in general be well approximated by xRL. However, if we were prepared to assume that $\bar{\varepsilon}\psi^*(\tau) \approx \pi'(p)\bar{E}\psi^*(\tau)$, $\bar{\varepsilon}\psi(0,\tau) \approx \pi'(p)\bar{E}\psi(0,\tau)$ and $\bar{\varepsilon}\psi'_{t-} \approx \pi'(p)\bar{E}\psi'_{t-}$, then the approximation $q/(1-q) \approx x\text{RL}$ would remain legitimate. Clearly, given the assumed linearity of $\pi(p)$, the case for approximating the operator ε by $\pi'(p)\text{E}$ depends upon the size of $\lim_{p \to 0+} \pi(p)$. If this limit is sufficiently small then the approximation will be good; otherwise it will not.

Bearing in mind this caveat concerning the interpretation of RL, let us return to the expression for $m_{1-}\Delta p_1^* \text{RL}$ given in (3.107). First, notice that since by definition $\psi^*(1) > \psi(0,1)$

$$\frac{\bar{\text{E}}\psi(0,\tau) - \psi(0,1)}{\bar{\text{E}}\psi^*(\tau) - \psi^*(1)} > \frac{\bar{\text{E}}\psi(0,\tau) - \psi^*(1)}{\bar{\text{E}}\psi^*(\tau) - \psi^*(1)}. \tag{3.110}$$

Furthermore, from (3.105),

$$1 - \frac{\Delta p_1^*}{1 - \bar{p}_1} = \frac{\pi'(p)\bar{\text{E}}\psi^*(\tau) - \pi'(p)\psi^*(1) - \bar{\varepsilon}\psi^*(\tau) + \bar{\varepsilon}\psi(0,\tau)}{\pi'(p)\bar{\text{E}}\psi^*(\tau) - \pi'(p)\psi^*(1)}. \tag{3.111}$$

Now suppose that the operator ε can indeed be well approximated by $\pi'(p)\text{E}$. Equation (3.111) then simplifies to

$$1 - \frac{\Delta p_1^*}{1 - \bar{p}_1} \approx \frac{\bar{\text{E}}\psi(0,\tau) - \psi^*(1)}{\bar{\text{E}}\psi^*(\tau) - \psi^*(1)} \tag{3.112}$$

so that, from (3.107), (3.110) and (3.112), it would appear legitimate to conclude that

$$m_{1-} \Delta p_1^* \text{ RL} > 1 - \frac{\Delta p_1^*}{1 - \bar{p}_1} \tag{3.113}$$

which is a result that (almost precisely) parallels that obtained on the assumption of expected utility maximization. Furthermore, the assumption that $\varepsilon(.) \approx \pi'(p)\text{E}(.)$ implies that a version of the argument leading to (3.43) also goes through, so that given this assumption it would again appear to be legitimate to conclude that for the majority of individuals $m_{1-}\Delta p_1^* \text{ RL} \approx 1$. In fact, this conclusion is not so surprising because if $\varepsilon(.) \approx \pi'(p)\text{E}(.)$ then, from a structural point of view, decision theory and expected utility theory are very similar. To be sure, value functions are assumed to have singularities, so that it is necessary to distinguish between left and right derivatives, but with $\varepsilon(.) \approx \pi'(p)\text{E}(.)$ a decision-weighted value function is effectively a constant fraction of its corresponding mathematical expectation.

It would therefore appear that decision theory produces results concerning the individual valuation of safety that are, in general, broadly similar to those of expected utility theory and that, under certain not altogether implausible simplifying assumptions concerning the decision-weighting function $\pi(p)$, the implications of the two theories are virtually identical.

3.8.2   Ratio-form Theory

Chew and MacCrimmon have shown that, provided an individual's choices obey a set of axioms that are effectively a weakened version of those entailing expected utility maximization, then the individual will choose as if maximizing a function[47] $E\theta(.)/E\Phi(.)$ where the functions θ and Φ are defined on consequences and can be transformed by, at most, multiplication by positive constants. For choices in which consequences are levels of wealth, it would seem appropriate to assume that $\theta(w)$ and $\Phi(w)$ are both differentiable with, $\forall w$, $\theta(w) > 0$, $\Phi(w) > 0$, $\theta'(w) \geq 0$, $\Phi'(w) \leq 0$.[48] In addition, for the usual reasons it would appear necessary to assume that θ is bounded above. Notice that expected utility theory is the special case of ratio-form theory in which $\Phi'(w) = 0$.

In applying ratio-form theory to the analysis of individual valuation of safety, θ and Φ will be defined on non-negative (w,τ) pairs with, in particular.

1   $\forall w,\tau$, $\theta(w,\tau) > 0$ and $\Phi(w,\tau) > 0$.

2   $\forall w,\tau$, $\dfrac{\partial\theta}{\partial w} > 0$, $\dfrac{\partial\theta}{\partial\tau} > 0$, $\dfrac{\partial\Phi}{\partial w} < 0$ and $\dfrac{\partial\Phi}{\partial\tau} < 0$.

3   $\tau_2 > \tau_1 \Rightarrow \theta^*(\tau_2) > \theta^*(\tau_1)$ where $\theta^*(\tau)$ denotes $\sup_w[\theta(w,\tau)]$.

4   $\tau_2 > \tau_1 \Rightarrow \Phi^*(\tau_2) < \Phi^*(\tau_1)$ where $\Phi^*(\tau)$ denotes $\inf_w[\Phi(w,\tau)]$.

The compensating variation v for a perturbation in the vector of conditional probabilities of death $(\bar{p}_1, \bar{p}_2, \ldots, \bar{p}_T)$ will, in this case, be given by the solution to

$$\max_{v,w} v \text{ subject to } \frac{E\theta(w-v,\tau)}{E\Phi(w-v,\tau)} = \frac{\bar{E}\theta(\bar{w},\tau)}{\bar{E}\Phi(\bar{w},\tau)} \text{ and } \bar{E}w = \bar{E}\bar{w}.$$

Now notice that the essential difference between this constrained maximization problem and that considered in section 3.3 is that the constraint $EU(w-v,\tau) = \bar{E}U(\bar{w},\tau)$ of expected utility theory has been replaced by

$$\frac{E\theta(w-v,\tau)}{E\Phi(w-v,\tau)} = \frac{\bar{E}\theta(\bar{w},\tau)}{\bar{E}\Phi(\bar{w},\tau)}.$$

However, denoting $\bar{E}\theta(\bar{w},\tau)/\bar{E}\Phi(\bar{w},\tau)$ by k, the ratio-form constraint can be written as $E\theta(w-v,\tau) = kE\Phi(w-v,\tau)$ or, equivalently, as $E[\theta(w-v,\tau) - k\Phi(w-v,\tau)] = 0$. Thus the constraint $EU(w-v,\tau) =$ constant of expected utility theory has been replaced by a constraint $E[\theta(w-v,\tau) - k\Phi(w-v,\tau)] =$ constant and these constraints are, of course, structurally identical. It follows that expressions for m_1, Δp_1^* and RL can be obtained directly from those derived in sections 3.3 and 3.4 by replacing $U(w-v,\tau)$, U_t', $EU(w-v,\tau)$ etc. by $\theta(w-v,\tau) - k\Phi(w-v,\tau)$, $\theta_t' - k\Phi_t'$, $E[\theta(w-v,\tau) - k\Phi(w-v,\tau)]$ etc. Thus

$$m_1 = \frac{\bar{E}[\theta(\bar{w},\tau)-k\Phi(\bar{w},\tau)] - [\theta(\bar{w}_1,1)-k\Phi(\bar{w}_1,1)]}{(1-\bar{p}_1)(\theta'-k\Phi')} \tag{3.114}$$

which, given the definition of k, simplifies to[49]

$$m_1 = \frac{k\Phi(\bar{w}_1,1) - \theta(\bar{w}_1,1)}{(1-\bar{p}_1)(\theta'-k\Phi')}. \tag{3.115}$$

Furthermore,

$$\Delta p_1^* = (1-\bar{p}_1) \frac{\bar{E}[\theta^*(\tau)-k\Phi^*(\tau)]-\bar{E}[\theta(\bar{w},\tau)-k\Phi(\bar{w},\tau)]}{\bar{E}[\theta^*(\tau)-k\Phi^*(\tau)] - [\theta^*(1)-k\Phi^*(1)]} \tag{3.116}$$

which simplifies to

$$\Delta p_1^* = \frac{(1-\bar{p}_1)\bar{E}[\theta^*(\tau)-k\Phi^*(\tau)]}{\bar{E}[\theta^*(\tau)-k\Phi^*(\tau)] - [\theta^*(1)-k\Phi^*(1)]} \tag{3.117}$$

In addition, the critical win–loss probability ratio $q/(1-q)$ that will just induce an individual to undertake a gamble with small stake x and large payoff y is given by

$$\frac{q}{1 - q} \approx \frac{x[\theta'-k\Phi']}{\bar{E}[\theta^*(\tau)-k\Phi^*(\tau)] - \bar{E}[\theta(\bar{w},\tau)-k\Phi(\bar{w},\tau)]} \tag{3.118}$$

which simplifies to

$$\frac{q}{1 - q} \approx \frac{x[\theta'-k\Phi']}{\bar{E}[\theta^*(\tau)-k\Phi^*(\tau)]} \tag{3.119}$$

so that it is natural to define RL in this context as

$$\text{RL} \equiv \frac{\theta'-k\Phi'}{\bar{E}[\theta^*(\tau)-k\Phi^*(\tau)]}. \tag{3.120}$$

It then follows from (3.115), (3.117) and (3.120) that

$$m_1\Delta p_1^* \, \text{RL} = \frac{k\Phi(\bar{w}_1,1) - \theta(\bar{w}_1,1)}{\bar{E}[\theta^*(\tau)-k\Phi^*(\tau)] - [\theta^*(1)-k\Phi^*(1)]}. \tag{3.121}$$

However, by the definition of θ^* and Φ^*,

$$\frac{k\Phi(\bar{w}_1,1) - \theta(\bar{w}_1,1)}{\bar{E}[\theta^*(\tau)-k\Phi^*(\tau)] - [\theta^*(1)-k\Phi^*(1)]} > \tag{3.122}$$
$$\frac{k\Phi^*(1) - \theta^*(1)}{\bar{E}[\theta^*(\tau)-k\Phi^*(\tau)] - [\theta^*(1)-k\Phi^*(1)]}.$$

Furthermore, from (3.117),

$$\frac{k\Phi^*(1) - \theta^*(1)}{\bar{E}[\theta^*(\tau)-k\Phi^*(\tau)] - [\theta^*(1)-k\Phi^*(1)]} = 1 - \frac{\Delta p_1^*}{1 - \bar{p}_1} \tag{3.123}$$

so that from (3.121), (3.122) and (3.123)

$$m_1\Delta p_1^* \, \text{RL} > 1 - \frac{\Delta p_1^*}{1 - \bar{p}_1} \tag{3.124}$$

which precisely reproduces the result derived in section 3.4.

Thus far, then, ratio-form theory has produced results that are precisely analogous to those of expected utility theory. However, when we attempt to obtain an expression for $m_1 \Delta p_1^*$ RL in terms of $\bar{p}_1$, Δp_1^* and $\hat{p}_1$ as in section 3.4 the parallel between the two theories apparently ceases to hold. It would seem that this occurs because, up to the present, all the analysis has been conducted with reference to the constraint

$$\frac{E\theta(w-v,\tau)}{E\Phi(w-v,\tau)} = \frac{\bar{E}\theta(\bar{w},\tau)}{\bar{E}\Phi(\bar{w},\tau)}$$

which, it has been shown, is structurally equivalent to the corresponding constraint in expected utility theory. However, the ratio-form equality implied by indifference between options A and B specified in section 3.4 (from which $\hat{p}_1$ was derived) is of a fundamentally *different* structure from its counterpart in expected utility theory specified in equation (3.40). In particular, while the latter entails a linear restriction on $\hat{p}_1$, the former is non-linear. Thus, while the results of prospect theory appeared broadly to parallel those of expected utility theory, but to do so *precisely* only under rather strong simplifying assumptions, the situation with ratio-form theory is rather different. Up to a certain point ratio-form theory produces results concerning the relationship between m_1, Δp_1^* and RL that are *identical* with those of expected utility theory, but thereafter the analyses appear to diverge markedly.

However, all things considered, the results of this section would suggest that, in the context of individual valuation of safety, the impact of variation in the underlying choice theory may be nowhere near as dramatic as might have been supposed and that the approximation $m_t \, \Delta p_t^*$ RL ≈ 1 may indeed be quite robust with respect to such variations.

3.9 Summary and Concluding Comments

The principal focus of concern under the willingness-to-pay approach is the individual compensating variation v for a change in the probability of death or injury during some forthcoming period or periods. While it would be possible to investigate the function $v(p_t)$ in an exclusively empirical manner, it seems sensible to explore the a priori implications of the more plausible theories of choice under uncertainty. As it happens, not only does theoretical analysis provide a source of explanation for some of the more puzzling empirical observations and a basis for organizing thought about policy issues, but it also turns out to be possible to use theoretical analysis to arrive at quite concrete conclusions concerning some of the key properties of $v(p_t)$ for the 'typical' individual. Thus, for example, theoretical work surveyed in Chapter 2 indicates that under fairly general conditions on individual preferences and attitudes to risk, marginal rates of substitution of wealth for probability of death will exceed human capital. Such results constitute a potentially very important check upon the findings of empirical studies, especially in view of the notorious difficulty of obtaining reliable empirical estimates in this area.[50]

The analysis in this chapter has therefore been largely aimed at obtaining results that provide this sort of 'cross-check' on empirical work. In particular it has been shown that, on the assumption that individuals behave as expected utility maximizers, then for values of t for which Δp_t^* is well defined the approximation $m_t \, \Delta p_t^* \, \text{RL} \approx 1$ will apply in the vast majority of cases. This means that if, as seems likely, for most people $\Delta p_1^* < 10^{-2}$ and $\text{RL} < 2 \times 10^{-4}$, then m_1 will tend to exceed £500,000.[51] In short, the concreteness of the relationship between m_t, Δp_t^* and RL allows one to place a lower bound on m_t (which is relatively difficult to think about or measure) in terms of upper bounds on Δp_t^* and RL (which, it would seem, are conceptual entities that most people find much more straightforward to deal with and are hence, in principle, much easier to measure). This result concerning a lower bound for m_t is particularly significant in that it provides independent confirmation of conclusions reached elsewhere in this book concerning the magnitude of the value of statistical life based on the results of empirical work.

An obvious objection to the kind of argument just adduced is that individuals may not, in the main, behave as expected utility maximizers. Indeed, there is growing empirical evidence of widespread systematic violation of the axioms of expected utility theory (although, in the author's opinion, in the context of somewhat contrived choices). In view of this, it seemed appropriate to explore the implications of reworking the central analysis of this chapter on the basis of some of the theories of choice under uncertainty that have been proposed in response to the observed violations of the axioms of expected utility theory. It is somewhat surprising, but nonetheless gratifying, to discover that the main results of this chapter appear to survive this major transplant surgery largely unscathed.

Finally, a variety of other results have been established. The potentially more significant of these for policy purposes concern the relative valuation of multiperiod and single-period variations in physical risk, the relative valuation of reductions in risks of morbidity and mortality, and the complete specification of $v(p_t)$ – given $\bar{p}_t$, $\bar{w}$, Δp_t^* and RR – for the exponential and homogeneous utility of wealth functions for the separable form of $U(w,\tau)$. While the latter is, *prima facie*, a rather special case, it has nonetheless been argued that it may give a broad indication of the 'shape' of $v(p_t)$ for the general (non-separable) case. One of the more interesting implications of separability of $U(w,\tau)$ is the effective linearity of $v(p_t)$ for $p_t < \bar{p}_t$ (and, indeed, for a quite significant range of values of $p_t > \bar{p}_t$) given that Δp_t^* is not small in relation to $\bar{p}_t$. If this is, in fact, a prevalent property of $v(p_t)$, then it would substantially increase the generality of the concept of the 'value of statistical life', rendering it applicable to a wide range of non-marginal as well as genuinely marginal variations in risk. It would also, incidentally, largely remove the empirical substance of one of Broome's more significant objections to the willingness-to-pay approach.[52]

Notes

1 This is essentially the position adopted in Mishan (1982).
2 See, for example, Prescott-Clarke (1982), pp. 146–7; Thaler (1982); or Jones-Lee *et al.* (1985).
3 The basic framework of this analysis was first discussed by Jones-Lee (1980a, 1980b, 1981) and Jones-Lee and Poncelet (1982), although what follows represents a considerable refinement and extension of the argument presented in these papers.
4 Notice that this way of setting up the model takes no account of the possibility that the individual may be markedly more averse to dying in one way rather than another. However, while it would be possible to modify the analysis that follows so as to distinguish between different causes of death, the gain in insight from doing so would probably not be adequate to justify the substantial additional technical complexity.
5 This type of utility function is unique up to an affine transformation. That is, if U is an admissible utility function for a particular individual then so too is the function $\hat{U}$ where $\hat{U}(w,\tau) = \alpha + \beta U(w,\tau)$, $\beta > 0$. This means that the origin and scale of the utility function can be arbitrarily chosen or, equivalently, that one can assign arbitrary utility indices to any two pairs (w_1,τ_1) and (w_2,τ_2) subject only to the condition that

$$(w_1,\tau_1) \ P \ (w_2,\tau_2) \Leftrightarrow U(w_1,\tau_1) > U(w_2,\tau_2)$$

where P denotes the relation of strict preference. In the special case in which U takes the separable form $U(w,\tau) = u(w) + \ell(\tau)$, admissible transformations will be given by $\hat{U}(w,\tau) = \alpha + \beta[u(w) + \ell(\tau)]$, $\beta > 0$. If we now let $\alpha = \gamma + \eta$, then we can write $\hat{U}(w,\tau) = \gamma + \beta u(w) + \eta + \beta \ell(\tau)$. Thus, defining $\hat{u}(w) = \gamma + \beta u(w)$ and $\hat{\ell}(\tau) = \eta + \beta \ell(\tau)$ it is clear that in the separable case we can choose an arbitrary origin and scale for u together with an arbitrary origin for ℓ or we can choose an arbitrary origin and scale for ℓ together with an arbitrary origin for u. Equivalently, we can assign arbitrary values to any two $u(w_1)$ and $u(w_2)$ together with one $\ell(\tau)$ or to any two $\ell(\tau_1)$ and $\ell(\tau_2)$ together with one $u(w)$ subject only to the conditions that

$$w_1 > w_2 \Leftrightarrow u(w_1) > u(w_2)$$

and

$$\tau_1 > \tau_2 \Leftrightarrow \ell(\tau_1) > \ell(\tau_2)$$

assuming that more is preferred to less of both w and τ.
6 For example, consider the highly simplified two-period case in which an individual's lifetime utility of consumption is given by the undiscounted sum of period utilities, $u(c_1) + u(c_2)$, if he lives for two periods and by $u(c_1)$ if he survives for only one period, with $u' > 0$ and $u'' < 0$. Suppose further that the individual finances consumption out of total wealth w. If the individual knows that he will survive for only one period then he will set $c_1 = w$ and $c_2 = 0$, so that the indirect utility of wealth is given by $u(w)$. If, by contrast, the individual knows that he will survive for two periods then he will set $c_1 = c_2 = w/2$ and the indirect utility of wealth will then be $2u(w/2)$.

Now suppose that the individual must plan consumption knowing only that there is a probability p that he will die at the end of the first period. Assuming that he is an expected utility maximizer then he will choose c_1 and c_2 as the solution to

$$\max_{c_1,c_2} pu(c_1) + (1-p)[u(c_1)+u(c_2)]$$

subject to $c_1 + c_2 = w$. The optimal consumption plan (c_1^*,c_2^*) will therefore be such that $u'(c_1^*)/u'(c_2^*) = 1-p$ which, with $u' > 0$, $u'' < 0$ and $0 < p < 1$, implies that $c_1^* > c_2^*$. It is therefore clear that the optimal consumption plan for the case of uncertainty is different from the plans for each of the cases in which the individual knows how long he will survive. Furthermore, notice that since $u(w) > u(c_1^*)$ and $2u(w/2) > u(c_1^*) + u(c_2^*)$, it will necessarily be the case that

$$pu(w) + (1-p)2u(w/2) > pu(c_1^*) + (1-p)[u(c_1^*)+u(c_2^*)]$$

so that the expected utility of the optimal consumption plan under uncertainty is different from the expectation of the indirect utility of wealth derived for each of the 'certainty' cases.

7 See, for example, Allais and Hagen (1979), Kahneman and Tversky (1979), Schoemaker (1982), or Machina (1983), pp. 62–86.

8 Areas in which expected utility theory has been successfully applied include portfolio theory and the analysis of capital market behaviour, optimal consumption under uncertainty, theory of the firm, the economics of insurance, information economics, tax evasion, tax avoidance, and so on. Furthermore, Brookshire *et al.* (1985) show that evidence concerning the purchase of earthquake insurance in California is consistent with the predictions of expected utility theory and conclude that their results '. . . demonstrate that the expected utility hypothesis is a reasonable description of behavior for consumers who face a low-probability, high-loss natural hazard event, given that they have adequate information'.

9 This example is taken from Kahneman and Tversky (1979).

10 In particular, the 'independence' axiom implies that if B is preferred to A then a 10% chance of B will be preferred to a 10% chance of A. Since a 10% chance of B is precisely what is afforded by option D and a 10% chance of A is equivalent to C, it follows that anyone whose preferences obey the independence axiom and who prefers B to A must also prefer D to C.

11 See, for example, Savage (1954), Chapter 5.

12 Drèze (1974b) makes a similar point in relation to paradoxes of this type.

13 See Kahneman and Tversky (1979). Specifically, the value function, which is defined on increments and decrements in the level of wealth, is assumed to have a singularity or 'kink' at the origin. Since this is tantamount to having a kink that 'moves about' with the current level of wealth, prospect theory will almost certainly be capable of predicting dynamically inconsistent choices. As far as the discontinuities in the weighting function are concerned, Kahneman and Tversky themselves acknowledge that under certain circumstances this may entail violation of first-order stochastic dominance.

14 It is assumed that $\bar{\rho}(\tau)$ is sufficiently well behaved to ensure that the above integrals are well defined. Notice also that since both expected utility *and* expected wealth are defined with respect to $\bar{\rho}(\tau)$, it is being implicitly assumed that insurance companies' views concerning the individual's survival prospects coincide with his own.

15 The assumption that we have an interior extremum is tantamount to ignoring the possibility that the individual will plan life insurance and annuity purchases so as to bankrupt himself (i.e. have $w = 0$ for some value(s) of τ). This does not seem to be an unreasonable assumption.

16 Equations (3.6) to (3.9) are an approximation to the extent that w and $U(w,\tau)$ are being treated as *invariant* within each of the T periods. However, the error involved will be small provided that the periods are sufficiently short.

17 The 'constraint qualification condition' – which ensures that (3.11) and (3.12) hold at a constrained maximum – requires that the Jacobian of the constraint functions is of rank 2. It is easy to check that this condition is fulfilled since (a) v is an argument of expected utility but not of expected wealth and (b) all partial derivatives of expected utility and expected wealth are, by assumption, non-zero.

18 This is most easily seen by writing $w_t - v$ as x_t so that the constrained maximization problem becomes

$$\max_{v,x_t} v \text{ subject to } EU(x_t,\tau) = \bar{E}U(\bar{w},\tau) \text{ and } \bar{E}x_t = \bar{E}\bar{w} - v$$

which is, in turn, equivalent to

$$\min_{x_t} \bar{E}x_t \text{ subject to } EU(x_t,\tau) = \bar{E}U(\bar{w},\tau).$$

19 Notice that the argument just developed is based upon the assumption that the terms of life insurance and annuity contracts do not vary in response to changes in a particular individual's safety, though the individual is free to vary the number and nature of such contracts held. Suppose, by contrast, that the terms of insurance and annuity contracts *do* vary with changes in individual safety so as, in particular, to maintain actuarial fairness. Those who have analysed such a case have done so on the implicit assumption that the terms of *all* insurance and annuities *including contracts that the individual has already entered into* vary in this way – see, for example, Cook and Graham (1977) or Dehez and Drèze (1982). Within the context of the model being used here this assumption is tantamount to requiring that

$$w_1 p_1 + w_2(1-p_1)\bar{p}_2 + \ldots = \hat{w}_1 p_1 + \hat{w}_2(1-p_1)\bar{p}_2 + \ldots$$

where $\hat{w}_1$, $\hat{w}_2$ etc. denote conditional levels of wealth *without* insurance or annuities. Differentiating through this constraint with respect to p_1 and rearranging gives

$$E\frac{\partial w_t}{\partial p_1} = \frac{\hat{w}_1 - w_1}{1 - p_1}.$$

But, from the necessary conditions for maximizing v subject to the expected utility equality constraint and the constraint specified above,

$$E\left(U_t'\frac{\partial w_t}{\partial p_1}\right) = \frac{1}{\lambda} E\left(\frac{\partial w_t}{\partial p_1}\right)$$

so that substituting into (3.15) and rearranging gives

$$\frac{\partial v}{\partial p_1} = \frac{U(w_1-v,1) - EU(w-v,\tau)}{(1-p_1)EU_t'} + \frac{\hat{w}_1 - w_1}{1 - p_1}$$

and, setting $p_1 = \bar{p}_1$, $v = 0$, $w_1 = \bar{w}_1$ etc.,

$$m_1 = \frac{\bar{E}U(\bar{w},\tau) - U(\bar{w}_1,1)}{(1-\bar{p}_1)\bar{E}U_t'} + \frac{\bar{w}_1 - \hat{w}_1}{1 - \bar{p}_1}.$$

Thus, the assumption that the terms of insurance and annuities adjust so as to maintain actuarial fairness, and that such adjustment applies to existing as well as new contracts, causes m_1 to be augmented by a sum (approximately) equal to the individual's first-period insurance cover if $\bar{w}_1 > \hat{w}_1$ or decreased by the amount paid for annuities if $\bar{w}_1 < \hat{w}_1$. This occurs essentially because it is being assumed that an increase in safety improves the terms on which all insurance (existing and new) is made available to the individual and worsens the terms on which all annuities are made available, so that such variations will be reflected in the individual's willingness to pay for the safety improvement.

The assumption that the terms of *all* insurance and annuity contracts vary in response to a change in safety does, however, seem somewhat implausible. If the terms of such contracts are to vary with a change in safety then it seems altogether more reasonable to suppose that such variations would apply only to *new* contracts, the terms of existing contracts being unaffected. If this is so, then assuming that new contracts are actuarially fair, we shall have

$$w_1 p_1 + w_2(1-p_1)\bar{p}_2 + \ldots = \bar{w}_1 p_1 + \bar{w}_2(1-p_1)\bar{p}_2 + \ldots$$

where, as above, $\bar{w}_1$, $\bar{w}_2$ etc. denote conditional levels of wealth prior to the variation in p_1. In this case it follows that

$$\frac{\partial v}{\partial p_1} = \frac{U(w_1 - v, 1) - EU(w - v, \tau)}{(1 - p_1)EU_t'} + \frac{\bar{w}_1 - w_1}{1 - p_1}$$

so that, setting $p_1 = \bar{p}_1$, $v = 0$, $w_1 = \bar{w}_1$ etc. gives *precisely the same* expression for m_1 as was obtained in the main text under the assumption of invariance of the terms of life insurance and annuity contracts.

20 See, for example, Jones-Lee (1976).

21 Notice that with $p_1 = \bar{p}_1$, $p_2 = \bar{p}_2$ etc. it follows from (3.14) that $U_1' = U_2' = \ldots = U_T'$ so that, with separable U, $\bar{w}_1 = \bar{w}_2 = \ldots = \bar{w}_T$. The separable form of U therefore corresponds to the case in which the individual *fully covers* his human capital with life insurance in the sense that his wealth, including discounted lifetime labour income and the payoff from life insurance, is independent of the time of death. Given all this, in the separable case we shall therefore have $\bar{E}U(\bar{w}, \tau) = u(\bar{w}) + \bar{E}\ell$, $\bar{E}U^*(\tau) = u^* + \bar{E}\ell$, $U(\bar{w}, 1) = u(\bar{w}) + \ell(1)$ and $U^*(1) = u^* + \ell(1)$. Substitution of these expressions in (3.19) and (3.23) and a little algebraic manipulation then yields (3.28).

22 Notice that, like the Pratt–Arrow coefficient of absolute risk aversion RA, the magnitude of RL depends upon the units in which w is measured. In Jones-Lee (1980b) various other properties of RL are established. For example, it is shown that if, as is usually assumed, RA is positive and decreasing with wealth, then RL < RA, and that if RA is constant then RL = RA.

23 While it may at first seem strange to suggest that m_1 and Δp_1^* might be connected in such a simple and direct way, the result is, on reflection, intuitively quite plausible. In the first place m_1 is the rate at which the individual is willing to trade wealth for safety, at the margin. Δp_1^*, in turn, reflects the rate at which the individual is willing to trade safety for a very large increase in wealth. It is therefore not surprising that m_1 and Δp_1^* should be connected by a measure of the odds at which the individual would be willing to trade wealth at the margin for the chance of a very large increase in wealth. In order to see why one might expect the relationship between m_1, Δp_1^* and RL to take the

form shown in (3.30), notice first that m_1 is effectively the modulus of the marginal utility of p_1 divided by the marginal utility of wealth. If the marginal utility of p_1 is roughly constant, then multiplying its modulus by Δp_1^* will give the change in utility that will occur if $\bar{p}_1 \to \bar{p}_1 + \Delta p_1^*$. But, by the definition of Δp_1^*, this change in utility is precisely offset by, and is therefore equal to, the increase in utility due to a large increase in wealth. The product $m_1 \Delta p_1^*$ will therefore be equal to this increase in utility divided by the marginal utility of wealth and this ratio is none other than the reciprocal of RL.

24 The increase in wealth is assumed to be sufficiently large that we can write $U(w_2,2) \approx U^*(2)$ etc.

25 Thus, for example, the individual will *not* be permitted to select option A and then purchase a very large one-period term-insurance policy, thereby substantially augmenting $U(w_1,1)$. Notice also that under option B the individual will not be able to enjoy directly any of the large increase in wealth that will accrue to his estate should he die during period 1. Nonetheless, it seems reasonable to suppose that, if the marginal utility of wealth conditional on death during period 1 is significantly positive, then it will be so principally because of the individual's concern for the material well-being of surviving dependants, and if this is so then it will be justifiable to set $U(w_1,1) \approx U^*(1)$ under option B.

26 Notice that since, from (3.43), $m_1\, \Delta p_1^*$RL is an unambiguously decreasing function of $\hat{p}_1$, the lower bound to $m_1\, \Delta p_1^*$RL can alternatively be obtained by setting $\hat{p}_1 = 1$ in (3.43).

27 The argument for the existence of $\hat{p}_2$ is similar to but slightly more complicated than that given for $\hat{p}_1$ above. First, denote the expected utility for option A' for any value of p_2 by $EU_{A'}(p_2)$ and that for option B' by $EU_{B'}(p_2)$. Since with $\bar{w}_t$ finite $U^*(t) > U(\bar{w}_t,t)$, it follows that $EU_{A'}(1) < EU_{B'}(1)$. Now notice that

$$EU_{A'}(0) = U(\bar{w}_1,1)\bar{p}_1 + U^*(3)(1-\bar{p}_1)\bar{p}_3 + \ldots$$

and

$$EU_{B'}(0) = U^*(1)\bar{p}_1 + U(\bar{w}_3,3)(1-\bar{p}_1)\bar{p}_3 + \ldots$$

so that

$$EU_{A'}(0) > EU_{B'}(0) \Leftrightarrow \frac{[U^*(1)-U(\bar{w}_1,1)]\bar{p}_1}{[U^*(3)(1-\bar{p}_1)\bar{p}_3+\ldots]-[U(\bar{w}_3,3)(1-\bar{p}_1)\bar{p}_3+\ldots]} < 1.$$

But with $\bar{p}_1$ and $\bar{p}_2$ small, T large and $U^*(1) < U^*(2) < U^*(3)$ etc.

$$[U^*(3)(1-\bar{p}_1)\bar{p}_3+\ldots]-[U(\bar{w}_3,3)(1-\bar{p}_1)\bar{p}_3+\ldots] \approx \bar{E}U^*(\tau) - \bar{E}U(\bar{w},\tau).$$

The condition for $EU_{A'}(0) > EU_{B'}(0)$ is therefore (almost) equivalent to the requirement that

$$\frac{[U^*(1)-U(\bar{w}_1,1)]\bar{p}_1}{\bar{E}U^*(\tau) - \bar{E}U(\bar{w},\tau)} < 1.$$

Now from (3.42)

$$\frac{[U^*(1)-U(\bar{w}_1,1)]\bar{p}_1}{\bar{E}U^*(\tau) - \bar{E}U(\bar{w},\tau)} = \frac{(1-\hat{p}_1)\bar{p}_1}{\hat{p}_1 + \bar{p}_1 - 2\hat{p}_1\bar{p}_1}$$

and the expression on the right-hand side is strictly less than unity provided that $\hat{p}_1 > 0$ and $\bar{p}_1 < 1$. Since it has already been demonstrated that $\hat{p}_1 > 0$ and since $\bar{p}_1 < 1$ holds in almost all cases, we can conclude with some confidence that, typically, $EU_{A'}(0) > EU_{B'}(0)$. Thus, since $EU_{A'}(p_2)$ and $EU_{B'}(p_2)$ are both continuous linear functions of p_2, the existence of a unique $0 < \hat{p}_2 < 1$ is effectively guaranteed for the vast majority of individuals. Furthermore, for a given value of $EU_{B'}(1) - EU_{A'}(1)$, $\hat{p}_2$ will tend to be larger the greater the difference between $EU_{A'}(0)$ and $EU_{B'}(0)$. This difference will, in turn, increase with $(1-\hat{p}_1)\bar{p}_1/(\hat{p}_1 + \bar{p}_1 - 2\hat{p}_1\bar{p}_1)$ and, since the latter is a strictly decreasing function of $\hat{p}_1$ provided that $\bar{p}_1 > 0$, it therefore follows that larger (smaller) values of $\hat{p}_2$ will tend to be associated with larger (smaller) values of $\hat{p}_1$. Finally notice that the justification for setting $U(w_1,1) \approx U^*(1)$ and $U(w_2,2) \approx U^*(2)$ under option B is similar to, although admittedly somewhat weaker than, that given in note 25.

28 This section is based upon an argument first developed by Jones-Lee and Poncelet (1982).

29 Though Sussman (1984) argues that there may be circumstances under which it is more appropriate to treat the risks of death by different causes as *independent*. Denoting the conditional probability of death during period t due to cause j $(j = 1, \ldots, m)$ by p_{jt}, we shall then have

$$p_t = 1 - \prod_{j=1}^{m} (1-p_{jt}).$$

However, notice that with $\forall_j$, p_{jt} small,

$$1 - \prod_{j=1}^{m} (1-p_{jt}) \approx \sum_{j=1}^{m} p_{jt}$$

so that the distinction between mutually exclusive and independent risks becomes of only limited significance.

30 A similar argument leads to the conclusion that $M/m_1 > \bar{E}\tau$ in the case in which $U(\bar{w}_t,\tau)$ is an increasing and strictly convex function of τ.

31 The material in this section is a generalized version of an argument first presented by Jones-Lee (1981).

32 The argument developed in this section applies only to those values of t for which Δp_t^* is well defined.

33 It will be recalled that the additive-separable case is that in which the individual fully covers his or her human capital with life insurance when the latter is actuarially fair, so that $\bar{w}_1 = \bar{w}_2 = \ldots = \bar{w}_T = \bar{w}$ (see note 21). It is also instructive to appreciate that additive-separability of U is tantamount to *Fishburn marginality* (see Raiffa, 1969, section 6) which entails that for any $\bar{w}$, $\hat{w}$, t_1 and t_2 the individual will be indifferent between (a) a 50:50 chance of $(\bar{w},t_1)$ or $(\hat{w},t_2)$ and (b) a 50:50 chance of $(\bar{w},t_2)$ or $(\hat{w},t_1)$.

34 From (3.43), the necessary and sufficient condition for the equality $m_1\Delta p_1^*RL = 1$ to be exact is $\hat{p}_1 = \frac{1}{2}$ which, in turn, is equivalent to $\bar{E}U(\bar{w},\tau) - U(\bar{w}_1,1) = \bar{E}U^*(\tau) - U^*(1)$. While separability of U is sufficient for this equality to hold, it is by no means necessary. Furthermore, for the case in which $t = 2$, figure 3.3 indicates quite clearly that a variety of $(\hat{p}_1,\hat{p}_2)$ pairs – only one of which corresponds to the case of separability – will entail $m_2\Delta p_2^*RL = 1$.

35 Notice that given the two degrees of freedom associated with $U(w,\tau)$ (see note 5), $u^* = \sup[u(w)]$ can be chosen arbitrarily. Throughout this section u^* is set equal to zero.

36 See, for example, Arrow (1971), Chapter 3.

37 And indeed there is some empirical evidence supporting this conclusion – see Chapter 2.

38 Recall that u^* has been set equal to zero.

39 As in the previous case, we have chosen to scale u so that $u^* = 0$.

40 See Chapter 2, section 2.1.

41 This is essentially a form of insurance which gives cover against the possibility that the insured will be unable to maintain regular employment as a result of injury or illness.

42 Though in the case of risks of non-fatal injury or illness, it must be admitted that expectations of regret and disappointment might well have a marked influence on individual decision making.

43 For example, as in the kind of questionnaire approach discussed in Chapters 2 and 4.

44 In order to avoid confusion with notation used elsewhere in the book, the notation in this section differs from that employed by the original proponents of the theories discussed.

45 The condition $|\delta w| < |v|$ ensures that for risk reductions $\psi(\delta w - v, \tau) < \psi(0, \tau)$ for *all* τ and that for increases in risk $\psi(\delta w - v, \tau) > \psi(0, \tau)$ for *all* τ. The significance of this is that all the partial derivatives of ψ with respect to x in the denominator of m_{1-} will be unambiguously *left* derivatives, while those in the denominator of m_{1+} will be unambiguously *right* derivatives. If the assumption that $|\delta w| < |v|$ is relaxed, then the denominators of m_{1-} and m_{1+} may contain mixtures of right and left derivatives. However, since these mixtures will almost certainly differ between m_{1-} and m_{1+} it will again be the case, as in (3.104), that $m_{1-} \neq m_{1+}$.

46 Notice that since, in general, $\pi(p) \neq p$ it will *not* be possible to generalize the argument developed in section 3.3 to conclude that $\partial \psi(x,t)/\partial x$ is constant, given actuarially fair life insurance and annuities.

47 Again, the notation here differs from that originally employed by Chew and MacCrimmon.

48 Notice that with $\Phi'(w) < 0$, if Φ were allowed to become negative then it would be possible to find distributions $F(w)$ and $G(w)$ such that F stochastically dominated G and yet $E\theta(w)/E\Phi(w)$ for F was *negative* while the corresponding ratio for G was positive.

49 Notice that, given the assumed properties of θ and Φ, it will necessarily be the case that $k > \theta(\bar{w}_1, 1)/\Phi(\bar{w}_1, 1)$ and that $\theta' - k\Phi' > 0$. It follows from (3.115) that m_1 is unambiguously positive. By a similar argument it can be shown that the expressions for Δp_1^* and RL derived below also have the 'right' signs.

50 A difficulty that is, incidentally, greatly exacerbated by the emotive and politically sensitive nature of such estimates. In order to be persuaded to abandon traditional ways of thinking about safety in favour of what they naturally perceive to be a somewhat radical alternative, public sector decision makers need to be doubly convinced of the reliability of empirical estimates of values of safety and costs of risk derived under that alternative.

51 Recall that the magnitude of RL depends upon the units in which w is measured.

52 It will be recalled that Broome objects to the fact that under the willingness-to-pay approach the cost associated with the exposure of m people to incremental individual risks of death of 10^{-m} each over the coming year will be different from the cost associated with exposing n ($\neq m$) people to incremental individual risks of 10^{-n}, in spite of the fact that the expected loss of life is identical in the two cases. However, if in fact $v(p_t)$ is effectively linear over the range of risks involved, then the difference between the costs referred to will be negligible.

4

The Empirical Estimation of Individual Valuation of Safety: Results of a National Sample Survey

by P. R. PHILIPS, I. T. RUSSELL AND
M. W. JONES-LEE[1]

As indicated in Chapter 2, the empirical estimation of individual marginal rates of substitution of wealth for risk – and hence values of statistical life – has been based upon two broad avenues of approach. These, for want of better terms, have been described as the 'revealed-preference' (or 'implicit value') and 'questionnaire' (or 'contingent market') methods.

After extensive discussion and correspondence with the author of this book, the UK Department of Transport (DTp) decided to fund a two-phase programme of research into the questionnaire approach, to be conducted by a research team at the University of Newcastle upon Tyne.[2] The first phase of the programme, carried out during 1980, consisted of a study designed to assess the general feasibility of a survey of this kind, the quality of individual perception of transport risks, and the likely reliability of valuation responses. The non-random sample of 120 subjects for the feasibility study was drawn from the Newcastle area and was generated principally by advertisements in the local news media. Each subject was interviewed at length by a research associate and paid a modest sum (£3.00) for his or her time and trouble. The findings of the study, summarized in Hammerton et al. (1982a), were, on the whole, encouraging.

As a result, the DTp decided to proceed to the second and main phase of the research programme. This was to consist of a nationally representative sample survey, intended principally to provide estimates of the value of statistical life. It was to be conducted by a professional survey organization using a questionnaire designed in Newcastle and piloted both locally by a research associate and in the Crowthorne area of Berkshire by interviewers from the Transport and Road Research Laboratory (TRRL). The survey was put out to tender early in 1982. Responses from those survey organizations approached were mixed. Two organizations submitted tenders but expressed reservations about the feasibility of such an exercise given the nature of some of the questions involved. One recommended substantial revision of the questions in a manner that would have rendered the responses virtually unusable for the purpose intended and two declined to submit any tender (one because of doubts about feasibility in general and the reliability of responses in particular and the other on the grounds that a survey of this kind was regarded as unethical). Largely because of the care and insight that its staff had shown in thinking through the various potential difficulties involved, NOP Market Research Ltd was awarded the contract. After satisfying themselves of the likely feasibility of the survey, following careful piloting and interviewer debriefing, representatives of NOP extensively 'refined' the questionnaire – in consultation with the Newcastle research team and DTp – in order to improve its intelligibility to the layman.

The main survey was conducted in June and July of 1982 using a three-stage, stratified random sample drawn from some 90 parliamentary constituencies in England, Scotland and Wales. The questionnaire was administered by professional NOP interviewers in the respondents' own homes and the effective sample size was 1,718, designed to produce 1,000 interviews at an assumed response rate of about 60%. In the event, the actual response rate of 67% was higher than expected, producing 1,103 fully and 47 partially completed questionnaires. The latter resulted from interviews terminated before completion, usually because the respondent was old and unable to understand the more difficult questions. The number of outright refusals to participate in the survey was 209 and the number of interviews terminated before completion because of objections to the questions was six. The overall picture was therefore rather similar to that reflected in an earlier Health & Safety Executive survey on attitudes to work-related, industrial and other risks (Prescott-Clarke, 1982) (effective sample size 1,563; response rate 76%; outright refusals 251).

Finally, a follow-up survey was conducted about a month after the main study on a subsample of 210 of the original respondents who were presented with some of the questions from the main questionnaire. This exercise was intended to test for the temporal consistency of responses.

4.1   The Questionnaire

The questionnaire, parts of which are reproduced in the Appendix to this chapter, contained 37 questions (many multipart) and took, on average, about 45 minutes to complete.[3] Broadly speaking, the questions fall into three categories, namely valuation questions, perception and consistency questions and factual questions.

4.1.1   Valuation Questions

These questions were intended to provide estimates of individual marginal rates of substitution, relative valuation of avoidance of fatal and non-fatal accidents, and information concerning factors likely to have a significant influence upon valuations. More specifically, the valuation questions were designed to shed light on the following issues.

1   How do people view various categories of non-fatal injury in relation to death? In particular

    (a)   What kinds of injury are regarded as serious?

    (b)   What are people's *relative* valuations of risk reduction for fatal and serious injury accidents?

2   How much are individuals willing to pay for various risk reductions and how are the sums affected by

    (a)   The nature of the risk and its existing level?

    (b)   The size of the change in risk?

    (c)   The extent to which the change in risk applies to others?

    (d)   The income of the individual at risk?

    (e)   The age of the individual at risk?

    (f)   Other factors such as social class, education and accident experience?

3   To what extent do individuals take account of direct economic effects (e.g. material damage, medical and police costs, and output losses) in assessing their willingness to pay for risk reduction?

4   Do people have a marked preference for the avoidance of loss of 'anonymous' life (i.e. the death of one as yet unidentified person) as opposed to the avoidance of the loss of 'statistical' life (i.e. the exposure of n people to independent incremental risks of death of $1/n$ each)?

In order to test for the possibility that the ordering of multipart valuation questions might systematically affect responses, half of the sample was presented with these questions in a particular order and the other half with the questions in reverse order. This explains the reference to 'versions 1 and 2' of the questionnaire later in this chapter.

4.1.2   Perception/Consistency Questions

The aim of these questions was to test the quality of individual perception of transport risks and ability to handle probability concepts, to examine the veracity and stability of valuation responses, and finally to test conformity with the standard axioms of rational choice under uncertainty in this context.[4] The main issues addressed in these questions were as follows.

1   How good are individuals' perceptions of transport risks? In particular

    (a)   To what extent do individual perceptions of the *relative* risk of different transport modes correspond with the 'objective' ranking reflected in historical accident rates?

    (b)   To what extent do individual perceptions of *absolute* accident rates correspond with actual accident rates?

    (c)   To what extent are individual perceptions improved by the provision of reference data (e.g. how are individual perceptions of motorcycle risks affected by the provision of statistics concerning accident rates for cars)?

(d)   To what extent are individuals' responses to valuation questions affected by their subjective overestimation or underestimation of transport risks?

2   How good are people at handling probability concepts? In particular, are people consistent in dealing with probabilities per se?

3   Do individual responses satisfy minimal conditions of rationality (or
'coherence')?

4   To what extent are the answers to willingness-to-pay questions
affected by the nature of the question? For example, does the
hypothetical situation described in the question markedly affect the
implied values of statistical life?

4.1.3   Factual and Other Questions

These questions concerned such matters as vehicle ownership, annual
mileage and accident experience as well as the usual questions about age,
income and other personal details. Questions about the respondent's
reaction to the questionnaire and the difficulty or ease of answering the
questions were also included.

4.1.4   Problems of Questionnaire Design

Many of the questions raised and problems encountered in designing the
questionnaire were unique, if only because at the time of the study no
exercise of this kind had ever been undertaken before on this scale.[5] For
example, in the course of early design and piloting it became clear that,
with questions of the type it would be necessary to ask, we faced a
difficult trade-off between simplicity and intelligibility on the one hand
and lack of ambiguity on the other. Early versions of the questionnaire
contained questions which, on careful reading, were largely unambiguous
but which were also far too complex and contained too much detailed
information for the average respondent to assimilate. However, simplification tended to introduce the possibility of more than one interpretation of the question and hence of the responses. In consequence,
refinement of the questions involved a careful, and therefore lengthy,
process of experimentation. A related problem was that of credibility of
the hypothetical situations and choices presented in many questions.
Ideally, hypothetical choices should be made as 'real' as possible. For
example, in asking how much a respondent would be willing to pay for a
car safety feature it is clearly desirable to be quite specific about the
nature of the device (e.g. that it is 'a kind of shock-absorbing bumper or
body panel'). If one does this, however, there will always be a proportion
of respondents who will simply not believe that any conceivable feature of
that type 'could possibly reduce risk by that amount'. One is then driven
back to less specificity and less realism.

Another problem encountered in early questionnaire design concerned
the precise means by which valuation responses, in particular, were to be

elicited. It was found that if respondents are simply asked, 'How much would you be willing to pay?', some experienced great difficulty in answering without some sort of prompt from the interviewer. One possibility considered was to provide respondents with a choice of boxes to tick, e.g.:

£0	£1	£2	£5	£10	£20	£50

This is certainly a simple device and experience in the feasibility phase showed that it would successfully generate a response in a large majority of cases. Unfortunately, however, it suffers from a notorious limitation, namely central tendency bias, in that subjects tend to pick the middle boxes in the belief that extremes are just that (see Poulton, 1975).

A further possibility is 'sequential (or iterative) bidding'. For example, the interviewer begins by asking, 'Would you pay more than £5 or less?' If the respondent says 'more', then the interviewer proceeds to ask, 'Would you pay £10 or less?' and so on. The difficulty with this procedure is that it is time consuming and tedious, and is likely to lead to boredom on the part of the respondent, especially if a number of valuation questions have to be asked.[6]

In the end it was decided to ask valuation questions unprompted in the first instance. If the respondent gave an answer, it was recorded. If the respondent hesitated, then the interviewer was instructed to use the following prompt:

'I'll read out some amounts of money. Please stop me when I get to an amount beyond which you would not be prepared to pay.'
Read out figures quickly and steadily
'Nothing, £1, £2, £5, £10, £20, £50, £100, £200, £1,000.'
When respondent stops you, ask
'You stopped me at . . . . Can you tell me how much you would actually be prepared to pay?'
If 'less than . . .' ask
'How much would you be prepared to pay?'
Probe for an estimate

The interviewer then recorded the fact that the prompt had been used.

Early piloting indicated that some respondents gave answers to valuation questions that represented the sums that they felt they *ought*, in some ideal or model sense, to be willing to pay rather than the amount they would actually be willing and able to pay, taking account of their budget constraints. Later versions of the valuation questions therefore stressed that respondents were to give the amount they would be willing to pay, *bearing in mind what they personally could afford*.

Presentation of probabilities also raised difficulties. The basic issue was whether respondents find it easier to have probabilities presented in the form '1 in x' or as 'y in 100,000'. Some tests were carried out to try to resolve this question and, while the results gave no indication of a clearly preferred or more intelligible mode of presentation, it was finally decided to use the 'y in 100,000' format. In the event, this proved to be a fortunate choice because it led to the suggestion by members of NOP (who were also somewhat worried about the intelligibility of probability concepts to the typical respondent) that all probability statements in the questionnaire should be supplemented by a pictorial representation in which the appropriate number of squares had been 'blacked out' on a piece of graph paper containing 100,000 squares. This proved to be a very successful method of conveying probability information and respondents in the NOP pilot said that they had found it to be of considerable help in understanding questions involving probabilities. Finally, in addition to the pictorial representation of probabilities, respondents were also provided with written versions of the more difficult or complex questions.

4.2 The Sample

Under our contract with NOP the sample was selected by their standard procedure. This is used to select the samples not only for their monthly political opinion polls but also for their regular 'omnibus' surveys. In principle, the procedure operates in three stages.

At the first stage a systematic sample of 90 parliamentary constituencies is selected from a sample frame of 621 constituencies, excluding Northern Ireland, Orkney and Shetland, and the Western Isles. Within this sampling frame, constituencies are ordered:

1 By region (Strathclyde, rest of Scotland, Northern, Northwest, Yorkshire and Humberside, East Midlands, West Midlands, East Anglia, Southeast Wales, rest of Wales, Southeast or Southwest).
2 Within region, by type (metropolitan, other urban, mixed or rural).
3 Within region and type, in descending order of the ratio of Conservative votes to Labour votes at the 1979 General Election.

Denote the electorate of the ith constituency by n_i and the total electorate of the 621 constituencies by N. The procedure selects a random number between 1 and $N/180$ and uses it to identify a single anonymous elector in the (putative) cumulative list of N electors. The constituency to which this elector belongs becomes the first constituency in the sample. The sampling interval $N/180$ is then added 179 times to the original random number. The 179 anonymous electors thus identified yield a further 179 constituencies. From this sample of 180 constituencies, a systematic subsample of 90 constituencies is then selected. (The reason for the prior selection of the sample of 180 constituencies is essentially one of economy and convenience for NOP. Given that NOP has to select regular stratified random samples from x constituencies – where $x < 180$ –

it is clearly far less complicated and costly to select these as systematic subsamples from the 'standard' sample of 180 constituencies rather than by repeated sampling from the complete sampling frame of 621 constituencies.) This first-stage sampling procedure has two desirable properties. First, it samples constituencies with probability proportional to their electorates; provided that second-stage samples of equal size are chosen from each selected constituency, this gives each of the N electors an equal probability of being selected. Secondly, the regional stratification ensures that the sample of electors is representative of the regions of Great Britain. In contrast, the procedure does not guarantee (although it increases the probability) that the sample of electors is representative of the types of constituency and of the political allegiance of those constituencies. If the sample were to be representative in these last two respects then both type of constituency and political allegiance should define independent strata rather than mere substrata within regions.

At the second stage, a cluster sample of 18 electors is selected from the electoral register of each of the 90 constituencies. The procedure selects a random number between 1 and n_i and uses it to identify the first elector in the subsample. A sampling interval of 15 is then added 17 times to the original random number, thus yielding a further 17 electors.

At the third stage, one non-elector aged 16 or over is sampled at random from each household containing both a selected elector and other non-electors. To correct for the unequal probabilities of selecting a non-elector which this third-stage procedure implies, each non-elector is given a weight of

$$\frac{\text{Number of non-electors in household}}{\text{Number of electors in household}}.$$

In contrast with the desirable properties of the first stage of sampling, the second stage is based on the cheap but statistically less desirable technique of cluster sampling and the third stage has to use disproportionate sampling as the only practical means of selecting non-electors. It is therefore important to take account of the extent to which the adverse effects of cluster sampling and disproportionate sampling have been offset by the stratified sampling of the first stage. This is done by means of the 'design effects' described in the next section.

4.3 Analysis of the Data and Results

In the main body of this section results are given for complete interviews ($n = 1,103$) and do not include the results of the 47 partial interviews terminated before completion.

Responses have been weighted both to correct for the differential probability of selecting electors and non-electors in our sampling procedure and to ensure that the adjusted sample is representative of the population of Great Britain as judged by age, sex, occupational group and region. This gives a weighted sample of 1,057 complete interviews.[7]

In the statistical package that we employed for data analysis (SPSS) standard errors are computed on the assumption that one is dealing with a simple random sample. In fact, as already noted, NOP's sampling procedure involved stratification, clustering and disproportionate sampling of non-electors, so that it is necessary to adjust for these factors in computing confidence intervals. This is done by multiplying by $\sqrt{\text{deff}}$, where deff is the 'design effect' of a sampling procedure and is the ratio of the true variance of the sampling distribution to that which would have been obtained from a simple random sample of the same size (see Moser and Kalton, [1971]). NOP suggested that $\sqrt{\text{deff}}$ should be taken as 1.3, this being the average value found in NOP's Random Omnibus Survey which involves a broadly similar sample design. However, the Health & Safety Executive survey referred to earlier employed the more conservative value of 1.5 for $\sqrt{\text{deff}}$ and we followed a similar path, computing all confidence intervals as $\pm$ 3 standard errors.[8]

4.3.1 Valuation Questions

Death versus Injury   Because the DTp's definition of serious injury is so broad and includes, for example, all injuries involving an overnight stay in hospital, it was felt to be important to obtain information concerning the types of injury that the public regards as serious. Respondents were therefore given a list of various injuries and asked which they regarded as serious and which not (Question 12). The results (with types of injury arranged in apparent order of seriousness rather than the order in which they were presented to respondents) are given in table 4.1.

As shown in Chapter 3, section 3.7, if an individual is indifferent between an incremental risk of 10^{-x} of being killed and an incremental risk of 10^{-y} of serious injury then

$$\frac{m_\mathrm{D}}{m_\mathrm{I}} \approx 10^{x-y}$$

where m_D is the individual's marginal rate of substitution of wealth for risk of death and m_I is his marginal rate of substitution of wealth for risk of serious injury. It follows that if the individual would rather face the incremental risk of 10^{-x} of death than the incremental risk of 10^{-y} of serious injury then $m_\mathrm{D}/m_\mathrm{I} < 10^{x-y}$ and that if he would rather face the incremental risk of serious injury then $m_\mathrm{D}/m_\mathrm{I} > 10^{x-y}$.

Question 16 asked 'If you had to choose between them, which one of these risks would you rather face:

a risk of 10 in 100,000 of being killed;
a risk of 1,000 in 100,000 of serious injury?'

The responses are given in table 4.2. In this question the term 'serious injury' was quite deliberately left undefined – before the survey we had

Table 4.1 Perceived severity of non-fatal injuries

Type	Not serious (%)	Serious but death worse (%)	As bad as death (%)	Slightly worse than death (%)	Much worse than death (%)	Very much worse than death (%)
Cut and bruised but can leave hospital after a couple of days and recover fully within a month	81.3 (±3.6)[a]	18.7 (±3.6)	0.0	0.0	0.0	0.0
Break an arm	63.1 (±4.5)	36.7 (±4.5)	0.1 (±0.3)[b]	0.1 (±0.3)	0.0	0.0
In hospital for a year but recover fully	15.3 (±3.3)	83.7 (±3.4)	0.6 (±0.7)	0.4 (±0.6)	0.0	0.0
Lose an eye	3.1 (±1.6)	89.0 (±2.9)	5.0 (±2.0)	1.9 (±1.3)	0.6 (±0.7)	0.3 (±0.5)
Lose a leg	3.2 (±1.6)	86.7 (±3.2)	6.2 (±2.2)	2.4 (±1.4)	1.2 (±1.0)	0.3 (±0.5)
Badly scarred for life and in hospital for a year	3.1 (±1.6)	84.4 (±3.4)	7.7 (±2.5)	3.0 (±1.6)	1.2 (±1.0)	0.5 (±0.6)
Confined to a wheelchair for the rest of your life	0.3 (±0.5)	48.3 (±4.7)	27.7 (±4.2)	10.8 (±2.9)	8.7 (±2.7)	4.3 (±1.9)
Permanently bed-ridden	0.2 (±0.4)	36.5 (±4.6)	33.4 (±4.5)	11.9 (±3.1)	11.2 (±3.0)	6.9 (±2.4)

[a] Here and throughout this chapter figures in brackets are 95% confidence intervals computed as ±3 standard errors (recall that the square root of the design effect for the NOP sampling procedure has been taken as 1.5).

[b] Here and at certain other points in the presentation of results the lower bound of the confidence interval gives a negative value for a variable that is, by definition, non-negative. This is because the normal approximation to the sampling distribution is strictly speaking inappropriate. In such cases a binomial confidence interval should, ideally, have been computed, but this would have been tedious and would have had little effect on the upper bound of the interval.

Table 4.2 Preferences between fatal and non-fatal injury

Prefer 10 in 10⁵ chance of being killed (%)	*Prefer 1,000 in 10⁵ chance of serious injury (%)*
63 ($\pm$4)	37 ($\pm$4)

Table 4.3 Preferences between improvements in mortality

Cause of death	*Prefer to have reduced (%)*
Motor accidents	11 ($\pm$3)
Heart disease	13 ($\pm$3)
Cancer	76 ($\pm$4)

no clear idea of what kinds of injury were commonly regarded as 'serious'. The responses summarized in table 4.2 must therefore be interpreted as indicating that substantially more than 50% of the respondents have marginal rates of substitution of wealth for risk of serious injury (where 'serious' is to be construed in the sense reflected in table 4.1) of more than one-hundredth the corresponding rate of substitution for risk of death.[9]

Valuation of Safety The questionnaire contained five different questions (some multipart) intended to estimate individual willingness to pay for reduction in the risk of death or requirement of compensation for increased risk. Specifically, Question 14(a) asked which of three UK death rates for individuals below the age of 55 – from cancer, heart disease or road accidents – the respondent would most wish to see reduced next year. Question 14(b) then asked how much the respondent would be willing to contribute to achieve a reduction of 100 such deaths were it possible to do so. The results of Question 14(a) are presented in table 4.3.

Question 18 asked the respondent to suppose that he had to make a foreign journey by coach and that he had been given travelling expenses equal to the fare charged by a particular coach firm with a specified risk of fatal injury. The respondent was then asked how much he or she would pay over and above allowed expenses for each of two different reductions in risk. The respondent was also asked how much of the fixed expenses he or she would expect to keep to be induced to accept each of two different increments in risk. Respondents were also permitted to say that they would not use the riskier modes at all. Version 1 of the questionnaire, administered to 52% of the sample, presented the questions in the following order: 18(a) smaller risk reduction; 18(b) larger risk reduction; 18(c) smaller risk increase; 18(d) larger risk increase. Version 2, administered to the remaining 48% of the sample, was ordered as follows: 18(a) larger risk increase; 18(b) smaller risk increase; 18(c) larger risk reduction; 18(d) smaller risk reduction. This was done in order to test for the possibility that ordering significantly affected the responses.

Question 20 asked how much the respondent would be willing to pay for a car safety feature which would reduce the risk of fatal injury in various ways. In verison 1 of the questionnaire Question 20(a) had the feature reducing driver risk by a given amount, 20(b) had the feature reducing driver risk by a smaller amount, and 20(c) had the feature reducing driver *and* passenger risk by an amount equal to that specified in Question 20(a). In version 2, the questions were put in reverse order. By comparing the results for 'driver *and* passenger' with those for 'driver only', one can derive estimates of willingness to pay for other people's safety.

Question 21 asked about willingness to change car tyres at 2-mm tread depth (rather than the then current legal limit of 1 mm) if it were demonstrated that doing so would reduce accident risks by 15%. Responses, together with information concerning the price of tyres and typical frequencies of tyre replacement, provide the basis for estimating willingness to pay for risk reduction.

Question 22 was intended to test for the 'free rider/non-revelation' effect in cases in which safety was perceived to be a public rather than a private good. It simply asked how much individuals would be willing to contribute to a door-to-door collection intended to finance local road safety improvement. A second part asked how much individuals thought would be a reasonable fixed sum to collect from each household in a universal levy.

Questions 14, 18, 20, 21 and 22 are reproduced verbatim in the Appendix to this chapter.

Responses to the willingness-to-pay questions are given in table 4.4. Estimates of the population mean and median of individual marginal rates of substitution of wealth for risk of death computed from these responses[10] are then given in tables 4.5–4.8. The ith individual's marginal rate of substitution for risks to self-only is denoted by m_i, for self plus (average) number of passengers carried by m_i^+, for self plus all others by m_i^* and, finally, the ith individual's marginal rate of substitution for risks to one other person only (where the other person is a car passenger – presumably normally a close relative or friend) by $\bar{m}_i$. 'Trimmed' means were computed with outliers removed. The principle employed in trimming was to remove any upper-tail responses that were very much larger than other responses, the suspicion being that these were either fanciful responses or (more probably) instances of coding errors. In particular, one response of £9,990 was removed from Question 14(b). It is worth noting that the code for 'Don't know' in this question was 9999. In Question 18(a) all the seven responses removed were coded 9998. This was the code for 'would pay over £9,997' and differed in only one digit from the code for 'Don't know' (9999). Similarly, all the six responses removed from 18(b), the two removed from 20(a) and the three removed

Table 4.4 Responses to valuation questions (£-sterling, 1982)

Question	Mean	Trimmed mean	Median
14(b) All	67.80 (±38.43) $n = 982$	56.13 (±20.36) $n = 981$	9.53 (+2.78) (−1.56) $n = 982$
14(b) Motor accidents[a]	24.51 (±14.77) $n = 113$	24.51 (±14.77) $n = 113$	5.23 (+3.91) (−2.26) $n = 113$
14(b) Heart disease[a]	44.09 (±38.13) $n = 120$	44.09 (±38.13) $n = 120$	9.60 (+7.30) (−4.27) $n = 120$
14(b) Cancer[a]	77.18 (±50.19) $n = 742$	61.77 (±28.33) $n = 741$	9.59 (+3.11) (−1.88) $n = 742$
18(a)[b]	136.96 (±81.39) $n = 988$	64.04 (±8.30) $n = 981$	49.55 (+13.55) (−10.66) $n = 988$
18(b)	155.58 (±73.02) $n = 1005$	97.36 (±14.00) $n = 999$	50.14 (+13.36) (−10.24) $n = 1005$
18(c) 18(c)	For those who would use ($n = 204$) 63.14 (±9.22)	63.14 (±9.22)	50.34 (+23.16) (−14.84)
18(d)	For those who would use ($n = 134$) 68.68 (±12.54)	68.68 (±12.54)	50.43 (+33.57) (−19.63)
20(a)	198.55 (±51.00) $n = 953$	176.72 (±24.11) $n = 951$	99.75 (+27.25) (−21.45) $n = 953$
20(b)	137.77 (±21.78) $n = 958$	137.77 (±21.78) $n = 958$	50.25 (+14.15) (−11.25) $n = 958$
20(c)	252.83 (±61.56) $n = 966$	220.47 (±29.24) $n = 963$	100.29 (+26.71) (−20.69) $n = 966$

Table 4.4   (Continued)

Question	Mean	Trimmed mean	Median
22(a)	6.00	6.00	1.01
	(±2.07)	(±2.07)	(+0.19)
			(−0.13)
	$n = 986$	$n = 986$	$n = 986$
22(b)	8.39	8.39	2.00
	(±1.78)	(±1.78)	(+0.42)
			(−0.35)
	$n = 955$	$n = 955$	$n = 955$

[a] Cause of death chosen to be reduced.
[b] Throughout the presentation and analysis of results, the order of the multipart valuation
Questions 18 and 20 is that given in Version 1 of the questionnaire.

from 20(c) were coded 9998, the code for 'Don't know' being again 9999. None of these extreme responses were given by individuals with high incomes.

The percentage of respondents reporting that their household owned a car or van was, in fact, 72%. Given that the percentage of households in Great Britain owning cars at the time of the survey was 61%[11] it appears that our sample is over-representative of car owners. However, it is clearly possible that larger households are more likely to own a car than are smaller households. If this is so, then because our sampling procedure selected *electors* with equal probability (so that larger households were more likely to be sampled than smaller households), one would expect the proportion of respondents in our sample living in car-owning households to exceed 61%. We therefore computed an estimate of households owning a car from our data using weights to correct for the number of electors in the household. The estimate was 66.7% (±4.5%), which, being less than 72%, tends to confirm the hypothesis that larger households are more likely to own a car, but also indicates that having taken account of this effect our sample is still over-representative of car owners. This is almost certainly because the sample does not include the 47 partial interviews terminated before completion, and the respondents in these interviews were from predominantly *non*-car-owning households. However, correction for this over-representation has relatively little impact on estimates of marginal rates of substitution: in the case of Question 20(a), for example, the trimmed mean of m_i falls from £1,210,000 to £1,170,000, the latter being well within the confidence interval given in table 4.5.

Regression Analysis of Valuation Results   The proportion of 'zero' responses to the various valuation questions ranged from about 14% in Question 20 to 30% in Question 22.[12] As suggested by Frankel (1979), such responses may reflect a fatalistic belief that life-spans are, in some

Table 4.5 Estimates of the population mean and median of m_i (self only; £-sterling, 1982)

	Mean of m_i	Trimmed mean of m_i	Median of m_i
18(a)	3,420,000 ($\pm$2,030,000)	1,600,000 ($\pm$210,000)	1,240,000 (+340,000) ($-$270,000)
	$n = 988$	$n = 981$	$n = 988$
18(b)	2,220,000 ($\pm$1,040,000)	1,390,000 ($\pm$200,000)	720,000 (+190,000) ($-$150,000)
	$n = 1,005$	$n = 999$	$n = 1,005$
18(c)	For those who would use ($n = 204$) 790,000 ($\pm$120,000)	790,000 ($\pm$120,000)	630,000 (+290,000) ($-$190,000)
	For those who would not use, $m \geqslant 2,500,000$		
18(d)	For those who would use ($n = 134$) 290,000 ($\pm$50,000)	290,000 ($\pm$50,000)	210,000 (+140,000) ($-$ 80,000)
	For those who would not use, $m \geqslant 830,000$		
20(a)	1,430,000 ($\pm$500,000)	1,210,000 ($\pm$220,000)	500,000 (+ 90,000) ($-$ 80,000)
	$n = 952$	$n = 950$	$n = 952$
20(b)	2,210,000 ($\pm$400,000)	2,210,000 ($\pm$400,000)	770,000 (+160,000) ($-$130,000)
	$n = 957$	$n = 957$	$n = 957$

Table 4.6 Estimates of the population mean and median of m_i^+ (self and passengers; £-sterling, 1982)

	Mean of m_i^+	Trimmed mean of m_i^+	Median of m_i^+
20(c)	1,770,000 ($\pm$540,000)	1,500,000 ($\pm$270,000)	500,000 (+100,000) ($-$80,000)
	$n = 966$	$n = 962$	$n = 966$
21(c)		'Change $\geqslant$ 2 mm' ($n = 301$) $m_i^* \geqslant 330,000$ 'Change $<$ 2 min' ($n = 89$) $m_i^* < 330,000$	

Table 4.7 Estimates of the population mean and median of $\tilde{m}_i$ (average passenger; £-sterling, 1982)

	Mean of $\tilde{m}_i$	Trimmed mean of $\tilde{m}_i$	Median of $\tilde{m}_i$
20(c) and 20(a)	500,000 ($\pm$200,000) $n = 945$	500,000 ($\pm$200,000) $n = 943$	0.0[a] $n = 945$

[a] This figure reflects the fact that 14% of respondents gave answers to Questions 20(a) and 20(c) that implied a negative valuation of passengers' lives; 47% gave answers that implied a value of zero and 39% gave answers that implied a positive value.

Table 4.8 Estimates of the population mean and median of m_i^* (self plus all others; £-sterling, 1982)

	Mean of m_i^*	Trimmed mean of m_i^*	Median of m_i^*
14(b) All	20,340,000 ($\pm$11,520,000) $n = 982$	16,840,000 ($\pm$6,110,000) $n = 981$	2,860,000 (+830,000) (−470,000) $n = 982$
14(b) Motor accidents[a]	7,350,000 ($\pm$1,480,000) $n = 113$	7,350,000 ($\pm$1,480,000) $n = 113$	1,570,000 (+1,700,000) (−680,000) $n = 113$
14(b) Heart disease[a]	13,230,000 ($\pm$11,440,000) $n = 120$	13,230,000 ($\pm$11,440,000) $n = 120$	2,880,000 (+2,190,000) (−1,280,000) $n = 120$
14(b) Cancer[a]	23,120,000 ($\pm$15,060,000) $n = 742$	18,530,000 ($\pm$8,500,000) $n = 741$	2,880,000 (+930,000) (−560,000) $n = 742$
22(a)	200,000 ($\pm$70,000) $n = 986$	200,000 ($\pm$70,000) $n = 986$	30,000 (+6,000) (−4,000) $n = 986$
22(b)	280,000 ($\pm$60,000) $n = 955$	280,000 ($\pm$60,000) $n = 955$	70,000 (+14,000) (−12,000) $n = 955$

[a] Cause of death chosen to be reduced.

way, predetermined so that there is simply no point in spending on safety. Alternatively, and more probably, zero responses may be what Smith and Desvousges (1987) describe as 'protest bids', i.e. responses reflecting a basic unwillingness to engage in a hypothetical valuation exercise related to a topic as sensitive as safety. Whatever the reason for the zero responses, it seems appropriate to assume, as did Smith and Desvousges, that for any particular valuation question stated willingness to pay y_i is related to various personal characteristics and other explanatory variables x_{ij} in the manner proposed by Heckman (1979), i.e.

$$\left. \begin{array}{l} y_i = \beta_0 + \beta_1 x_{i1} + \ldots + \beta_m x_{im} + u_i \\ \quad \text{if } \gamma_0 + \gamma_1 x_{i1} + \ldots + \gamma_m x_{im} + \epsilon_i > 0 \\ y_i = 0 \text{ otherwise} \end{array} \right\} \quad (4.1)$$

where the β_j and γ_j are parameters, γ_j reflecting the manner in which x_{ij} influences the probability of a non-zero response from the ith individual, while β_j reflects the way in which x_{ij} influences the magnitude of such a response, if it occurs. In addition, u_i and ϵ_i are each independently and normally distributed with mean zero, but $\text{cov}(u_i, \epsilon_i)$ is *not* necessarily zero.

It can then be shown (Heckman, 1979; Johnson and Kotz, 1972, pp. 112–13) that

$$E(y_i/y_i \neq 0) = \beta_0 + \beta_1 x_{i1} + \ldots + \beta_m x_{im} + \frac{\text{cov}(u_i, \epsilon_i)}{[\text{var}(\epsilon_i)]^{1/2}} \lambda_i \quad (4.2)$$

where E is, as usual, the expectation operator, $\lambda_i = f(z_i)/F(z_i)$, $f(.)$ and $F(.)$ are, respectively, the standard normal density and distribution functions and

$$z_i = \frac{1}{[\text{var}(\epsilon_i)]^{\frac{1}{2}}} (\gamma_0 + \gamma_1 x_{i1} + \ldots + \gamma_m x_{im}).$$

To the extent that the term $\{\text{cov}(u_i, \epsilon_i)/[\text{var}(\epsilon_i)]^{\frac{1}{2}}\} \lambda_i$ effectively corrects for the bias that would occur if the positive responses y_i were regressed on the explanatory variables x_{ij} by ordinary least squares, λ_i is typically referred to as a 'sample selection bias correction' variable.

With a view to estimating this model using the standard Heckman two-stage procedure, probit analyses were first conducted on the responses to the valuation questions[13] using the following explanatory variables:

1 Household's annual income from all sources before tax (£).
2 Missing income dummy (= 1 if no income given).
3 Income minus mean income all squared.
4 Respondent's age minus mean age (years).
5 Age minus mean age all squared.
6 Social class dummy (= 1 if AB).
7 Social class dummy (= 1 if C1).
8 Social class dummy (= 1 if C2).
9 Social class dummy (= 1 if D).

10   Marital status dummy (= 1 if married).
11   Number of people in respondent's household.
12   Number of people in household minus 3 all squared.
13   Age at which respondent finished full-time education.
14   Respondent's total consistency score.[14]
15   Regional dummy (= 1 if lives in GLC).
16   Regional dummy (= 1 if lives in Scotland).
17   Regional dummy (= 1 if lives in Southeast).
18   Regional dummy (= 1 if lives in Midlands).
19   Car ownership dummy (= 1 if household owns).
20   Miles driven last year.
21   Missing mileage dummy (= 1 if no miles driven last year).
22   Accident experience dummy (= 1 if respondent involved in a car accident).
23   Accident experience dummy (= 1 if respondent knows someone involved in a car accident).

The results of the first-stage probit analyses were, to say the least, mixed, in that with one or two exceptions none of the explanatory variables was clearly significant. In particular, there was very little evidence of significance in the various parts of Question 20 and, while there was some weak evidence in Question 18, those variables that showed signs of significance tended to differ between the two parts of the question. In fact, the only case in which the explanatory variables appeared to be at all effective in discriminating between zero and positive responses was Question 22 where it transpired that the probability of a positive response was a significantly *declining* function of age in both parts of the question.

These first-stage probit results therefore indicate that for Questions 18, 20 and 14(b) the probability of a positive response is effectively *independent* of the various explanatory variables and, in terms of the model specified in (4.1), is equal to $p(\epsilon_i > -\gamma_0)$. Notice that if the probability of a non-zero response is *completely* independent of the x_{ij}, then λ_i is constant and equal to $f(\gamma_0)/F(\gamma_0)$. In spite of this, it is still important to include λ_i in the regression analysis in view of the possibility that $cov(u_i, \epsilon_i) \neq 0$ since exclusion of λ_i in this case would yield a biased estimate of the intercept term β_0. Furthermore, to the extent that there is *any* relationship between the probability of a non-zero response and the x_{ij}, however weak, then λ_i will display some variability, so that it is again important that λ_i should be included in the specification of the regression relationship. In the case of Question 22 matters are somewhat different. Here, it is plain that the probability of a positive response *does* depend on at least one of the explanatory variables, though it is again the case that the first-stage results leave open the question of whether and how λ_i will influence the magnitude of a positive response if it occurs.

In order to settle the question of the relationship between y_i and λ_i for the various valuation questions, the second stage of the Heckman procedure was carried out. This involved regressing the positive valuation responses on the explanatory variables listed above, together with values of λ_i computed from the first-stage estimates of z_i. In questions 18, 20 and 14(b) the Heckman sample selection bias correction variable λ_i was insignificant, indicating that $cov(u_i, \epsilon_i) \approx 0$. It thus transpires that for those questions, ordinary least squares *without* Heckman sample selection bias correction is the appropriate estimation procedure. In Questions 22(a) and 22(b), by contrast, the coefficient of λ_i was significantly *negative*. This suggests that, for Question 22, u_i and ϵ_i in (4.1) are negatively correlated. However, it should be noted that in regressions run on the positive responses *with λ_i omitted*, the coefficient of 'age minus mean age' was negative and significant at the 1% level in Question 22(b) and negative and significant at the 20% level in Question 22(a). Given that λ_i and 'age minus mean age' were strongly positively correlated, it is therefore clearly possible that the negative association between responses to Question 22 and λ_i is, in fact, a reflection of collinearity between λ_i and 'age minus mean age'. If this is so, then taken together with the first-stage probit results it suggests that both the probability of a positive response *and* the magnitude of such a response, if given, were declining functions of age for Question 22.

In view of the results of the Heckman two-stage analysis we therefore present the following regression results in table 4.9: positive marginal rates of substitution for Questions 18, 20, 14(b) and 22 regressed on all explanatory variables *excluding* λ_i; positive marginal rates of substitution for Question 22 regressed on all explanatory variables *including* λ_i.

For comparison, table 4.10 reports the results of regression analysis of *all* marginal rates of substitution (including zero and positive) on all explanatory variables *excluding* λ_i. In this table we also report regression results for $\bar{m}_i$, which yields the value placed by respondents on other people's safety and took on negative as well as zero and positive values.

In all cases the regression procedure employed was *stepwise* ordinary least squares with mean substitution. The stopping rule used in the stepwise procedure required that the last variable entered should be nominally significant at the 10% level.

Semilogarithmic specifications of the regression relationships produced no marked improvement in fit and the results of these analyses are therefore not reported here.

Output Losses In order to determine whether or not respondents took account of direct economic effects in assessing their willingness to pay for safety improvements, Question 23 asked:

> At the earlier questions you were asked to think only about death and injury. However, traffic accidents can have other effects beside death and injury and they are listed on this page. Now although you were *not* asked to, did you in fact take any of these things into account when giving your answer to the earlier questions?

Table 4.9 Multiple regression results, positive responses only[a]

	m_i (self only)				m_i^+ (self and passengers)		m_i^+ (self and all others)			
	18(a)	18(b)	20(a)	20(b)	20(c)	14(b)	22(a)	22(b)	22(a)	22(b)
Constant	2,540,000 (336,000)	1,630,000 (131,000)	1,130,000 (250,000)	2,120,000 (500,000)	1,410,000 (295,000)	4,220,000 (6,800,000)	585,000 (204,000)	267,000 (37,000)	558,000 (92,800)	507,000 (73,400)
Household's annual income from all sources before tax (£)	–	–	82.6 (26.1)	103 (65.1)	76.4 (31.2)	–	–	–	–	–
Missing income dummy (= 1 if no income given)	–	–	–	–	–	2,000 (736)	–	–	–	–
Income minus main income all squared	–	–	–	0.020,9 (0.012,2)	–	–	0.005,31 (0.001,49)	–	0.006,18 (0.001,50)	–
Respondent's age minus mean age (years)	–	–	–	–	–	–	–	–3,840 (1,520)	6,230 (2,110)	–
Age minus mean age all squared	–	–442 (234)	–987 (271)	–1,750 (535)	–1,160 (325)	–	–	–	–	–
Social class dummy (= 1 if AB)	–	–	–	–	–	–	–	292,000 (74,400)	–	249,000 (76,500)
Social class dummy (= 1 if C1)	–	–	–	–	–	–	–	–	–	–
Social class dummy (= 1 if C2)	–	–	–	–	–	–	–	132,000 (60,800)	–	112,000 (61,500)
Social class dummy (= 1 if D)	–	336,000 (191,000)	–	–	–	–	–	–	–	–
Marital status dummy (= 1 if married)	–	–	–	–	–	–	–	–	–	–
Number of people in respondent's household	–	–	–	–	–	–3,090,000 (1,550,000)	–	–	–	–
Number of people in household minus 3 all squared	–	35,600 (19,600)	–	–	–	–	–	–	–	–

Table 4.10 Multiple regression results, all responses[a]

	m_i (self only)				m_i^+ (self- and passengers)	$\bar{m}_i$ (average passenger)	m_i^* (self and all others)		
	18(a)	18(b)	20(a)	20(b)	20(c)	20(a) and 20(c)	14(b)	22(a)	22(b)
Constant	2,460,000 (293,000)	1,320,000 (112,000)	956,000 (220,000)	3,210,000 (1,100,000)	1,320,000 (268,000)	244,000 (269,000)	5,730,000 (6,170,000)	324,000 (147,000)	277,000 (39,900)
Household's annual income from all sources before tax (£)	–	–	73.9 (23.4)	161 (45.0)	77.2 (28.5)	–	1,380 (697)	–	–
Missing income dummy (= 1 if no income given)	–	–	–	–	–	–	–	–	–
Income minus mean income all squared	-0.006,74 (0.004,09)	–	–	–	–	–	–	0.003,19 (0.001,06)	–
Respondent's age minus mean age (years)	12,100 (4,060)	–	–	–	–	–	–	–	-4,360 (1,090)
Age minus mean age squared	-641 (226)	-420 (202)	-822 (239)	-1,070 (432)	-1,090 (291)	-564 (201)	–	–	–
Social class dummy (= 1 if AB)	–	–	–	–	–	–	10,200,000 (6,120,000)	–	229,000 (56,100)
Social class dummy (= 1 if C1)	–	–	–	–	–	–	–	–	–
Social class dummy (= 1 if C2)	–	–	–	–	–	–	–	–	86,500 (44,900)
Social class dummy (= 1 if D)	–	398,000 (166,000)	–	–	–	–	–	–	–
Marital status dummy (= 1 if married)	–	–	–	–	–	–	–	–	–
Number of people in respondent's household	–	–	–	–	–	–	-2,780,000 (1,420,000)	41,500 (14,400)	–

	(1)	(2)	(3)	(4)	(5)	(6)	(7)	(8)	(9)
Number of people in respondent's household minus 3 all squared	31,700 (17,700)	31,700 (17,000)	—	—	—	—	—	—	-10,800 (5,380)
Age at which respondent finished full-time education	—	—	—	-120,000 (71,700)	—	—	—	—	-16,800 (9,370)
Respondent's total consistency score[b]	-109,000 (46,300)	—	—	—	—	78,600 (43,900)	—	—	—
Regional dummy (= 1 if live in London)	—	—	—	884,000 (386,000)	—	—	—	221,000 (53,300)	177,000 (58,000)
Regional dummy (= 1 if live in Southeast)	—	—	—	—	—	—	13,100,000 (4,920,000)	—	—
Regional dummy (= 1 if live in Midlands)	—	352,000 (178,000)	—	—	—	—	—	—	—
Regional dummy (= 1 if live in Scotland)	—	—	—	—	—	—	—	-108,000 (37,900)	-94,900 (42,200)
Car ownership dummy (= 1 if household owns)	—	—	—	—	—	—	8,340,000 (4,850,000)	—	—
Miles driven last year	—	—	—	—	—	—	—	—	-5.02 (2.67)
Missing mileage dummy (= 1 if no miles driven)	—	—	—	—	—	—	—	—	—
Accident experience dummy (= 1 if respondent involved in a car accident)	—	—	—	—	—	—	—	—	—
Accident experience dummy (= 1 if respondent knows someone involved in a car accident)	—	—	—	—	—	—	—	-59,800 (35,900)	—
Adjusted R^2	0.019	0.015	0.033	0.031	0.031	0.010	0.023	0.045	0.057
n	981	999	950	957	962	943	981	985	955

[a] Figures in parentheses are standard errors.
[b] For details of the calculation of consistency scores, see section 4.3.2.

	(1)	(2)	(3)	(4)	(5)	(6)	(7)	(8)	(9)	(10)
Age at which respondent finished full-time education	–	–	–	–	–	–	-25,300 (12,900)	–	–	–
Respondent's total consistency score[b]	-129,000 (56,000)	–	–	–	–	–	–	–	–	–
Regional dummy (= 1 if live in London)	–	–	–	838,000 (443,000)	–	–	276,000 (71,300)	–	–	–
Regional dummy (= 1 if live in Southeast)	–	–	–	–	–	14,100,000 (5,340,000)	–	280,000 (73,300)	–	–
Regional dummy (= 1 if live in Midlands)	444,000 (233,000)	556,000 (214,000)	–	–	–	–	–	–	–	–
Regional dummy (= 1 if live in Scotland)	–	–	–	–	–	–	-119,000 (53,800)	–	–	–
Car ownership dummy (= 1 if household owns)	355,000 (182,000)	–	–	–	–	9,770,000 (5,260,000)	–	–	–	–
Miles driven last year	–	–	–	–	–	–	–	–	–	–
Missing mileage dummy (= 1 if no miles driven)	–	–	–	–	–	–	–	–	–	–
Accident experience dummy (= 1 if respondent involved in car accident)	–	–	–	–	420,000 (229,000)	–	–	–	–	–
Accident experience dummy (= 1 if respondent knows someone involved in car accident)	–	–	–	–	–	–	–	–	–	–
Sample selection bias correction variable λ	Not included	Not included	Not included	Not included	Not included	Not included	Not included	Not included	-876,000 (205,000)	-428,000 (140,000)
Adjusted R^2	0.013	0.017	0.040	0.044	0.037	0.023	0.050	0.050	0.038	0.034
n	736	805	826	782	861	893	687	671	687	671

[a] Figures in parentheses are standard errors.
[b] For details of the calculation of consistency scores, see section 4.3.2.

Table 4.11   Proportions of respondents who took account of direct economic effects

Effect	Took account (%)	Did not take account (%)
Lost working hours	19 (±4)	81 (±4)
Inconvenience	11 (±3)	89 (±3)
Cost of repairs	14 (±3)	86 (±3)
Police and medical costs	12 (±3)	88 (±3)

Table 4.12   Preferences between re-injecting and gritting

Would not care (%)	Would care (%)	Prefer re-injecting (%)	Prefer gritting (%)
17 (±4)	83 (±4)	56 (±5)	44 (±5)

The results are shown in table 4.11. It is clearly possible that propensity to take account of output effects in particular is related to social class, income, education or responses to valuation questions. Chi-squared tests indicate no significant difference at the 5% level between those who did and those who did not take account of output effects on the basis of social class, income or education. There do, however, appear to be significant differences between the responses of the two groups to some valuation questions, notably 14(b) and 20, with those who did take account of output effects giving larger values.

Anonymous versus Statistical Life   In order to determine whether people prefer the avoidance of anonymous death (the death of one as yet un-identified person) to statistical death (exposure of n people to independent incremental risks of $1/n$ each), respondents were asked to suppose that they lived in an area with 100,000 inhabitants. All inhabitants of the area have been given an immunizing injection but one injection is known to be faulty (though it is not known to whom it was administered) and the recipient will certainly die unless re-injected. The government of the area faces the choice of *either* re-injecting everyone *or* gritting the roads in the winter, which it is estimated will reduce the risk of road deaths by 1 in 100,000 for each person. Respondents were asked whether they would care which alternative was chosen and if so which they would prefer (Question 24). The responses are given in table 4.12.

4.3.2   *Perception/Consistency Questions*

Perception of Transport Risks   In order to investigate people's *qualitative* perception of transport risk, respondents were asked to rank six different

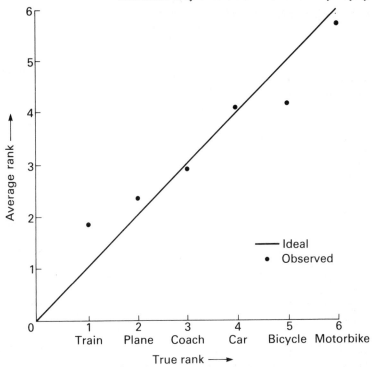

Figure 4.1   Average rank given by respondents in comparing risks of transport modes versus true rank. Under ideal circumstances, in which all respondents estimate the true ranks precisely, their average rank would be equal to the true rank; 'train', the safest mode, would be given an average rank of 1 and 'motorbike', the most dangerous, an average rank of 6.

transport modes in terms of the risk of being killed on a journey of 500 miles (Question 11). In fact, the ratio of the 'objective' risk of being killed on the most dangerous mode (motorbike) to the 'objective' risk of being killed on the safest mode (train) is about 400:1. The results are summarized in figure 4.1.

Respondents were then asked:

About how many times more dangerous is (the mode you judged most dangerous) than (the mode you judged safest) in terms of the risk of being killed in a journey of 500 miles?

The mean response was 11,300 and the median 20. However, with the 10 highest responses trimmed out, the mean falls to 1,060.

To investigate the nature of *quantitative* perceptions and the effect of 'reference' data, half the sample was asked to estimate (1) the number of car drivers and passengers killed in Great Britain during the previous

Table 4.13   Respondents' estimates of the number of transport deaths

		Version 1		Version 2	
	Actual	*Mean*	*Median*	*Mean*	*Median*
Car drivers and passengers	2,500	33,515[a] (±22,000)	4,000 (+1,500) (−1,150)	Given as reference	
Motorcycle riders and passengers	1,160	29,000[a] (±19,000)	2,999 (+1,331) (−939)	7,347 (±7,050)	3,498 (+742) (−608)
Coach drivers and passengers	60	4,907[a] (±7,380)	250 (+106) (−80)	660 (±351)	300 (+89) (−69)

[a] In the version 1 responses five estimates of car deaths, five estimates of motorcycle deaths and one estimate of coach deaths were given the code for 'one million or more', 999998. This code differed in only one digit from the code for 'Don't know', 999999. If these were, in fact, coding errors then the version 1 means for car and motorcycle deaths would each fall by over 13,000 and the mean for coach deaths would fall by over 2,600.

year, (2) the number of motorcycle riders and passengers killed and (3) the number of coach drivers and passengers killed. The other half of the sample was first given the information that about 2,500 car drivers and passengers were killed and then asked to estimate the number of motorcycle deaths and coach deaths (Question 13). The results are given in table 4.13.

Question 15, designed in part to 'educate' the respondent in the concept of risk, gave the risk of a car driver being killed as 10 in 100,000 per year and then asked for estimates of the risk to motorcyclists. The respondent, having answered, was then told that the risk is, in fact, 75 in 100,000. The respondent was then asked for an estimate of the risk to bus and coach passengers and was finally told that the risk is in fact less than 1 in 100,000. Responses are given in table 4.14.

Probability Concepts   In order to investigate people's ability to process simple probability information (as opposed to the relatively complex information contained in conditional probability statements – see Hammerton, 1973), Question 17 asked:

Imagine that you have to face two different risks of being killed:

in one, your risk of death is 2 in 100,000
in the other your risk of death is 20 in 100,000.

You cannot avoid either of these risks but you can choose to have one of them reduced. Which would you prefer:

Table 4.14 Respondents' estimates of motorcycle and bus/coach fatalities

	Actual	*Mean*	*Median*
Motorcyclists	75 in 10^5	1,874 in 10^5 ($\pm$3,287)	30 in 10^5 (+4) (−5)
Bus and coach passengers	< 1 in 10^5	26 in 10^5 ($\pm$15)	5 in 10^5 ($\pm$1)

Table 4.15 Preferences between probability reductions

Prefer 2 in 10^5 reduced to 1 in 10^5(%)	*Prefer 20 in 10^5 reduced to 15 in 10^5(%)*	*Don't know(%)*
47 ($\pm$5)	48($\pm$5)	5 ($\pm$2)

Table 4.16 Proportions of consistent and inconsistent responses to Question 25

Consistent (%)	*Inconsistent(%)*
75 ($\pm$4)	25 ($\pm$4)

the risk of 2 in 100,000 reduced to 1 in 100,000
the risk of 20 in 100,000 reduced to 15 in 100,000?

The results are given in table 4.15.

Coherence In order to investigate the extent of people's conformity with the standard axioms of expected utility theory in situations which do not involve the assimilation of relatively complicated probability information, respondents were asked about their preferences in a sequence of three simple pairwise choices (Question 25).[15] The results are shown in table 4.16.

Overall Consistency Scores The questionnaire contained six separate consistency or perception tests. These consisted of the following:

1 Two tests of the consistency of respondents' relative valuation of different risk reductions or increments, e.g. respondents who reported lower willingness to pay for larger risk reductions in multi-part valuation questions were treated as inconsistent (Questions 18 and 20).
2 Two tests of the quality of respondents' estimates of the relative magnitudes of accident rates for different transport modes –

Table 4.17   Frequency distribution of overall consistency scores

Consistency score	Cumulative frequency (%)
0	0.0
0.5	0.0
1.0	0.1
1.5	0.4
2.0	1.8
2.5	3.2
3.0	7.7
3.5	10.9
4.0	19.5
4.5	27.0
5.0	42.9
5.5	50.7
6.0	70.5
6.5	74.9
7.0	84.6
7.5	89.0
8.0 (maximum)	100.00

respondents who estimated motorcycle deaths as fewer than bus/coach deaths in Question 13 and respondents who estimated the motorcycle fatality rate as less than the car fatality rate in Question 15 were all treated as inconsistent.

3   A test of respondents' ability to compare two different changes in the probability of a given event (Question 17).
4   A test of respondents' conformity with the standard axioms of rational choice under uncertainty or 'coherence' (Question 25).

In order to get a feel for the degree of consistency of a subject's responses taken as a whole, it was decided to construct an 'overall consistency score' for each respondent. In our judgement, the last two of the six consistency tests described above were qualitatively more important than the first four so that, in the interests of simplicity, we decided to award *one* point for each consistent response to the first four tests and *two* points for each consistent response to the last two tests. When a consistency test could not be conducted because of a non-response to a particular question, we awarded a score equal to the mid-range (i.e. 0.5 for the first four tests and 1 for the last two). The distribution of consistency scores for the full sample is given in table 4.17.

4.3.3   Other Questions

Question 1 asked whether the respondent thought that over the past ten years the risk of car drivers and passengers being killed on Britain's roads

Table 4.18   Beliefs concerning the time trend of risks to car drivers and passengers

Increased (%)	Decreased (%)	Same (%)	Don't know (%)
78 (±4)	5 (±2)	15 (±3)	2 (±1)

Table 4.19   Beliefs concerning the effect of compulsory seat-belt legislation

Reduce risk (%)	Increase risk (%)	No difference (%)	Don't know (%)
69 (±4)	5 (±2)	23 (±4)	3 (±2)

Table 4.20   Attitudes to re-testing of car drivers

Should be re-tested (%)	Should not be re-tested (%)	Don't know (%)
76 (±4)	23 (±4)	1 (±1)

had increased, decreased, or stayed much the same. The responses are given in table 4.18.

Question 2 asked what effect the respondent thought the compulsory wearing of seat-belts would have on the risk of death for car drivers and passengers. The results are shown in table 4.19.

Question 19, concerning the possibility of additional driving tests, was originally intended to provide estimates of marginal rates of substitution of wealth for risk. Although this was found to be impractical in the course of piloting, the question was retained because respondents appeared to enjoy the opportunity to give their views on this subject and the question was therefore judged to be valuable in establishing a rapport between interviewer and respondent. Question 19(a) asked whether the respondent thought that drivers should be re-tested at certain intervals after passing the driving test. The responses are given in table 4.20.

For those who thought that drivers should be re-tested (or did not know), Question 19(b) told the respondent that currently the driving test costs the driver about £15. The respondent was then asked whether he thought it reasonable that drivers should be re-tested at age 60. The responses are given in table 4.21.

In Question 19(c) those who thought it reasonable to re-test at 60 were asked whether they thought such a re-test would reduce the risk of car drivers being killed. The responses are given in table 4.22.

Those who thought the risk would be reduced were then asked in Question 19(d) to what level, having been reminded that the current risk

Table 4.21 Attitudes to re-testing at age 60

Reasonable (%)	Unreasonable (%)	Don't know (%)
89 (±3)	10 (±3)	1 (±1)

Table 4.22 Beliefs about the effectiveness of re-testing

Reduce risk (%)	No difference (%)	Don't know (%)
72 (±5)	26 (±5)	2 (±2)

to the average driver is 10 in 100,000. The mean response was 6.93 in 100,000 and the median 7.60 in 100,000.

Finally, in order to examine respondents' reactions to the questionnaire, two questions were put to the respondent at the end of the interview and three to the interviewer. The results are given in tables 4.23–4.26.

4.3.4 The Follow-up Survey

Questions in the follow-up survey, conducted on 210 of the original respondents, represented a graded sequence through:

- simple demographic question (age)
- more complex demographic question (social class)
- simple opinion question (Question 1: have risks to car drivers increased, decreased etc?)
- more difficult opinion question (Question 14(a): should we reduce deaths from motor accidents, heart disease or cancer?)
- valuation question (Question 14(b): willingness to pay for the reduction identified in Question 14(a)).

The percentages of the follow-up sample whose answers differed between the original and recall questions are given in table 4.27. Frequency distributions of absolute and percentage changes in response to Question 14(b) are shown in figures 4.2 and 4.3. While the distribution for absolute differences between responses is effectively symmetrical, with mean, median and mode in the interval $[-5, +5]$, the distribution of *percentage* changes in responses is, at first sight, more puzzling. However, given that responses are bounded below by zero but have no upper bound, it is clear that the percentage

$$\frac{\text{recall} - \text{original}}{\text{original}} \times 100$$

Table 4.23 Respondents' reactions to questionnaire

Question to respondent	All (%)	Most (%)	Some (%)	None (%)
How much of this interview have you found interesting?	32 (±4)	31 (±4)	31 (±4)	6 (±2)
How many of the questions did you find difficult to answer?	2 (±1)	10 (±3)	73 (±4)	15 (±3)

Table 4.24 Interviewers' assessments of respondents' interest in questionnaire

Question to interviewer	Generally interested (%)	Interested in some parts, not in others (%)	Generally uninterested (%)
How did the respondent react to the subject of the survey?	77 (±4)	18 (± 4)	5 (± 2)

Table 4.25 Interviewers' assessments of respondents' understanding of probability concepts

Question to interviewer	Yes (%)	No (%)	Intervewer uncertain (%)
In your opinion did the respondent understand the y in 100,000 risk concept?	79 (±4)	4 (±2)	17 (±4)

Table 4.26 Interviewers' assessments of respondents' ability to provide monetary valuations

Question to interviewer	Yes, quite unable to give value (%)	Yes, but gave values (%)	Yes, some questions but not others (%)	No (%)	Interviewer uncertain (%)
Did the respondent have difficulty in giving monetary values for the various changes in risk?	4 (±2)	32 (±4)	20 (±4)	43(±5)	1(±1)

Table 4.27   Percentages of responses differing between original and follow-up surveys

Age	Class	Q.1	Q.14(a)	Q.14(b)
2%	7%	20%	20%	57%

itself has a lower bound of -100 but *no* upper bound. Given a symmetrical distribution of absolute changes, one would therefore expect a right-skewed distribution of percentage changes. In turn, the bi-modal nature of the distribution is clearly a consequence of the fact that any pair of responses in which the recall was much smaller than the original would generate a percentage change equal or close to -100%.

4.4   Evaluation of Reliability of the Results

Before we can proceed to assess the policy implications of the results, it is necessary to form a view on the apparent veracity and reliability of the valuation responses and also on the apparent quality of perception of risk and ability to handle probability concepts.

At the first and most obvious level, the distribution of consistency scores shown in table 4.17 is quite encouraging. Respondents with a consistency score of 5 or more out of 8 form more than 70% of the sample. In order to score 5 or more, it is necessary *either* to be consistent on both of the more important consistency tests and one of the less important tests *or* to be consistent on one of the more important tests and three of the others.

4.4.1   Validity and Reliability of Valuation Responses

At a more detailed level, the valuation results show a number of interesting features. These are best dealt with in separate categories of estimated marginal rates of substitution, m_i, m_i^+, $\bar{m}_i$ and m_i^*.

Estimates of m_i   The estimates of m_i (marginal rates of substitution of wealth for *own* risk of death) indicate that for the sample as a whole the distribution of responses is heavily skewed in most questions. One cause of this is a few (usually between 1 and 7) outliers whose responses had been coded as, for example, 'would pay £10,000 or more'. Unfortunately, the code for this response differed in only one digit from the code for 'don't know' so that the responses could simply be cases of miscoding. Alternatively, these outliers might have been fanciful responses, not at all indicative of what the respondents concerned would truly be willing to pay. It was essentially for these reasons that it was decided to compute 'trimmed' means with these outliers removed. It is clear from table 4.5

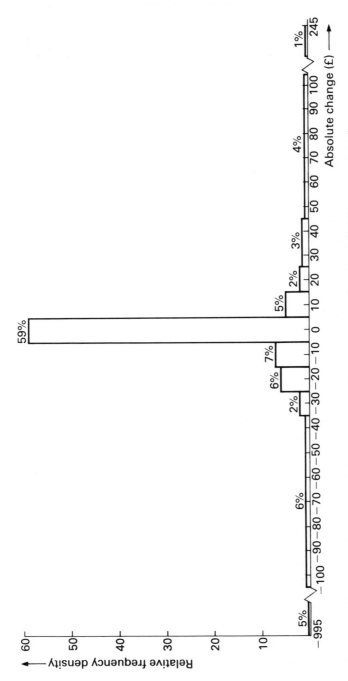

Figure 4.2 Frequency distribution of absolute changes in responses to Question 14(b) (recall − original).

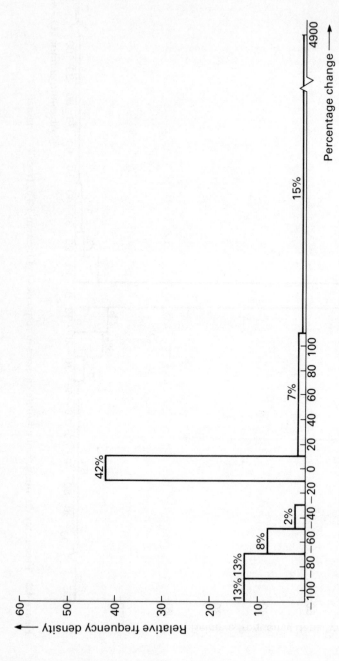

Figure 4.3 Frequency distribution of percentage changes in responses to Question 14(b) ((recall − original) × 100/original).

that the range of estimates of trimmed mean m_i from Questions 18(a), 18(b), 20(a) and 20(b) is substantially smaller than the range of estimates of mean m_i and that the range of estimates of median m_i is much smaller still. Indeed, the relatively compact range of estimates of median m_i (£1,240,000, £720,000, £500,000 and £770,000) encourages us to believe that respondents were, in the main, attempting to be truthful in their responses to these questions. Certainly, the nature of the valuation questions does appear to have had some effect upon the responses, as one would expect. In particular, Question 18, concerning the foreign coach journey, was deliberately constructed so as to involve a higher level of initial risk than would normally be encountered in car or coach travel in the UK. (A risk of 8 in 10^5 of dying in a coach journey of, say, 1,500 miles is approximately 30 times the risk of a corresponding journey in the UK.) The generally higher estimates of m_i from Question 18 therefore tend to confirm the theoretical prediction that marginal rates of substitution of wealth for physical risk will be an increasing function of initial risk.[16] Unfortunately, to quantify the relationship between m_i and initial risk we would have required many more valuation questions than could reasonably have been included in a single questionnaire.

Other arguments lend credence to the estimates of m_i from Questions 18 and 20. First, if respondents were simply guessing or 'pulling numbers out of the air' in their answers to valuation questions, then one would have expected responses *either* to show little variation between different valuation questions *or* to vary more or less randomly. In short, if the majority of respondents were guessing then one would not expect valuation responses to vary in the systematic way predicted by the theory summarized in Chapter 2. However, tables 4.5–4.8 indicate that on the whole the central tendency measures of valuation responses do vary in the way predicted by theory. In the first place, the results reported in table 4.4 clearly indicate that, far from being invariant between different questions, responses differed substantially and usually in the 'right' direction. In addition, estimates of the mean (and median) of m_i from the parts of Questions 18 and 20 relating to smaller reductions in risk are larger than the corresponding estimates from the parts involving larger risk reductions. This is precisely the relationship predicted by expected utility theory which implies that, under a wide range of conditions, willingness to pay will be a *strictly concave* function of risk reduction.[17] Furthermore, as explained below, the responses to Questions 18(c) and 18(d), involving compensation required for increases in risk, are also consistent with the predictions of theory.

If, on the other hand, valuation responses were systematically biased then the most obvious source of such bias would be misperception of risk. Suppose, for example, that in spite of the fact that they were told the size of the risks involved, respondents nonetheless tended to overestimate the risk of a fatal car accident in Question 20. The valuation responses (and hence estimates of m_i) would then tend to be biased upwards. Similar comments apply to systematic underestimation of risks. However, if this kind of bias was present, then one would expect a significant relationship between individual marginal rates of substitution derived from the responses to Question 20 and individual subjective estimates of car deaths in Question 13(a) (version 1) or motorcycle deaths in Question 13(a) (version 2). Regression analysis[18] revealed *no* significant relationships, suggesting that, in spite of their overestimation (or underestimation) of car or motorcycle deaths in Question 13, respondents nonetheless assimilated the risk information given in Question 20 and in consequence gave valuation responses that were largely free from bias due to misperception of risk. Regression analysis also indicated the absence of any significant relationship between valuation responses to Question 18 and subjective estimates of coach fatalities in Question 13.

The multiple regression analysis reported in tables 4.9 and 4.10 indicates apparently quite strong relationships between willingness to pay for safety improvement, income and age (an 'inverted-U' life-cycle) in some questions. Furthermore these relationships are essentially of the kind predicted by theory. We believe that, taken together, these regression results are not consistent with the hypothesis that respondents were generally either guessing or systematically misrepresenting their true willingness to pay.

The responses to Questions 18(c) and 18(d), involving risk *increases*, together with the theory underlying the willingness-to-pay approach, which predicts that individual compensating variation versus risk change functions will be strictly decreasing and concave, can also be used as a direct test of the estimates of m_i from 18(a) and 18(b). For example, consider the estimate of £720,000 for median m_i from 18(b). If valuation functions are decreasing and concave then required compensation for the risk increase in 18(c) (8×10^{-5}) should be *more* than £720,000 $\times$ 8 $\times$ 10^{-5} (i.e. £58) for at least 50% of respondents, and the required compensation for the risk increase in 18(d) (24×10^{-5}) should be *more* than £720,000 $\times$ 24 $\times$ 10^{-5}, i.e. £173. (The extent to which required compensation exceeds these numbers depends on the degree of concavity of the valuation function.) The fact that 81% of respondents were *not* willing to travel at all in 18(c) (implying that required compensation exceeded the fixed expenses of £200) and that 87% were unwilling to travel at all in 18(d) is therefore clear evidence in support of values of m_i as large as those derived from 18(a) and 18(b).

The responses to Question 21 can also be regarded as providing (admittedly somewhat weaker) support for the estimates from Questions 18 and 20, in that a majority of those who answered this question gave responses that implied values of $m_i^+ \geqslant$ £330,000.

The most disturbing feature of the valuation responses to Questions 18 and 20 is the relatively high proportion of respondents (42% on Question 18 and 47% on Question 20) who gave the *same* answers to questions involving two different reductions in a given base risk (fortunately, only about 10% of the sample moved in the *wrong* direction on these questions).[19] The first point to be made about these 'no change' responses is that almost half of those for Question 18 and a quarter of those for

Question 20 were *zero* responses. Since the psychological factors that produce a zero valuation response to one part of a given question are also likely to be at work on another part, these unchanged zero responses do not give serious cause for concern. However, unchanged *positive* responses are altogether more worrying. There would seem to be two possisble explanations for such responses. In the first place, it may be that in these cases the relevant valuation functions had become effectively 'flat' for the risk reductions considered. Alternatively, these really could be people who were either 'pulling numbers out of the air' or failing to assimilate the probability information given to them. Fortunately, the central tendency measures of the responses of those individuals who were entirely consistent on valuation questions (i.e. whose responses for larger risk changes exceeded their responses for smaller changes) were broadly similar to the remaining responses.[20] Furthermore, the responses of individuals with consistency scores of 5 or more out of the maximum possible 8 were also broadly similar to the remaining responses.

One might be tempted to think that the similarity between the valuation responses of apparently consistent respondents and those of the doubtful consistency respondents could be adduced *either* as evidence in favour of reliability of the doubtful respondents *or* as evidence detracting from reliability of the consistent respondents. However, we believe that this kind of argument, which essentially involves 'exoneration (or guilt) by association', is spurious for the following reasons. In the first place, with the exception of obviously absurd answers, the reliability of a *particular* person's response to a *particular* valuation question *cannot* be determined by reference to that response alone. Similarly (and again with the exception of obviously absurd answers), the reliability of a group of people's responses to a particular valuation question cannot be determined by reference to the frequency distribution of responses, and central tendency measures in particular. It follows that the *relative* reliability of two different people's (or groups') responses to a particular valuation question cannot be determined by a comparison of their responses.

In fact, an assessment of the reliability of a person's valuation responses can only be made by comparing his responses to two or more *different* questions (or his responses to the same question on two or more different occasions). It is by this legitimate criterion that the 'no change' responses to the various parts of Questions 18 and 20 appear to be of doubtful reliability. The real significance of the similarity between the central tendency measures of this group's responses and those of apparently consistent individuals is that it obviates the necessity to *weight* responses to take account of the relative reliability of the two groups.

Estimates of m_i^+ Estimates of m_i^+ (marginal rates of substitution of wealth for risk to self plus passengers) were derived from the responses to Question 20(c), and display much the same properties as the estimates of m_i from Questions 20(a) and 20(b), so that similar comments would seem to apply to their apparent reliability.

Estimates of $\bar{m}_i$ The estimates of $\bar{m}_i$ (marginal rates of substitution of wealth for risk to an 'average' passenger) are rather interesting. While the estimate of the mean of $\bar{m}_i$ is £500,000 (the trimmed mean is the same because there were no outliers), the estimate of median $\bar{m}_i$ is zero, reflecting the fact that 14% of the sample gave *lower* answers to Question 20(c) than to 20(a), implying a negative valuation of passenger safety (these responses must obviously be regarded as highly suspect), while a substantial number of respondents (47%) gave the same answers to Questions 20(a) and 20(c). We initially supposed that the latter might be predominantly drivers or unmarried. However, the proportions of these respondents who were drivers (61%) or unmarried (31%) are not significantly different from the corresponding proportions for the sample as a whole.

Estimates of m_i^*   Question 22 involved a safety improvement that was quite clearly a public good. It is therefore not at all surprising that the estimates of m_i^* (marginal rates of substitution of wealth for risk to self and everyone else) derived from this question are very low relative to estimates of m_i or m_i^+ from other questions, reflecting the usual non-revelation of preferences for public goods. This effect is, as one might expect, particularly marked in Question 22(a) which referred to a non-compulsory door-to-door collection (Question 22(b), by contrast, involved a fixed sum to be collected from every household.)

Taken as a whole, the estimates of m_i^* from Question 14(b) display enormous variability and clearly have a heavily skewed distribution with a large upper tail (the 22 largest responses contributed more than £10,000,000 to the overall mean of £20,340,000). To this extent, these must be regarded as the least reliable of all the estimates of marginal rates of substitution from the survey. It is also clear that the nature of the risk of greatest concern to the respondent has had a marked effect, with mean willingness to pay to reduce cancer deaths more than double that for road deaths (it should be recalled that respondents were asked how much they would be willing to pay to reduce by 100 the number of deaths next year *from the source of risk of greatest concern* – motor accidents, heart disease or cancer). Thus, while the overall mean and median of m_i^* for this question are substantially larger than mean and median marginal rates of substitution estimated from other valuation questions, the discrepancy is nowhere near as marked for those respondents reporting willingness to pay to reduce road deaths (as opposed to deaths from cancer or heart disease). In fact the lower bound of the interval estimate for the mean of m_i^* for this group is quite close to the larger estimates of the mean of m_i in table 4.5 and the difference is even less pronounced in the case of medians. Even so, these results are still rather puzzling because it would not be unreasonable to assume that, as in Question 22, the safety improvement involved here is also in the nature of a public good. However, two points may explain the discrepancy between the responses to Questions 14(b) and 22. First, as far as non-revelation effects are concerned, it must be remembered that in Question 14(b) respondents were asked how much they *individually* would contribute to reduce fatalities, no reference being made to contributions from anyone else or, for that matter, to the way contributions would be collected (in marked contrast with Question 22). This may explain why non-revelation effects, so obviously present in responses to Question 22, appear not to have arisen in Question 14(b). Secondly, Question 14(b) was in a very real sense different in kind from Question 22 in that it referred to the avoidance of a given number of deaths, whereas Question 22 explicitly involved (small) individual risk reductions.

Finally, the fact that such a large proportion of respondents opted for the avoidance of cancer deaths, coupled with the very large value of m_i^* implied by these responses, suggests that people are indeed markedly more averse to some causes of death rather than others and would be willing to pay very large sums to avoid the protracted period of physical and emotional suffering that precedes cancer death.

Drivers versus Non-drivers For the purposes of our study, non-drivers were defined as those who had not driven during the 12 month period prior to the survey and constituted 42% of the sample of full interviews. Since the majority of non-drivers, thus defined, did not hold a valid driving licence, there are clearly doubts about whether or not it is appropriate to treat non-drivers' responses to Questions 20(a) and 20(b) – which concern risks to car *drivers* – on a par with other responses. Three factors seem to us to be relevant in this connection. First, the questionnaire contained a clear instruction to interviewers to tell non-drivers to answer Question 20 *as if they were car drivers*. The second point is that the general insignificance of the 'missing mileage' dummy in the regression analysis suggests that there was, in fact, no significant difference between drivers' and non-drivers' responses in *any* of the valuation questions. Finally, in preliminary analysis, separate regressions were run for drivers and non-drivers and F tests for structural change rejected the hypothesis of a significant difference in *all* parts of Question 20.[21] All things considered, then, it would appear to be unnecessary to distinguish between the valuation responses of drivers and non-drivers.

The Effect of Prompts Breakdowns of the responses to valuation questions suggest that prompting had a significant effect on these responses. Non-parametric tests tend to confirm that this is so. In addition, it is clear that respondents requiring prompts (between 13% and 29% on Question 20 and 32% on Question 14(b)) generally gave lower values than those who did not need to be prompted. One possible explanation for this is that respondents requiring prompts were from lower income, social class or education groups. The results of chi-squared tests are mixed, but where these are significant they suggest that individuals from lower income, social class or education groups are more likely to require prompts.

Reported Tyre-change Behaviour One final piece of evidence appears to be pertinent to an assessmment of the validity and reliability of responses

Table 4.28   Claimed behaviour in changing tyres

Change tyres at the legal limit (including response when the garage tells me (%)	Change tyres above the legal limit (%)	Change tyres below the legal limit (%)	Don't know (%)
43	44	3	10

to the valuation of questions and, indeed, to the questionnaire as a whole. Question 21(a) asked respondents who were drivers ($n = 612$) whether they changed car tyres at, above or below the legal limit of tread depth. The responses from those drivers who claimed responsibility for the tyre change decision are shown in table 4.28.

These responses can be compared with results given in *TRRL Report LR449*, 'The Condition of Tyres in Use on Cars' (Lowne, 1972), based on a survey of car tyres carried out during 1969–70. The report concluded that

> . . . it appears that about 25% of tyres are changed only when the tread depth is less than 1 mm and 50% at 1 mm or more. The remaining 25% are changed because of irreparable damage. As a first approximation it may be assumed that the tyres failing prematurely are owned by drivers of the two classes postulated in 4.2 [those who change above and those who change below the legal limit of 1 mm] in the same proportions as the tyres changed because of tread wear. Thus the data are consistent with approximately one third of drivers being prepared to let their tyres wear until the tread depth is below 1 mm. (Lowne, 1972, p. 7)

The report enters the caveat that

> . . . although too many assumptions and simplifications have had to be introduced to permit any claims to be made for the accuracy of the results, they are probably of the right order of magnitude. (Lowne, 1972, p. 7)

Given that one would not expect many people to admit to illegal behaviour in answering a questionnaire, the proportions shown in table 4.28 appear to be broadly consistent with the findings of the TRRL report. However, given the life of modern car tyres, many people will change cars well before the tyres have worn to the legal limit so that for some respondents the tyre change decision is entirely hypothetical.

4.4.2   Quality of Perception of Risks

As with the valuation responses, there are both encouraging and discouraging features in the results relating to the quality of perception of transport risks and ability to handle probability concepts. First, the quality of respondents' perceptions of the *ordering* of transport risks is surprisingly high. Although the graph in figure 4.1 shows the kind of 'hysteresis' effects found over a wider range of risks by Slovic *et al.* (1981), the closeness between the actual and ideal average ranking scores suggests that most people have a good qualitative understanding of the relative risks of different transport modes. When we asked for quantitative estimates of relative risk, however, we obtained heavily skewed distributions of responses for version 1 respondents who were not provided with reference data. The mean responses are substantially above the true figures but the median responses are of the right order of magnitude.

The provision of reference data on car risk had an encouraging effect, the results shown in table 4.13 suggesting that provision of such data had a significant impact on the mean estimates of motorcycle and coach deaths but had little effect upon medians. However, when we applied non-parametric tests to the results, a Mann–Whitney test indicated *no* significant difference at the 5% level between the responses to the two versions of the questionnaire, whereas a Kolmogorov–Smirnov test did indicate a significant difference, especially in estimates of motocycle deaths. These results imply that, while there is no significant difference between the medians of the two distributions of responses, the distributions *are* significantly different in other respects. Inspection of the frequency distributions themselves shows that the provision of reference data produces a substantial reduction in the spread of the distributions, especially in the upper tail.

In short, without reference data, individual estimates of transport risks are widely spread but have medians that are not too seriously biased. Provision of reference data appears to cause these estimates to concentrate more closely around the true figures, leaving medians largely unaffected. Thus, given that all the valuation questions included reference data concerning the magnitude of risks, it seems reasonable to suppose that the provision of these data will have served the intended purpose of minimizing variability in valuation responses owing to misperception of risk. The absence of a significant relationship between individual valuation responses and subjective estimates of the number of transport deaths given in response to Question 13 lends further support to this view.

When we examine the results of Question 17, intended to test for ability to compare probabilities, and Question 25, intended to test for coherence, the picture becomes more cloudy. While a substantial majority of respondents displayed coherence, a disappointingly large proportion gave what is, *prima facie*, the 'wrong' answer to the probability question. These results are clearly in stark contrast with each other and lead one to wonder whether there is some explanation for the responses to Question 17. Of the various possible explanations, two seem most plausible. First, in spite of the fact that the question stressed that the respondent had to face both risks, it may be that some people failed to register this point and thought that they were ultimately being asked whether they would rather face a risk of 1 in 10^5 or 15 in 10^5, in which case selection of the first option would be entirely rational.[22] Secondly, some respondents may have treated the risks as *multiplicative* rather than additive. This would not be entirely unreasonable, because the question did not (for obvious reasons) say that the events which would involve death under each of the two risks were 'mutually exclusive'. If a respondent had supposed that the events involved were in fact *independent* and that death would result only if both occurred together (i.e. that a train in which the respondent is travelling crashes *and* he happens to be in the coach in which fatalities occur) then again it would be quite rational to prefer to have the risk of 2 in 10^5 halved rather than the risk of 20 in 10^5 reduced to 15 in 10^5 (if the events involved are independent then halving the smaller risk would give an overall risk of death of 20×10^{-10} whereas reducing the larger risk would give an overall risk of 30×10^{-10}).

Although we are not entirely convinced by either of these arguments, they do represent plausible explanations for what is, at face value, one of the more disappointing results of the survey.

4.4.3   NOP's Comments on Reliability of the Results

In assessing the reliability and credibility of our results, it seems relevant to consider the views expressed in NOP's *Fieldwork Report* submitted following completion of the main and follow-up surveys. Broadly speaking, NOP's main conclusions were that

1   contrary to their initial fears, the survey was generally successful in avoiding alienation on the part of respondents (or interviewers) and in maintaining their interest and willingness to participate,
2   the survey was generally successful in getting across the probabilistic concept of risk, and
3   the survey was somewhat less successful in eliciting reliable valuation responses.

We agree with the first of these conclusions. Indeed, the success of the questionnaire in eliciting responses surprised us less than it did NOP, simply because it confirmed our experience in the feasibility study and in early piloting. However, we are somewhat less sanguine than NOP about the success of the survey in getting across the risk concept and rather *more* optimistic about the reliability of valuation responses. NOP's evaluation of respondents' performance with the risk concept is based largely, if not exclusively, on respondents' and interviewers' answers to the question asking how well or badly they had coped. Certainly, these responses are encouraging, but the results of the questions concerning perception of transport risks, comparison of probability reductions and coherence are also relevant to this issue. As we have argued, these results are rather less clear-cut.

On the subject of the valuation questions, the NOP report argues that the responses to Question 18 (about the coach trip) reveal some 'rotation' effects from the order of presentation of the four parts of the question,

Table 4.29   Results of tests for the significance of rotation effects

Question	Mann–Whitney test for differences in distributions	Kolmogorov–Smirnov test for differences in distributions
18(a)	Significant	Significant
18(b)	Significant	Significant
18(c)	Insignificant	Insignificant
18(d)	Insignificant	Significant
20(a)	Significant	Insignificant
20(b)	Significant	Significant
20(c)	Significant	Insignificant

but that there would appear to be no rotation effects in the responses to the various parts of Question 20 (about the car safety feature). However, NOP's comments seem to be based on inspection of the data without formal tests of significance. In fact, Mann–Whitney and Kolmogorov–Smirnov tests give the results shown in Table 4.29 concerning significance of rotation effects at the 5% level. Thus, while there is unequivocal evidence of rotation effects in Questions 18(a), 18(b) and 20(b) and little, if any, in 18(c), the evidence in other cases is somewhat mixed. These findings, together with inspection of the results broken down by the two versions of the questionnaire, suggest that, while the order of presentation of multipart valuation questions did have some effect upon responses, these effects were not large enough to cause serious concern.

NOP also appears to be rather disturbed by the relationship between the original and follow-up responses to Question 14(b). We do not share this concern. First, the results in tables 4.4–4.8 indicate that 14(b) is by far the least reliable of the valuation questions. (Though it was thus an unfortunate choice for the follow-up study, neither we nor NOP had any way of knowing this at the time at which it was decided which question to use in that study.) Secondly, NOP's comments are again not based on any formal test of significance of the difference between original and recall responses but simply on a comparison of the extent of movement in responses to this question with movements in other (non-valuation) responses. It is not surprising that the differences between original and recall responses to a valuation question are greater than in responses to questions concerning age, social class or opinions. Furthermore, although the spread of these differences is large, they are distributed about zero with a very sharp peak. It is also the case that a Wilcoxon matched-pairs, signed-ranks test fails to reject the hypothesis that original and recall responses to Question 14(b) are identically distributed.

4.4.4   Summary of the Evidence Concerning Credibility

The various results enhancing and detracting from the credibility of the estimates of marginal rates of substitution and, indeed, other responses to the questionnaire are summarized in table 4.30. Clearly, it would be inappropriate simply to regard the case in favour of credibility as having been established by the fact that the number of positive points in table 4.30 outweighs the number of negatives: one must also consider the question of the qualitative importance of the various pieces of evidence and this is ultimately a matter of personal judgement. Our view is that the balance of the arguments and evidence is in favour of regarding the estimates of marginal rates of substitution of wealth for physical risk derived from the responses to Questions 18 and 20 as an adequate indication of the order of magnitude of the 'true' rates of substitution. Taken as a whole, and with some notable exceptions, the valuation results display an overall pattern and degree of conformity with the predictions of theory and the dictates of commonsense that would be highly improbable if people were generally muddled about the more basic and elementary notions of probability, or prone to mendacity or mere randomness in their answers to valuation questions. Certainly, the first and third points in the negative column of table 4.30 are rather disturbing, but in neither case was it a clear majority of respondents that gave implausible or 'wrong' responses and in any case, as we have already noted, estimates of marginal rates of substitution for this subsample do not appear to be markedly different from the estimates derived from the sample as a whole.

Finally, we are encouraged by the fact that the order of magnitude of our estimates of mean marginal rates of substitution of wealth for own risk, m_i, are broadly consistent with those reported in Marin and Psacharopoulos (1982) which is the most recent and comprehensive 'revealed preference' study carried out to date in the UK.

4.5 Policy Implications

If our evaluation of the reliability of the results is accepted, then it seems to us that six clear policy implications follow. These concern:

- The definition of 'serious' injury.
- The relative values of the avoidance of serious and fatal injury.
- The appropriateness or otherwise of including allowances for police, damage and other resource costs, as well as losses of net output, in the definition of values of safety.
- The relative values of avoidance of 'statistical' and 'anonymous' death.
- The magnitude of the value of statistical life.
- The relationship between individual valuation of safety, age and income and the implied effects of distributional weighting.

The remainder of this section considers these policy implications in more detail.

Table 4.30 Summary of the various results enhancing and detracting from the credibility of estimated marginal rates of substitution

Results enhancing credibility	*Results detracting from credibility*
1 High proportion of respondents scoring 5 or more out of 8 on consistency tests	1 42% of respondents giving same valuation response for different risk reductions in Questions 18(a)/(b) and 47% in Questions 20(a)/(b). However, of these, 18% and 13% respectively were zero responses
2 Broadly similar nature of distributions of estimates of m_i from Questions 18(a), 18(b), 20(a) and 20(b)	
3 Relationship between central tendency measures of valuation responses to Question 18(a)/(b) and 20(a)/20(b) in accord with the predictions of theory (i.e. strictly decreasing, strictly concave function of p_t – see Chapter 3).	2 8% of respondents moving in 'wrong' direction in Questions 18(a)/(b), 11% in Questions 20(a)/(b) and 14% in Questions 20(a)/(c)
	3 47% of respondents giving 'wrong' answer to the probability question
	4 High variability of responses to Question 14(b)
4 Supporting evidence for estimates of m_i provided by proportions of respondents 'unwilling to travel' in 18(c) and 18(d) and who would change tyres at ≥ 2 mm in 21(c)	5 Some evidence of 'rotation' effects in multipart valuation questions (18 and 20)
5 Regression results, especially for Questions 20(a), 20(b) and 20(c) in accord with predictions of theory	6 Large spread of the distribution of differences between original and recall responses to Question 14(b)
6 Generally accurate qualitative perception of relative transport risks in Question 11	
7 Apparent effectiveness of risk 'reference data' in reducing variability of estimates of fatality rates	
8 Absence of significant relationship between individual valuation responses to Question 20(a) and subjective estimates of transport fatalities in Question 13, suggesting that valuation responses not biased by misperception of transport risks	
9 High proportion of respondents 'coherent' in Question 25	
10 Symmetry and central tendency of the distribution of differences between original and recall responses to Question 14(b). Also no significant difference between original and recall responses to	

Table 4.30   (Continued)

Results enhancing credibility	*Results detracting from credibility*
Question 14(b) on Wilcoxon matched-pairs, signed-ranks test	
11 Broad correspondence between responses to tyre change question (21(a)) and results of TRRL survey of tyre tread thickness	
12 Respondents' and interviewers' generally favourable comments on understanding of probability concept and ease of providing valuation responses	

4.5.1   The Definition of Serious Injury

Given the results reported in table 4.1, the Department of Transport should re-define its category of 'serious injury' to *exclude* injuries that are not permanent and involve only short stays in hospital.

4.5.2   The Value of Avoidance of Serious Injury

The results reported in table 4.2 indicate that rather more than 50% of the population have marginal rates of substitution of wealth for risk of serious injury that are more than one-hundredth of the corresponding rate of substitution for risk of death. This, together with the fact that some categories of serious injury were viewed by a substantial proportion of respondents as being 'as bad as or worse than death', suggests that values of avoidance of serious injury should be *at least* one-hundredth of the corresponding values of avoidance of statistical death.

4.5.3   Resource Costs and Losses of Net Output

If the Department of Transport can be persuaded to abandon its current output-based definition of the cost of accidents and the value of accident prevention in favour of a willingness-to-pay definition, then the fact that so few respondents appear to have taken account of the resource costs of accidents and effects on net output (see table 4.11) suggests that it *will* be appropriate to include an allowance for such effects in the definition of the value of statistical life, as suggested in Chapter 1.

4.5.4   Values of Statistical and Anonymous Life

The results reported in table 4.12 indicate that respondents are about equally split in their preferences between the avoidance of 'statistical' and 'anonymous' deaths. This suggests that the Department of Transport need not be too concerned by the question of whether the risk reductions afforded by a particular safety improvement are, or are not, independent of each other and that the principal focus should be, as it is at present, on the *expected* number of accidents avoided. In particular, there seems to be no clear majority preference for compact as opposed to widely spread distributions of the number of accidents avoided, given that the identities of potential victims are unknown.[23]

4.5.5   The Value of Statistical Life

Although Questions 14(b), 18, 20 and 22 all provide estimates of mean marginal rates of substitution, it is our view that most weight should be given to the estimates derived from Question 20 and, to a somewhat lesser degree, those from Question 18. Question 22 was designed to test for non-revelation of preferences in the case of safety improvements that are obviously public goods and was never intended to form the basis for obtaining estimates of the value of statistical life. Question 14(b) is different in kind from the other valuation questions since it relates to the saving of anonymous lives rather than risk changes and since for 76% of respondents the relevant cause of death was cancer rather than road accidents. In addition, the distribution of responses to Question 14(b) suggests that these responses were substantially less reliable than those for other questions. Finally, wherever the estimates derived from Questions 18 and 20 conflict, those from Question 20 should be given greater weight simply because Question 18 referred to foreign rather than UK travel and had a base risk that was deliberately set well above the corresponding level for the UK.

Conventional cost–benefit analysis (without distributional weights) requires that the value of statistical life should be defined in terms of the population mean of individual marginal rates of substitution together with resource cost and net output components (see Chapter 1). However, we are disinclined to recommend that the value of statistical life be based on mean marginal rates of substitution, largely because means may have been artificially inflated, either by coding errors or by fanciful responses on the part of a very few respondents and also because of the highly skewed nature of the distribution of valuation responses.

Instead, we believe that the value of statistical life should be based upon estimates of either the *trimmed* mean *or* the median values of m_i, m_i^+ and $\bar{m}_i$ obtained from the various parts of Questions 20 and, with less emphasis, 18. The case in favour of using trimmed means is essentially that this would represent an attempt to get at the value appropriate for a conventional cost–benefit analysis without allowing the more blatantly 'suspect' responses to bias the estimates. The case against trimming is that there is a certain arbitrariness about what one treats as 'suspect'. Since the estimates of the trimmed mean of m_i from 18(a) and 18(b) lie between those from 20(a) and 20(b) there is no obvious conflict between these estimates, and it would seem appropriate simply to take their average which is £1,600,000. To this it would be necessary – subject to the caveats discussed in Chapter 2, section 2.1.7 – to add the mean marginal rate of substitution of wealth for risk to other people, $\bar{m}_i$, the major component of which will presumably be for risk to family and friends. The estimate of the trimmed mean of $\bar{m}_i$ from Question 20(a) and 20(c) is £500,000. Adding this to the average of the four estimates of the trimmed mean of m_i gives an overall value of statistical life (excluding real re-source and net output components) of £2,100,000 in 1982 prices.

Alternatively, one could depart somewhat from strict adherence to the requirements of utilitarian welfare economics and conventional cost–benefit analysis and proceed instead along lines implied by more direct considerations of democracy and majority voting. Suppose, in particular, that the public could be led to an understanding of the meaning of a 'value of statistical life' and the manner in which such a value would be used in the process of allocative decision making. It is then clear that given the highly right–skewed nature of the frequency distributions of marginal rates of substitution, a majority of people would regard the value of statistical life implied by mean m_i as being *too high*. In short, setting the value of statistical life at this level would result in a situation in which a minority of people with high marginal rates of substitution would be 'dominating' an unwilling majority. In addition, given the difficulty of identifying those with higher marginal rates of substitution, there would be no way of arranging for compensating taxes and transfers. This leads one to wonder what value of statistical life would *not* meet with majority disapproval – or, more accurately, which value would command majority support in comparison with any other particular value. The answer is, of course, the value implied by the *median* of m_i, by the standard 'median-voter' type of argument.[24]

A further possible reason for focusing on the median of m_i rather than on the mean is that this is the value to which the latter would tend in a progressive process of trimming the top and bottom of the frequency distribution of m_i. The argument for this sort of trimming (rather than removing only those responses that look like coding errors) is that in a survey of this kind extreme responses, both very small (including zero) and very large, are a priori more suspect than moderate responses. This raises the question of how far it is appropriate to go in the process of progressive trimming. Figures 4.4 and 4.5 show the way in which values of mean m_i, m_i^+ and $\bar{m}_i$ vary with x when the bottom $x\%$ and top $x\%$ of observations are removed from the distributions of responses for the various parts of Questions 18 and 20.[25] In all cases, it is clear that, by the time the bottom 15% and top 15% of responses have been removed, the means of the remaining marginal rates of substitution have already moved substantially closer to the median of the original distribution than to the original trimmed mean. Thus, even if one rejects the majority voting kind of argument, there are nonetheless cogent reasons for setting values of statistical life at levels closer to the median of m_i than to the trimmed mean.

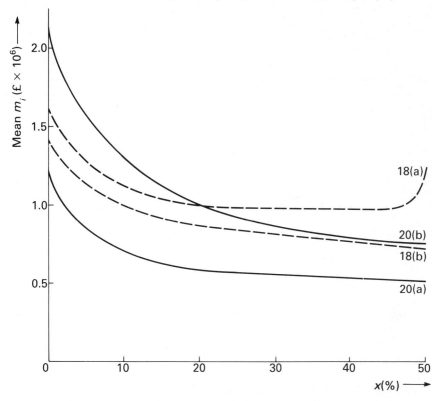

Figure 4.4 Mean of m_i after removal of the bottom $x\%$ and top $x\%$ of observations – 'own life' questions.

In fact, the estimates of the median of m_i from Questions 18(a) and 18(b), are, taken together, somewhat higher than those from Questions 20(a) and 20(b), but as with trimmed means the discrepancy does not appear to be sufficient to warrant differential weighting and the position can again be summarized in terms of the average of the four estimates which is £810,000. Notice that since the estimate of median $\tilde{m}_i$ given in table 4.7 is zero, it would seem inappropriate to augment the median of $\tilde{m}_i$ to reflect willingness to pay for other people's safety.

All of these are very large numbers. In addition, the estimate of the value of statistical life based on trimmed means is more than twice that based on medians. This difference is due in large part to the highly skewed nature of the distribution of individual marginal rates of substitution.[26] Thus, selection of an appropriate value of statistical life is not a question of choice between estimators of a given parameter but, rather, is a choice concerning the appropriate statistic to use as a summary

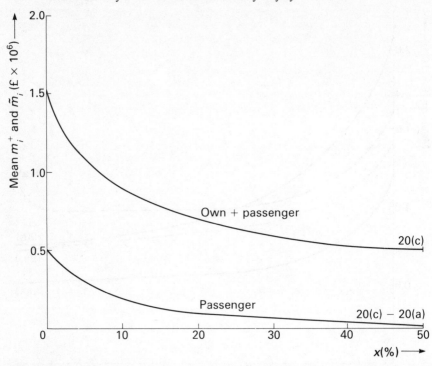

Figure 4.5   Mean of m_i^+ and $\tilde{m}_i$ after removal of the bottom $x\%$ and top $x\%$ of observations – 'own plus passenger's life' and 'passenger's life' questions.

description of the distribution of individual marginal rates of substitution. As we have already said, if values of safety are to be defined in strict accordance with the principles of conventional social cost–benefit analysis without distributional weights, then by the argument developed in Chapter 1 the value of statistical life should be based on the (trimmed) mean of individual marginal rates of substitution. If, by contrast, one wished to base decisions about transport safety on values that would command majority support in relation to any proposed alternative, then the median would seem to be the more appropriate statistic. Finally, it has been shown that if one elects to adopt a more draconian form of trimming involving the removal of the bottom $x\%$ and top $x\%$ of the distributions, then even with relatively modest values of x the mean of the 'top and tailed' distributions will be significantly closer to the median than to the original (more modestly) trimmed mean.[27]

In summary, we feel considerable confidence in asserting that unless one rejects the results of the survey out of hand, then whether trimmed means or medians are used there would appear to be a very strong case indeed in favour of setting the value of statistical life *no lower than*

£500,000 in 1982 prices (the lowest estimate of the median of m_i in Table 4.5). Indeed the evidence points towards a value of nearer £800,000 if medians are held to be the appropriate basis for the calculation and a value of £1,700,000 (i.e. 80% of £2,100,000)[28] if trimmed means are used. These values are all in mid-1982 prices and updated to 1987 become, in round terms, respectively, £600,000, £1,000,000 and £2,000,000. All of these figures are, of course, exclusive of any allowance for the avoidance of real resource costs and net output losses.

It is clear, therefore, that the range of results generated by our study is remarkably similar to the range of estimates taken *across* the various different studies carried out to date and summarized in Chapter 2.

4.5.6 The Relationship between Values of Safety, Income and Age

The regression results reported in section 4.3 also have potentially significant policy implications, the most important of which are associated with the relationship between individual marginal rates of substitution, household income and age. For Questions 18(a) and 18(b) the regression coefficients of income do not differ significantly from zero at the 5% level. However, for the various parts of Question 20 the income coefficients are, in the main, highly significant[29] and for reasons given above we are inclined to give rather more weight to the estimates from this question. The implied income elasticities for m_i from Question 20 (calculated at average income) range from about 0.3 to 0.5, which is consistent with the empirical estimate given by Blomquist (1979) and also with that implied by regression results reported by Smith and Desvousges (1987). While these results confirm the theoretical prediction that safety is a normal good (see, for example, Jones-Lee, 1976) it may seem surprising that the elasticities are so modest. However, it should be borne in mind that these are elasticities for *very* large marginal rates of substitution, so that, in spite of the fact that the elasticities themselves are relatively small, they nonetheless imply substantial absolute increases in the value of statistical life per £1,000 increase in annual household income. For example, with m_i equal to £1,500,000, an income elasticity of 0.4 implies that an increase in annual household income from £7,000 to £8,000 will raise m_i by over £85,000 (or, equivalently, that willingness to pay for a 1 in 10^5 reduction in risk for the coming year will rise from £15.00 to over £15.85).

All of this suggests that it may be important to take explicit account of distributional considerations in the cost–benefit analysis of transport safety, though the question of precisely how this should be done is clearly a matter for political judgement. Nonetheless, it would be illuminating to explore the way in which various different distributional adjustments would affect the value of statistical life. Accordingly, we have performed two separate sets of calculations related to the distribution of income:

1 We have computed the effect upon the unweighted aggregate willingness-to-pay values of statistical life implied by the responses

to the various parts of Questions 18 and 20 under the hypothesis of a redistribution of income to *complete equality* and a non-linear specification of the relationship between marginal rates of substitution and income.[30]

2   We have computed values of statistical life for Questions 18 and 20 based upon *distributionally weighted* aggregate willingness to pay using weights that are *inversely related to income*.

More specifically, the weights in 2 were defined as follows. Denote by Y_i the ith respondent's household income from all sources before tax. Let $X_i = (Y_i)^{-n}$, $n > 0$. Distributional weights a_i were then defined as $a_i = X_i/\bar{X}_i$, where $\bar{X}_i$ is the sample mean of X_i.[31] Notice that with distributional weights defined in this way their mean value, taken over the sample, will be precisely equal to unity. It seems to us to be essential to ensure that any distributional weighting scheme, *applied to a particular cost or value in isolation*, should satisfy this property. This is so because if the weights had a mean that was, say, greater than unity, then the cost or value to which the weighting scheme was applied would receive an unwarranted upward bias in relation to other (unweighted) costs and values, including values of statistical life computed on an unweighted basis. The necessity to ensure that distributional weights have a mean of unity does not, of course, arise if the weighting scheme is applied *simultaneously* to all the costs and benefits involved in the appraisal of a particular project or group of projects.[32]

For illustrative purposes distributionally weighted values of statistical life were computed for $n = 1, 2, 4, 6, 8$ and 10.

The results of the various distributional experiments are reported in table 4.31. Values of statistical life based on unweighted (trimmed) mean marginal rates of substitution are also shown for comparison. The effects of these distributional adjustments can hardly be described as dramatic, at least for the smaller values of n, and do little to alter our earlier conclusion concerning the appropriate order of magnitude of the value of statistical life.

As far as the relationship between marginal rates of substitution and age are concerned, the results for the various parts of Questions 18 and 20 are encouragingly consonant with the predictions of theory and the dictates of commonsense. In the first place, on the hypothesis that marginal rates of substitution are an increasing function of wealth, a simple life-cycle theory of individual wealth – defined as net assets plus human capital (equal to discounted expected future labour income) – predicts that, quite apart from other age-related variations in attitudes to physical risk, marginal rates of substitution will themselves tend to follow an 'inverted-U' life-cycle. At a somewhat more sophisticated level, Shepard and Zeckhauser (1982), using a discounted utility of lifetime consumption model, have also derived 'inverted-U' life-cycle results. Furthermore, Arthur (1981), using a steady-state growth model (see Chapter 2), predicts that marginal rates of substitution will tend to be declining function

Table 4.31 Values of statistical life from various distributional experiments (£-sterling, 1982)[a]

	Own life				Own plus passengers' lives	Average passenger's life
	18(a)	18(b)	20(a)	20(b)	20(c)	20(a)/(c)
Unweighted aggregation	1,600,000	1,390,000	1,210,000	2,210,000	1,500,000	500,000
Unweighted aggregation with redistribution to complete equality	1,680,000	1,390,000	1,210,000	2,210,000	1,500,000	500,000
Weighted aggregation $a_i = X_i/\bar{X}_i, X_i = (Y_i)^{-1}$	1,390,000	1,200,000	940,000	1,770,000	1,230,000	430,000
Weighted aggregation $a_i = X_i/\bar{X}_i, X_i = (Y_i)^{-2}$	1,310,000	1,080,000	750,000	1,490,000	1,020,000	390,000
Weighted aggregation $a_i = X_i/\bar{X}_i, X_i = (Y_i)^{-4}$	1,180,000	910,000	590,000	1,250,000	830,000	350,000
Weighted aggregation $a_i = X_i/\bar{X}_i, X_i = (Y_i)^{-6}$	1,130,000	850,000	540,000	1,180,000	770,000	340,000
Weighted aggregation $a_i = X_i/\bar{X}_i, X_i = (Y_i)^{-8}$	1,110,000	830,000	530,000	1,170,000	760,000	340,000
Weighted aggregation $a_i = X_i/\bar{X}_i, X_i = (Y_i)^{-10}$	1,100,000	830,000	530,000	1,160,000	750,000	330,000

[a] All cases of suspect coding have been removed.

of age with m_i falling by roughly 50% between the ages of 20 and 50. However, this model does not allow for variation in annual income over the life-cycle and one suspects that if such variation were introduced, with income growing in early working years, then the steady decline of m_i with age might well be replaced by a tendency for m_i to rise initially and then subsequently to fall, as in the 'inverted-U' cycle.

Finally, Cropper and Sussman (1985, 1987), using a model similar to that employed by Shepard and Zeckhauser, but extended to incorporate a head of household's concern for the consumption of his dependants, predict that m_i will decline with age beyond early adulthood, falling to a level at or close to zero by about age 90.

Theoretical considerations therefore provide rather strong grounds for expecting that m_i will follow some sort of life-cycle, peaking between early adulthood and middle age and falling off quite rapidly thereafter. The estimated regression coefficients for Questions 18(a), 18(b), 20(a) and 20(b) reported in tables 4.9 and 4.10 offer some support for this theoretical prediction. In particular, while the coefficient of 'age minus mean age all squared' tends to be negative and highly significant, 'age minus mean age' itself is generally insignificant. This means that for our sample m_i did indeed follow an 'inverted-U' life-cycle of the type predicted by theory. For illustration, figure 4.6 shows the relationship between m_i and age implied by the regression results for all responses (zero and positive) for Question 20(a). The graph is plotted only for ages above 16 – the minimum required for inclusion in our sample; extrapolation to ages below this minimum is almost certainly unwarranted. We have also refrained from completing the graph at the upper end of the age spectrum because of doubts about the relative reliability of valuation responses in this age range (it will be recalled that, of the 47 interviews terminated before completion, most were abandoned because the respondents were old and could not cope with the more difficult questions).

It is not for us to say precisely how these results should be incorporated in decisions about public sector expenditure on safety improvement. However, the evidence of a significant relationship between valuation of safety and age is so strong as to convince us that, if it is important to take explicit account of distributional considerations in public sector safety decisions, then one ought also to consider how such decisions affect the safety of different age groups.

4.6   Summary and Concluding Comments

This chapter has presented and analysed the results of a nationally representative sample survey of individual perception and valuation of transport safety. Given the wide variety of issues addressed by the survey, it seems inappropriate to attempt to provide a comprehensive summary of all the results. In this concluding section we shall therefore limit ourselves to drawing out what we consider to be the three most significant *general* findings of the study.

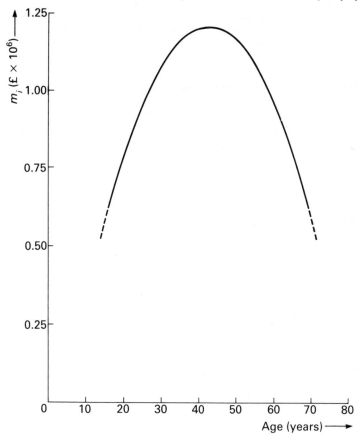

Figure 4.6 m_i versus age for Question 20(a) (all responses).

In our view, the first important lesson to be learned from this exercise is that, in spite of the gravity and difficulty of some of the questions involved, the survey proved to be feasible. In particular, a substantial majority of respondents appear not to have been offended by the questionnaire, to have found it generally interesting, and, finally, to have attempted to answer it in a sensible and careful manner. Undoubtedly, the skill and patience of the NOP interviewers – and the fact they had been extensively briefed prior to the survey by an NOP executive[33] – contributed substantially to the success of the survey in generating answers to the questions put to respondents.

The second important general conclusion to emerge from the study is that, as had been feared, a number of respondents experienced difficulty with the valuation questions and risk concepts and in some cases gave apparently inconsistent answers. While various factors detailed in section 4.4 lead us to believe that these do not constitute adequate grounds for rejecting the results of the study out of hand, we do think that they warrant the exercise of some caution in the interpretation of results. Furthermore, the evidence of inconsistency on the part of some respondents suggests that in future studies of this sort it will be most important to make provision for 'follow-up' interviews in order to probe respondents for the reasons for apparent inconsistencies.

Finally, to the extent that one is persuaded that the results of the survey are sufficiently reliable to permit the inference of at least the broad order of magnitude of the value of statistical life for transport risks, then these results point towards values of safety that are substantially larger than those currently employed by the UK Department of Transport. In particular, we believe that our results very strongly support the conclusion that, in 1987 prices, the value of statistical life for transport risks should be, at a minimum, £600,000 and more probably well in excess of £1,000,000. Furthermore, these values appear to be relatively robust with respect to other than very extreme forms of distributional weighting.

Notes

1 My co-authors are, respectively, members of the Health Care Research Unit, University of Newcastle upon Tyne and the Health Services Research Unit, University of Aberdeen. We acknowledge our debt to Max Hammerton and Vicki Abson (née Abbott) of the Department of Psychology, University of Newcastle upon Tyne, for their substantial contribution to the work reported in this chapter and particularly to the design of the questionnaire which was used to collect the data. The opinions expressed in this chapter are those of the authors and do not necessarily reflect the views of the Department of Transport.

2 Originally, this team was drawn from the Department of Economics and Department of Psychology, but at the final questionnaire and survey design stage, and throughout subsequent data analysis, was expanded to include some members of the Health Care Research Unit.

3 This figure is for full interviews and does not include the 47 interviews terminated before completion.

4 While there is growing evidence that some people will behave incoherently (i.e. will violate the Von Neumann–Morgenstern or Savage axioms) when faced with particular kinds of choice (see, for example, Kahneman and Tversky, 1979) we believe that the valuation questions in our survey were not of this type. Thus, while our questions related to awesome, unwanted events, they also involved somewhat simpler choices than those that tend to give rise to incoherence. It was for this reason that we decided to test for coherence in relatively simple choices under uncertainty.

5 While there had been many earlier attempts to investigate attitudes to and valuation of safety using the questionnaire approach (see Chapters 2 and 5 for summaries) to the best of our knowledge, only one of these, namely Prescott–Clarke (1982), employed a large national random sample survey conducted by professional interviewers. Unfortunately, the wording of the valuation questions in the latter was such as to preclude the possibility of inferring unambiguous values of statistical life.

6 However, it should be noted that Cummings *et al.* (1986) appear to regard iterative bidding as being effectively essential if one is to elicit true maximum willingness to pay. For a contrary view, see Mitchell and Carson (1986).

7 The weighted sample is smaller than the number of complete interviews because the weights applied to non-electors were typically less than one.

8 In those cases in which distributions are heavily skewed, confidence intervals for medians were estimated by first transforming variables to produce more nearly normal distributions and then computing a confidence interval for the median of the *transformed* variable using the result that, for a normally distributed random variable, the standard error of the median is approximately 1.25 times the standard error of the mean. The inverse of the original transformation was then used to convert this to a confidence interval for the median of the original variable.

9 While the theoretical result concerning the relationship between m_D and m_I proved in Chapter 3 related to *incremental* risks of death and serious injury, it is possible to show that the same result applies, at least to a good approximation, to *absolute* risks of death and injury (see Jones-Lee *et al.*, 1983, 1987, Appendix C). Thus, our inference conerning the relative magnitudes of the marginal rates of substitution of wealth for risk of death and risk of serious injury is effectively independent of whether respondents interpreted the risks in Question 16 as incremental or absolute.

10 Estimation of marginal rates of substitution from the responses to the various parts of Question 18 (the coach journey question) was straightforward and simply involved dividing each respondent's required variation in the coach fare by the corresponding change in risk quoted in the question. In the case of Question 20 (the car safety feature question) marginal rates of substitution for 'own' and 'own plus passengers' safety were estimated by (a) dividing reported willingness to pay for the car safety feature by the respondent's reported frequency of car replacement – this yielded an effective annual payment for the safety feature – and then (b) dividing the effective annual payment by the reduction in annual risk of death afforded by the feature. To the extent that step (a) involved no discounting the resultant estimates will, if anything, be biased downwards. In cases in which no frequency of car replacement was reported, the sample mean frequency was used.

In order to estimate marginal rates of substitution of own wealth for risk to one other person, extra willingness to pay for a halving of passenger as well as own risk – again converted to an effective annual payment – was divided by average passenger mileage per car multiplied by the passenger fatality rate per mile for the UK.

In the case of the other valuation questions, namely 14(b), 21(c) and 22, estimation of marginal rates of substitution was again fairly straightforward once appropriate assumptions had been made concerning the size of the population at risk (for Question 14(b)) and frequency of tyre replacement and tyre prices (for Question 21(c)).

It should also be noted that last-minute editing of the questionnaire introduced an unintended and unfortunate ambiguity in the wording of Question 22. As it was presented to respondents this question did not make clear for how long the safety improvement would be effective nor whether the door-to-door collection in part (a) would be once and for all or repeated annually. Marginal rates of substitution for this question have been computed on the assumption that respondents understood all information to apply to a *single year*. If, by contrast, respondents took it that the safety improvement would

208   *Estimation of Individual Valuation of Safety*

be effective over a number of years *and* treated the payment in 22(a) as once and for all, then the implied marginal rates of substitution for Question 22 would be even lower than those given in table 4.8.

11 From *Transport Statistics Great Britain 1971–1981* published by HMSO. This figure is based on the 1981 Census of Population.

12 In fact the percentages of zero responses were as follows: Question 14(b), 9%; Question 18(a), 25%; Question 18(b), 19%; Question 20(a), 13%; Question 20(b), 18%; Question 20(c), 10%; Question 22(a), 30%; Question 22(b), 30%.

13 In fact, because of the need to adjust for length of car ownership in computing marginal rates of substitution from valuation responses in Question 20, probit analyses for this question were conducted on estimated marginal rates of substitution rather than directly on valuation responses.

14 For details of the calculation of consistency scores, see section 4.3.2.

15 These choices were between pairs of bets on the nature of the weather on Christmas Day 1982, and essentially represented direct tests of Savage's postulates P2 (the first part of the 'sure thing' principle) and P4 (a postulate ensuring robustness of subjective probabilities).

16 See Jones-Lee (1976), Chapter 5. However, note the reservations concerning the generality of this result discussed in Chapter 2, section 2.1.1.

17 See Jones-Lee (1976), Chapter 5, but, again, note the reservations concerning the generality of this result discussed in Chapter 3, section 3.3.

18 For obvious reasons the results of this and many other subsidiary statistical analyses are not reported in detail.

19 These are, of course, unequivocally unreliable responses.

20 The similarity between the responses of consistent and other individuals also applied to the majority of other (non-valuation) questions.

21 Though it should be noted that these regressions were based on a rather more restricted set of explanatory variables than are listed in tables 4.9 and 4.10.

22 We understand that when this question was put to a sample of Swedish respondents, results very similar to those reported in table 4.15 were obtained. However, when the question was modified so as to stress the fact that the two risks had to be borne *simultaneously* then the proportion of 'wrong' responses fell substantially. This would seem to confirm the supposition that the wording of Question 17 was not entirely successful in getting across the idea that the risks were not alternatives. We are grateful to Ulph Persson of the Swedish Institute for Health Economics for drawing this point to our attention.

23 See Chapter 5, section 5.2.1, for further discussion of preferences over the saving of statistical and anonymous life.

24 Consider a pairwise vote between $\bar{m}$ (the median value of m_i) and any other value – say $\hat{m}$. If $\bar{m} > \hat{m}$, then given well-behaved individual valuation functions, all individuals for whom $m_i > (\bar{m} + \hat{m})/2$ will vote for $\bar{m}$, so that the latter will receive a majority of the votes cast. If, by contrast, $\bar{m} < \hat{m}$, then all of those for whom $m_i < (\bar{m} + \hat{m})/2$ will vote for $\bar{m}$ and the latter will again receive a majority of the votes cast.

25 Note that these distributions have *already* been trimmed of cases of suspected coding error.

26 It should also be stressed that there is nothing inherently perverse about a skewed distribution of marginal rates of substitution: with the exception of pathological cases, willingness to pay for safety is bounded below by zero, but there is no corresponding upper bound save, in the last analysis, the constraint imposed by an individual's ability to pay.

27 Before reaching final conclusions about the value of statistical life for transport risks, we should mention a possibility which, if it is the case, would tend to depress somewhat the estimated values of statistical life for road safety improvements under the 'mean of m_i' definition. It has been suggested to us that more cautious people experience smaller risk reductions as a result of road safety improvements (simply because they already drive more carefully) *and* tend to be more averse to physical risk and so have higher marginal rates of substitution. If this is so then cov $(m_i, \delta p_i)$ will be *positive* – recall that $\delta p_i < 0$ for a risk reduction – and from equation (1.5) the value of statistical life will be *less* than the population mean of m_i. In order to assess the possible impact of such an effect we have computed the value of statistical life on the 'worst-case' assumption that variations in risk δp_i are perfectly positively correlated with marginal rates of substitution m_i and that risk reductions go to zero as we move towards the upper tail of the frequency distribution of marginal rates of substitution, i.e.

$$\delta p_i = a + bm_i \qquad a < 0, \, b > 0$$

and

$$a + bm_{max} = 0$$

where m_{max} denotes the maximum of m_i over the affected population. It then follows that

$$\text{cov}(m_i, \delta p_i) = b \, \text{var}(m_i).$$

Furthermore, since we are considering the saving of one statistical life we shall have $\Sigma \delta p_i = -1$ so that summing over the expression for δp_i given above and using the condition that $a + bm_{max} = 0$

$$b = \frac{1}{n(m_{max} - \bar{m})}$$

where $\bar{m}$ denotes the mean of m_i. Hence, substituting for cov$(m_i, \delta p_i)$ and b into equation (1.5) of Chapter 1 gives

$$V = \bar{m} - \frac{\text{var}(m_i)}{m_{max} - \bar{m}}$$

where V, as in earlier chapters, denotes the value of statistical life under the 'aggregate willingness-to-pay' definition.

For Question 20(a) the survey results gave $\bar{m}$ (trimmed) = £1.21 × 10⁶, m_{max} (trimmed) = £24 × 10⁶ and var(m_i) (trimmed) = 5.18 × 10¹² so that, using the result just established, the value of statistical life is £983,000 – a reduction of 19% on the value given by the mean of m_i. The corresponding reductions for Questions 20(b), 18(a) and 18(b) are, respectively, 25%, 16% and 15%. While we cannot estimate the relationship between m_i and δp_i empirically, it seems unlikely that there would exist more than a weak positive correlation between these variables so that we doubt that the appropriate values of statistical life would be significantly below those given by the mean of m_i. Certainly, we would be very surprised if cov($m_i, \delta p_i$) were larger than implied by the rather extreme assumptions made above, so that we are convinced that the mean of m_i overestimates the value of statistical life for road safety by, at the most, about 20%.

28 See the argument developed in note 27.

29 In fact, the only case in which the coefficient of income is not significant at the 5% level is Question 20(b) (positive responses only). Furthermore, in this case the last variable to enter under the 10% significance stopping rule in the stepwise regression procedure is the 'income minus mean income all squared' variable. If this variable is omitted then the coefficient of the linear income variable is significant at the 1% level.

30 Clearly, such redistribution will have no effect whatsoever if the relationship is linear. This is essentially because aggregate willingness to pay will then depend *only* upon aggregate income and will be quite independent of its distribution. In fact, our calculations were based upon the estimated coefficients of the 'income minus mean income all squared' variable in the regression analysis for 'all' valuation responses (zero and positive) reported in table 4.10. As can be seen from this table, the coefficient of the 'income minus mean income all squared' variable was significant only in the case of Question 18(a).

31 Where data concerning Y_i were missing, the sample mean of Y_i was substituted in this procedure.

32 Indeed, we would go so far as to say that if distributional weights are to be employed at all in cost–benefit analysis, then they *ought* to be applied simultaneously to all the costs and benefits of a project or group of projects. Our purpose in computing distributionally weighted values of statistical life should therefore be seen *not* as an attempt to provide a part of the information necessary for a distributionally weighted cost–benefit analysis but rather as an illustration of the way in which such weighting might be expected to affect values of safety in relation to their unweighted counterparts. We are grateful to Ian Dobbs for drawing this point to our attention.

33 Apparently, each briefing session lasted about five hours.

Appendix

While the questionnaire together with its visual displays and interviewer instructions is too lengthy to reproduce in full (60 pages), it seems appropriate to provide details of the key valuation questions. These questions are therefore reproduced in this Appendix, though code boxes and instructions to interviewers have been omitted. The ordering of the various parts of Questions 18 and 20 is that given in version 1 of the questionnaire.

Q 14(a)   Each year in England and Wales, motor accidents, heart disease and cancer cause roughly these number of deaths among people under the age of 55:

motor accidents cause 4,000 deaths,
heart disease, 11,000 deaths,
and cancer, 16,000 deaths.

Suppose that, for a given amount of money, it were possible to reduce the number of deaths from just one of these causes by 100 next year. Which one cause would you choose to have reduced?

Q 14(b)   If *you* were asked to make a single payment to help raise the money needed to avoid these 100 deaths, what is the most that you personally would be prepared to pay, bearing in mind how much you can afford?

Q 18
Imagine that you have to make a long coach trip in a foreign country. You have been given £200 for your travelling expenses, and given the name of a coach service which will take you for exactly £200. The risk of being killed on the journey with this coach firm is 8 in 100,000.

You can choose to travel with a safer coach service if you want to, but the fare will be higher, and you will have to pay the extra cost yourself.

(a) How much extra, if anything, would you be prepared to pay to use a coach service with a risk of being killed of 4 in 100,000 – that is, half the risk of the one at £200?

(b) How much extra, if anything, would you be prepared to pay to use a coach service with a risk of being killed of 1 in 100,000 – one-eighth the risk of the one at £200?

Instead of paying extra to travel by safer coach service, you could keep some of the £200 and use a cheaper, but more dangerous, coach service.

(c) How much of the £200 travelling expenses would you expect to keep if you used a coach service with a risk of being killed of 16 in 100,000 – twice the risk of the service at £200 – or would you not travel on this service?

(d) How much of the £200 travelling expenses would you expect to keep if you used a coach service with a risk of being killed of 32 in 100,000 – four times the risk of the service at £200 – or would you not travel on this service?

Q 20
Suppose that you are buying a particular make of car. You can, if you want, choose to have a new kind of safety feature fitted to the car at extra cost. The next few questions will ask about how much extra you would be prepared to pay for some different types of safety feature. You must bear in mind how much you personally can afford.

(a) As we said earlier, the risk of a car driver being killed in an accident is 10 in 100,000. You could choose to have a safety feature fitted to your car which will halve the risk of the *car driver* being killed, down to 5 in 100,000. Taking into account how much you personally can afford, what is the most that you would be prepared to pay to have this safety feature fitted to the car?

(b) An alternative safety feature would reduce the risk of *the driver* being killed by 20% – to 8 in 100,000. Taking into account how much you personally can afford, what is the most you would be prepared to pay for that safety feature?

(c) I now want to ask you about a safety feature which would reduce the risk of death for not only the *driver, but also the passengers* in the car. Bear in mind that the average car journey involves one passenger as well as the driver, and the passenger's risk of being killed is broadly the same as the driver's.

Suppose you could choose a safety feature which would halve the risk of the *driver* and *any passengers* in the car being killed in an accident. Bearing in mind how much you personally can afford, what is the most you would be prepared to pay to have this safety feature fitted to the car?

The following question was put to drivers only:

Q 21(b)   Suppose it were proved that changing your tyres when the treads were 2 mm deep, instead of waiting until they reach the legal (1 mm) limit, would reduce the risk of a fatal accident by 15%. Would you change your car tyres sooner, or not?

If sooner

Q 21(c)   At what tread depth would you change your tyres?

When treads at or above 2 mm deep
When treads less than 2 mm but more than
Probe as necessary   1 mm deep
When 1 mm deep
When less than 1 mm deep
Don't know

Q 22   A road improvement scheme has been designed for a town of half a million people. The improvements will cut by one-quarter the risk of death or serious injury on the roads for everyone in the town – including drivers, passengers, riders of motorbikes and bicycles, and pedestrians. It will cut the risk from 12 to 9 in 100,000. However, the Council do not have enough money to pay for the scheme, and two suggestions have been made for collecting money.

(a)   It could be raised by a single door-to-door collection. Everyone in the town would be asked to contribute but it would not be compulsory. How much do *you* honestly think your household would be prepared to give to this single *voluntary* collection?

(b)   On the other hand, the money would be collected by raising the rates or taxes for a year. Some households could afford to pay more than others. Bearing in mind how much your household could afford, what do you think would be a reasonable sum to collect from every household?

5

Physical Risk: Psychological and Decision-theoretic Perspectives

Previous chapters have been largely concerned with the application of the tools of economic analysis to the problems posed by the phenomenon of physical risk in public sector and government decision making. That is, the principal focus has been upon the question of the appropriate way in which to trade off safety improvement against other desirable uses of scarce resources. Given the essentially utilitarian nature of the fundamental premises of welfare economics and the consequent importance accorded to ensuring that social choices reflect private preferences, this focus has narrowed even further to a specific concern with *individual* valuation of safety and, more particularly, with individual willingness to pay for reductions in the probability of particular types of death or injury during a forthcoming period or periods.

As such, this way of structuring and analysing the problem of physical risk has many features that are typical of the economist's approach to the study of social phenomena. For example, the analysis of earlier chapters has involved a fairly high level of abstraction and simplification in that it has been assumed that the multifaceted concept of 'risk' can be adequately summarized in terms of more or less well-behaved individual subjective probabilities for the occurrence of each of a limited number of well-defined events (i.e. types of death or injury). It has also been taken that people have sufficiently clear-cut, systematic and stable preferences for one to be able to talk sensibly about the rate at which individuals are willing to trade off variations in such probabilities against other desirable uses of scarce resources. However, the economic approach begs a number of important and interesting questions. For example, is it in fact legitimate to summarize individual perceptions of physical risk in terms of well-behaved subjective probabilities for well-defined events, or is the human cognitive process in reality too complex or too fickle or subject to too many biases to admit of such an ordered and simple characterization? As to preferences, are they on the whole as clear-cut, systematic and stable as is presupposed by the economist's approach[1] or are they in fact so fuzzy, perverse and capricious as to render the concept of a reasonably stable marginal rate of substitution virtually meaningless, thereby removing the very foundation of the social welfare maximization/cost–benefit analysis approach to the definition of values of safety and costs of risk?

It is tempting to think of the contributions to risk analysis that have come from other disciplines, particularly psychology and decision theory, as having originated in largely negative answers to questions such as these, i.e. from dissatisfaction with the extreme abstraction and over-simplification of economic analysis. One suspects, however, that this is not so. In reality, these very different approaches to the problem are probably more a reflection of fundamentally different perspectives and paradigms and hence *a different starting point in the analytical process*. In any case, whatever the origins and *raison d'être* of these other approaches, they result in a body of analysis that sheds light on some of the questions posed above and, more significantly, yield a set of results that are essentially complementary to, rather than substitutes for, those of economic analysis. The purpose of this chapter is to summarize some of the more significant results of the psychological and decision-theoretic approaches to risk analysis and to assess their implications for the discussion in earlier chapters.

5.1   Contributions from Psychology

The main thrust of work by cognitive and experimental psychologists in the area of physical risk has been directed towards investigation of the way that people – especially the 'non-expert' public – *perceive* physical risks and hazards, i.e. how they think and feel about such risks and what determines their overall attitudes towards them. This work appears to a significant degree to have been prompted by the growing realization during recent years that there is a marked divergence between the way that the public thinks about and reacts to various potential hazards – such as nuclear power generation and waste disposal – and the way that 'experts' characterize and evaluate such phenomena.

At the risk of grossly over-simplifying their methodological stance, cognitive psychologists appear to model overall attitude formation in a way that broadly (but *only* broadly) resembles expected utility theory. That is, psychologists postulate that an individual's overall attitude to an activity or entity depends (a) upon his *stength of belief* that the activity or entity is associated with each of a number of characteristics or will result in various possible consequences and (b) upon his *attribute evaluation* or feeling of favourability or unfavourability towards each of these characteristics or consequences. Clearly then, overall attitudes, belief strengths and attribute evaluations can be seen as the counterparts to expected utilities, subjective probabilities and Von Neumann–Morgenstern utilities respectively. However, the parallel is only loose. The axioms of expected utility theory entail fairly rigid restrictions on the properties of subjective probabilities and utilities (the former must behave like mathematical probabilities, the latter are cardinally measurable and the two must be combined in an expectations operation). In addition, economists tend to be draconian, parsimonious and one might even say presumptuous (in the literal sense of the word) in specifying what are and are not to constitute relevant consequences. The net result of all this is, not surprisingly, a rather concrete set of positive and normative conclusions (as in the $m \triangle p * \text{RL} = 1$ result and its policy implications discussed in Chapter 3). By contrast, psychologists appear to take an altogether less restrictive approach to the analysis of beliefs and evaluations – typically these are measured on simple $2n + 1$-point scales (e.g. $-2, -1, 0, +1, +2$) such as 'very unlikely' $(-n)$ to 'very likely' $(+n)$ or 'very bad' $(-n)$ to 'very good' $(+n)$. In addition there is no rigid specification of the way in which the resulting measures of belief strength and attribute evaluation are to be combined to arrive at a measure of overall attitude. Finally, and perhaps most significantly, psychologists are far more permissive and open-minded about *what* consequences people will regard as relevant and important (or 'salient').

Another distinctive feature of the psychologist's approach to the study of individual perception of risk is the identification of a limited number of inferential rules of thumb or 'heuristics' that people appear to employ in order to simplify the complex task of processing (often partial) data and information in order to reach intuitive judgements under conditions of uncertainty. Not surprisingly, it has been found that such heuristics tend to lead to various systematic biases in individual perception of risk and before proceeding to consider the results of empirical investigation of beliefs and attitudes it seems appropriate to give a brief summary of the nature of these heuristics and biases.

5.1.1   Heuristics and Biases in the Public's Perception of Physical Risk

Some of the most substantial insights into the nature of the public's perceptions of the risk of various activities and technologies have come from a series of contributions by Slovic *et al.* (e.g. Slovic *et al.*, 1981). The focus in these contributions tends to be upon beliefs and belief strength (rather than overall attitude and attribute evaluation) and upon the sort of inferential rules or heuristics that people appear to employ in arriving at their beliefs and judgements under conditions of uncertainty.

According to Slovic *et al.*, one of the most significant heuristics in the context of physical risk is *availability*. This refers to the tendency for people to judge a particular type of event to be more likely to occur if actual instances of the event are easy to imagine or remember or for whatever reasons 'come to mind' more readily. Examples of this phenomenon are (a) the tendency for people living in areas at risk of natural disasters (such as floods or earthquakes) to underestimate these risks – and hence, for example, to underinsure against them – simply because no instance of the disaster has occurred in recent memory and (b) the tendency for people to overestimate the frequency of dramatic, sensational – and hence widely reported – causes of death (such as murder) relative to statistically more frequent but less sensational causes (such as disease). It is apparently also the case that a majority of people view themselves as safer than average drivers, more likely to live longer than normal life expectancy, less likely than average to succumb to the dangers of smoking or excessive drinking and so on. These unrealistic views can readily be explained in terms of the availability heuristic in that, for most people, daily experience of driving, smoking, drinking etc. produces no adverse consequences for the person concerned and they are hence judged to be 'safe'.

Another heuristic that has potential relevance in the formation of perceptions of physical risk is *anchoring*. Numerical estimates and judgements are often arrived at by adjusting from a starting point that is either given or is the result of a 'first-guess' partial solution to a problem. 'Anchoring' refers to a tendency for people to make insufficient adjustment from such starting points. Thus, if asked first to judge whether the weight of an object is more or less than 10 kg and then asked for a precise estimate of its weight, people will tend to give higher estimates than if asked first whether the weight is more or less than 5 kg. Similarly, if asked to give a 95% confidence interval for tomorrow's stock-market index, investors apparently proceed by first selecting a 'best guess' and then making upward and downward adjustments to this. Once again there is an apparent tendency for people to 'anchor' on their best guess and make insufficient adjustment from it, thereby ending up with estimated confidence intervals that are too narrow relative to the 'true' intervals implied by observed data. The net result of this is that people tend to be over-confident and over-precise in judgements under uncertainty.

A third heuristic that is perhaps of less interest for our purposes is *representativeness*. Essentially, this is a tendency for people to judge the conditional probability $P(H|E)$ of an hypothesis H, given certain evidence E, *exclusively* on the basis of the likelihood $P(E|H)$, *ignoring* both the prior probability $P(H)$ and the reliability of the evidence. For example, in judging the probability that a particular person is an airline pilot, given a description of his or her characteristics, people tend to focus upon the extent to which those characteristics are typical of airline pilots in the population. A variant of this type of phenomenon that may have more relevance in the context of assessment of physical risk is the tendency for people to ignore sample size in reaching judgements about sample statistics, focusing exclusively upon the corresponding population statistics.

Finally, though it is not generally regarded as a heuristic, the phenomenon of *cognitive dissonance* is directly relevant to our discussion of the public's perception of risk. The basic premise of the theory of cognitive dissonance is that people like to hold beliefs that are mutually reinforcing and are uncomfortable if their ideas are apparently contradictory. Thus, there is a tendency to discount new information that appears to conflict with beliefs that have already been formed, or to discount the adverse potential consequences of a course of action once that course has been chosen after a weighing of its pros and cons. An example of the impact of cognitive dissonance is the tendency for people who have chosen to work in a dangerous occupation to discount the dangers because the cognition that it was a sensible decision to choose that occupation sits uncomfortably with the cognition that the job is, in fact, dangerous.

5.1.2 Beliefs and Attitudes Concerning Physical Risk

Having considered the various heuristics and biases that seem to be at work in the formation of beliefs about and attitudes towards physical risk, let us now turn to the empirical investigation and estimation of such beliefs and attitudes.

The most immediately striking finding concerning the public's perception of risk is that, whereas for some activities and technologies the public's beliefs correspond closely with those of experts (these being, not surprisingly, very closely related to statistical frequencies), in other cases, notably nuclear power, there are very substantial differences. In particular Slovic *et al.* (1981) asked one group of experts and three groups of non-experts in the USA to rank 30 activities, substances and technologies in terms of the risk of death from each. In terms of mean rankings within the groups, two of the non-expert groups judged nuclear power to be the most risky of the 30 activities, and the third non-expert group judged it the eighth most risky activity. Experts, by contrast, placed nuclear power in twentieth place.

This might, of course, simply indicate that the public's subjective estimates of fatality rates from various causes differ substantially from statistical frequencies or other technical estimates. However, Slovic *et al.* also asked non-expert subjects for estimates of annual fatalities and found that their rankings in terms of 'risk of death' were no more closely related to their estimates of fatality rates than to statistical frequencies and technical estimates. They therefore concluded that:

> Apparently, lay people incorporate other considerations besides annual fatalities into their concept of risk. (Slovic *et al.*, 1981, p. 24)

This speculation was reinforced by the finding that, while two of the non-expert groups had judged nuclear power to be the most risky activity, they had also judged it likely to produce the smallest number of fatalities during the coming year. This strongly suggests that factors other than fatality rates are instrumental in determining people's overall perception of risk. In the case of nuclear power, an obvious candidate is the potential for large-scale disaster involving extensive loss of life. In order to test this hypothesis, Slovic *et al.* asked experts and various groups of non-experts to rate the 30 activities considered in their earlier study on nine characteristics thought likely to be key determinants of perceptions of risk. These included the degree to which the activity was judged to be voluntary, and the extent to which its potential adverse consequences were controllable, known to science, known to potential victims, familiar, dreaded, certain to be fatal, catastrophic and immediately manifested. While experts' judgements of risk – based, as already noted, largely on statistical frequencies – turned out not to be related to *any* of the nine risk characteristics, some very interesting relationships emerged in the case of the non-expert groups. In the first place, mean ratings were similar for all groups, including experts. Second, nuclear power (by contrast with other power sources and X-rays) scored at or near the extreme of all undesirable characteristics. Third, non-expert judgements of risk turned out to be closely related to two characteristics, namely 'dread' and the likelihood of a mishap proving to be fatal. In addition, the ratings for many pairs of characteristics turned out to be correlated with each other across the 30 activities, suggesting that the ratings of the nine characteristics might be explained in terms of a smaller number of basic 'dimensions' of risk. Factor analysis confirmed that this was indeed the case, indicating that the nine characteristics could be represented by two underlying factors that Slovic *et al.* describe as 'dread risk' and 'unknown risk'. Activities scoring at the high end of the 'dread risk' scale tended to be associated with adverse consequences judged likely to be fatal and affecting large numbers of people (e.g. nuclear power and commercial aviation). Activities with high 'unknown risk' scores tended to be new, involuntary and to have unknown adverse consequences with delayed effects (e.g. food colouring and pesticides). Interestingly, the scores for nuclear power were high on both risk dimensions.

More recently Slovic *et al.* have conducted similar but more extensive studies involving 80–90 activities and 18 characteristics. Again, it transpires that ratings for the 18 characteristics could be largely explained in terms of a smaller number of underlying factors, namely 'dread risk', 'unknown risk' and the number of people (including the respondent) exposed to the risk. These studies confirm that lay people's overall perceptions of risk are closely related to dread risk: 'The higher an activity's score on this factor, (a) the higher its perceived risk, (b) the more people want its risks reduced and (c) the more they want to see strict regulation employed to achieve the desired reduction in risk . . .'. By contrast, experts' judgements of risk appear not to be closely related to any of the three factors.

The importance of 'dread risk' in the determination of the public's beliefs and attitudes has been confirmed by studies conducted in the UK by van der Pligt *et al.* (1986) and in Austria by Thomas *et al.* (1980) and Thomas (1981). Broadly speaking, the analytical approach employed in these studies is similar to that used by Slovic *et al.*, though the psychological dimensions considered were somewhat wider, including overall attitudes and attribute evaluations as well as belief strengths. By contrast, the focus in terms of activities was rather narrower in that only energy systems and industrial activities were considered.

The study of van der Plight *et al.* was based upon a random sample of 450 drawn from the electoral registers of three areas proposed as potential sites for a new nuclear power station in southwest England. Respondents received a postal questionnaire and the response rate was 70%.

Respondents were first asked to rate their overall attitude to the construction of a new nuclear power station (both in their own locality and elsewhere in England) together with various other industrial developments (such as the construction of a coal-fired power station or a chemicals factory). Ratings were on a seven-point scale ranging from 'very strongly opposed' to 'very strongly in favour'. In the event, approximately 75% of respondents indicated a negative attitude to the construction of a nuclear power station in their own neighbourhood and there was a similar degree of opposition to the construction of a chemicals factory, the most favourable response being to the construction of windmills as a source of electricity. Respondents were then presented with various potential immediate and long-term consequences and asked (a) to rate these in terms of the extent to which they would change life in the neighbourhood for the better or for the worse and (b) to select the five immediate and five long-term consequences they thought to be most important. Clearly, the rating exercise was intended to establish the nature of belief strengths while the selection of 'most important' consequences is intended to reveal information concerning attribute evaluation or 'salience'.

In general terms, it turned out that those with generally 'pro' attitudes to nuclear power tended to regard potential economic benefits as being amongst the most important consequences while those with 'anti' attitudes tended to stress risk factors. More specifically, as far as short-term consequences were concerned, with a few exceptions there were not major differences between the pro and anti groups. The exceptions were 'road building' and 'workers coming into the area' (both seen as more important and more favourable by the pros) and 'conversion of land from agricultural use' (seen as more important and more unfavourable by the antis). Both pro and anti groups thought that transportation of nuclear waste was important but differed in their beliefs concerning its impact. However, results concerning longer-term consequences revealed more marked differences between pros and antis in terms of both their assessments of importance and their belief ratings. In particular, the belief rating for the item 'personal peace of mind' had a very high predictive power for overall attitude scores (the correlation coefficient for these two variables was 0.79). Finally, it is interesting to note that, in general, respondents' attitudes to the construction of nuclear power stations in their own locality were more adverse than to their construction elsewhere and that these attitudes were in turn more adverse than to nuclear energy in general. These results were, of course, obtained prior to the occurrence of the Chernobyl disaster.

The study by Thomas *et al.* is probably the most comprehensive attempt to apply the concepts of attitude theory to the study of perceptions of physical risk. The study, carried out during the late 1970s, involved a stratified sample of 224 subjects drawn from the Austrain public and questionnaires were administered in personal interviews, thereby permitting full instruction of subjects in the use of scales. Essentially, respondents were asked, for each of five energy systems (coal, oil,

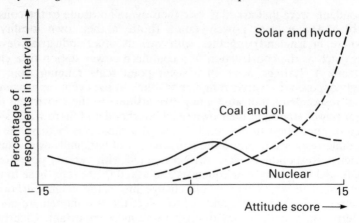

Figure 5.1   Frequency distributions of attitude scores.

hydro, solar and nuclear), to rate the following on a series of seven-point scales (−3 to +3).

1   Overall attitude – this was rated on the basis of five different criteria and an aggregate rating was then constructed, giving a range of −15 to +15.
2   Attribute evaluations for each of 39 possible consequences of the energy systems (i.e. ratings of the favourability or unfavourability with which the consequences are viewed by the subject). These consequences were selected on the basis of the results of earlier open-ended interviews with members of the Austrian public and from a pilot survey of the beliefs and attitudes of nuclear experts. Consequences included 'increased standard of living', 'production of noxious waste', 'increasing rate of mortality', 'new forms of industrial development', 'accidents that affect large numbers of people' and 'exposure to risk that I cannot control'.
3   Belief strengths for each of the 39 possible consequences (i.e. ratings of the subject's assessment of the likelihood of occurrence of the consequences).

The frequency distributions of overall attitude scores (on a scale from −15 to +15) for coal and oil were very similar to each other, as were those for solar and hydro energy. For solar and hydro there were very few negative scores and for coal and oil scores were predominantly, though less markedly, positive. However, the distribution for nuclear energy was quite different, being effectively tri-modal with clusters at the middle and near the end-points of the scale. Smoothed versions of the frequency distributions are shown in figure 5.1.[2]

Factor analysis indicated that the set of 39 possible consequences of the five energy systems could be partitioned into five[3] underlying 'dimensions', namely (i) environmental risk, (ii) indirect risk (future oriented and political), (iii) psychological and physical risk, (iv) general economic benefits and (v) future-oriented benefits of technological development.

Beliefs about the energy systems were then compared by focusing upon the 'pro nuclear energy' group (those 50 respondents with the highest attitude ratings for nuclear energy) and the 'con nuclear energy' group (the 50 respondents with the lowest attitude ratings). For each individual in the pro and con groups the belief strength scores for the five consequences most characteristic of each underlying dimension were summed to yield a total belief strength score for the individual on that particular dimension. The main findings were as follows:

1. With the exception of nuclear energy, beliefs of the pro and con groups concerning the energy systems were remarkably similar.
2. Belief strengths concerning the three-risk and two-benefit dimensions differed significantly across the five energy systems.
3. Both pro and con groups tended to have negative belief strength scores for the risk dimensions for the four non-nuclear energy sources (i.e. thought the adverse consequences associated with these risks *unlikely* to materialize). The only exceptions were positive belief strength scores for environmental risk in the cases of coal and oil.
4. On the whole, both pro and con groups tended to take the view that *all* energy systems would lead to probable benefits. The exceptions were the beliefs that coal will *not* lead to technological development (both groups), that coal will *not* lead to economic benefits (con group) and that hydro and oil will *not* lead to technological development (con group). In general, the pro group's belief strength scores for probable benefits were higher than those for the con group.
5. Beliefs about the risks of nuclear energy were different from those for the other energy systems in that it was the only system strongly associated with indirect risk (con group) and psychological and physical risks (both groups).
6. The pro and con groups perceived both risks and benefits of nuclear energy very differently. As far as risk is concerned, the con group had positive belief strength scores for *all three* dimensions of risk while the pro group had a positive score only for psychological and physical risk, though this score was lower than for the con group. In the case of benefits, while both groups took the view that nuclear energy would lead to economic and technological benefits, the con group believed so less strongly, particularly in the case of economic benefits.

Thomas *et al.* also examined the relationship between overall attitude to the five energy systems and attribute evaluation ratings. In general, it appeared that attribute evaluations, weighted by belief strength scores and summed across the relevant dimensions, acted as a good predictor

of overall evaluation, confirming the interpretation of attribute evaluations as being, in some sense, measures of 'favourability/unfavourability'
and belief strength scores measures of 'degree of belief' or subjective
probability.

Finally, in a separate study Thomas *et al.* examined the quality of
policy makers' assessments of the public's attitudes and perceptions. A
sample of 40 senior civil servants (each of whom advised the government
on energy matters) was partitioned randomly into one of two role-play
conditions and asked to complete the same questionnaire as used in the
study described above, but in the role of a typical Austrian citizen pro (or
anti) nuclear energy. The instructions to participants were framed in such
a way as to discourage the role-playing of militant extremists.

While the policy makers tended, on the whole, to have a fairly accurate
assessment of the pro and con groups' beliefs and attitudes, there were
some notable exceptions. In the case of belief strengths, for example,
they tended to underestimate the belief that nuclear energy is associated
with psychological risk for *both* pro and con groups, the underestimation
in the case of the pro group's belief being the most marked. In addition,
the policy makers underestimated both the pro and con groups' strength
of belief that nuclear energy leads to economic and technological benefits.
The policy makers' assessments of the public's attribute evaluation was
also inaccurate in the case of risk. For example they underestimated the
negative value that both pro and con groups associated with psychological
risk and with environmental and physical risk as well as the pro group's
negative evaluation of socio-political risk.

5.1.3 *The Psychologists' Approach – The Problem of Measurement*

Probably the most worrying feature of the psychologists' approach is the
status of the measurements that result from their empirical investigations.
These measurements tend to be subjected to statistical tests and form
the basis for inferences that, strictly speaking, require the measurements
to be at least on an *interval* scale which is, in addition, *interpersonally
comparable*. For example, a regression analysis of individual n-point
ratings for overall attitude to 'construction of a nuclear power plant in
one's neighbourhood' or the m-point scores for beliefs in and attribute
evaluations of the various consequences of such construction requires (a)
that individual ratings and scores cannot be subjected to arbitrary mono-
tonic transformations (otherwise correlation coefficients, t statistics and so
on will be effectively meaningless) and (b) that an attitude rating or belief
score of x for individual i should 'mean' much the same as a rating or
score of x for individual j. As far as measurement of attitudes and beliefs
on an interval scale is concerned, there are precise 'consistency' conditions on such beliefs and attitudes that have been shown to be necessary
and sufficient for the legitimacy of such measurement. (For example, the
axioms for 'additive conjoint measurement' give conditions for the cardinal measurement of different factors where the measures can simply be

added together to arrive at an overall effect or impact of the factors (Krantz *et al.*, 1971).) To the best of the author's knowledge, there exists no direct evidence to support the proposition that attitudes and beliefs concerning physical risk tend to satisfy these axioms, and indeed it seems somewhat implausible, a priori, that they would do so. (The axioms for additive conjoint measurement, for instance, require an absence of inter-action between variables or factors in the determination of their overall effect and one doubts that these conditions would be fulfilled in the case of beliefs and attribute evaluations.)

However, even if one could be satisfied that cardinal measurement of attitudes, evaluations and beliefs was in fact legitimate, there would remain the thorny question of interpersonal comparability. For example, on what grounds is it legitimate to treat two people who claim to be 'very strongly opposed' to the construction of a nuclear power station – and hence are each given equal negative attitude ratings – as being, in fact, *equally* opposed? One may be genuinely averse and concerned while the other is, in truth, only marginally so but given to hyperbole in the expression of his views. While the same sort of criticism can, in principle, be levelled against interpersonal comparisons of individual monetary valuations (who knows, ultimately, whether the additional well-being generated by an extra £1 to *i* is the same as an extra £1 for *j*?) it nonetheless seems altogether more plausible and persuasive to conclude that two individuals with similar incomes, who would each be willing to pay the same amount for some particular good or service, do in a very real sense, 'value' it equally relative to other ways in which they might spend their income.

In spite of all this, introspection suggests that attitudes, evaluations and beliefs often seem to be more than merely ordinal. Furthermore, *faut de mieux*, it also seems appropriate to treat one person's expression of extreme aversion (or favourability) as being more or less equivalent to another's provided that their circumstances are broadly similar. Thus, some sort of cardinal measurement of individual attitudes, evaluations and beliefs is probably ultimately justified, as is some sort of interperson-al comparison of these measurements. What psychologists have done to date might therefore be viewed as a first tentative step in the analysis of a necessarily complex problem.[4]

5.1.4 *The Rationality of Individual Perceptions of Physical Risk*

Given the evidence of biases and of discrepancies between the public's perception of risk and the assessments of experts, one is bound to wonder whether there are grounds for regarding the non-expert public as in-herently irrational in this context and, indeed, whether the degree of irrationality is so serious as to render invalid the underlying assumptions of the economic approach.

As far as the general charge of irrationality is concerned, Lee (1981) has argued that this is largely unwarranted. Lee's contention is that individual perceptions and attitudes are typically formed on the basis of a rather wider set of considerations and criteria than the limited number of relatively easily quantifiable variables employed by experts in forming their estimates and assessments. For example, experts will tend to focus upon the probability distribution of the number of deaths in assessing the seriousness of a hazard. By contrast, for members of the non-expert public, less easily quantifiable considerations such as pain, suffering and emotional impact, the identity of potential victims, the voluntary or involuntary nature of the risks and a variety of moral and ethical considerations (including questions of blame, responsibility, the preservation of civilization and the sanctity of life) will also have a significant impact in the formation of perceptions. In addition, members of the public must necessarily rely upon partial information, personal experience, and imperfect memory as well as limited information processing and computational ability in forming their beliefs and attitudes. All of this leads Lee to conclude that '. . . the public's perception of risk and so-called objective risk assessment are different but complementary forms of rationality . . .' although he does emphasize the desirability of a convergence of the two processes through (a) provision of objective data capable of assimilation by the public and (b) the incorporation of the public's subjective perceptions in 'expert' risk assessment.

Turning to the question of whether divergence between the public's perception and 'objective' estimates of risk do irreparable damage to the economic approach, one can be fairly brief. In fact, all that is required by the economic approach is (a) that individuals should have reasonably well-defined preferences, (b) that these preferences should be fairly stable over time and (c) that individuals should have a broad awareness and understanding of the trade-offs involved in their decisions concerning safety. Little, if anything, in the results of the studies summarized in sections 5.1.1 or 5.1.2 leads one to suppose that these requirements will not be fulfilled. Certainly, there would be cause for concern if there were indications that individual beliefs were seriously mistaken or if attitudes (and hence preferences) were based upon false information, but by and large this seems not to be the case. In summary, the fact that the public appears to view certain sources of physical risk with considerably greater alarm than others and that this differentiated perception does not entirely accord with the 'objective' estimates of expected fatality rates, and so on, is really neither here nor there for the economic approach. What *is* important is that if people are, for whatever reasons, more averse to risk from nuclear power generation than to an 'objectively' equivalent risk from, say, a natural disaster, then this comparative aversion should be reflected in decisions concerning the allocation of resources to reactor safety and disaster prevention and this is precisely what the economic approach seeks to do.

It would appear, then, that the results of work by cognitive psychologists in the field of physical risk give no cause for serious concern about the robustness of the underlying assumptions of the economic approach.[5]

There is another body of experimental work, however, whose results are altogether more disturbing. The following section therefore outlines and examines these results and their implications for individual choice in situations involving physical risk.

5.1.5 *Preference Reversal, Compensating versus Equivalent Variations and Willingness to pay versus Willingness to Accept*

Consider an individual in situation A who is presented with the possibility of changing to a preferred situation B. The individual's *compensating variation* (CV) for the move from A to B is the maximum sum he would be willing to pay to make the change while his *equivalent variation* (EV) is the minimum sum that he would require to compensate him for forgoing the change. In a very obvious sense, therefore, the compensating and equivalent variations both provide monetary measures of the value to the individual of the move from A to the preferred situation B. It is well known that the standard theory of consumer choice tells us the following things about the relationship between CV and EV:[6]

1 The only difference between CV and EV for a given change will be due to income or wealth effects.[7] Thus, if the change from A to B involves only the reduction in the price of a particular good, then if that good is normal EV will exceed CV and vice versa if the good is inferior.[8] However, while the two variations will be equal if and only if the income effect is zero, in many cases income effects can be assumed to be sufficiently small that CV and EV will be *approximately* equal.

2 If we consider a third situation, C, that is preferred to B, then the EV for the change from A to C will *necessarily* exceed the EV for the change from A to B. However, it is *possible* for the CV for the change from A to C to be less than that for the change from A to B,[9] although one would suppose that this case would be the exception rather than the rule.

Unfortunately, in choices involving certain kinds of financial gamble, there is evidence that many people behave in a way that is not in accord with the predictions of the standard theory of choice. For example in a series of experiments (some of which were played for real monetary payoffs) Lichtenstein and Slovic (1971, 1973) found that when presented with the choice between a gamble involving a high probability of a modest win and one involving a low probability of a substantially larger win (e.g. 0.99 to win \$4 and 0.01 to lose \$1 vs 0.33 to win \$16 and 0.67 to lose \$2) a significant proportion of subjects would express a preference for the former kind of gamble *but* indicate a larger EV for the latter. A somewhat more modest number of subjects exhibited the same kind of pathological response in relation to CVs. Now while the CV responses could *just possibly* be a reflection of the kind of phenomenon discussed in note 9, the EV responses are definitely contrary to the predictions of standard choice theory and appear to reflect a kind of 'preference reversal'. The explanation afforded by Lichtenstein and Slovic for such responses (and confirmed, to some extent, by in-depth interviewing of subjects) is that individuals do not in general behave according to the axioms of standard choice theory (and expected utility theory in particular) but instead may, for example, tend to focus upon *probabilities* when expressing preferences or making choices and, by contrast, upon *payoffs* when deciding upon EVs and CVs.

Almost as worrying as Slovic and Lichtenstein's findings are those of a sequence of experiments and empirical work by Hammack and Brown (1974), Rowe *et al.* (1980) and more recently by Knetsch and Sinden (1984). The results of this work cast doubt upon the predicted relationship between the relative magnitudes of the CV and EV for cases in which it would seem entirely reasonable to assume that income effects will have been negligible. For example, Knetsch and Sinden, conducting experiments with real monetary payoffs, found that in one group of subjects who were offered the opportunity to participate in a financial gamble with a modest payoff (e.g. $50), 50% refused to pay $2 for the right to participate, thereby revealing that their CVs were less than $2. However, in a similar group of subjects who had been given the right to participate in the same gamble and then asked if they would be prepared to sell that right for $2, 76% refused, thus revealing EVs of more than $2. While it is just possible that the CVs of those who refused in the former group were only marginally less than $2 and the EVs of refusers in the latter group only marginally more than $2, so that responses could be no more than a reflection of income effects, this seems unlikely, to say the least. Knetsch and Sinden unequivocally reject this explanation and argue instead that there is a sort of 'bird in the hand' effect at work in relation to levels of income on wealth. The essential idea seems to be that, given a particular starting level of income, an individual will be somewhat more circumspect in contemplating a definite reduction in that level in exchange for a less well-defined gain (such as the right to participate in a particular gamble) than in speculating about the increase from the existing level of income or wealth that would be equivalent to the uncertain gain. While this explanation seems to drift rather close to reliance upon the notion of diminishing marginal utility of income or wealth (effectively, the influence of income effects in another guise) there does seem to be a grain of truth in the suggestion that, psychologically, people react in a fundamentally different way to reductions in wealth on the one hand and increases on the other.

It must be conceded that all of this is, in its own right, interesting, puzzling and somewhat disturbing. However, the crucial question in the current context is whether or not these apparently paradoxical propensities in individual choice have significant implications for the economic approach to the analysis of physical risk. One suspects not. As in the case of the Allais paradox discussed in Chapter 3, the 'preference reversal' phenomenon seems to be somewhat in the nature of an optical illusion peculiar to the particular kind of financial gambles contrived by Lichtenstein and Slovic, and one is at something of a loss to imagine a counterpart in the case of physical (as opposed to financial) risk. As for the CV–EV disparity identified by Knetsch and Sinden and others, one might be tempted to argue that since the kind of exercise discussed in Chapter 4 deals exclusively with *compensating* variations (i.e. willingness to pay for risk reductions and required compensation for increases in risk) the problem does not arise. However, the major objection to this line of reasoning is that the real conflict in the Knetsch and Sinden results is not that which exists between the CV and EV measures of value but derives instead from the relationship between willingness to pay (WTP) on the one hand and willingness to accept compensation (WTA) on the other. In understanding this point it is important to appreciate that there is a very real difference between the CV–EV and WTP–WTA distinctions. While willingness to pay for a desirable change is unequivocally a CV, willingness to pay to avoid an undesirable change is equally clearly an EV. Similarly, willingness to accept compensation may, depending on context, be either a CV or an EV: such compensation is, in fact, the CV that would 'just make up for' an undesirable change as well as being the EV that would be judged 'just as good as' a desirable change.

Various explanations have been offered for the WTP–WTA disparities observed by Knetsch and Sinden and others. Apart from Knetsch and Sinden's own suggestion that cognitive biases may be at work which lead people to think about reductions in wealth from existing levels in a fundamentally different way from that in which they contemplate increases, other possibilities are discussed by various contributors to Cummings *et al.* (1986). For example, Randall suggests that because of a sort of 'bounded rationality' people will tend to suboptimize in their 'solution' to the problem of expenditure minimization subject to a utility constraint and will hence *under*estimate the maximum sum that they would be willing to pay for a desirable change and *over*estimate the minimum sum that they would accept as compensation for an undesirable change. If this is so, then even if 'true' WTP and WTA were equal, reported values could be expected to diverge in the way that they in fact do. By contrast, Kahneman argues that the WTP–WTA discrepancy is primarily attributable to the kind of 'kinked' value function discussed in Chapter 3, section 3.8.

In spite of these arguments, it remains the author's firm conviction that expected utility theory provides a perfectly adequate explanation for the difference between observed WTP and WTA in the context of physical risk. Thus, the theory developed in Chapter 3, sections 3.3–3.6, indicates that a modest WTP for a 'small' risk reduction from a given base may be quite consistent with a very substantial (and indeed possibly infinite) WTA for a corresponding increase from the same base. In any case, whatever the reason for the difference between WTP and WTA, there can surely be little doubt that *in principle* the former constitutes the appropriate basis for the definition of values of safety improvement while the latter has direct relevance for the specification of costs of increases in risk. The fact that empirical estimates of WTA obtained by direct questioning may, as suggested by Cummings *et al.*, tend to be less reliable than their WTP counterparts is not in itself grounds for wholesale rejection of the WTA definition of cost or value. Cummings *et al.* seem to acknowledge this much in the concluding chapter of their book.

Finally, a version of the preference reversal phenomenon that seems to the author to be distinctly more worrying than Lichtenstein and Slovic's results or the CV–EV disparity is a result reported by Tversky and Kahneman (1981). A group of practising physicians was presented with the following choices:

> Imagine that the United States is preparing for the outbreak of an unusual Asian disease, which is expected to kill 600 people. Two alternative programs to combat the disease have been proposed. Assume that the consequences of the programs are as follows:
>
> > If program A is adopted, 200 people will be saved.
> >
> > If program B is adopted, there is one-third probability that 600 people will be saved, and two-thirds probability that no people will be saved.
>
> Which of the two programs would you favor?

> Imagine that the United States is preparing for the outbreak of an unusual Asian disease, which is expected to kill 600 people. Two alternative programs to combat the disease have been proposed. Assume that the consequences of the programs are as follows:
>
> > If program C is adopted, 400 people will die.
> >
> > If program D is adopted, there is one-third probability that nobody will die, and two-thirds probability that 600 people will die.
>
> Which of the two programs would you favor?

In spite of the fact that A is equivalent to C and B is equivalent to D, most of those presented with the choices expressed a preference for A over B *and* a preference for D over C, thereby providing stark evidence of a kind of preference reversal phenomenon at work in the assessment of physical risk. However, it seems clear that factors that give rise to preference reversal in this sort of case are somewhat different from those suggested by Lichtenstein and Slovic in explanation of their results. Here, rather than having people focus on different aspects of alternative options in different kinds of decision context, it would appear that the 'framing', or way in which the options are described, is responsible for the paradoxical responses. At the very least, this should alert us to the extreme importance of the wording of any questionnaire on the subject of safety and to the need to interpret the responses to such a questionnaire with great caution.

5.2 The Decision Theory Approach

The economist's approach to the problem of risk assessment is essentially based upon the premise that social decisions affecting individual risk should be taken in such a way as to reflect the interests, preferences and attitudes of those who are affected by the decisions. As already noted, economists also tend to proceed on the assumption that risks can be adequately summarized in terms of one or another kind of probability and that individual preferences meet certain minimal requirements of consistency and stability. Ultimately, the conventional economic approach seeks to establish the rate at which individuals are willing to trade off safety against other desirable uses of scarce resources and then recommends that society's corresponding rate of trade-off should be based upon some appropriately weighted average of the individual rates.

Like economists, psychologists are principally concerned with individual attitudes and wishes but, in contrast with economists, they appear to approach the risk assessment problem in a somewhat more eclectic and less highly structured manner with, in particular, far fewer preconceived notions about what constitutes rationality and what is and is not relevant to the individual. As such, and as already remarked in the introductory section of this chapter, the economists' and psychologists' approaches are probably best seen as complementary rather than competing. Thus, while the economic approach, if successful, will provide hard information about a relatively narrow but highly pertinent range of questions concerning the individual valuation of safety, the efforts of psychologists in this field can be expected to shed light on a rather wider, less rigidly prescribed set of questions concerning the way that people think about and react to different kinds of risk and hazard.

The approach advocated by decision theorists is rather different. Under this approach, the focus shifts away from individual wishes and attitudes and rests instead upon the preferences of the social decision-making agent or agency. The essence of the approach is first to identify the main potential consequences of decisions related to disasters and accidents, such as number of lives lost, number of fatal injuries, extent of material damage and the resource cost of attenuating or mitigating these potential adverse consequences. On the assumption that the decision-making agent's preferences are sufficiently well behaved to justify treating the agent as an expected utility maximizer, a multi-attribute 'organizational' utility function is then defined, with the various potential consequences as the relevant arguments. It is important to appreciate that this utility function is essentially that of the relevant decision maker(s) and, as such, its properties will be determined by his or her value judgements concerning the appropriate trade-offs between desirable and undesirable consequences.

The most comprehensive development of the decision theory approach has been undertaken in a series of articles by Keeney (1980a, b, c, 1982) whose programme has been essentially (a) to specify a limited number of value judgements which he believes will have wide appeal to decision makers and then to establish the *general* properties of the organizational utility function implied by these value judgements, and (b) to delineate a limited number of hypothetical questions concerning decisions and choices which, when answered by a particular decision maker, will permit the determination of the various parameters of the organizational utility function.

As a subsidiary component of (a) Keeney has also demonstrated the mutual inconsistency of three value judgements which, on the face of it, most people would probably wish the organizational utility function to exhibit, namely (i) the desirability of minimizing the expected number of lives lost, (ii) the desirability of ensuring an equitable distribution of risks across society and (iii) the desirability of avoiding catastrophes.

5.2.1   Equity Proneness, Catastrophe Aversion and Minimizing Expected Lives Lost

In order to get a feel for the way in which Keeney's argument is developed, it is probably best to begin by outlining the argument by which he demonstrates the inconsistency of the three value judgements referred to in the preceding paragraph. Keeney starts by adopting the notational convention that the vector $(p_1, p_2, \ldots, p_N)$ denotes an ordered set of *statistically independent* probabilities of death during a forthcoming period for each of N individuals. Using this notation, a situation in which each of N individuals is exposed to independent risks of $1/N$ each would be represented by $(1/N, 1/N, \ldots, 1/N)$ whereas the case in which there is a probability $1/N$ that every one of N people would be killed (and a probability $1 - 1/N$ that they would all survive) would be represented by a 'lottery' involving a probability of $1/N$ of $(1, 1, \ldots, 1)$ and a probability of $1 - 1/N$ of $(0, 0, \ldots, 0)$. Notice that both the situations just described involve individual risks of $1/N$ and expected loss of life equal to unity. In the parlance of the decision theory literature, the former has come to be referred to as the loss of one 'statistical' life while the latter is termed a 'catastrophe' risk. A third kind of situation involving individual risks of $1/N$ and expected loss of life equal to unity is that in which one as yet unidentified member of a population of N will certainly die during a forthcoming period. In Keeney's notation this would be represented by a lottery involving a probability $1/N$ of $(1, 0, \ldots, 0)$, a probability $1/N$ of $(0, 1, \ldots, 0)$ and so on, and is referred to as the loss of one 'anonymous' life.[10]

Having introduced a simple notational convention that rather neatly permits the description of various different kinds of risk, Keeney then postulates the value judgement that all individuals are to be equally valued so that $(1, 0, \ldots, 0)$ is equivalent to $(0, 1, \ldots, 0)$ and so on. This means that in assessing different kinds of risk the decision maker's ultimate concern will be exclusively with the probability distribution of *number of fatalities* and not with the identity of potential victims. On the

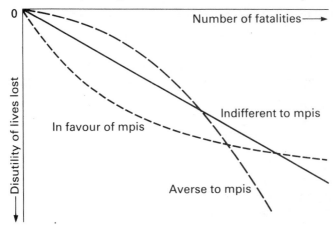

Figure 5.2 Disutility versus number of fatalities (mpis, mean-preserving increase in the spread).

assumption that the decision maker can be treated as an expected utility maximizer, it then follows that his preferences can be represented by the expectation of a cardinal 'disutility of lives lost' function. Clearly, if fewer deaths are preferred to more, then this function will be strictly decreasing in x, the number of fatalities. The crucial question is then whether the function is linear, convex or concave. By the usual argument, it is clear that this will depend upon the decision maker's attitude to a mean-preserving increase in the spread of the probability distribution of number of fatalities. In particular, if the decision maker is indifferent to such increases, then the disutility of lives lost function will be *linear*. Correspondingly, if he is averse to a mean-preserving increase in spread then the function will be *strictly concave*, and if in favour of, then it will be *strictly convex*. The situation is summarized in figure 5.2.

Now it is clear that the relationship between the probability distributions of number of lives lost corresponding to (i) the loss of one anonymous life, (ii) the loss of one statistical life and (iii) a catastrophe risk involving an expected loss of life equal to unity is that, while all three distributions have the same mean, they have successively larger variances. It therefore follows that we shall have the situation shown in table 5.1.

A further and rather significant implication of the correspondence between attitudes to a mean-preserving increase in spread of the probability distributions of number of fatalities and the curvature of the disutility of lives lost function concerns the inconsistency of the three value judgements referred to earlier, each of which appears to have substantial appeal in its own right. Specifically, these value judgements are as follows:

1   Given any two alternative risks to a population, it is desirable to pick that which minimizes the expected loss of life. .

Table 5.1 Preferences over different risks

Disutility of number of lives lost function	*Preference ordering over different kinds of risk*[a]
Linear	(i)I(ii)I(iii)
Convex	(iii)P(ii)P(i)
Concave	(i)P(ii)P(iii)

[a] I denotes the relation of indifference and P denotes the relation of strict preference.

2 Given two vectors of independent probabilities of death $(p_1, \ldots, p_i, \ldots, p_j, \ldots, p_N)$ and $(p_1, \ldots, p_i+\varepsilon, \ldots, p_j-\varepsilon, \ldots, p_N)$, the former will be preferred whenever the difference between p_i and p_j is smaller than that between $p_i+\varepsilon$ and $p_j-\varepsilon$. In other words, a situation in which risks are more evenly or equitably spread over the population is to be preferred. (Keeney refers to this as the 'risk equity assumption'.)

3 A probability π of x fatalities is preferred to a probability π' or x' fatalities whenever $x < x'$ given that $\pi x = \pi'x'$. (Keeney describes this as the 'catastrophe avoidance assumption'.)

Now clearly, a decision maker who subscribes to the first of these value judgements must have a *linear* disutility of lives lost function (i.e. must be indifferent to a mean-preserving increase in spread). By contrast, the 'risk equity assumption' requires that the disutility function should be strictly convex (entailing a preference for a mean-preserving increase in spread) and finally the 'catastrophe avoidance assumption' implies that the function should be strictly concave. Thus, in spite of their individual appeal, the three value judgements are mutually incompatible so that a decision maker who subscribes to one must, perforce, reject the other two *or* must accept that his choices will not obey the axioms of expected utility theory.

5.2.2 Structuring and Calibrating the Organizational Utility Function

Turning now to procedures by which one might set about structuring and estimating the parameters of the disutility of lives lost function or some more comprehensive organizational utility function for a particular decision maker or group, this section summarizes the approach advocated by Keeney (1980a). The procedure developed by Keeney is intended more as an illustrative guide to the general way in which one might proceed rather than as a comprehensive prescription covering all factors that might conceivably be of relevance to a particular decision maker. Thus, Keeney focuses upon possible fatalities and does not explicitly consider other potentially relevant consequences such as injury, illness or environmental and economic effects, although the clear implication is that a suitably generalized version of the same sort of approach could also accommodate such effects.

Keeney begins by distinguishing between the number of fatalities x due to involuntary risks and the number y due to voluntary risks. As Keeney observes, the distinction between these two kinds of risk is not always clear-cut, but archetypal examples would be the risk of death in a nuclear war initiated by a hostile power (involuntary) and the risk of death in a climbing accident (voluntary). An example of a risk in the 'grey area' in between would be the possibility of melt-down of a nuclear reactor located in the vicinity of one's home (since one *could* choose to live elsewhere, there is clearly an element of voluntariness about continuing to bear the risk).

Given that x and y are assumed to be the ultimate objects of concern, it follows that if the decision maker values all lives equally and behaves as an expected utility maximizer, then the organizational utility function u will be defined on (x, y) pairs. The next stage in the argument is thus to structure and specify $u(x, y)$. As a first step in this process, Keeney suggests that 'there should be two major governmental concerns regarding impact of fatalities on the public', namely (a) the direct effects of pain, suffering and economic hardship for victims, friends and relatives together with the grief, sorrow and anxiety experienced by others less directly involved (personal impacts) and (b) indirect societal effects, including political, social and economic turmoil (societal impacts). Keeney proposes that there will exist *separate* component utility functions, $u_p(x, y)$ and $u_s(x, y)$, for personal and societal impacts respectively, and assumes that the decision maker's preferences over probability distributions of x and y satisfy 'independence' conditions which ensure that $u_p(x, y)$ and $u_s(x, y)$ will each be quasi-additive[11] with, in particular,

$$u_p(x, y) = \alpha_p f_p(x) + \beta_p g_p(y) + (\alpha_p + \beta_p - 1)f_p(x)g_p(y) \quad (5.1)$$

and

$$u_s(x, y) = \alpha_s f_s(x) + \beta_s g_s(y) + (\alpha_s + \beta_s - 1)f_s(x)g_s(y) \quad (5.2)$$

Furthermore, Keeney assumes that $u(x, y)$ is *itself* additive[12] in $u_p(x, y)$ and $u_s(x, y)$, i.e. with appropriate choice of scaling

$$u(x, y) = u_p(x, y) + \gamma u_s(x, y) \quad (5.3)$$

Keeney then proceeds to refine the structure of $u_p(x, y)$ and $u_s(x, y)$ still further. For example in the case of $u_p(x, y)$ he assumes that

1 as far as personal impacts are concerned, the decision maker will be indifferent between any two options that yield the same involuntary risks of death for each individual. Thus, using the notation introduced earlier, in terms of personal impacts the decision maker would be indifferent between independent involuntary risks $(1/N, 1/N, \ldots, 1/N)$ and involuntary risks involving a $1/N$ chance of $(1, 0, \ldots, 0)$, $1/N$ of $(0, 1, \ldots, 0)$ etc.
2 similar conditions apply to the personal impact of voluntary risks.
3 viewed from the perspective of their personal impacts, the decision

maker will be indifferent between the following joint distributions of x and y:

A, a 50/50 chance of $(0, 0)$ and (x', y')
B, a 50/50 chance of $(0, y')$ and $(x', 0)$.

From conditions (1) and (2) it follows immediately that $f_p(x)$ and $g_p(y)$ will both be *linear* functions and condition (3) (known as 'Fishburn marginality') implies that $u_p(x, y)$ will be additive (rather than quasi-additive). With appropriate choice of scaling, $u_p(x, y)$ can therefore be written as

$$u_p(x, y) = -x - \lambda y \qquad \lambda > 0. \qquad (5.4)$$

In the case of $u_s(x, y)$ Keeney assumes that

1   in terms of the societal impact, the certain loss of x lives due to involuntary risks is less desirable than a 50:50 chance of $2x$ fatalities or 0 fatalities.
2   as the number of deaths, x, due to involuntary risks gets increasingly large, the difference in societal impact between x and $2x$ approaches zero.
3   there is a constant probability p, independent of x, such that the societal impact of the loss of x lives due to involuntary risks is the same as a probability p of the loss of $x + 1$ lives and a probability $1 - p$ of the loss of $x - 1$ lives.
4   similar conditions apply to the societal impact of voluntary risks.

Given (4), conditions (1) and (2) imply that $f_s(x)$ and $g_s(y)$ will both be strictly convex and bounded below, while condition (3) implies that these functions will also display a property corresponding to constant Pratt–Arrow absolute financial risk aversion.[13] Keeney therefore proposes to adopt the following specific functional forms that embody these properties:

$$f_s(x) = \frac{1}{h}[(1 - h)^x - 1] \qquad 0 < h < 1 \qquad (5.5)$$

and

$$g_s(y) = \frac{1}{d}[(1 - d)^y - 1] \qquad 0 < d < 1. \qquad (5.6)$$

Given appropriate choice of scale and on the further assumption that the societal impact of (x, y) approaches the societal impact of $(x, 0)$ for all y as x becomes increasingly large, Keeney shows that $u_s(x, y)$ will then simplify to

$$u_s(x, y) = \frac{1}{h}[(1 - h)^x - 1] + \frac{\mu}{d}[(1 - d)^y - 1](1 - h)^x \quad (5.7)$$

where μ is a parameter.

Thus, assuming that the conditions underpinning (5.3) are satisfied, $u(x, y)$ can be written as

$$u(x, y) = -x - \lambda y + \gamma \left\{ \frac{1}{h}[(1 - h)^x - 1] \right.$$
$$\left. + \frac{\mu}{d}[(1 - d)^y - 1](1 - h)^x \right\} \qquad (5.8)$$

In order to complete the specification of $u(x, y)$ for a given decision maker, it is then necessary to determine the parameters λ, γ, h, μ and d. Basically, these parameters reflect the decision maker's relative evaluation of the impacts of different kinds of risk. In particular[14]

λ is the weight given to the personal impact of one fatality due to voluntary risks relative to the personal impact of one fatality due to involuntary risks.

γ is the weight given to the societal impact of an involuntary risk involving one fatality relative to the personal impact of that fatality.

h is the weight given to the societal impact of an involuntary risk involving one fatality relative to the societal impact of a large number of fatalities due to involuntary risks (notice from (5.5) that, with $x = 1$, $f_s(x) = -1$ while $\lim_{x \to \infty} f_s(x) = -1/h$).

μ is the weight given to the societal impact of a voluntary risk involving one fatality relative to the societal impact of an involuntary risk involving one fatality.

d is the weight given to the societal impact of a voluntary risk involving one fatality relative to the societal impact of a large number of fatalities due to voluntary risks (notice from (5.6) that, with $y = 1$, $g_s(y) = -1$ while $\lim_{y \to \infty} g_s(y) = -1/d$).

Keeney then shows how λ, γ, h, μ and d can, in principle, be determined for any particular decision maker by presenting him with appropriately framed hypothetical choices. For example, in the case of h, one could attempt to establish the numbers of fatalities x_1 and x_2 such that the decision maker judged the societal impact of x_1 fatalities for certain to be equivalent to the societal impact of a $50:50$ chance of x_2 fatalities and no fatalities. From (5.5) it would then follow that

$$(1 - h)^{x_1} - 1 = 0.5[(1 - h)^{x_2} - 1] \qquad (5.9)$$

which can then be solved for h. The parameters d, λ and μ can similarly be estimated by establishing the appropriate equivalences between the specific impacts of different kinds of risk. In the case of γ, however, things are a little more complicated since this parameter reflects the relative evaluation of societal and personal impacts. In principle, what one wants to do is to find levels of $u_p(x, y)$ and $u_s(x, y)$ that are judged to be equivalent in terms of undesirability by the decision maker. But, as Keeney notes, such levels have no direct '. . . physical interpretation . . .' so that we cannot frame choices explicitly in terms of $u_p(x, y)$ and $u_s(x, y)$. However, if the parameters λ, h, μ and d have already been estimated, then γ can be determined by (a) establishing levels of involuntary and voluntary risks x_1 and y_1 that the decision maker judges equivalent (taking account of personal *and* societal impacts) to risks x_2 and y_2 and then (b) equating the resultant expressions for $u(x_1, y_1)$ and $u(x_2, y_2)$.

So much for the mechanics of Keeney's proposed procedure for structuring and estimating the organizational utility function, but what of its practicability and potential effectiveness as a means of dealing with safety effects in government and industrial decision making? At the level of practicality, the major limitation of the kind of approach proposed by Keeney lies in its high degree of complexity, abstraction and formalism. In short, the suggestion that a procedure as intricate and tortuous as that described above could possibly constitute a successful substitute for (or adjunct to) the exercise of experienced judgement would probably evoke a reaction somewhere on a spectrum from mirth to outrage on the part of most public sector and industrial decision makers. In this author's experience, it is a frequently frustrating but nonetheless hard fact of life that, if formalized decision procedures are to stand any chance of being accepted by those involved in government or industrial decision making, then they have to be capable of succinct explanation and must, above all else, carry a strong and direct commonsense appeal. Not to put too fine a point on it, Keeney's approach would almost certainly be viewed as a fantastical concoction of mathematical and philosophical legerdemain by those actively engaged in the kind of decisions that it is supposed to assist. Also, as already noted in Chapter 1, senior decision makers would be understandably reluctant to surrender their active decision-making role to what they would perceive as the inexorable grinding of a mathematical abstraction. Finally, one suspects that many decision makers would become impatient with the failure of Keeney's approach to shed any light whatsoever on many of the more difficult ethical questions that one inevitably confronts in decisions affecting safety. For example, the approach gives no guidance at all as to *how* one ought to go about trading off safety improvement against other kinds of benefit – or weighing voluntary against involuntary risks – or assessing the relative costs of fatal and non-fatal injury. Indeed, far from shedding light on these crucial questions, the decision theory approach advocated by Keeney simply repackages them in what, for many decision makers, will appear to be a rather arcane and opaque mathematical obfuscation.

In practical terms, then, one doubts that Keeney's approach stands much chance of arousing more than passing curiosity and ultimate irritation on the part of those seriously involved in decisions concerning safety, especially when they come to appreciate that the approach simply begs many of the really difficult questions. However, even if one sets aside these reservations concerning the practical feasibility of Keeney's approach, there remain further more fundamental doubts about his proposals. For example, is the distinction between 'personal' and 'societal' impacts really sustainable? In particular, what *are* 'societal' impacts if other than effects upon victims and other individuals more or less closely associated with them? At one stage in his argument, Keeney is emphatic that the preferences that are reflected in the component utility function u_p '. . . are those of individuals directly impacted by the fatalities' so that, by implication, the essential distinction between u_p and u_s lies in the constituencies whose preferences are represented by these functions. But this way of looking at things would seem to sit rather uncomfortably with the fundamental *raison d'être* of the decision theory approach which is to structure and estimate a utility function representing the *decision maker's* preferences.

Another more technical difficulty associated with Keeney's 'personal/ societal' impact distinction lies in the justification for the structure of $u(x, y)$ specified in (5.3). While it is one thing to argue that the Fishburn marginality condition implying the additive structure of u_p given in (5.4) applies to joint distributions of x and y, it is entirely another matter to suggest that this condition also applies to joint distributions of u_p and u_s, as does Keeney.[15] Thus, the choice between a $50:50$ chance of $(0, 0)$ and (x', y') and a $50:50$ chance of $(0, y')$ and $(x', 0)$ is clear and unambiguous. However, what is one supposed to make of a choice between a $50:50$ chance of $(0, 0)$ and (u_p', u_s') and a $50:50$ chance of $(0, u_s')$ and $(u_p', 0)$? In order for this choice to be meaningful, u_p and u_s have to be capable of independent variation, but how can this be so if both are defined on the same (x, y) pair?

5.3 Summary and Concluding Comments

Given the multifaceted nature of the subject, it is not surprising that risk analysis has attracted the attention of a number of different disciplines. Thus, in addition to work by economists, significant contributions have also come from psychology, decision theory, philosophy, natural science, engineering and medicine. Clearly it is beyond the scope of this book – and the ability of its author – to attempt to provide a summary of all of these diverse contributions. However, the issues addressed by psychologists and decision theorists are so closely related to, and bear so directly upon, those considered by economists that it seems especially important to try to understand the relationship between developments in these three particular disciplines.

This chapter has therefore attempted to summarize and evaluate some of the more significant contributions to risk analysis that have come from cognitive and experimental psychology and decision theory.

As far as the way in which the three disciplines relate, it has been argued that the contributions from psychology and decision theory are most fruitfully viewed as complements to, rather than as substitutes for, the approach adopted by economists. Thus, the insights gained from work by psychologists on the nature of beliefs and attitudes concerning different sources of risk illuminate dimensions of individual perception that have been largely neglected by economists, but are nonetheless of vital importance if we are to have an adequate understanding of the way in which people think about and react to risk. It is rather as if economists, concerned with a rather narrow range of questions related to the problem of resource allocation, focus a spotlight on a limited area, while psychologists play a less intense beam, more widely cast.

The relationship between economics and decision theory is somewhat different. Thus, while contributions from decision theory appear to contain no obvious counterpart to economists' and psychologists' *positive* analysis of individual preferences and attitudes, there is a clear parallel between decision theory and the *normative* aspects of the economic approach. In particular, like economists (and in notable contrast with psychologists) decision theorists explicitly address the question of how a government or similar decision-making agency *ought* to make decisions concerning safety. However, there are again notable differences in emphasis. For example, economists have, in the main, tended to argue that social choices should as far as possible reflect individual preferences and attitudes (hence the economists' preoccupation with the positive analysis of the latter). By contrast, decision theorists appear to be somewhat less concerned to ensure that social choices reflect individual wishes and concentrate instead upon the sorts of criteria by which different probability distributions of fatalities (and other desirable and undesirable consequences) might be compared by a decision-making agency.

In spite of such differences in emphasis, there is once more a significant potential complementarity between the two approaches. Thus, as suggested in Chapter 1, it may well be that a blend of economics and decision theory will provide the most effective way of informing resource allocation decisions in the case of potential catastrophes.

Finally, it is worth remarking that there are certain similarities between the way in which Keeney, in particular, structures the problem of organizational decision making in the context of physical risk and Broome's advocacy of the *ex post* (or *exostochastic*) approach in welfare economics summarized in Chapter 1. Specifically, both approaches focus upon the decision maker's evaluation of the probability distribution of *ex post* outcomes (such as number of fatalities) rather than upon individual evaluations of *ex ante* risks.

Notes

1 Arguably, the assumption of stable, well-behaved individual preferences is *the* hallmark of mainstream (neoclassical) positive and normative economic analysis.
2 Reproduced from Thomas (1981) with kind permission of Dr Thomas and the Royal Society.
3 A second factor analysis of belief strength ratings for nuclear energy alone indicated that in this case the 39 consequences could be reduced to just *four* underlying dimensions, namely 'socio-political risk', 'psychological risk', 'environmental and physical risk' and 'economic and technical benefit'.
4 For an interesting discussion of measurement in experimental psychology, see Cliff (1982).

5 Though it will be recalled from Chapter 1, section 1.6.3, that Fischer (1979) is somewhat less sanguine on this score.

6 See, for example, Gravelle and Rees (1981), Chapter 4, and Foster and Neuberger (1974).

7 These reflect the way in which an individual's consumption of a good is affected by variations in his or her income or wealth.

8 A normal good is one whose consumption increases with income, while an inferior good is one whose consumption decreases with income.

9 For example, in a simple two-goods consumption problem consider first a reduction in the price of one good for which the CV is precisely half the consumer's income. Then, as an alternative, consider a 49% reduction in the price of *both* goods. The CV for the latter will clearly be equal to 49% of the consumer's income. However, it is a straightfoward matter to construct an indifference map such that the two-goods price reduction is preferred to the one-good price reduction.

10 In Keeney (1980b) the term 'loss of anonymous life' was used to describe what is here being referred to as loss of statistical life, and vice versa. Keeney has since agreed in conversation that his usage in that paper was inappropriate.

11 Consider a situation in which x is random and y deterministic. Suppose that for all distributions $\theta(x)$, $\phi(x)$ and all y_0, y_1, $\theta(x)$ preferred to $\phi(x)$, given $y = y_0 \Rightarrow \theta(x)$ preferred to $\phi(x)$, given $y = y_1$. Then x is said to be 'strongly conditionally utility independent of y' (x s c u i y). It can be shown (see Keeney and Raiffa, 1976) that if x s c u i y and y s c u i x then the Von Neumann – Morgenstern utility function on (x, y) pairs will have the sort of structure specified in (5.1) and (5.2).

12 A sufficient condition for the additive structure, known as 'Fishburn marginality', is discussed below. Keeney assumes that this property applies to joint distributions of u_p and u_s.

13 The Pratt–Arrow measure of absolute risk aversion RA is defined as RA $\equiv - u''(w)/u'(w)$ where $u(w)$ denotes an individual's cardinal utility of wealth. Amongst other things it can be shown that the win probability π that will just induce an individual to pay a small stake x to participate in a financial gamble with a possible net win of x is well approximated by $\pi = 1/2 + (RA/4)x$. If RA is constant, then π is independent of wealth.

14 These are Keeney's definitions.

15 See note 12.

6

Applications and Implications

The body of analysis that constitutes the subject matter of this book is ultimately intended as an aid to the formation of public policy. It would therefore seem appropriate to explore the policy implications of some of the more significant conclusions reached in previous chapters. Accordingly, this chapter considers the application of earlier analysis and results to a selection of problems in three areas of public policy, namely nuclear power, medical care and transport.

6.1 The Economics of Radiological Protection

Of all scientific discoveries and technological advances to date, few, if any, can have been as controversial as nuclear power. In its favour, it is claimed of nuclear power that it represents the solution to the problem of finite reserves of fossil fuels and the damaging environmental and atmospheric effects that may be a consequence of continued extensive reliance on these sources of energy.[1] For those opposed to the use of nuclear power, undoubtedly the major concern is with the adverse health effects of ionizing radiation emitted both in the course of normal operation of nuclear plants and as a result of catastrophic accidents such as recently occurred at Chernobyl.

The purpose of this section is not to argue the grand economic case for or against the use of nuclear power – others have already painted on that broad canvas[2] – but rather to focus upon the safety dimension and to explore the extent to which the analysis of earlier chapters might shed light on this confused and contentious issue.

6.1.1 The Nature of Ionizing Radiation and its Effects on Tissue

The most common forms of ionizing radiation are alpha particles, beta particles, neutrons, gamma rays and X-rays, the first three being subatomic particles (with electric charges in the case of alpha and beta particles), while gamma rays and X-rays are electromagnetic waves. An alpha particle, for example, consists of two protons and two neutrons while a beta particle can take the form of either an electron or a particle with the same mass as an electron but opposite charge. Gamma rays and X-rays, by contrast, have no mass or charge and are essentially quantities of energy.

Ionizing radiation is produced when an atom of an inherently unstable type of element spontaneously transforms into an atom of another type, emitting subatomic particles or quantities of energy as it does so.[3] This process of transformation is known as 'decay' and occurs because the forces within the atomic nucleus of the unstable element are incapable of preserving the particular configuration of protons and neutrons that characterize that type. Unstable elements exist naturally but may also be created by bombarding stable elements with neutrons or in the course of nuclear fission and fusion.

The human body may become irradiated in one of two distinct ways. First, the radiation may come from a source *external* to the body, as in the case of cosmic radiation or radiation generated in the workplace. The second possibility is that radioactive materials (contained in the air or in food) may be taken into the body by inhalation, ingestion or through the skin and thereafter retained for various periods of time in different organs, the latter being subjected to the radiation emitted by these materials during their period of retention in the body.

When ionizing radiation passes through tissue it gives up energy along its path, dislodging electrons from the atoms of the water molecules in tissue cells and hence causing these atoms to become electrically charged or 'ionized'. These irons in turn pass on energy to the tissue cells, thereby damaging them, mainly by breaking one or both strands of the DNA double helix[4] that makes up the chromosomes within the cell, or by causing other kinds of chemical change in the cell. The nature and extent of this damage depends, amongst other things, upon the size of the radiation dose. At high doses the damage may be so extensive as to result in cell death. At lower doses, the cell will not die but the damage may be such as to be incapable of repair by the cell's enzyme systems, in which case, if the cell divides and multiplies, the damage will be transmitted to descendant cells. Usually, this will have no significant adverse impact in view of the large number of undamaged cells elsewhere in the affected tissue. However, there are two sets of circumstances in which the multi-plication of damaged cells can have significant consequences. First, it is possible that the damage causes the cell to become immune to the processes that control the rate of cell multiplication and, as a conse-quence, a cancerous growth develops. Alternatively, the damage may occur to cells that are the originators of the reproductive process, in which case genetic changes, some of which may be detrimental, will result.

The damage that the body sustains because of cell death depends upon the number of cells killed and the organs in which they are located. It has been established that for each of the body's organs there are threshold doses of radiation below which cell death is insufficiently pervasive to cause severe and lasting injury. However, above these thresholds damage will certainly occur, and its extent will increase with the size of the dose up to that point at which the dose is lethal. These are known as the 'non-stochastic' effects of radiation.

In contrast with the non-stochastic effects, which occur only above threshold doses and whose severity then varies with the size of the dose, the carcinogenic and hereditary effects that may result from unrepaired chromosome breaks are thought to have no thresholds. Furthermore, it is the *probability* of occurrence – rather than the severity – of such effects that increases with the size of the dose. These are therefore referred to as 'stochastic' effects.

Not surprisingly, day-to-day activities involving the routine emission of ionizing radiation are strictly regulated to ensure that the thresholds for non-stochastic effects are not even approached. However, if it is the case that stochastic effects have no thresholds, then it must be accepted than even the most minute doses will entail increased risks of cancer and hereditary defects. Indeed, it should also be remembered that even if man-made doses are very small, these effects will be *cumulative* with those of the unavoidable background doses from natural sources, such as the earth's crust and cosmic radiation.

6.1.2   Measures of Radiation Dose

The basic unit of radiation dose is the gray (Gy), which is a measure of the energy transferred by radiation to a given mass of tissue and is equal to one joule per kilogram.[5] However, the cell damage caused by 1 Gy differs from one type of ionizing radiation to another. For example, 1 Gy of alpha radiation gives rise to a much denser path of ionizations within tissue than does 1 Gy of beta radiation and hence is much more likely to cause the hard-to-repair two-strand breaks in the DNA double helix. A measure of radiation dose, weighted for this differential capacity for damage of different kinds of radiation, has therefore been introduced and is known as a 'dose equivalent'. The most common unit of dose equivalent is the sievert (Sv)[6] which, for example, is equal to 1 Gy of X-rays, gamma rays or beta particles but to only 10^{-1} Gy of neutron radiation or to 5×10^{-2} Gy of the potentially far more damaging alpha particles.

As one might expect, the risk of harm from 1 Sv of radiation varies from one part of the body to another. For example, it is lower for bone surfaces and the thyroid gland than for the bone marrow. To take account of this factor, weights have been estimated which allow given doses to particular parts of the body to be converted to 'whole-body' equivalents (i.e. uniform doses to the whole body that would carry the same risk of harm expressed in terms of fatal cancer in the exposed individual and hereditary defects in his or her offspring). For example, while 1 Sv to the red bone marrow is equivalent to a whole-body dose of 0.12 Sv, the same dose to the thyroid gland is equivalent to a whole-body dose of only 0.03 Sv (reflecting the fact that a thyroid is less vulnerable to damage from a given radiation dose than is the bone marrow). Thus a dose of x Sv to the red bone marrow and y Sv to the thyroid gives a whole-body 'effective dose equivalent' of $(0.12x + 0.03y)$ SV.

6.1.3 The Dose–Response Relationship

Empirical estimation of the relationship between radiation dose and the risk of inducing fatal cancers or hereditary defects requires observation – over a period long enough for such adverse effects to manifest themselves – of groups exposed to known doses of radiation over and above background doses, together with observation of similar 'control' groups not exposed to such additional doses. Clearly, the chances of detecting statistically significant differences between the rates of cancer induction (or genetic defects) in the exposed and control groups and of arriving at reliable estimates of incremental risks depends (a) upon the size of these incremental risks and (b) upon the number of people in the respective groups. Intuitively, it is clear that in order to detect smaller differences one will require observations on larger groups. What is perhaps less obvious is that as the difference between the 'true' exposed and control risk is reduced, so the group size required for a given level of reliability of estimation increases substantially more than in proportion. In fact, if the differential risk is reduced by a factor of x then the group size will need to be increased by a factor of x^2.

The long and short of all this is that statistically significant differences between exposed and control groups – and hence reliable estimates of the extent of such differences – have so far been found only in the case of cancer risks at relatively high radiation doses (i.e. in the region of 1 Sv). For cancer risks at lower doses and for genetic defects at all doses so far observed (including those to the victims of Hiroshima and Nagasaki) the groups concerned have been too small to permit the detection of statistically significant differences. This means that for radiation doses of the size normally encountered in the course of radiological protection decisions there is simply no direct empirical evidence concerning the carcinogenic or hereditary effects of such doses. Those concerned with radiological protection have therefore been driven to base their estimates of such effects on extrapolation of curves fitted to observations of incremental risk at high and moderate doses.[7] Theoretical analysis of the nature of radiation-induced cell damage and observations of low-dose mutation rates in other species lend some support to the legitimacy of such extrapolation.

For forms of radiation that produce a high density of ionizations along their path (referred to as high 'linear energy transfer' or LET) such as alpha particles, empirical evidence indicates that risk of induction of fatal cancer is *proportional* to dose, whereas for low LET radiation such as beta particles, X-rays and gamma rays, the relationship is non-linear with, in particular, the risk per unit dose increasing with increasing dose. Straightforward extrapolation therefore suggests dose–response relationships of the type depicted in figure 6.1.

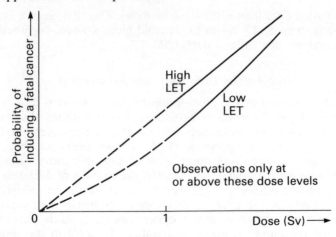

Figure 6.1   Dose–response relationships.

In fact, the pedictions of theory are intriguingly consonant with these empirical observations. In the case of high LET radiation, ionizations along the radiation path are sufficiently dense that a *single* track of radiation can cause the potentially harmful two-strand breaks in the DNA double helix referred to earlier. Since the number of tracks is proportional to dose, the frequency of two-strand breaks, and hence risk of harm, can also be expected to display a proportionality relationship. For low LET radiation, however, ionizations are so spaced out that no single track is likely to cause a double-strand break. Instead, two separate tracks must coincide closely in space and time in order to cause a two-strand break.[8] With number of tracks again proportional to dose, the probability of such coincidence clearly depends on the *square* of the dose so that, for low LET radiation, theory once again predicts the kind of relationship depicted in figure 6.1.

In the case of genetic defects, experimental studies of mice, fruit flies and plants have indicated that the number of cell mutations is proportional to radiation dose down to very low doses (i.e. as low as 3×10^{-3} Sv in plants).

In view of this empirical and theoretical evidence, the various nuclear advisory and regulatory agencies such as the United Nations Scientific Committee on the Effects of Atomic Radiation (UNSCEAR), the International Commission on Radiological Protection (ICRP) and the UK National Radiological Protection Board (NRPB) have opted for the 'worst-case' assumption that, for both fatal cancers and hereditary defects, risk is *proportional to dose at all doses, without thresholds*. The specific risk factors recommended by the ICRP are 1.25×10^{-2} per sievert for fatal cancer risks (NRPB, 1981, p. 23) and about 8×10^{-3} per sievert for genetic defects in all future generations (or about 4×10^{-3} per sievert if only the first two generations are taken into account) (ICRP, 1977, p. 12) giving an overall risk factor for fatal cancers and genetic defects in all future generations of about 2×10^{-2} per sievert.

Given the assumption of proportionality in the dose–response relationship together with a specific risk factor of 2×10^{-2} per sievert, it follows that the *expected* number of fatal cancers and genetic defects in any irradiated population is given by $[\Sigma_i x_i f(x_i)] \times 2 \times 10^{-2}$ where $f(x_i)$ is the number of people receiving a dose level of x_i Sv. The sum $\Sigma_i x_i f(x_i)$ is referred to as a 'collective effective dose equivalent' and is normally measured in 'man sieverts.' Thus, for example, 1 man Sv might involve ten people each receiving 10^{-1} Sv *or* five people each receiving 0.05 Sv and five people each receiving 0.15 Sv *or* a million people each receiving 10^{-6} Sv and so on. In each case the expected number of health effects is the same and is given by the product of the collective dose and the risk factor, *regardless* of the way in which the collective dose is distributed over the affected population.[9] Notice that this would *not* be the case if the dose–response relationship were other than one of proportionality.

6.1.4   The ICRP, NRPB and the ALARA Principle

Although the recommendations of the ICRP have no statutory force, they are significantly influential in the formation of radiological protection policy in most of those countries that use nuclear power. The fundamental principles underpinning the ICRP's recommendations are the following (ICRP, 1977, p. 3):

1   no practice shall be adopted unless its introduction produces a positive net benefit;
2   all exposures shall be kept as low as reasonably achievable, economic and social factors being taken into account (this is commonly referred to as the ALARA principle); and
3   the dose equivalent to individuals shall not exceed the limits recommended for the appropriate circumstances by the Commission.

As far as recommendations (1) and (2) are concerned, the ICRP has explicitly indicated that the concepts and techniques of conventional social cost–benefit analysis are to be employed in determining appropriate levels of expenditure on radiological protection. In the case of recommendation (3) the ICRP has set specific dose limits: (a) for those exposed to radiation in the course of their employment and (b) for members of the general public. The rationale for the occupational dose limit is to set a level of annual dose which, when treated as a maximum permissible dose, will result in *average* annual doses yielding incremental risks that are comparable with those in 'other occupations recognized as having high standards of safety' (ICRP, 1977, p. 19). The ICRP identifies this incremental occupational risk as being about 10^{-4} per annum so that given a risk factor of 2×10^{-2} per sievert it is clear that, according to the ICRP criterion, average annual doses from occupational exposure should not exceed 5×10^{-3} Sv. Given that annual doses in large groups of workers

have been found to be approximately log-normally distributed in circumstances in which its recommendations have been applied, the ICRP
has therefore set its dose limit for workers at ten times the level of the
average dose which it does not wish to exceed, i.e. at 50×10^{-3} Sv.

In the case of the general public, dose limits are set so as to ensure that
incremental risks from radiation do not exceed those that individuals
appear to run in the normal course of everyday life (ICRP, 1977, p. 23).
The ICRP identifies such risks as lying in the range $10^{-6} - 10^{-5}$ p.a. and
accordingly sets the lifetime dose limit at 70×10^{-3} Sv (or 1×10^{-3} Sv
p.a. on average) and the absolute limit to annual dose at one-tenth of the
limit for workers, i.e. at 5×10^{-3} Sv. Again, it would appear that the
rationale for these limits is that if they are observed then *average* exposures will be very much lower.

Clearly, in order to implement the ICRP recommendations, and the
ALARA principle in particular, it is necessary to associate costs with
incremental risks from exposure to radiation and values with reductions
in these risks so that standard procedures of allocative decision making
may be applied to the selection of appropriate levels of expenditure on
radiological protection. The specific recommendations of the ICRP and
NRPB concerning such costs and values, while differing in detail, are
broadly similar in principle. Basically, both involve the specification of a
'baseline' cost per collective dose equivalent, applicable at low individual
doses, which then rises as individual doses increase to reflect '. . . the
aspect of individual risk aversion towards increasing levels of individual
dose' (NRPB, 1986). Thus, for example, NRPB (1986) recommends a
baseline cost of £3,000 per man sievert at individual doses of less than
10^{-5} which then rises as a *convex* function of dose to about £45,000 per
man sievert at doses in the region of 1 Sv.[10]

Qualitatively, these recommendations, together with the ICRP dose
limits, are *entirely consonant* with the precepts of the willingness-to-pay
approach to the valuation of life and safety. Indeed, early versions of the
NRPB argument *explicitly appealed* to the results of work by the author
in order to rationalize its recommendations (NRPB, 1980, pp. 35–6,
66–71; 1981, pp. 31–3).

To be more explicit, suppose that as argued in Chapter 3, willingness to
pay v is a decreasing concave function of the probability of death p_t
during the tth future period, with a graph of the general form shown in
figure 6.2. Now consider an increase in risk to a group of people such that
the expected number of deaths in the group during period t rises by 1.
By the argument developed in Chapter 3, under the willingness-to-pay
approach the cost of this 'statistical fatality'[11] will be given by the population mean of m_t, *provided that individual increments in risk are small*.
Suppose, however, that these individual increments are not sufficiently
small to justify using a first-order Taylor's series approximation. It will
then be necessary to define the cost of the increase in risk, not in terms of
the mean of m_t, but rather as the mean of the modulus of the slope of
a *chord* to the graph in figure 6.2. In particular, denoting the 'non-

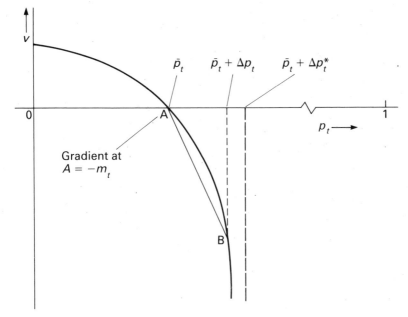

Figure 6.2 v as a function of p_t.

marginal' increment in individual probability of death by $\triangle p_t$, the overall cost of the increase in risk will be given by the mean, over the affected group, of the modulus of the slope of the chord AB. Clearly, for any given individual, the chord AB will be steeper the larger is $\triangle p_t$, so that the cost of a statistical fatality will tend to rise as individual increments in risk get larger. This means, for example, that the cost of exposing 10^3 people to individual increments of 10^{-3} in the probability of death during any given period will, other things being equal, be greater than the cost of exposing 10^6 people to increments of 10^{-6}. It is clear, then, that under the willingness-to-pay approach the cost of a statistical fatality will be related to increments in individual risk by a function whose graph has the general form shown in figure 6.3.

Notice (a) that the intercept[12] on the vertical axis will be given by the population mean of the relevant marginal rate of substitution m_t and (b) that the level of the increment in individual risk at which the cost of a statistical fatality becomes unbounded will depend on individual maximum acceptable increases in risk, $\triangle p_t^*$, within the affected group and, strictly speaking, will be equal to the *smallest* of these maximum acceptable increases.[13]

As already noted, the assumed proportionality of the dose–response relationship implies that the expected number of fatal cancers and serious genetic defects depends only on collective dose and is equal to about 2×10^{-2} per man sievert. Assuming that people are about equally averse to

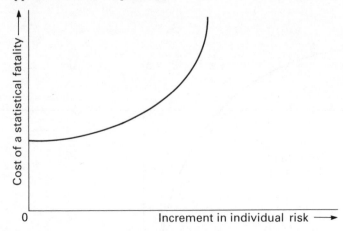

Figure 6.3 Cost of a statistical fatality versus increment in individual risk.

the prospect of developing fatal cancers themselves and passing on serious genetic defects to their descendants,[14] this allows the NRPB cost
per man sievert to be converted directly to an equivalent cost of statistical
death simply by dividing by 2×10^{-2}. Similarly, individual annual dose in
sieverts converts directly to incremental individual risk of death by multi-
plication by 2×10^{-2}. The NRBP proposal that the cost per man sievert
should be an increasing, convex function of individual dose, together with
the ICRP dose limits, therefore, as suggested, squares rather well in
qualitative terms with the shape of the graphs in figures 6.2 and 6.3.
However, when one comes to examine the precise *quantitative* nature of
the ICRP and NRPB recommendations, things look somewhat less satisfactory.

In the first place, given a coefficient of proportionality of 2×10^{-2} in
the dose–response relationship, the NRPB cost per man sievert of £3,000
at low doses converts directly to a cost of a statistical fatality of £150,000.
This, incidentally, is very similar to the Department of Transport's 1986
cost of a fatality and indeed this is hardly surprising since the NRPB cost,
like the Department of Transport figure, is derived by the gross output
method (NRPB, 1986, section 4). One is therefore bound to wonder why
the NRPB has based its estimate on a patently deficient methodology.
The answer is not easy to discern. One possible explanation is that gross
output costs and values can be estimated with considerable precision, and
precise estimates are luxuries that natural scientists have traditionally
enjoyed – and have therefore come to expect – to a far greater degree
than their counterparts in the social sciences. Would it, then, be so
surprising that the NRPB staffed, as it is, predominantly by natural
scientists, should succumb to the temptation to opt for a precise estimate
of the wrong thing rather than an imprecise indication of the broad order
of magnitude of an entirely more appropriate concept of cost? A rather

different and probably more persuasive explanation is suggested by the rationale offered in NRPB (1980) for selection of the gross output approach. In particular, it is argued that:

> work carried out by Jones-Lee has indicated that where individuals are aware of any change in risk, even at very low levels, their subjective valuations will dominate the costing, possibly exceeding the direct monetary costs by an order of magnitude.
>
> There are therefore three possible evaluations of the value to be assigned to increments of collective dose equivalent made up entirely of dose equivalents below an insignificant dose level.
> (a)   A value of zero, based on pragmatic arguments that any finite value will divert resources to reducing doses which are already insignificant.
> (b)   A value of about £1,000 per man Sv (£10 per man rem) using only the direct costs of objectively predicted statistical health effects.
> (c)   A value of about £5,000 to £10,000 per man Sv (£50 to £100 per man rem) using in addition subjective valuations of very low levels of risk.
>
> The Board feels that on balance option (b) represents the most reasonable choice and suggests a value of £1,000 per man Sv (£10 per man rem) for practical use. (National Radiological Protection Board, 1980, p. 10)

The first thing to notice about this passage is its clear indication of the NRPB's awareness of the willingness-to-pay approach and the fact that it would yield a cost of per man sievert very significantly larger than the figure given by the gross output method. The other striking feature of the passage is that its structure and conclusion bear all the hallmarks of a *compromise*. But this leads one to wonder why it was felt necessary to compromise in the first place and why, having decided to compromise, the NRPB should do so by picking a manifestly inappropriate and by now largely discredited methodology. One explanation for the decision to compromise is that it reflects doubts about the proportionality hypothesis for the dose–response relationship and concern over the possibility that there may, in fact, exist threshold doses below which there are no stochastic effects at all, which, if it were the case, would imply a cost per man sievert of *zero* at low doses. The reference to '. . . doses that are already insignificant' in (a) seems to suggest that the NRPB may indeed harbour such doubts, and if this is so then it would certainly be appropriate to 'compromise' between a cost of zero and the level of cost implied by the willingness-to-pay approach together with the proportionality hypothesis. However, it is surely *not* appropriate to effect such a compromise by basing cost estimates on the gross output approach. If the NRPB is, in fact, uncertain about whether the dose–response relationship involves proportionality at all doses on the one hand or thresholds on the other, then a rational (rather than arbitrary) way to reflect such uncertainty would be to assign the proportionality and threshold hypotheses prior probabilities of π and $1 - \pi$ respectively and then set the risk factor at $\pi \times 2 \times 10^{-2}$ adverse health effects per man sievert for low doses. With the cost of a statistical fatality set at the minimum level implied by the willingness-to-pay approach[15] (i.e. about £500,000) π would then have to be in the region of 0.3 in order to justify a cost per man sievert as low as the NRPB's latest figure of £3,000. One doubts that the NRPB has *that* little faith in the proportionality hypothesis.

Having established that the NRPB's recommended cost per man sievert at low doses does not accord with the cost that would be implied by the willingness-to-pay approach, let us now turn to the recommendations for higher doses. While the NRPB's proposals concerning costs at higher doses make no direct allowance for dose limits, it is clearly intended that the ICRP limits appropriate to particular circumstances should form an upper bound to permissible doses (NRPB, 1986, section 4) so that any project or activity that violated the relevant limit would be rejected out of hand, however beneficial it might be in other respects. These limits therefore effectively determine the level of individual dose at which the cost per man sievert – and hence the implied cost of a statistical fatality – *becomes infinite*. As such, the ICRP limits can be viewed as public sector decision-making counterparts to individual maximum acceptable increases in risk and indeed, if the dose limits are to accord with the wishes and attitudes of those they will affect, then there is a good case for setting the limits so as to reflect the typical order of magnitude of individual maximum acceptable increments in risk. Now it will be recalled that the ICRP's annual dose limit for occupational exposures is 50×10^{-3} Sv, while that for the general public is 5×10^{-3} Sv. Given a risk factor of 2×10^{-2} fatal cancers and hereditary defects per sievert, these limits therefore mean that projects which raise the risk of fatal cancer or hereditary defects by more than 10^{-3} p.a. for workers, or 10^{-4} for the general public, will be rejected. Could such increases in risk possibly be taken to reflect the typical order of magnitude of individual maximum acceptable increments? The first thing to say is that the figure of 10^{-4} for the public does seem improbably small given that most people already face an annual risk of death from all causes of more than 10^{-3}, although, in the absence of hard empirical evidence concerning the typical magnitude of $\triangle p_t^*$, one has to concede that such an assessment can be little more than an expression of hunch or casual speculation. However, things can be made somewhat more concrete by employing the relationship between m_t, $\triangle p_t^*$ and RL derived in Chapter 3. In particular, suppose that we set m_t at the sort of level suggested by revealed preference and questionnaire studies. Given that the latter, strictly speaking, provide estimates of m_1, then to the extent that m_t decreases with t, this will if anything overestimate m_t. Nonetheless, setting $m_t = £1.5 \times 10^6$ (a value that is broadly reflective of the central tendency measures of the more reliable estimates reported in Chapters 2 and 4) and $\triangle p_t^* = 10^{-4}$ (the level implied by the ICRP dose limit), the relationship $m_t \triangle p_t^* \text{RL} = 1$ then gives RL $= 1/150$. Now recall that RL can be interpreted as an approximation to the critical odds at which an individual would *just* be willing to undertake a £1 stake large payoff financial gamble. Would the reader have any hesitation about paying a £1 stake for a possible multimillion pound payoff if the chances of winning were 1 in 150? One strongly suspects not, and this leads inexorably to the conclusion that one or other (or both) of $m_t = £1.5 \times 10^6$ or $\triangle p_t^* = 10^{-4}$ are serious *underestimates*. Indeed, to drive RL down to a level that begins to sound plausible it would seem to be necessary to increase m_t or $\triangle p_t^*$ by at least an order of magnitude. While it is just possible that people are so averse to risks from nuclear power that marginal rates of substitution for such risks are typically as high as £15 $\times$ 10^6, this does seem rather unlikely. What is altogether more credible is that $\triangle p_t^*$ is substantially closer to 10^{-3} than to 10^{-4}. Notice that this conclusion concerning the magnitude of $\triangle p_t^*$ becomes even more persuasive if one sets m_t at the lower end of the range of estimates reported in Chapters 2 and 4, namely £500,000.

All things considered, then, it would appear that the NRPB's recommended cost per man sievert at low doses is almost certainly at least an order of magnitude too small and that the same can probably be said for the ICRP dose limit for members of the general public. What seems absolutely clear, however, is that if the cost associated with a man sievert at low doses and the dose limit for members of the general public are to reflect individual attitudes and wishes then, given the relationship between m_t, $\triangle p_t^*$ and RL, the NRPB's cost and the ICRP's dose limit cannot *both* be appropriate. Indeed, setting $m_t = £150,000$ (the value implied by the NRPB cost per man sievert) and $\triangle p_t^* = 10^{-4}$ (the level implied by the ICRP dose limit) gives RL = 1/15 which is absurdly large. It therefore follows that if these recommendations are implemented then they will tend to lead to a misallocation of resources in that too little will be spent on the attenuation of low doses relative to the amount devoted to keeping higher doses within the ICRP limits.

6.1.5 *The implications of Broome and Keeney's Arguments*

Having explored the implications of the willingness-to-pay approach for the ICRP and NRPB recommendations, it would seem appropriate to evaluate these recommendations from the alternative perspective of the arguments adduced by Broome and Keeney and summarized in earlier chapters. Amongst other things Broome believes that government decisions under uncertainty ought to obey the 'sure thing' principle and that in consequence the value of statistical life (or the cost of a statistical fatality) should be *independent* of the size of the group at risk. Thus, according to Broome, a variation in individual risk of 10^{-3} for each of a thousand people should be accorded precisely the same cost or value as a variation of 10^{-6} for each of a million people. The essential reason that Broome gives for this recommendation, it will be recalled, is that if the cost of a statistical fatality increases with the size of individual increments

in risk (as implied by the willingness-to-pay approach) then the anticipated loss of one anonymous life from a population of size n will be
accorded a higher cost than the loss of one life in a population of size $2n$,
thereby violating the 'sure thing' principle.

The implications of Broome's argument for the ICRP and NRPB
recommendations are therefore even more dramatic than those already
reached in this section. In particular, Broome's position entails (a) that
the cost of a man sievert should be *independent* of individual dose and (b)
that there should be *no* dose limits. As was noted in Chapter 1, there is
therefore a clear conflict between the requirements of coherence (including the sure-thing principle) in government decision making and democracy (i.e. ensuring that government decisions take account of individual
wishes and attitudes to risk). The reader must simply make up his or her
own mind about how this conflict should be resolved. However, it is
worth remarking that any government that persistently ignored people's
wishes and attitudes in a matter as sensitive as nuclear safety would
almost certainly do so at its peril and the author's view (for what it is
worth) is that, since considerations of democracy are paramount, then
that is precisely as it should be.

As far as Keeney's proposals are concerned, these would involve rejection of the ICRP's recommendation that allocative decisions related
to radiological protection should be taken according to the principles of
conventional social cost–benefit analysis. Instead, Keeney would presumably have the relevant bodies structure and calibrate an appropriate
organizational utility function and then allocate resources to radiological
protection in such a way as to maximize the mathematical expectation of
this function. The various practical and other objections to Keeney's
proposed approach have already been developed in Chapter 5, but nonetheless, it would be interesting to know whether the kind of approach
recommended by Keeney would lead to a radically different allocative
outcome from that which can be expected to emerge from the use of
cost–benefit analysis. The answer, it would seem, depends crucially upon
whether the relevant component 'disutility of lives lost' function satisfies
'risk equity', 'catastrophe avoidance' or a preference for minimizing the
expected loss of life (three moral principles that are, it will be recalled,
mutually incompatible). The 'risk equity' principle entails a preference
for mean preserving increases in spread of the probability distribution of
lives lost, so that an increase in risk of 10^{-3} for each of a thousand people
would be regarded as worse than an increase in risk of 10^{-6} for each of a
million people. This principle would therefore, like the ICRP and NRPB
recommendations – as well as the willingness-to-pay approach – effectively require that the cost of a man sievert should *increase* with individual
dose. By contrast, 'catastrophe avoidance' would lead to the opposite
conclusion, namely that the cost of a man sievert should *decrease* with
individual dose, essentially because the exposure of one person to 1 Sv
could, at most, result in one death whereas the exposure of a million
people to 10^{-6} Sv each could (just possibly) result in a million deaths.

Finally, adoption of the principle of minimizing expected loss of life leads to precisely the same kind of conclusion as that reached by Broome, i.e. that the cost of a man sievert should be *independent* of individual dose. It is perhaps worth reminding the reader that as far as involuntary risks are concerned Keeney appears to favour minimization of expected loss of life for what he calls 'personal' impacts, so that in this respect his proposals are qualitatively similar to Broome's, whereas for 'societal' impacts he advocates the 'risk equity' principle which is qualitatively in line with the ICRP and NRPB recommendations as well as the willingness-to-pay approach.

6.1.6   Summary

As the studies summarized in Chapter 5 indicated, nowhere is the public's concern over issues of safety more acute than in the case of nuclear power. One suspects that the main anxiety relates to the kind of catastrophic accident that occurred at Chernobyl, but the publicity associated with that event will no doubt also have made people more aware of the dangers associated with lower levels of radiation emitted in the course of normal operation of nuclear power plants. Given that such emissions can be attenuated – but only at a cost – the question of the optimal level of safety in nuclear power generation and other activities that give rise to ionizing radiation clearly has an important economic dimension.

This fact has been explicitly recognized by the various regulatory agencies concerned with radiological protection and the ICRP, in particular, has recommended that conventional procedures of social cost–benefit analysis should be employed in decisions concerning the optimal level of protection from the effects of ionizing radiation.

In order to implement the ICRP recommendations, the UK NRPB has defined costs of collective doses of ionizing radiation that start from a base level at low individual doses and rise thereafter as individual doses increase. Given that the ICRP has also laid down individual dose limits for various sets of circumstances, these limits effectively determine the level of individual dose at which the cost of a given collective dose becomes infinite.

Theoretical considerations supported by empirical evidence strongly suggest that the risk of inducing fatal cancers and serious hereditary defects increases with individual dose at all non-zero dose levels and, in fact, the various regulatory agencies work on the 'worst-case' assumption that risk is *proportional* to dose. Given this and given the estimated coefficient of proportionality, it is possible to convert the NRPB's recommended cost per unit collective dose at low individual doses directly into a cost of a statistical fatality and the ICRP's dose limits into maximum permissible increments in individual annual probability of death. In particular, the NRPB's recommended figure corresponds to a cost of a statistical fatality of £150,000 in 1986 prices, while the ICRP's dose limit for members of the general public implies a maximum permissible increase in individual annual probability of death of 10^{-4}. The central contention of the argument developed in this chapter is that *both* of these figures are almost certainly too low, probably by at least an order of magnitude, with the consequent clear implication that their use will tend to lead to an allocation of scarce resources that is not reflective of the wishes and attitudes of those who will be affected by the decisions. Specifically, too little will be spent on protection against low-dose emissions relative to the costs incurred in ensuring that dose limits are not exceeded.

As far as the implications of alternative approaches are concerned, it has been noted that Broome's insistence that public sector decisions should obey the 'sure thing' principle entails even more dramatic modifications to the NRPB and ICRP recommendations. Not only would the cost per unit collective dose be *invariant* with individual dose, but it would also seem that dose limits would have to be abandoned. One doubts that such modifications would meet with very widespread approval if they were understood by members of the general public and, indeed, this is hardly surprising as it has already been shown in Chapter 1 that adherence to the 'sure thing' principle may well result in government decisions that fail to comply with the wishes of those affected by the decisions.

In the case of the 'decision theory' approach advocated by Keeney, it turns out that things depend crucially upon which of the three mutually exclusive principles – 'risk equity', 'catastrophe avoidance' and minimizing expected loss of life – is required to be reflected in the relevant 'disutility of lives lost' function. The first of these principles leads to conclusions that are qualitatively identical to the ICRP/NRPB recommendations, in that the exposure of a small group to 1 man Sv would be regarded as worse than the exposure of a large group to the same collective dose. 'Catastrophe avoidance' leads to the opposite result and minimizing expected loss of life squares precisely with the conclusion of Broome's argument.

6.2   The Post-marketing Surveillance of New Drugs

In addition to their intended beneficial effects of cure, symptomatic relief or attenuation of disorder, many drugs have harmful side effects of varying severity and likelihood of occurrence. In some cases these adverse effects may be very serious, resulting in permanent disability or even death. Thalidomide and Opren are but two tragic examples. It is therefore clearly important that, before a new drug is marketed, it should be tested to establish whether or not it produces adverse effects and, if so, to determine their nature and frequency of occurrence. In the UK such 'pre-marketing' trials are normally carried out on a sample of 1,000–2,000 patients and the results of these trials then form the basis for the UK Committee on the Safety of Medicine's decision about whether or not to recommend that the drug should be licensed for general use.

However, it is clear that with a sample of this size, only the more prevalent adverse effects are likely to be detected. For instance, given a sample of 1,000, only effects occurring with a frequency of more than 1 in 333 cases will give a better than 95% chance of detection. For this reason, even if a new drug has 'passed' its pre-marketing trials, the Committee on the Safety of Medicines continues to monitor the drug for possible adverse effects, principally by asking medical practitioners to report any instances of such effects.[16] However, this is a relatively inefficent detection procedure – especially for rarer effects – in that practitioners may fail, for various reasons, to notice the effects or to attribute particular effects to use of the drug concerned or simply to accede to the Committee's request for notification. As a result, unusual adverse effects may take a very long time to detect and, indeed, may not be identified at all.

A far more efficient method of detecting the rarer adverse effects of new drugs – and one that has been recommended by leading pharmacologists[17] – would involve the systematic monitoring of a large cohort of patients, together with an appropriate control group, over a period following the introduction of a new drug.[18] The costs of such a 'post-marketing' surveillance, however, would be substantial and would ultimately be borne in large part by the National Health Service, either directly or as a result of an increase in the price of the drug if the pharmaceutical industry was required to carry out the surveillance. The problem is therefore to establish the nature of the conditions under which a post-marketing surveillance would, on balance, be warranted. The purpose of this section is to develop a simple model of the post-marketing surveillance decision that will facilitate the identification of these conditions.

6.2.1   A Simple Model of the Post-marketing Surveillance Decision

It will be assumed that a new drug is either 'safe', in which case it will produce no significant adverse effects, or 'dangerous', in which case it will, if licensed, produce n instances of a particular adverse effect before evidence from practitioners' reports indicates that the drug is dangerous.[19] Although this characterization somewhat abstracts from the full complexity of the situation with regard to a new drug, it is intended to capture the key features while at the same time making for ease of analysis.[20]

It will also be assumed that a post-marketing surveillance will, within a given period, establish *with certainty* whether the drug is safe or dangerous but, if the latter is the case, that the drug will by then have produced m ($< n$) instances of the adverse effect. Finally, it will be assumed that, following pre-marketing trials, the Committee on the Safety of Medicines can make one of three mutually exclusive recommendations, namely (a) that the drug should be licensed, (b) that the drug should not be licensed and (c) that a post-marketing surveillance should be conducted.

In the terminology of decision theory, the Committee's 'act–state–consequence' matrix[21] will then be as shown in table 6.1. Notice that

Table 6.1   The act–state–consequence matrix

	Drug dangerous	Drug safe
License	$kB - nV$	B
Not license	0	0
Post-marketing surveillance	$hB - C - mV$	$B - C$

B, aggregate benefits of cure, symptomatic relief etc. over anticipated lifetime of drug, if safe.

kB, aggregate benefits of cure, symptomatic relief etc. up to the time at which evidence from medical practitioners' reports indicates that drug is dangerous. $0 < k \leqslant 1$.

hB, aggregate benefits of cure, symptomatic relief etc. up to the time at which post-marketing survillance indicates that drug is dangerous. $0 < h < 1$.

C, cost of post-marketing surveillance.

V, cost associated with occurrence of one adverse effect.

since the post-marketing surveillance will detect dangerous drugs more rapidly than the procedure that relies on practitioners' reports, we shall have $h < k$ and, as already remarked, $m < n$.

Now suppose that the Committee on the Safety of Medicines adopts a decision criterion that is consonant with social welfare maximization. It will then clearly be appropriate to define B and V in terms of individual willingness to pay or requirement of compensation. In particular, if the 'adverse effect' is, in fact, death (i.e the drug, if dangerous, can be lethal) then V will be none other than the cost of a statistical fatality as defined in Chapter 1.[22] Suppose also that the Committee is able, on the basis of evidence from the pre-marketing trials and past experience with the type of drug under consideration, to associate a prior probability π with the state 'drug dangerous' (and hence a prior probability $1 - \pi$ with the state 'drug safe').[23] With a little algebraic manipulation, maximization of expected net benefits then entails the following:

'License' preferred to 'Not license' $\Leftrightarrow \pi < \dfrac{B}{nV + (1 - k)B}$ \hfill (6.1)

'Post-marketing surveillance'
preferred to 'Not license' \quad $\Leftrightarrow \pi < \dfrac{B - C}{mV + (1 - h)B}$ \hfill (6.2)

'Post-marketing surveillance'
preferred to 'License' \quad $\Leftrightarrow \pi > \dfrac{C}{(n - m)V - (k - h)B}$ \hfill (6.3)

Clearly while π, B, m, n, h and k will tend to vary from one drug to another, C will, to all intents and purposes, be constant and V will, in turn, be invariant for particular kinds of adverse effect. Let us therefore

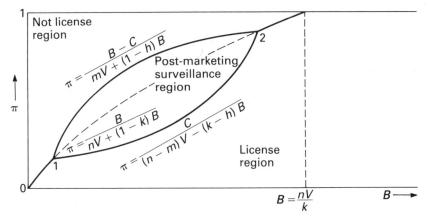

Figure 6.4 The (B, π) space partition.

focus upon various combinations of B and π and establish, for each combination, the optimal choice from the license, not license, post-marketing surveillance options. In fact, it is straightforward to show that (6.1), (6.2) and (6.3) partition the (B, π) space in the manner shown in figure 6.4. Notice that the common coincidence of the three boundaries at points 1 and 2 occurs becuase at these points we have expected net benefits from 'License' equal to expected net benefits from 'Not license' *and* expected net benefits from 'Not license' equal to expected net benefits from 'Post-marketing surveillance'. It will therefore necessarily be the case that *at the same points* we shall have expected net benefits from 'License' equal to expected net benefits from 'Post-marketing surveillance'. In fact, much of what is implied by figure 6.4 is intuitively quite plausible. In the first place, for any given level of π, 'Not license' will tend to be the optimal strategy for low values of B, Post-marketing surveillance' for intermediate values of B and 'License' for high values of B. Furthermore, the range of values of B for which 'Post-marketing surveillance' is optimal will be larger the greater the degree of uncertainty associated with the possibility of adverse effects (i.e. the closer is π to 0.5). Finally it is worth noting that if $B > nV/k$ then 'License' is unambiguously optimal even if $\pi = 1$. This is because with $B > nV/k$ the benefits of cure, symptomatic relief etc. outweigh the costs of the side effects *even if the drug is dangerous*. The most extreme example of this situation would be that in which pre-marketing trials indicated that a drug designed to cure or alleviate an otherwise potentially fatal condition would have fatal side effects in some cases but would, on balance, avoid more fatalities than it caused, so that $kB > nV$.

Not surprisingly, for given values of C and V, the size of the post-marketing surveillance region in figure 6.4 depends upon $n - m$, i.e. upon the number of instances of the adverse effect that are avoided by having a post-marketing surveillance, as opposed to licensing the drug directly and relying upon practitioners' reports to detect any adverse effects. More significantly, as $n - m$ increases, so the proportion of the (B, π) space above the interval $[0, nV/k]$ on the B axis occupied by the post-marketing surveillance region increases. Conversely, as the difference between n and m decreases, so the post-marketing surveillance region shrinks, and in fact it vanishes when

$$[(n - m)V - (1 - k)C]^2 - 4(k - h)nCV < 0. \tag{6.4}$$

It follows that a sufficient condition for the existence of a non-empty post-marketing surveillance region is that V should exceed the larger of the two roots of the quadratic equation

$$[(n - m)V - (1 - k)C]^2 - 4(k - h)nCV = 0 \tag{6.5}$$

i.e. V should satisfy

$$V > \frac{2[(n - m) + k(n + m) - 2h]C + \{4[(n - m) + k(n + m) - 2h]^2C^2 - 4(1 - k)^2(n - m)^2C^2\}^{1/2}}{2(n - m)^2} \tag{6.6}$$

or

$$\frac{V}{C} > \frac{[(n - m) + k(n + m) - 2h] + \{[(n - m) + k(n + m) - 2h]^2 - (1 - k)^2(n - m)^2\}^{1/2}}{(n - m)^2} \tag{6.7}$$

But since $n > m$ and $0 < h < k \leqslant 1$, a sufficient condition for (6.7) is, in turn,

$$\frac{V}{C} > \frac{2[(n - m) + k(n + m)]}{(n - m)^2} \tag{6.8}$$

so that with $0 < k > 1$ the following condition will ensure the existence of a non-empty post-marketing surveillance region:

$$\frac{V}{C} > \frac{4n}{(n - m)^2}. \tag{6.9}$$

For illustrative purposes, consider the case of a new drug which, if dangerous, would have potentially lethal side effects. Setting $V = £500,000$ (a value at the lower end of the range of results reported in Chapters 2 and 4) and $C = £2,500,000$ (a figure towards the upper end of a range suggested in conversation with a senior member of the Committee on the Safety of Medicines), the implications of equation (6.9) are as in table 6.2. With $C = £250,000$ (a figure nearer the bottom of the range referred to above) the minimum values of n for which a non-empty post-marketing surveillance region exists are precisely one-tenth of those shown in table 6.2.

6.2.2 A Special Case

In order to get a further 'feel' for the way in which the size of the post-marketing surveillance region varies with the number of adverse reac-

Table 6.2 Minimum values of *n* for the existence of a post-marketing surveillance region

$\dfrac{m}{n}$	Post-marketing surveillance region exists if n *greater than*
0.1	25
0.25	36
0.5	80
0.75	320
0.9	2,000

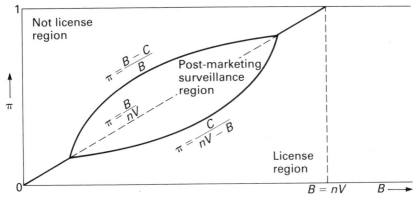

Figure 6.5   The (B, π) space partition for a special case.

tions that such a surveillance would avoid if a new drug turned out to be dangerous, consider the limiting case in which the surveillance would be perfectly *efficient* (i.e. would detect adverse effects without delay, so that $h = m = 0$) and the practitioners' reporting procedure would be perfectly *inefficient* (i.e. would completely fail to detect adverse effects so that $k = 1$). The 'License – Not license' boundary in (B, π) space then becomes linear and the other two boundaries are 'skew' symmetrical about the latter, as illustrated in figure 6.5. In this case the necessary and sufficient condition for existence of a non-empty post-marketing surveillance region is $V/C > 4/n$.

To make things even more concrete, again consider the case in which the new drug would, if dangerous, have potentially lethal adverse effects. Setting $V = £500,000$ and $C = £2,500,000$ as before, a non-empty post-marketing surveillance region then exists if and only if $n > 20$. Accordingly, the (B, π) partitions for $n = 50$ and $n = 100$ are shown by the solid curves in figure 6.6. As can be seen, the proportion of the (B, π) space above the interval $[0, nV]$ on the B-axis occupied by the post-marketing surveillance region increases substantially with n, and in fact grows from about 36% when $n = 50$ to over 60% when $n = 100$. Not surprisingly, with $C = £250,000$ (which, it will be recalled, is towards the lower end of the probable range) the post-marketing surveillance region is substantially larger for each value of n. In this case the boundaries of the region are shown by the chain-dotted curves in figure 6.6, the region now occupying 89% of the space above $[0, nV]$ for $n = 50$ and 94% for $n = 100$, so that a post-marketing surveillance will be indicated in all cases save those having either very high values of B or very low values of B combined with high values of π.

6.2.3   Estimating V and B

Clearly, implementation of the analysis developed above requires estimates of V and B. While the empirical studies surveyed in Chapter 2 provide a guideline as to the order of magnitude of V for cases in which adverse effects result in increased mortality, they do not do so for less serious effects. Similar comments apply to B, in that if the beneficial effect of a new drug is to cure an otherwise fatal disorder then the results summarized in Chapter 2 have direct relevance but otherwise do not. To the best of the author's knowledge, the only empirical study to have attempted to obtain empirical estimates of willingness-to-pay based values of avoidance of non-fatal illness is that conducted by Berger *et al.* (1987), and this study considered only a limited range of mild disorders. Clearly, further research on this matter is urgently needed, not only to illuminate the topic under discussion, but also in the interests of the efficient allocation of resources in the context of medical care in general.

6.2.4   Summary

Current practice in the UK is to subject all new drugs to 'pre-marketing' trials to test for the possibility of adverse side effects. However, since these trials are carried out on a sample of only 1,000–2,000 patients, they are unlikely to detect the rarer adverse effects of new drugs. The Committee on the Safety of Medicines therefore attempts to monitor new drugs after they have been marketed by asking practitioners to notify the Committee of any adverse effects through the 'yellow card system'. For various reasons, this reporting system is less than wholly efficient, so that some adverse effects will be detected, if at all, only after a considerable delay – by which time it is possible that serious damage will have been done to some patients' health.

A potentially far more efficient procedure for monitoring a drug that has 'passed' its pre-marketing trials would be to conduct a systematic 'post-marketing' surveillance of a large cohort of patients to whom the drug is being administered, together with an appropriate control group. Such an exercise, however, would be very costly to conduct – estimates range from £250,000 to £2,500,000. Given that many of the drugs on

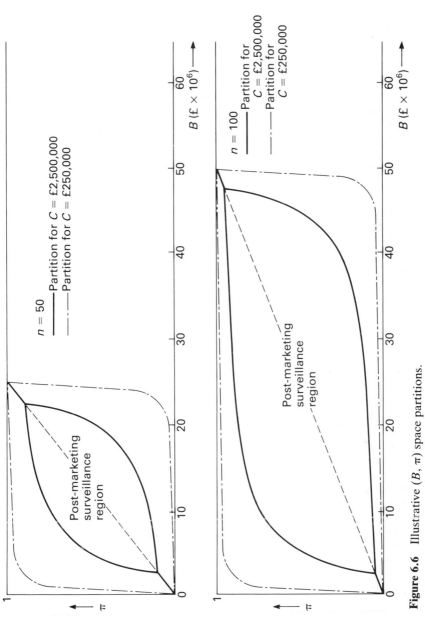

Figure 6.6 Illustrative (B, π) space partitions.

which a post-marketing surveillance might be conducted would turn out not to have significant adverse effects, the problem is therefore to identify the conditions under which it would (or would not) be appropriate for the Committee on the Safety of Medicines to recommend such a surveillance. Clearly, the Committee's decision has something of the structure of a classic hypothesis-testing problem in which the type-1 and type-2 errors involve both real resource costs and increases in the kind of physical risk with which this book is concerned. Thus, provided that one is prepared to view the Committee's problem from the standpoint of social welfare maximization, then it should be amenable to analysis using willingness-to-pay based costs and values to render the variations in physical risk commensurate with real resource costs. In this section a model of the Committee on the Safety of Medicine's decision has been developed along precisely these lines.

Most of the qualitative results of the analysis are intuitively quite plausible. For example, the set of combinations of B (the benefits of symptomatic relief, cure etc. afforded by the drug) and π (the Committee's prior probability that the drug will turn out to have significant adverse effects) under which it will be appropriate for the Committee to recommend a post-marketing surveillance will be larger (a) the larger the number of instances of the adverse effect that would be avoided by such a surveillance, (b) the larger the value accorded to the avoidance of one such effect and (c) the lower the cost of the surveillance. What is perhaps less obvious is the precise nature of the quantitative properties of this set of (B, Π) pairs and their relationship with the other parameters of the problem. The main purpose of the analysis in this section has been to draw out these quantitative properties and relationships.

6.3   The Sensitivity of Transport Project Rankings to Variations in the Value of Safety

In deciding upon an appropriate definition of the cost of accidents and the value of accident prevention in public sector decision making – and, indeed, in choosing a 'best' estimate under any given definition – it is natural to wonder to what extent variations in the magnitude of such costs and values might affect the ranking of public sector investment projects. In particular, if project rankings are largely unaffected by whether one chooses a gross output or willingness-to-pay definition (or, say, vary little within the rather wide range of values reported in Chapter 2) then for all practical purposes there would be little point in agonizing over the choice of definition or estimate. If, by contrast, project rankings turn out to be highly sensitive to the magnitude of the costs and values associated with variations in safety, then selection of a definition and estimate of these costs and values is clearly a matter of considerable consequence.

While it is well known that replacement of gross output based costs and values by figures such as those generated by the willingness-to-pay approach could be expected to have a significant impact on the allocation of resources in a developed economy,[24] this is less obvioulsy the case for *developing* countries where the absolute magnitude of the difference between such measures is likely to be very much smaller. As part of a study of traffic accidents in less developed countries carried out by the author and others for the World Bank,[25] it therefore seemed natural to conduct a sensitivity analysis to assess the impact of variations in accident costs and values on the ranking of the kind of transport projects that one might expect to encounter in the developing country context. The present section summarizes the key features and results of this sensitivity analysis.

6.3.1   The Projects

In order to assess the impact of variations in accident costs and values in the appraisal of developing country transport projects, one would ideally require data concerning expected effects on accident rates as well as capital, maintenance and vehicle-operating costs, time savings and anticipated traffic demand for a set of 'typical' projects. Unfortunately, no data meeting all these requirements were available to us at the time of the study. Accordingly, we constructed a data set by 'grafting' expert estimates of expected safety effects onto cost and traffic flow data for a group of projects in India, detailed by Adler (1971) and which were judged to be fairly typical of developing country highway investment schemes. The estimated safety effects were arrived at on the basis of correspondence and discussion with developing country transport specialists in the World Bank and the UK Transport and Road Research Laboratory (TRRL). In some cases, the data reported in Adler were simplified somewhat in the interests of analytical tractability.

In essence, the key features of the four mutually exclusive projects were as follows:

Project 1   (The 'do nothing' case.) Retain an existing 190 km two-lane stabilized gravel road connecting two cities in India, with populations of about 1,000,000 and 400,000 respectively.

Project 2   Pave the existing gravel road with minor improvements to alignment and some widening.

Project 3   Pave the existing gravel road with substantial improvements to alignment and width and reconstruction of bridges, drainage culverts and so on.

Project 4   Construct an entirely new, shorter road (145 km) between the two cities with the old road remaining in use, mainly for local traffic. The new road would incorporate a number of prupose-built safety features.

In all cases 1969 was used as the base year, with a time horizon of 1990. All costs and values are in 1969 rupees (the 1969 rupee–sterling exchange rate was approximately 18 Rs/£). Project 2 was assumed to have a capital cost of Rs61 million, spread over one year, project 3 a capital cost of Rs86 million, spread over two years and project 4, Rs145 million over three years. While it seems unnecessary to burden the reader with full details of maintenance costs, time saving and traffic growth, it is perhaps relevant to note that in each of projects 2, 3 and 4 existing traffic (275 trucks, 50 buses and 110 cars per day in 1969) was taken to grow at 10% p.a., while generated traffic was assumed to grow over the first few years of use to about 20% of the level of existing traffic and then at 10% p.a. thereafter.

As far as safety effects are concerned, as already noted, these were not explicitly considered in Adler's original discussion so that it was necessary to rely upon expert advice from the World Bank and TRRL in arriving at estimates of the sort of effects that might be expected in a case such as this. In the event, it was assumed that adoption of project 2 would lead to a 30% increase in accident rates vis-à-vis the status quo (project 1), while project 3 would have no net effect on accident rates and project 4 would *reduce* accident rates by 30%. The fatality rate for project 1 was taken to be 0.4 fatalities per 10^6 vehicle-km and it was assumed that, on average, the non-fatal accident rate was ten times as large. No distinction was drawn between various severities of non-fatal injury.

6.3.2   *A Digression on the Incorporation of Safety Effects in Transport Project Appraisal*

Before proceeding to assess the sentitivity of project rankings to variations in the values accorded to safety improvements, it is necessary to be clear about the way in which such values should be combined with estimated safety effects in the process of estimating overall benefits and costs. As it happens, things turn out to be less straightforward than might at first appear to be the case.

To make matters concrete, consider a transport facility on which the current number of journeys per period is n, the generalized cost per journey (including time, fuel and other costs but *excluding* safety effects) is c and the accident rate (expressed in accidents per *journey*) is x. Suppose, then, that a particular improvement to this transport facility would reduce the generalized cost to $c - \delta c$ and the accident rate to $x - \delta x$. Suppose also that, as a result of the improvement, journeys per period would increase to $n + \delta n$. Finally, denote by V the value of avoiding a statistical accident of the type under consideration (alternatively, V can be thought of as an average value of avoidance of accidents of varying severity).

The crucial question is then whether users of the transport facility have, or have not, taken account of the reduction δx in the accident rate in their decision to increase journeys from n to $n + \delta n$. If they have *not* done so then, ignoring income effects and treating the demand curve as linear, *their own perception* of the value of the improvement (i.e. their aggregate willingness to pay), will be given, by the usual argument, by the area FGKJ in figure 6.7, i.e. by $(n + \delta n/2)\delta c$. Given that users are effectively

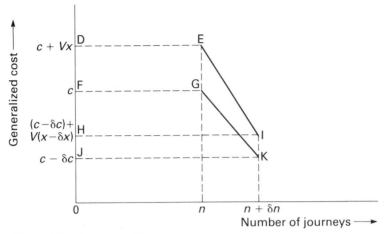

Figure 6.7   The demand for journeys.

ignoring safety effects, it seems appropriate for a responsible decision maker to *impute* a value to the safety improvement and *add* this to the users' aggregate willingness to pay. Furthermore, the appropriate sum to add is clearly the difference between total accident costs per period before the safety improvement and total accident costs after the improvement, i.e. areas DEGF in figure 6.7 minus area HIKJ, or $nVx - (n + \delta n) V(x - \delta x)$. Under this approach the overall benefit per period, B, due to the improvement to the transport facility would then be given by

$$B = \left(n + \frac{\delta n}{2}\right)\delta c + nVx - (n + \delta n)V(x - \delta x). \tag{6.10}$$

Now suppose, by contrast, that users have taken full and accurate account of safety effects in determining their demand for journeys. Suppose, in addition, that V has been defined on a conventional willingness-to-pay basis and is therefore equal to the mean of individual marginal rates of substitution of wealth for risk. Aggregated willingness to pay will then be given by the area DEIH in figure 6.7, i.e. by $(n + \delta n/2)(\delta c + V\delta x)$. Furthermore, since this is the aggregate willingness to pay for *all* the beneficial effects of the improvement, this will constitute the appropriate measure of the per period benefit of the improvement for a conventional social cost–benefit analysis. Denoting this measure of benefit by $\hat{B}$, we can therefore write

$$\hat{B} = \left(n + \frac{\delta n}{2}\right)(\delta c + V\delta x). \tag{6.11}$$

Now comparing (6.10) and (6.11) it is clear that, with $V > O$, B and $\hat{B}$ constitute *different* measures of benefit unless $\delta n = 0$. Furthermore, a little algebra indicates that since, perforce, $\delta x \leqslant x$, we shall necessarily have $\hat{B} > B$ when $\delta n > 0$. In fact the difference between $\hat{B}$ and B can be illustrated directly in figure 6.7 since, in terms of the various areas in the diagram,

$$\hat{B} - B = \text{DEIH} - (\text{FGKJ} + \text{DEGF} - \text{HIKJ}) \qquad (6.12)$$

or

$$\hat{B} - B = (\text{DEIH} + \text{HIKJ}) - (\text{FGKJ} + \text{DEGF}) \qquad (6.13)$$

so that

$$\hat{B} - B = \text{EIKG}. \qquad (6.14)$$

A further point to note is that while the measure $\hat{B}$ accords the safety improvement a positive value *if and only if* $\delta x > 0$, the measure B will treat a reduction in the accident rate as a net *cost* whenever $(n + \delta n)$ $(x - \delta x)$ exceeds nx.

Finally, notice that it would be possible to develop variants of the measure $\hat{B}$ for those cases in which users did not ignore safety effects but rather had only partial perceptions of these effects or had marginal rates of substitution of wealth for risk that, on average, differed from V.

All of this may, at first sight, seem to be of little more than academic interest. However, the difficulty identified in this section could turn out to be quite important given that the conventional wisdom in transport project appraisal appears to be that the appropriate way to incorporate safety effects is by use of a measure such as B rather than $\hat{B}$. Thus, for example, the UK Department of Transport's *COBA 8 Manual* assets that:

> Accident savings from a road improvement scheme equal the flow multiplied by the accident rate multiplied by the average personal injury accident cost on a link 'before' less the same 'after', summed over all links. (Department of Transport, 1979, Section 1.7)

The measure of accident savings recommended by the Department of Transport is therefore clearly equivalent to the term $nVx - (n + \delta n)$ $\times V(x - \delta x)$ in measure B. The discussion in this section therefore indicates that, to the extent that users *do* take account of safety effects in determining their demand for journeys on a particular facility, then the conventional measure will tend to *under*estimate the benefits of safety improvement.[26] This – allied to the fact that the values of accident avoidance currently employed in the UK and elsewhere are a disturbingly low fraction of the estimates summarized in Chapters 2 and 4 – is surely cause for some concern.

In order to give an indication of the numerical magnitude of the impact of using measure $\hat{B}$ as opposed to B, the sensitivity analysis reported in the next section was conducted for *both* benefit measures.

6.3.3 The Sensitivity Analysis

Annual incremental benefits for each of projects 2, 3 and 4 vis-à-vis the 'do nothing' option were computed using, as alternatives, measures B and

$\hat{B}$. These annual benefits were discounted to a 1969 base year present value using a discount rate of 12% and then compared with capital costs to derive discounted incremental net benefits with respect to the status quo. This exercise was repeated for various values of avoidance of a statistical fatality ranging from zero to about ten times the figure implied by the gross output measure in a middle-income country such as India, the latter being approximately Rs40,000 in 1969 prices. In addition, the value of avoidance of a statistical injury was set at, respectively, 0.05, 0.1 and 0.2 times the value of avoidance of a fatality.[27] Incremental net benefits for each of projects 2, 3 and 4 with respect to the status quo are shown as a function of the value ascribed to the avoidance of a fatality under benefit measure B in figure 6.8 and under the alternative benefit measure $\hat{B}$ in figure 6.9.

Inspection of figures 6.8 and 6.9 reveals a number of interesting features. In the first place, as expected, when $\delta n > 0$ measure $\hat{B}$ yields incremental net benefits that are clearly larger than those given by measure B for any particular project and configuration of parameter values.

Second, even for the lowest ratio of the value of avoidance of non-fatal to fatal injury, the ranking of projects is substantially affected by the value associated with safety improvements. In particular, at the lowest ratio of non-fatal to fatal injury values, project 4 moves from third to first place in the ranking as the value of avoidance of a statistical fatality increases from zero to a mere four times the relevant gross output measure under both the B and $\hat{B}$ definitions of benefit. At the highest ratio (0.2), project 4 moves from third to first place as this value increases from zero to about twice the gross output measure.

Finally, while choice of the B or $\hat{B}$ definition of benefit clearly has a substantial impact on the magnitude of incremental net benefit in any given case, it is equally clear that substitution of one definition for another does not markedly affect the project *rankings* at any particular value of avoidance of a fatality, at least for the particular group of projects under consideration. This, together with the point noted in the previous paragraph, suggests that it is selection of the definition and estimate of V – rather than choice of the B or $\hat{B}$ measure – that will be the crucial determinant of the final outcome of the project selection decision, at least within a given budget.

6.3.4 Summary

A sensitivity analysis conducted as part of the *Leitch Committee Report on Trunk Road Assessment* clearly indicates that transport project rankings in a developed country can be expected to be significantly affected by use of willingness-to-pay based accident costs and values of accident prevention rather than their gross output counterparts. However, given that all such costs and values will almost certainly be somewhat lower for a developing country, one is bound to wonder whether the willingness-to-pay/gross output distinction 'matters' to the same extent in such a context.

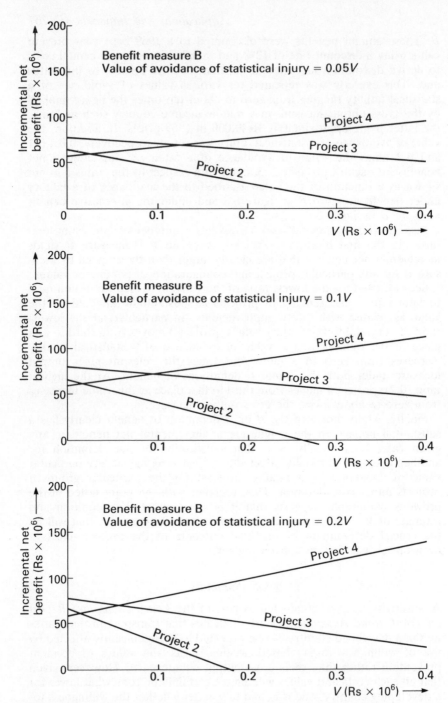

Figure 6.8 Incremental net benefit versus V for benefit measure B.

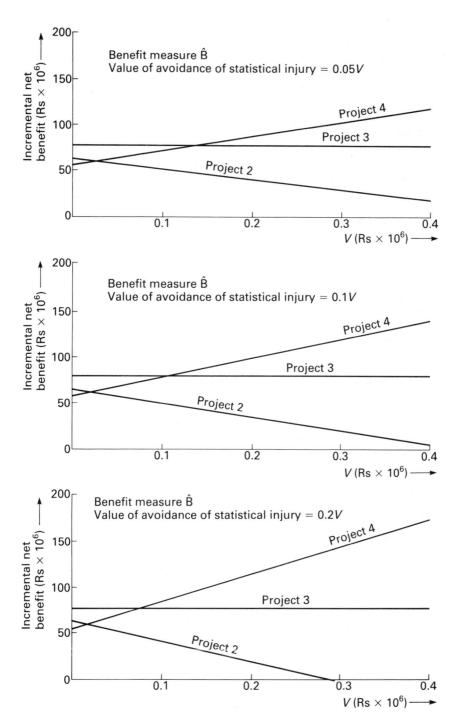

Figure 6.9 Incremental net benefit versus V for benefit measure $\hat{B}$.

This question is of more than academic interest because if the distinction does not matter – in the sense that it has a negligible impact on developing country transport project rankings or overall measures of net benefit – then it would be grossly inefficient (not to say downright wasteful) to devote desperately scarce resources to obtaining refined willingness-to-pay based estimates of the cost of accidents and the value of accident prevention. In fact, the analysis in this section strongly suggests that, far from being a matter of irrelevance, the magnitude of accident costs and values can be expected to have a significant impact on project rankings and measures of net benefit in transport project appraisal in developing countries. Specifically, as the value of accident prevention is increased from zero (the value implied by ignoring accident effects – which is, incidentally, a not uncommon practice in developing country transport project appraisal) through the level implied by the gross output definition, and then on towards the order of magnitude that would probably emerge under the willingness-to-pay approach, so the ranking of the group of projects considered in this section altered dramatically. In particular, the project that was ranked third out of four when accident effects were ignored moved up into first place at values of statistical life only a little in excess of those implied by the gross output definition. Thereafter, the difference in net benefits between this project and its competitors increased substantially as one moved towards the levels of the value of statistical life that might be expected under the willingness-to-pay approach.

This section has also considered a rather interesting dilemma concerning the appropriate means by which to combine estimated variations in accident rates and values of accident prevention in arriving at measures of overall benefit from transport safety improvement. It has been shown that the extent to which users of a transport facility do (or do not) take account of safety effects in determining their demand for journeys on the facility will significantly influence the expression for (and magnitude of) overall benefit from any particular safety improvement.

6.4   The Effect of Variations in the Value of Safety on the Overall Allocation of the Road Budget

Following its decision to increase the value accorded to time-savings in the light of the results of a willingness-to-pay based study designed to produce empirical estimates of the value of non-working time, the UK Department of Transport (DTp) recently recommended that values of safety should also be increased, with the value of avoiding a fatality, in particular, being raised from its current (1987) level of £192,000 to £269,000 (Department of Transport, 1987). The justification offered for this recommendation was that:

> The new values [of safety] have been set so as to ensure that, for the present, the existing overall balance between the benefits of road

investment from journey time savings and from accident savings is maintained. (DTp, 1987, p. 7)

In fact, the 'old' figure of £192,000 for the value of avoiding a fatality was derived under the gross output definition, with an allowance for 'pain, grief and suffering' constituting approximately 28% of the total.

Thus, in spite of the accumulated evidence from empirical work using the willingness-to-pay approach – including the study by the author and others that the DTp had itself commissioned[28] – the DTp has elected to derive its revised valuation of avoidance of a fatality by taking a figure based upon an almost completely discredited methodology and then inflating this by the proposed percentage increase in the value of time-savings.

In the author's opinion this proposal – by now, incidentally, endorsed by the Minister of Transport – is thoroughly misguided, involving, as it does, the implicit assumption that the 'old' value of safety was wrong by the same percentage as the 'old' value of time – an assumption for which there is no justification whatsoever. Fortunately, as noted earlier, at the time of going to press there are indications that the DTp may be reviewing its position on this matter.

Again in the author's view, the DTp, which has effectively acknowledged the marked conceptual superiority of the willingness-to-pay approach over its gross output counterpart (Department of Transport, 1987, pp. 6, 7), should in fact attempt to form a judgement concerning the appropriate order of magnitude of a willingness-to-pay based value of statistical life in the light of all the available theoretical and empirical evidence. As suggested in Chapters 2 and 4, it would seem very difficult indeed to conclude that this value should be much less than £500,000 and it should probably be well in excess of £1,000,000.

While the reasons given by the DTp for not so far having taken such a course of action relate mainly to its concern about the reliability of the empirical estimates summarized in Chapters 2 and 4, one suspects that a number of other factors may have militated against adoption of values such as those implied by the willingness-to-pay approach. One of these factors could be the concern, frequently expressed to the author by public sector decision makers in transport and other fields, that use of values of safety as large as those generated by the willingness-to-pay approach would lead to safety expenditures that represent an unacceptably high proportion of public sector budgets.[29]

6.4.1 The Cost of Increased Road Safety in the UK

Given the possibility that increased values of safety might lead to unacceptably large increases in safety expenditure, it would clearly be of considerable interest to establish what effect use of values of statistical life of £500,00 or larger might be expected to have upon overall road safety expenditure in the UK. Such an exercise, however, would require

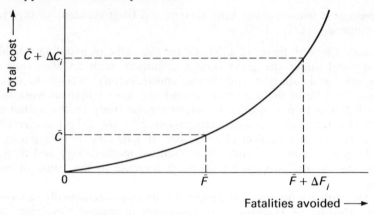

Figure 6.10 Total cost versus fatalities avoided.

an estimate of the UK cost function for road safety and, to the best of the author's knowledge, no such estimate exists. Nonetheless, a fairly recent OECD report (OECD, 1981) does contain estimates of the costs and effectiveness of various road safety countermeasures for the USA. These estimates are described in the following terms:

> A full-scale cost effectiveness ranking of safety countermeasures had been carried out by the Department of Transportation. . . . From a very large number of suggested countermeasures 37 . . . were finally distilled out as being the most promising. From a literature survey and on the basis of the opinions of a panel of experts the fatality . . . reducing capability over a 10 year period was estimated for each of these together with the cost of implementation. These estimates were arrived at on the assumption that present levels of expenditure on safety would continue but supplemented by an additional amount over a 10 year period. It was the accident reductions due to this supplementary amount that were being estimated. (OECD, 1981, pp. 100–101)

Thus, denoting the (then[30]) current level of expenditure on road safety in the USA by $\bar{C}$ and the fatalities avoided as a result of this expenditure by $\bar{F}$, the estimates referred to are essentially of the *incremental* costs, $\triangle C_i$, and the corresponding *incremental* avoided fatalities, $\triangle F_i$, depicted in figure 6.10.

The question is therefore whether there exists any basis on which these estimates of $\triangle C_i$ and $\triangle F_i$ might be used to derive an estimate of the counterpart incremental cost curve for the UK. In fact there would seem to be reasonably defensible grounds for deriving at least a rough approximation. In particular, most of the individual countermeasures in the list of 37 considered by the US Department of Transportation (such as 'mandatory safety belt usage', 'regulatory and warning signs', 'motorcycle rider safety helmets', 'upgrade traffic signals and systems', 'bridge widening' and so on) will almost certainly, at least to a good approximation, have the property of *constant returns to scale*. For example, mandatory safety belt usage for 1,000 deivers will presumably cost approximately 10 times that for 100 drivers and will save about 10 times as many lives, just as widening 20 bridges will be roughly twice as costly as widening 10 and will save approximately twice as many lives. If this is so, then given the broad similarity of road safety technology in the UK and USA, together with similarity of relative prices and approximate purchasing power partiy, it would seem legitimate to derive an estimate of a cost of safety curve for the UK simply by scaling down both $\triangle C_i$ and $\triangle F_i$ *in proportion to the ratio of the UK and US populations* (and, of course, making the appropriate currency conversion). Notice that this reflects the further implicit assumption that, since the population of the USA is approximately four times as large as that of the UK, there will be four times as many seat-belts in the USA under mandatory usage, as well as four times as many bridges to be widened and so on.

On the basis of this admittedly somewhat heroic set of assumptions, the estimates of $\triangle C_i$ and $\triangle F_i$, scaled down by the relative populations of the UK and US, converted to pounds sterling, 1987, and expressed on an annual (rather than 10 yearly) basis, yield the $\triangle C$ versus $\triangle F$ curve depicted in figure 6.11. Strictly speaking, the assumption of constant returns to scale within any given countermeasure implies that this curve should be piecewise-linear. However, given the scale dictated by the page size of a book, some of the linear segments would be very small and it therefore seemed preferable to depict the curve by a smooth approximation. Now it must be remembered that figure 6.11 shows *incremental* costs and *incremental* fatalities avoided with respect to the UK counterpart to the point $(\bar{F}, \bar{C})$ in figure 6.10. It will therefore be possible to use figure 6.11 to estimate the impact of increasing the value of safety *if and only if* the 1987 status quo for the UK lies to the right of this counterpart and hence to the right of the origin in Figure 6.11. Fortunately, it appears that this condition is fulfilled simply because maximization of net benefit requires that safety expenditure be undertaken up to the point at which the marginal cost of safety improvement equals its marginal value, and in the context of figure 6.11 this means that the status quo, given a value of avoidance of a fatality of £192,000 (the DTp's pre-revision figure), should be at point A.

6.4.2 The Implied Increases in Road Safety Expenditure in the UK

Assuming that we have arrived at a not entirely inaccurate representation of the UK's cost function for road safety, what then are its implications for various increases in the value of avoidance of a fatality? According to figure 6.11, use of the DTp's revised value of £269,000 will entail a move from A to B, thereby saving, on average, an additional 300 lives per annum at an incremental annual cost of £70 $\times$ 10^6 (i.e. about 4% of the

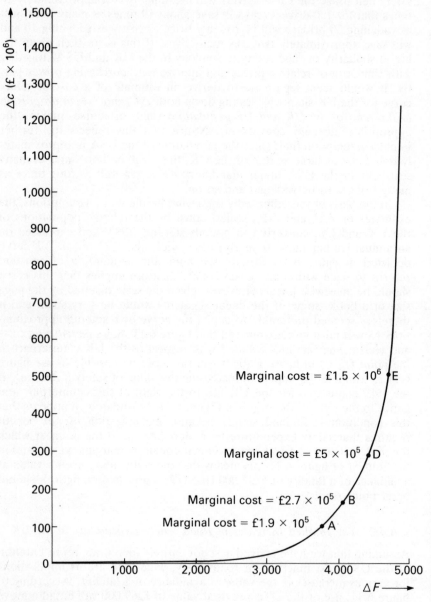

Figure 6.11 Incremental total cost versus incremental road fatalities avoided per annum for the UK.

central and local government annual budget for new road construction and improvements). By contrast, the lowest value that would appear to be consistent with the results of the various willingness-to-pay based studies (£500,000) would entail a move from A to D, saving roughly 600 lives per annum at an incremental annual cost of £180 × 10^6 (about 10% of the budget) while a willingness-to-pay value of £1.5 × 10^6 would take us from A to E, saving about 900 lives each year at an incremental annual cost of 390 × 10^6 (about 22% of the budget). While the reader must, of course, make up his or her own mind as to whether or not the increases implied by the willingness-to-pay approach are 'unacceptably large', it should be borne in mind that if all the various estimates concerned are broadly accurate, then these are incontrovertibly the sort of increases implied by the conventional procedure for 'aggregating' individual preferences and wishes.

Before leaving this topic, two final points deserve brief mention. The first concerns the possibility that, as suggested by Peltzman (1975), countermeasures such as mandatory seat belt usage, while improving driver and passenger safety, may also produce driver behavioural responses that markedly *reduce* predestrian safety. It is not clear whether those who produced the cost-effectiveness estimates used in this section took account of such behavioural responses. However, to the extent that they did not do so, then some of the countermeasures in the list of 37 would be less cost effective than supposed and this would have the overall effect of making the cost curve in figure 6.11 'flatter' than it should be.[31] If this is the case then the percentage increases in safety expenditure discussed in the preceding paragraph will, if anything, tend to be *over*estimates (direct computation indicates that this is certainly the case if, for example, the fatalities avoided by each countermeasure are reduced by a constant proportion). The second point relates to the possibility that, not only is increased safety expenditure likely to be choked off by rapidly increasing marginal costs (as in figure 6.11), but also, under the willingness-to-pay approach, by *decreasing marginal valuations*. While this may be so, it should be borne in mind that the analysis in Chapter 3, section 3.6, suggested that individual willingess to pay may well be (approximately) proportional to risk reduction over a quite substantial interval of the latter (although, of course, required compensation is most decidedly *not* proportional to increased risk). If this is the case, then willingness-to-pay based values of statistical life should show a negligible tendency to decline over the range of safety improvements involved in a move such as that from A to D in figure 6.11.

6.4.3 Summary

There can be little doubt that a *ceteris paribus* increase in the value accorded to any beneficial effect in public sector project appraisal is likely to lead to an increase in the level of provision of that effect and vice versa. Nonetheless, the relative and absolute magnitude of such variations in value will normally be such as to produce only small overall allocative adjustments: the DTp's recent increase in the value of non-working time, for example, is unlikely to have profound implications for the way in which the road budget is expended.

However, in the case of values of safety, things are rather different. In both relative and absolute terms, the magnitude of the increase in the value of avoidance of a fatality implied by a switch from the gross output to the willingess-to-pay definitions is very large indeed. Furthermore, as is clearly demonstrated by the results of the sensitivity analyses described in the *Leitch Committee Report* and in the previous section, such increases can be expected to have a substantial effect upon the rankings and measures of net benefit of transport projects in countries at all levels of development.

One is therefore bound to wonder just how large the increase in expenditure on road safety improvement would actually be if, say, the UK DTp could be persuaded to adopt the willingness-to-pay approach. The present section has attempted to provide a tentative answer to this question.

Given particular values of avoidance of death and injury, the implied optimal levels of expenditure on safety will be determined by the *costs* of reducing fatal and non-fatal injuries by various amounts. To the best of the author's knowledge, no data concerning such costs have been published for the UK. The estimates given in this section are therefore based upon the admittedly somewhat heroic assumption that US data concerning the costs and estimated effectivenss of various road safety counter-measures can legitimately be 'scaled down' to produce a rough and ready estimate of the cost curve for incremental fatalities avoided for the UK. It must also be admitted that the resultant estimates are only partial to the extent that they are based exclusively upon the cost of avoiding *fatalities* rather than all classes of injury. Nonetheless, the results of the exercise probably serve to give a reasonably reliable broad indication of how things would be if the DTp could be persuaded to use willingness to pay rather than gross output based values of safety. In fact, the implied increases in expenditure on avoidance of fatalities turn out to be significant, but by no means outrageous, simply because, beyond a relatively modest increase in expenditure, the marginal cost of avoiding additional fatalities increases very rapidly. There are at least some grounds for supposing that similar comments would apply to the cost of avoiding non-fatal injuries. However, all this is little more than partially informed speculation and it is clear that 'harder' estimates of the properties of cost functions for safety – in transport as well as other areas – are urgently needed.

Notes

1 Such as acid rain and the 'greenhouse' effect.
2 See, for example, Layfield (1987).

3 Strictly speaking, rather than referring to 'types of element' one should talk of *nuclides* which are elements with a specific mass number – determined by the number of protons and neutrons in the nucleus – such as carbon-12 or lead-208. For a fuller discussion of this and other technical points, see Pochin (1983), National Radiological Protection Board (1981) and International Commission on Radiological Protection (1977). The material in sections 6.1.1 to 6.1.3 draws heavily on these three sources.

4 DNA is the acronym for deoxyribonucleic acid. The genetic information that determines the characteristics of living matter is contained in chromosomes. The latter consist of two strands of DNA wound around each other with the form of a double helix. Each strand of DNA comprises an alternating sequence of sugar and phosphate groups linked together by pairs of bases. It is essentially the order in which these pairs occur in the strands that encodes the genetic information.

5 The older unit is the rad, which is equal to 10^{-2} Gy.

6 The older unit is the rem, which is equal to 10^{-2} Sv.

7 These observations have been obtained from (a) those subjected to occupational exposures (e.g. people engaged in luminizing the dials of watches and instruments and uranium and hard-rock miners), (b) patients undergoing radiation therapy, (c) the diagnostic use of X-rays and (d) the surviving victims of the Hiroshima and Nagasaki bombings.

8 The temporal coincidence is required in order that the cell does not have time to repair the first strand-break before the second occurs.

9 Provided, of course, that non-stochastic dose thresholds are not exceeded.

10 In fact there is a slight difference between the NRPB and ICRP's recommendations in that the former applies an increasing multiplicative factor to the baseline cost whereas the ICRP recommends an addition to the baseline.

11 This is the natural cost counterpart to the 'value of statistical life' in that the former is a measure of aggregate compensation for small increments in risk while the latter is the aggregate willingness to pay for small reductions in risk.

12 Strictly speaking there is no intercept on the vertical axis, as the function is discontinuous at an increment of zero. One should therefore speak of the *limit* of cost as the increment approaches zero.

13 To the extent that the cost of a statistical fatality is defined as the sum of the amounts that individuals require in compensation, this cost will become unbounded *as soon as any* individual requires infinite compensation. This would, of course, entail that the most timid person in any group would determine the group's limit to acceptable increases in risk and it might therefore be felt appropriate to relax the strict requirements of the willingness-to-pay approach and define the group's maximum acceptable increase in terms of some measure of the central tendency of individual maximum acceptable increases.

14 This assumption seems reasonable for the first two generations but is probably increasingly less so for later ones. However, given that the expected number of fatal cancers is 1.25×10^{-2} per man sievert and the expected number of genetic defects in the first two generations is 0.4×10^{-2} per man sievert the error involved in treating the overall risk factor as 2×10^{-2} will be relatively small.

15 It should, of course, be recalled that these estimates have been obtained principally for occupational and transport risks (see Chapter 2) and, to the extent that the public appears to be markedly more averse to risks from nuclear power than to other everyday risks (see Slovic *et al.*, 1981), the cost of a statistical fatality for nuclear risks can be expected to be substantially larger.

16 This is known as the 'yellow card' system.

17 See, for example, Rawlins (1984).

18 The need for a control group arises either because the disorder for which the drug is being prescribed is itself productive of abnormal morbidity or mortality or because the potential adverse side effects are themselves relatively common so that it is a question of establishing whether or not the drug causes a statistically significant increase in the frequency of occurrence of these effects.

19 n is, of course, the *actual* number of adverse effects rather than the number reported by practitioners, which will typically be substantially smaller than n.

20 In fact, the analysis that follows could, in principle, be modified to accommodate different degrees of safety and cases in which drugs, if dangerous, could produce a variety of different adverse effects. However, this would greatly add to the difficulty of the analysis without, one suspects, providing significant additional insights.

21 The formal description of decisions under uncertainty in terms of 'acts' (mutually exclusive courses of action open to the decision maker), 'consequences' (decision outcomes) and 'states of the world' (mutually exclusive and collectively exhaustive descriptions of the future course of events that are sufficiently complete to determine a unique consequence for each act) is originally due to Savage (1954).

22 It might, of course, be necessary to take account of the fact that the drug concerned would tend to be administered to a group of patients with particular characteristics, such as the elderly or pregnant women. The sort of results reported in Chapter 4 concerning the relationship between individual willingness to pay and age or sex would then be directly relevant to the definition of the cost of a statistical fatality. It would also seem important to recognize that some adverse effects might involve a lingering and painful death and that V should, so far as possible, be set to reflect this (again, the results reported in Chapter 4 concerning willingness to pay to avoid cancer death might have some relevance to this issue).

23 Apparently, in most cases the Committee will have at least a broad idea of the likelihood and nature of potential adverse side effects.

24 See Leitch (1977), especially sensitivity tests 24, 25 and 26.

25 For a summary of the main findings of the study, see Hills and Jones-Lee (1983).

26 Though it should be noted that B and $\hat{B}$ would be identical under COBA's 'fixed trip matrix' methodology which effectively treats the demand curve for journeys between particular origins and destinations as perfectly inelastic (so that $\delta n = 0$) – see COBA 9, Section 1. However, under the more sophisticated 'variable trip matrix' approach, which recognizes the possibility of generated traffic, the difference between B and $\hat{B}$ can be quite significant, as will be seen in the next section.

27 The reader may be surprised that the value of avoidance of a statistical injury was set at such relatively high proportions of the value of avoidance of a fatality. However, while the latter can be expected to be very much smaller than its counterpart in a developed economy under either the gross output or willingness-to-pay definitions, the medical costs and damage associated with a non-fatal injury will almost certainly be comparable with those incurred in a developed economy and will represent a very serious drain on scarce resources. For this reason, a ratio of even 0.2 may not be excessive.

28 See Chapter 4.

29 Indeed, a senior member of one developed country's transport ministry re-

marked that 'back of the envelope' calculations indicated that use of a value of statistical life of the order of £1,000,000 would result in expenditure of his country's *entire* road budget on safety!

30 OECD (1981) gives the publication date of the document reporting the Department of Transportation's estimates as 1976 so that one assumes that these estimates are in 1976 or slightly earlier prices.

31 I am grateful to James Foreman-Peck for drawing this point to my attention.

7

Final Reflections

If one is to reach firm conclusions concerning the appropriate way in which to deal with safety in public sector allocative and legislative decisions, then it would seem to be essential to adopt a clear and unequivocal prescriptive stance. Accordingly, this book has (almost) unreservedly espoused the precepts of *ex ante, welfarist consequentialism*. That is, it has been argued that public sector decisions affecting safety should, to a large degree, be based upon the current preferences and perceptions of those who will be affected by the decisions. This is in marked contrast with the position taken by, for example, John Broome or Ralph Keeney who both advocate (albeit for somewhat different reasons) that decisions concerning safety should be based upon the public sector decision maker's evaluation (and assessment of the likelihood) of the various possible *ex post* outcomes of those decisions.

It has to be admitted that if public sector decisions are to take account of people's current preferences and perceptions then, as demonstrated in Broome (1982), public decision makers will from time to time be driven to be 'incoherent' in the sense that – viewed from their own perspective – chosen options will be unambiguously dominated by available alternatives. However, such circumstances will almost certainly be the exception rather than the rule and, in the author's view, can be regarded as an acceptable price to pay for ensuring that public sector decisions are, in the wider sense, 'democratic'.

It is, of course, natural to qualify this commitment to the primacy of individual beliefs and preferences with the requirement that they should be 'rational' and 'well-informed'. Thus, the demonstrably false idea that inhaling sulphur dioxide is good for the health would be discounted. However, such aberrant beliefs apart, the argument developed in this book has been based upon the premise that in matters that affect their own health and safety people should effectively *be allowed to judge for themselves* what is and is not in their own best interests.

7.1 The Main Conclusions Concerning the Value of Safety

A natural and obvious way in which to take account of individual preferences in decisions affecting health and safety is in terms of the rate at which affected individuals are willing to trade off risk against some index of the value of alternative uses of scarce resources. How such rates of trade-off are to be combined or aggregated to arrive at an overall value of safety or cost of risk is, in the author's opinion, a 'second-order' problem reflecting the precise balance that the social decision maker chooses to strike in weighing off one person's interests against another's. In fact, as shown in Chapter 1, it turns out that the premises of both social cost–benefit analysis and social welfare maximization entail that, if one focuses exclusively on people's concern for their own safety, then the appropriate monetary value to place upon the saving of one statistical life is the distributionally weighted average of individual marginal rates of substitution m_i of wealth for risk. In the particular case of conventional cost–benefit analysis, the distributional weights are set equal to unity, so that the value of statistical life is given by the arithmetic mean of m_i over the affected population. This is the central result of the so-called 'willingness-to-pay' approach.

Interestingly, it transpires that there are two quite independent arguments for basing the value of statistical life, not on the mean of m_i, but rather upon its *median*. The first argument in favour of doing so is that, given the apparently highly right-skewed nature of the population distribution of m_i, a majority of people would regard a value of statistical life equal to the mean of m_i as too high and would, in fact, vote in favour of the median of m_i as opposed to any other particular value. Considerations of democracy (narrowly construed)[1] would therefore favour the use of the median rather than the mean of m_i. A rather different sort of argument for focusing upon the median of m_i in the definition of the value of statistical life – at least in the context of questionnaire-based studies – is that very large and very small (including zero) responses to valuation questions are inherently more suspect than 'intermediate' responses, so that there is a case for trimming *both* tails of the distribution of estimates of m_i. If one then computes the mean of the trimmed distribution, the result clearly approaches the *median* of the original distribution as the proportion of top and bottom responses trimmed out is increased. In the case of the questionnaire study reported in Chapter 4, the mean of the trimmed distribution approaches the median of the original distribution rather rapidly. Thus, even if in principle one sticks with the 'mean marginal rate of substitution' definition of the value of statistical life, doubts about the reliability of 'extreme' values of m_i might lead to adoption of a value closer to the median than to the mean of the overall distribution of m_i.

What has been said so far in this chapter relates exclusively to individuals' valuation of their own safety. If account is to be taken of the fact that people are typically also concerned – and therefore willing to pay – for others' safety, then subject to certain conditions on the nature of people's concern for others' safety,[2] an allowance for this additional willingness to pay should be added to the value of statistical life. Empirical evidence suggests that this will lead to an increase of between 30% and 50%. Finally, to the extent that people tend not to take account of such factors in assessing their own willingness to pay for safety, one should also add a further allowance for 'direct' economic effects like reductions in police and damage costs and the avoidance of losses of net output. However, the magnitude of these direct effects tends to be very small in relation to the other components of the value of statistical life.

Implementation of the willingness-to-pay approach clearly requires an empirical estimate of the population mean of m_i or – if any sort of weighting exercise is contemplated – of the population *distribution* of m_i broken down by various factors. As might be expected, empirical estimation in this area is a chancy business and reported results span a very wide range. It was suggested in Chapter 2 that there are two possible reactions to this state of affairs, provided one accepts that the willingness-to-pay approach is, in principle, the appropriate way in which to take account of safety effects in public sector decision making. The first possible response is to regard the variation in the estimates as being so large as to render the inference of a specific value, or even a working range, an impossibility. The alternative way in which to react to the various empirical estimates is to attempt to extract a 'best' estimate, or range of estimates, on the basis of a judgemental assessment of the relative reliablity of the various figures involved. In the author's opinion, there can be little doubt that the latter is the markedly superior stance on this issue.

Based upon a detailed evaluation of the relative reliability of the various estimates reported to date, Chapter 2 concluded that for 'everyday' risks, such as those encountered in transport or the non-nuclear workplace, a value of statistical life for 'own' risks of *at least* £500,000 in 1987 prices seems to be warranted and that a good case can be made for a figure in excess of £1,000,000. Much the same sort of conclusion emerges from an assessment of the results of the study reported in Chapter 4.

This interpretation of the findings of empirical work is, in turn, strongly supported by the results of theoretical analysis. In the first place, Conley (1976), Bailey (1978), Jones-Lee (1980a), Bergstrom (1982), Dehez and Drèze (1982) and Shepard and Zeckhauser (1982) have shown, within the context of a variety of models, that the typical individual's marginal rate of substitution of wealth for risk will exceed his or her human capital (the latter being the major component of cost or value under the 'gross output' approach), possibly by many multiples.[3]

The second source of theoretical support for the conclusion that the population mean of m_i almost certainly exceeds £500,000 – and may well be larger than £1,000,000 – lies in the result first proved for a special case in Jones-Lee (1980b) and generalized, as an approximation, in Chapter 3. This result is to the effect that, for the vast majority of people, the marginal rate of substitution m_i, the maximum acceptable increase Δp_i^* in physical risk and the coefficient of asymptotic risk aversion RL_i will satisfy the relationship $m_i \Delta p_i^* RL_i \approx 1$. Now it will be recalled that Δp_i^* is effectively the smallest increase in probability of death for the coming year that the individual would refuse to accept 'at any price'. RL_i is, in turn, approximately the win–loss probability ratio at which the individual would *just* be willing to pay a £1 stake to participate in a financial gamble with a very large prize. Thus, it seems reasonable to suppose that for most people Δp_i^* will probably be smaller than 1 in 100 while RL_i will be less than, say, 1 in 5,000. If this is so, then given $m_i \Delta p_i^* RL_i \approx 1$, it follows that m_i will typically exceed £500,000. Indeed, many people reveal themselves willing to engage in small stake–large prize financial gambles at win–loss probability ratios *very* much smaller than 1 in 5,000, so that for such people even with Δp_i^* as improbably large as, say, 1 in 10, m_i will still be well in excess of £500,000.

An alternative way in which the relationship $m_i \Delta p_i^* RL_i \approx 1$ can be used to place a lower bound on m_i is by recalling the result, proved in Jones-Lee (1980b), that if (as is usually assumed) the Pratt–Arrow measure of absolute risk aversion RA_i is a non-increasing function of wealth, then with the latter defined to include human capital, $RL_i \leqslant RA_i$. This in turn means that $RL_i \leqslant RR_i / w_i$, where w_i is wealth (including human capital) and RR_i is the Pratt–Arrow measure of *relative* risk aversion. Since the latter has been estimated to be typically less than 10, then with $m_i \Delta p_i^* RL_i \approx 1$, it follows that $m_i > w_i / 10 \Delta p_i^*$. Thus, even with Δp_i^* as large as 1 in 10, m_i would exceed human capital and, indeed, would do so by a factor of more than 10 if Δp_i^* were equal to 1 in 100.

All things considered, then, the case for believing that the value of statistical life for everyday risks should be at least £500,000 seems to be very powerful indeed, with a value in excess of £1,000,000 quite consistent with much of the empirical evidence and the findings of theoretical work.

It has to be acknowledged that a value of statistical life in excess of £1,000,000 would be more than four times as large as the Department of Transport's 1987 cost of a fatality or the figure implied by the National Radiological Protection Board's recommended cost of a unit collective dose of ionizing radiation at low per capita doses. It is therefore natural to wonder just how extensive the allocative implications of a switch to such a high value might actually be. Chapter 6, section 6.4, addressed precisely this question, at least for the case of transport risks, and concluded that the likely effect, though substantial, would not be outrageous. This is essentially because the marginal *cost* of safety improvement is, beyond a certain point, very rapidly increasing and this, together with falling marginal valuations,[4] will serve to choke off incremental safety expenditures at only relatively modest levels.

7.2   Some Further Policy Questions

Even if one accepts the ethical precepts on which the willingness-to-pay approach is based and is persuaded by the arguments that have been adduced in favour of values of statistical life of, at a minimum, £500,000 and more probably over £1,000,000 for everyday risks, there remain a number of difficult but important policy questions. In particular:

1   How should the value of statistical life for more emotive, involuntary 'dread' risks, such as those that are a consequence of nuclear power generation, relate to values for everyday risks which are, on the whole, more or less voluntary?
2   How should the possibility of catastrophes, such as occurred at Chernobyl or Bhopal, be fitted into the willingness-to-pay framework, if indeed they can be?
3   How should current risks be weighed against risks to future generations?

Apart from the question concerning willingness to pay for a reduction in cancer deaths asked as part of the survey reported in Chapter 4 and various questions concerning willingness to pay to reduce risks from nuclear power generation asked in a recent – and, as yet, unpublished – UK Health and Safety Executive pilot-scale survey, the author is not aware of any empirical work that permits unambiguous estimation of values of statistical life for 'dread' risks.[5] For different but fairly obvious reasons, the estimates derived from the two survey exercises referred to above must be treated with considerable caution – in the former case because of the nature of the question asked (which essentially related to the loss of anonymous rather than statistical life) and in the latter because of the extremely small and probably biased sample involved. Nonetheless, as it happens, both studies yield very large values indeed – the survey reported in Chapter 4 gave a value in the region of £20,000,000 and some of the Health and Safety Executive pilot results were of a similar order of magnitude.[6] This, together with the evidence from work in experimental psychology summarized in Chapter 5, suggests that, were it possible to obtain reliable empirical estimates of the value of statistical life for involuntary 'dread' risks, then these might well be many multiples of the value for everyday risks. However, a definitive conclusion on this subject must await further more extensive empirical work in this area.

The question of how values of safety and costs of risk might be defined and estimated for the case of catastrophes has already been addressed and tentatively answered in Chapter 1. Essentially, the suggestion was that a combination of the decision analysis and willingness-to-pay approaches might provide the basis for a solution to the problem. In particular, given an estimate of the monetary cost to be associated with the exposure of 10^n people to independent incremental risks of 10^{-n} each (i.e. the cost of the loss of one statistical) and given an estimate of a Keeney-type 'disutility of lives lost' function, it would be possible in principle to deduce the approximate cost to be associated with a catastrophe risk involving a probability of 10^{-n} that 10^n people would *all* be killed.

The assessment of risks to future generations raises a number of very difficult questions. Perhaps the most fundamental of these concerns the issue of whether or not current decisions should take any *direct* account of the interests of those who are, as yet, unborn. Some have argued that public sector project appraisal should take direct account *only* of the preferences of those currently alive.[7] Under this approach, the interests of future generations would be recognized only to the extent that members of the present generation care about those who are yet to be born. The alternative position, and the one to which the author is inclined to subscribe, is that current public sector decisions should, so far as possible, take direct account of the interests and preferences of *all* who are, or will be, affected by those decisions *whether or not they are currently alive* and that the welfare of future generations should rank *pari passu* with that of the present generation. If one adopts this position, however, there are two immediate difficulties. First, how is one to know the interests and preferences of people as yet unborn? Second, even if one could, by whatever means, establish the nature of these interests and preferences, how ought they to be aggregated with, or weighed against, the interests and preferences of the current generation? As far as the first of these difficulties is concerned, there really would seem to be no alternative to adoption of the working assumption that future attitudes to physical risk will, by and large, be straightforward projections of current attitudes, appropriately adjusted for increases in living standards and the level of real income. The aggregation problem, however, is somewhat more complex. In the first place, while current decisions can affect *only* the future for those currently alive, such decisions will affect both the future *and a part of the past* for those yet to be born. Thus, for someone born at time $t = T$ (> 0), not only may the future, $t > T$, be affected by a decision at $t = 0$, but so also will that period of the past represented by the interval between $t = 0$ and $t = T$. Given that people may legitimately hold preferences over their pasts,[8] should a public sector decision at $t = 0$, if it is to take account of the preferences of those who will be born at $t = T$ (> 0), do so for their preferences over what will have happened in their past between $t = 0$ and $t = T$, as well as reflecting their wishes concerning what might happen in their future, i.e. for $t > T$? Strictly speaking, the answer would seem to be 'yes'. Apart from anything else, if the anticipated consequences of decisions A and B differ only to the extent that a particular future generation can be expected to prefer the past that would ensue from A to that which would emerge under B, then according to the Pareto criterion A should be judged superior to B. In practical terms, however, it has to be acknowledged that we know very little of people's preferences over their pasts. Indeed, it would seem that, beyond their ordinal properties, such preferences would be extremely difficult to establish. Consider, for example, an attempt to determine an individual's compensating or equivalent variation at time T for a change in the course of events at some time prior to T. Plainly, save in the world of science fiction, no markets exist for 'backward' trades between the present and the past,[9] so that one cannot hope to estimate compensating or equivalent variations from observation of actual choices. This leaves direct questioning concerning willingness to pay or required compensation for *hypothetical* changes in the nature of the past as the only remaining possibility for empirical estimation. However, since most people would find the concept of such changes literally incredible, it seems probable that direct questioning would prove to be a somewhat fruitless endeavour. One is therefore left in the rather unsatisfactory position of either having to make more or less arbitrary *assumptions* about people's preferences over their pasts, or ignoring such preferences. Since the strategy of ignoring preferences (unless the latter are seriously misinformed) runs counter to the fundamental ethical premise of this book, there would seem to be no alternative but to grasp the bull by the horns and speculate about how future generations will retrospect about the past. The first point to note is that preferences over past events would seem to be capable of reflecting one of two types of consideration: *either* I would prefer that A rather than B had taken place in the past because the consequences of A *for my own future* would have been better than the consequences of B (these will be referred to as 'derived' preferences), *or* I would prefer A to B per se, there being no difference between A and B in terms of their implications for my future (these are probably best described as 'pure' preferences). An example of the 'derived' case would be my preferences concerning a past government's decision to build a nuclear reactor in the neighbourhood in which I was eventually born and brought up. An example of the 'pure' sort of effect is my current preference that Newcastle United rather than Liverpool should have won the 1974 FA Cup Final. Of course, some cases will involve a 'mixture' of derived and pure preferences, but it will be conceptually convenient to think of them as mutually exclusive cases.

I suspect that if we are to take account of people's preferences over their pasts, as well as their futures, then we need – and indeed ought – only to do so for the case of 'pure' preferences. This is so because those considerations that give rise to derived preferences over past events will be reflected, and therefore taken account of, in an assessment of people's preferences over their futures. Any attempt to take direct account of derived preferences over past events would therefore involve double counting. If this much is granted, then we can legitimately focus upon pure preferences over past events. In doing so, I would suggest that little will be lost if we ignore people's pure preferences over relatively 'trivial' past events and focus instead upon preferences over matters that will have had a significant bearing on the well-being of past generations.

Since it seems reasonable to suppose that any future generation will regard the level of safety experienced by its forebears as having made a significant contribution to the latter's degree of well-being and will prefer that this level of safety should have been higher rather than lower, then it would appear to follow that a value of safety improvement *defined with-*

out reference to future generations' pure preferences over their pasts would constitute an *under*estimate. Simply put, such a value would fail to take account of future generations' pure preferences for more rather than less safety for their forebears.

This is, admittedly, not a particularly strong conclusion but it is probably about as far as one can safely go without making what would be essentially arbitrary assumptions about the precise nature of people's pure preferences over their pasts. Accordingly, the remainder of the discussion will focus upon the current and future generations' preferences concerning their respective *futures*, since we at least now know the direction of the error involved in this simplification.

If, in fact, we do focus exclusively on each generation's preferences concerning future levels of safety, then it is clear that it is the current and future generations' respective *values of statistical life* (defined, as they are, in terms of attitudes to the *prospect* of risk) that ought somehow to be weighed against each other in the process of 'aggregation of preferences'. Viewed in this way, the aggregation problem is simply the 'distributional weighting' problem in another guise and is usually handled in practical terms by the use of some form of discounting.[10] This leads on to the final problem in the complex skein of conundrums that attends the question of the safety of future generations. If values of safety and costs of risk are to be discounted for futurity, then one must face the fact that the prospect of the saving of one statistical life in 50 or 100 years' time will, in general, be accorded a different present value from a corresponding safety improvement whose effects will be manifest in the current period. Of course, it is *just* possible that these values might be equal, but this would depend, inter alia, upon (a) the way in which individual valuation of safety varies with income, (b) the rate of growth of income per capita and (c) the magnitude of the public sector discount rate.

Suppose that, as suggested by the regression results reported in Chapter 4, the relationship between the population mean marginal rate of substitution of wealth for risk $\bar{m}$ and income per capita $\bar{y}$ (both expressed in real terms) takes the form

$$\bar{m} = \alpha + \beta\bar{y} \qquad \alpha, \beta > 0. \tag{7.1}$$

Thus, if real income per capita grows at rate g per annum and the public sector discount rate is ρ per annum, then the discounted present value of the saving of one statistical life n years hence, V_n, will be given by

$$V_n = \frac{\alpha + \beta\bar{y}_0 (1 + g)^n}{(1 + \rho)^n} \tag{7.2}$$

where $\bar{y}_0$ denotes the current level of real income per capita. Clearly, with $\rho \geqslant g$ we will have $V_n < V_0$. Given that, in fact, the public sector discount rate in the UK currently exceeds the rate of growth of real income per capita, it will therefore be the case that the discounted present value of statistical life will fall with futurity. This is, to say the least, a disturbing conclusion. Whatever the implications of the *ex ante*, welfarist–

consequentialist position that this book has espoused, one cannot deny the force of the ethical precept that the saving of one statistical life in a hundred years' time deserves to be treated, in the context of current allocative decision making, as being worth no less and no more than the saving of one statistical life now: this would seem to be a natural corollary to the principle of 'equal treatment of equals'.

If it is, in fact, the case that the public sector discount rate exceeds the rate of growth of real income per capita, then the only way in which it would be possible to get $V_n = V_0$ would be by having $\bar{m}$ depend on higher degree terms in $\bar{y}$. However, since the regression analysis reported in Chapter 4 gave little indication that individual willingness to pay for safety is significantly related to higher degree terms in income,[11] this would not seem to be a very promising route out of our dilemma.

The only other way in which it would be possible to ensure that V_n is equal to V_0 within the context of the willingness-to-pay approach, together with a conventional treatment of futurity in public sector allocative decision making, would be to set the discount rate lower than the rate of growth of real income per capita, at least in the assessment of effects on current and future levels of safety.

All things considered then, it would seem that if public sector decision makers are to use the willingness-to-pay approach in the evaluation of safety effects for future generations then they face an uncomfortable choice, given the apparent nature of the relationship between individual valuation of safety and income. *Either* they must place a lower value on safety for future generations than for those currently alive, *or*, if these values are to be equalized, they must discount safety effects at a rate that is lower than that currently being applied to other costs and benefits in public sector project appraisal.

7.3   A Tentative Agenda for Further Research

During recent years there has been a considerable advance in our understanding of the way in which individuals value their own and others' safety and of the arguments for and against basing public sector allocative and legislative decisions upon these individual valuations. However, it has to be conceded that there remain a number of important questions to which we have, at best, only partial answers and, at worst, no answers at all. Undoubtedly, the most pressing of these questions concerns the appropriate numerical magnitude of the value of statistical life for various different kinds of risk. Indeed, it would seem that the resistance of public sector decision makers to adoption of the willingness-to-pay approach owes far more to doubts about the reliability of existing empirical estimates than to serious reservations concerning the fundamental principles of the approach. While it is the author's strong belief that existing empirical and theoretical results allow one to reach fairly clear conclusions concerning the *range* in which 'true' values of statistical life, if they could be established, would lie, it must be admitted that this is an area that, as yet, lacks definitive empirical results. Given the large and varied range of empirical studies that have already been undertaken, one is bound to wonder just what would constitute a recipe for success in empirical estimation. I suspect that the answer lies in a version of the questionnaire approach that would, unfortunately, be rather costly to conduct. Essentially, this would involve assembling a representative sample or 'panel' of individuals who would, possibly over a period of more than one day, be (a) introduced to the basic conceptual apparatus and *raison d'être* of the willingness-to-pay approach, and then (b) asked a variety of valuation and other relevant questions.

Following analysis of the results, the panel would then be reassembled and subjected to in-depth questioning concerning 'first-round' answers including the rationale for apparently anomalous responses. In this way it might just be possible to arrive at estimates, together with explanations of peculiarities in responses, that would carry sufficient conviction to persuade sceptical public sector decision makers.

Other topics that might fruitfully be addressed in future research on the economics of safety and physical risk include the following:

1 The nature of the relationship between individual valuation of reductions in the risk of death and reductions in the risk of various kinds of non-fatal injury or illness. Hitherto, empirical research has focused almost exclusively upon the case of mortality risks. However, there is in principle no reason why the willingness-to-pay approach should not also be applied to risks of morbidity and it is incontrovertibly the case that, in purely numerical terms, cases of non-fatal injury and illness far outweigh fatalities in most public sector contexts.

2 The nature of the relationship between values of statistical life for 'everyday' voluntary risks such as those encountered in transport, and involuntary 'dread' risks such as those that arise in the course of nuclear power generation. A connected question concerns the relationship between values of statistical life for independent risks and the corresponding values for reduction in the risk of catastrophes. This and earlier chapters have examined some of the issues related to these questions, but clearly much remains to be done before we have anything remotely resembling satisfactory answers.

3 The nature of the relationship between subjective and objective probabilities in the context of physical risk. Strictly speaking, the marginal rates of substitution of wealth for physical risk that feature centrally in the willingness-to-pay approach should be defined in terms of *subjective perceptions* of physical risk. It is therefore of vital importance for successful application of the willingness-to-pay approach that we should have reliable information concerning the relationship between these subjective perceptions and 'objective'

measures of physical risk, such as historical relative frequencies of occurrence of accidents of various types.

4   The implications for the economics of safety of theories of choice other than expected utility maximization. Chapter 3, section 3.8, attempted to explore the consequences of replacing expected utility theory by prospect theory and ratio-form theory, but there are various other theories whose implications might fruitfully be investigated.

5   Procedures for evaluating safety effects on future generations. Again, this chapter has offered some tentative suggestions on this subject, but it is plain that many questions remain to be answered.

6   The properties of cost functions for safety improvement. The argument developed in this book has focused largely upon the question of *valuation* of safety improvement. However, in order to assess the allocative implications of adopting any particular valuation method it is necessary to know something of the relevant cost function. In particular, if safety improvement is carried out to the point at which the marginal value of additional safety is equated to its marginal cost, then knowledge of the behaviour of the latter is clearly a prerequisite for establishing the extent of the allocative adjustment that would result from the adoption of one, rather than another, valuation method. While an attempt was made in Chapter 6 to establish the properties of the cost function for road safety in the UK, it must be admitted that this was little more than a 'back of the envelope' calculation; far harder empirical estimates are urgently needed for transport and various other contexts.

7.4.   Conclusion

In spite of its limitations, the willingness-to-pay approach appears to be by far the most cogent procedure currently available for taking account of safety effects in public sector allocative and legislative decisions. This view is essentially founded on a belief in the importance of ensuring that such decisions should reflect the wishes and attitudes of those who will be affected by them. Since this is precisely what the willingness-to-pay approach is designed to do, it can fairly lay claim to being the natural vehicle for carrying the principles of 'democracy' (in the wider sense of the term) into the sphere of public safety. This having been said, two important caveats should be entered. First, few, if any, advocates of the willingness-to-pay approach have argued that it ought to be regarded as the *sole* criterion by which safety effects should be judged. Nonetheless, while there are plainly many other considerations that might sensibly be weighed in the decision-making process, a measure of society's aggregate valuation of safety is clearly a matter of central importance. The second reservation concerning the approach relates to the difficulties of empirical estimation. It is in the nature of the problem that empirical work is unlikely, within the near future, to yield 'hard' point estimates of the value of statistical life for various kinds of risk – or even to allow one to place these values within tight confidence intervals. Instead, I suspect that decision makers will have to face up to the fact that, at least for some time to come, there will be no substitute for the exercise of critical judgement on this question. However, the fact that difficult judgements are needed if the willingness-to-pay approach is actually to be implemented is surely no excuse for eschewing its use in favour of a manifestly inappropriate methodology, such as the gross output approach. Furthermore, while it is probably too much to expect that empirical work will quickly lead to definitive results, one can hope that with further refinement of estimation methods, the range of values within which judgement must be exercised will be substantially narrowed. I am encouraged in this hope not least by the fact that 15 years ago it would simply not have been possible to defend the confident assertion that the value of statistical life should be, at a minimum, £500,000 for everyday risks. To all of this can be added the reasonable speculation that theoretical work will provide further a priori grounds for believing that 'true' values lie within this range rather than that.

All in all then, there is still much to be done in this intriguing and important area of research. However, I perceive a significantly growing level of activity directed at the various questions involved and am therefore optimistic that we shall continue to make substantial progress towards the discovery of satisfactory answers.

Notes

1 In contrast to the 'wider' interpretation of the term that was used in the context of the justification for basing public sector safety decisions on private preferences and perceptions. The narrower meaning can be viewed as a special case, in that it entails a *particular way* of incorporating private preferences in public choices.

2 Bergstrom (1982) identifies conditions under which it would be unambiguously *in*appropriate to add an allowance to the value of statistical life to reflect valuation of other people's safety. For a detailed discussion of this point, see Chapter 2, section 2.1.7.

3 See particularly Jones-Lee (1980a).

4 Though as was argued in Chapter 3, section 3.6, these marginal valuations may not fall very rapidly.

5 While Mulligan (1977), Prescott-Clarke (1982) and Smith and Desvousges (1987) all asked valuation questions related to risks from nuclear power generation or the disposal of hazardous wastes, none permitted unambiguous inference of values of statistical life.

6 For example, some questions concerning willingness to pay to reduce risks from nuclear power implied values of statistical life well in excess of £20,000,000.

7 See, for example, Krutilla and Eckstein (1958) and Marglin (1963).

8 While one certainly cannot exercise *choices* over past events, I believe that it is

perfectly meaningful to assert that one would *prefer* that such and such had, or had not, happened. It might, of course, be objected that in relation to known historical facts the expression of such preferences is an essentially vacuous exercise. However, this objection would seem to lose its force in the case of past events whose outcomes are *unknown*. Thus, I feel it quite legitimate to claim that I would prefer that Mallory and Irvine should have reached the summit of Everest before meeting their deaths.

 9 Though, of course, 'forward' trades between the present and future are of the essence in financial markets.

10 For a very readable discussion of this and many other points related to cost–benefit analysis and social choice, see Layard (1972).

11 While there was substantial evidence of significance of the linear income variable in the various parts of the key valuation Question 20, in no case was the 'income minus mean income all squared' variable significant at the 5% level.

Postscript

Since the script of this book was delivered to the publisher, the UK Department of Transport has issued a consultative document, *Valuation of Road Accident Fatalities* (London, Department of Transport, 1988) in which it is proposed that the department's current procedure for valuing the avoidance of a fatality – based broadly upon the 'gross output' (or 'human capital') approach – should be abandoned in favour of the 'willingness-to-pay' approach, with the value of a statistical life for transport risks set at £500,000.

Bibliography and References

Abraham, C. and Thedié, J. (1960) Le prix d'une vie humaine dans les décisions économiques. *Revue Française de Recherche Opérationelle*, 20, 157–68.

Acton, J. P. (1973) *Evaluating Public Programs to Save Lives: The Case of Heart Attacks*. Research Report R-73-02. Santa Monica: Rand Corporation.

Acton, J. P. (1976) Measuring the monetary value of life saving programs. *Law and Contemporary Problems*, 40, 46–72.

Adams, J. G. H. (1974) And how much for your grandmother? *Environment and Planning A*, 6, 619–26.

Adler, H. A. (1971) *Economic Appraisal of Transport Projects*. Bloomington: Indiana University Press.

Akehurst, R and Culyer, A. J. (1974) On the economic surplus and the value of life. *Bulletin of Economic Research*, 26, 64–74.

Allais, M. and Hagen, O. (eds) (1979) *Expected Utility Hypotheses and the Allais Paradox*. Dordrecht: D Reidel.

Arnould, R. J. and Nichols, L. M. (1983) Wage–risk premiums and workers' compensation: a refinement of estimates of compensating wage differential. *Journal of Political Economy*, 91, 332–40.

Arrow, K. J. (1971) *Essays in the Theory of Risk Bearing*. Amsterdam: North Holland.

Arthur, W. B. (1981) The economics of risks to life. *American Economic Review*, 71, 54–64.

Atiyah, P. S. (1982) A legal perspective on recent contributions to the valuation of life. In M. W. Jones-Lee (ed.), *The Value of Life and Safety: Proceedings of a Conference held by the Geneva Association*. Amsterdam: North Holland, 185–220.

Bailey, M. J. (1978) Safety decisions and insurance. *American Economic Review*, 68, 295–8.

Bailey, M. J. (1980) *Reducing Risks to Life: Measurement of the Benefits*, Washington: American Enterprise Institute.

Barancik, J. I. and Shapiro, M. A. (1972) Pittsburgh burn study. Unpublished paper, Graduate School of Public Health, University of Pittsburgh.

Bell, D. (1982) Regret in decision making under uncertainty. *Operations Research*, 30, 961–81.

Bell, D. (1985) Disappointment in decision making under uncertainty. *Operations Research*, 33, 1–27.

Bergan, J. J. (1973) Current risks to the kidney transplant donor. *Transplantation Proceedings*, 5, 1131–4.

Berger, M. C., Blomquist, G. C., Kenkel, D. and Tolley, G. S. (1987) Valuing changes in health risks: a comparison of alternative measures. *Southern Economic Journal*, 53, 967–84.

Bergson, A. (1938) A reformulation of certain aspects of welfare economics. *Quarterly Journal of Economics*, 66, 366–84.

Bergstrom, T. C. (1974) Preference and choice in matters of life and death. In J. Hirshleifer, T. Bergstrom and E. Rappaport, (eds) *Applying Cost–Benefit Concepts to Projects which Alter Human Mortality*. UCLA-ENG-7478. Los Angeles: School of Engineering and Applied Sciences, University of California, Appendix 1.

Bergstrom, T. C. (1982) Is a man's life worth more than his human capital? In M. W. Jones-Lee (ed.) *The Value of Life and Safety: Proceedings of a Conference held by the Geneva Association*. Amsterdam: North Holland, 3–26.

Blackorby, C. and Donaldson, D. (1986) Can risk–benefit analysis provide consistent policy evaluations of projects invovling loss of life? *Economic Journal*, 96, 758–73.

Blomquist, G. (1979) Value of life saving: implications of consumption activity. *Journal of Political Economy*, 87, 540–58.

Blomquist, G. (1981) The value of human life: an empirical perspective. *Economic Enquiry*, 19, 157–64.

Blomquist, G. (1982) Estimating the value of life and safety: recent developments. In M. W. Jones-Lee (ed.) *The Value of Life and Safety: Proceedings of a Conference held by the Geneva Association*. Amsterdam: North Holland, 27–40.

Bodily, S. E. (1980) Analysis of risks to life and limb. *Operations Research*, 28, 156–75.

Borch, K. (1977) Optimal life insurance. *The Geneva Papers on Risk and Insurance*, 6, 3–16.

Borch, K. (1978) Consumption and saving: models and reality. *Theory and Decision*, 9, 241–53.

British Medical Association (1987) *Living With Risk*. Chichester: Wiley.

Brookshire, D. S., Thayer, M. A., Tschirhart, J. and Schulze, W. D. (1985) A test of the expected utility model: evidence from earthquake risks. *Journal of Political Economy*, 93, 369–89.

Broome, J. (1978a) Choice and value in economics. *Oxford Economic Papers*, 30, 313–33.

Broome, J. (1978b) Trying to value a life. *Journal of Public Economics*, 9, 91–100.

Broome, J. (1979) Trying to value a life: a reply. *Journal of Public Economics*, 12, 259–62.

Broome, J. (1982) Uncertainty in welfare economics and the value of life. In M. W. Jones-Lee (ed.) *The Value of Life and Safety: Proceedings of a Conference held by the Geneva Association*. Amsterdam: North Holland, 201–16.

Broome, J. (1983a) The price of life: where economics is out of its depth. *The Financial Times*, 17 August.

Broome, J. (1983b) Letter to the Editor. *The Financial Times*, 2 September.

Broome, J. (1983c) The economic value of life: a problem in the philosophy of population. Mimeo: University of Bristol.

Broome, J. (1984a) Uncertainty and fairness. *Economic Journal*, 94, 624–32.

Broome, J. (1984b) Selecting people randomly. *Ethics*, 95, 38–55.

Broome, J. (1985) The economic value of life. *Economica*, 52, 281–94.

Brown, C. (1980) Equalising differences in the labor market. *Quarterly Journal of*

Economics, 94, 113–34.

Brown, R. A. and Green, C. H. (1981) Threats to health and safety: perceived risk and willingness-to-pay. *Social Science and Medicine*, 15, 67–75.

Buchanan, J. and Faith, R. (1979) Trying again to value a life. *Journal of Public Economics*, 12, 245–8.

Calabresi, G. and Bolbit, P. (1978) *Tragic Choices*. New York: Norton.

Calne, P. (1967) *Renal Transplantation*. London: Williams & Wilkins.

Campbell, B. J. O'Neill, B. and Tingley, B. (1974) Comparative injuries to belted and unbelted drivers of subcompact, compact, intermediate and standard cars. Paper presented at the *Third International Congress on Auto Safety, San Francisco, July*.

Card, W. I. and Mooney, G. H. (1977) What is the monetary value of a human life? *British Medical Journal*, 281, 1627–9.

Carlson, J. W. (1963) *Evaluating Life Saving*. PhD dissertation, Harvard University.

Chase, S. B. (ed.) (1968) *Problems in Public Expenditure Analysis*. Washington: Brookings.

Chew, S. and MacCrimmon, K. (1979) Alpha–nu choice theory: a generalisation of expected utility theory. Working Paper No. 669: University of British Columbia, Faculty of Commerce and Business Administration.

Clark, M. J., Fleishman, A. B. and Webb, G. A. M. (1981) *Optimisation of the Radiological Protection of the Public*, NRPBR120. Chilton: HMSO.

Cliff, N. (1982) What is and isn't measurement. In G. Keren (ed.) *Statistical and Methodological Issues in Psychology and Social Sciences Research*. Hillsdale, NJ: Lawrence Erlbaum Associates.

Conley, B. C. (1976) The value of human life in the demand for safety. *American Economic Review*, 66, 45–55.

Conley, B. C. (1978) The value of human life in the demand for safety: extension and reply. *American Economic Review*, 68, 717–19.

Cook, P. J. (1978). The value of human life in the demand for safety: comment. *American Economic Review*, 68, 710–11.

Cook, P. J. and Graham. D. A. (1977) The demand for insurance and protection: the case of irreplaceable commodities. *Quarterly Journal of Economics*, 91, 143–56.

Council, F. M. and Hunter, W. W. (1974) *Seat Belt Usage and Benefits in North Carolina Accidents*. Chapel Hill, NC: Highway Safety Research Center.

Cropper, M. L. and Sussman, F. G. (1985) The role of families in valuing risks to life. Working Paper 85–10: University of Maryland, Department of Economics.

Cropper, M. L. and Sussman, F. G. (1987) Families and the economics of risks to life. Mimeo: University of Maryland.

Cummings, R. G, Brookshire, D. S. and Schulze, W. D. (1986) *Valuing Environmental Goods: An Assessment of the Contingent Valuation Method*. Totowa, NJ: Rowman and Allanheld.

Currie, D. A. and Peters, W. (eds) (1980) *Contemporary Economic Analysis*, Vol. 2. London: Croom Helm.

Currie, D. A. Peel, D. and Peters, W. (eds) (1981) *Microeconomic Analysis*. London: Croom Helm.

Dardis, R. (1980) The value of life: new evidence from the marketplace. *American Economic Review*, 70, 1077–82.

Dawson, R. F. F. (1967) *Cost of Road Accidents in Great Britain*. London: Road Research Laboratory, Ministry of Transport.

Dawson, R. F. F. (1971) *Current Costs of Road Accidents in Great Britain*. London: Road Research Laboratory, Department of the Environment.

Dehez, P. and Drèze, J. H. (1982) State-dependent utility, the demand for insurance and the value of safety. In M. W. Jones-Lee (ed.) *The Value of Life and Safety: Proceedings of a Conference held by the Geneva Association.* Amsterdam: North Holland, 41–65.

Department of Transport (1979) *COBA 8 Manual.* London: Economics Highways Division, Department of Transport.

Department of Transport (1981) *COBA 9 Manual.* London: Economics Highways Division, Department of Transport.

Department of Transport (1982) *Transport Statistics Great Britain 1971–1981.* London: HMSO.

Department of Transport (1987) *Values for Journey Time Savings and Accident Prevention.* London: Department of Transport.

Dillingham, A. E. (1979) *The Injury Risk Structure of Occupations and Wages.* PhD Dissertation, Cornell University.

Dillingham, A. E. (1980) The relationship between estimates of wage premiums for injury risk and the measurement of injury risk: results from one population. Illinois State University, Department of Economics.

Dobbs, I. M. (1985) Shadow prices, consistency and the value of life. *Journal of Public Economics*, 27, 177–93.

Dorfman, R. (ed.) (1965) *Measuring Benefits of Government Investments.* Washington: Brookings.

Dorsey, S. and Walzer, N. (1983) Workers' compensation, job hazards and wages. *Industrial and Labor Relations Review*, 36, 642–54.

Drèze, J. H. (1962) L'utilité sociale d'une vie humaine. *Revue Française de Recherche Opérationelle*, 22, 139–55.

Drèze, J. H. (ed.) (1974a) *Allocation under Uncertainty: Equilibrium and Optimality*, London: Macmillan.

Drèze, J. H. (1974b) Axiomatic Theories of Choice, Cardinal Utility and Subjective Probability: A Review. In J. H. Dréze (ed.) *Allocation under Uncertainty: Equilibrium and Optimality.* London: Macmillan, 3–23.

Drèze, J. H. (1981) Inferring risk tolerance from deductibles in insurance contracts. *The Geneva Papers on Risk and Insurance*, 6, 48–52.

Drèze, J. H. (1987) *Essays on Economic Decisions under Uncertainty.* Cambridge: Cambridge University Press.

Dublin, C. I. and Lotka, A. J. (1930) *The Money Value of a Man.* New York: Ronald Press.

Duval, H. (1979) Essai sur la valeur de la vie et la valeur du temps. Arcueil: Organisme National de Sécurité Routiére.

Duval, H. (1983) La valeur monétaire d'une vie humaine. Arcueil: Cahiers d'Etudes de l'Organisme National de Sécurité Routière.

Eisner, R. and Strotz, R. H. (1961) Flight insurance and the theory of choice. *Journal of Political Economy*, 69, 355–68.

Engel, E. (1893) Der Werth des Menschen. *Volkswirtschaftliche Zeitfragen.*

Farr, W. (1876) Contribution to *39th Annual Report of the Registrar General of Births, Marriages and Deaths for England and Wales.*

Fenn, P. (1987) Evaluating irreplaceable loss: some implications for insurance and liability rules. *The Geneva Papers on Risk and Insurance*, 12, 158–67.

Fischer, G. W. (1979) Willingness to pay for probabilistic improvements in functional health status: a psychological perspective. In S. J. Mushkin and D. W. Dunlop (eds) *Health: What is it Worth?* Elmsford, NY: Pergamon Press.

Fischer, G. W. and Vaupel, J. W. (1976) A lifespan utility model: assessing preferences for consumption and longevity. Working paper. Durham, NC:

Center for Policy Analysis, Institute of Policy Sciences and Public Affairs, Duke University.

Fischoff, B., Lichtenstein, S., Slovic, P., Derby, S. L. and Keeney, R. L. (1981) *Acceptable Risk*. Cambridge: Cambridge University Press.

Foster, C. D. and Neuberger, H. L. I. (1974) The ambiguity of the consumer's surplus measure of welfare change. *Oxford Economic Papers*, 26, 66–77.

Frank, R. H. (1982) Envy and the optimal purchase of unobservable commodities: the case of safety. In M. W. Jones-Lee (ed.) *The Value of Life and Safety: Proceedings of a Conference held by the Geneva Association*. Amsterdam: North Holland, 145–57.

Frankel, M. (1979) Hazard opportunity and the valuation of life. Mimeo: University of Illinois at Urbana-Champaign.

Fraser, C. D. (1980) Optimal compensating insurance, informational asymmetries and government discretionary behaviour. Mimeo: University of York.

Fraser, C. D. (1984) Optimal compensation for potential fatality. *Journal of Public Economics*, 23, 307–32.

Freeman, A. M. (1979) *The Benefits of Environmental Improvement*. Baltimore: Johns Hopkins University Press.

French, T. and Hofferberth, W. (1967) Tyre development and application. Paper presented to the *International Rubber Conference, Brighton, May 15–18*.

Fried, C. (1969) The value of human life. *Harvard Law Review*, 82, 1415–37.

Friedman, D. (1982) What is fair compensation for death or injury? *International Review of Law and Economics*, 2, 81–93.

Friend, J. and Blume, M. E. (1975) The demand for risky assets. *American Economic Review*, 65, 900–22.

Fromm, G. (1965) Civil aviation expenditures. In R. Dorfman (ed.) *Measuring Benefits of Government Investments*. Washington: Brookings, 172–230.

Ghosh, D., Lees, D. and Seal, W. (1975) Optimal motorway speed and some valuations of time and life. *Manchester School*, 43, 134–43.

Glover, J. (1977) *Causing Death and Saving Lives*. Harmondsworth: Penguin.

Glover, J. (1978) Assessing the value of saving lives. In G. Vesey (ed.) *Human Values*. Brighton: Harvester Press, 208–27.

Gould, W. and Thaler, R. (1980) Public policy toward life saving: maximise lives saved vs consumer sovereignty. Cambridge, MA: National Bureau of Economic Research Working Paper Series.

Gravelle, H. S. E. (1979) The value of changes in individual risk in a large mixed economy. *Economics Letters*, 3, 145–8.

Gravelle, H. and Rees, R. (1981) *Microeconomics*. London: Longman.

Greene, G. (1980) *Dr Fischer of Geneva or the Bomb Party*. London: Bodley Head.

Gregor, J. (1977) *Intra-urban Mortality and Air Quality: An Economic Analysis of the Costs of Pollution Induced Mortality*. EPA Research Report, EPA-60015-77-009. Washington: Environmental Protection Agency.

Grogan, R. J. and Watson, T. R. (1974) Tyre punctures – how, why and where. *Journal of the Forensic Science Society*, 14, 15–176.

Hamburger, J. and Crosnier, J. (1968) Moral and ethical problems in transplantation. In F. T. Rapaport and J. Dausset (eds) *Human Transplantation*. New York: Grune and Stratton, 37–44.

Hammack, J. and Brown. G. M. (1974) *Waterfowl and Wetlands: Toward Bioeconomic Analysis*. Baltimore: Johns Hopkins University Press for Resources for the Future.

Hammermesh, D. S. (1977) Economic aspects of job satisfaction. In O.

Ashenfelter and W. Oates (eds) *Essays in Labor Market and Population Analysis*, New York: Wiley, 53–72.

Hammerton, M. (1973) A case of radical probability estimation. *Journal of Experimental Psychology*, 101, 252–4.

Hammerton, M., Jones–Lee, M. W. and Abbott, V. (1982a) The consistency and coherence of attitudes to physical risk. *Journal of Transport Economics and Policy*, 16, 181–99.

Hammerton, M., Jones-Lee, M. W. and Abbott, V. (1982b) Equity and public risk: some empirical results. *Operations Research*, 30, 203–7.

Hammond, P. J. (1982) Utilitarianism, uncertainty and information. In A. Sen and B. Williams (eds) *Utilitarianism and Beyond*. Cambridge: Cambridge University Press, 85–102.

Hare, R. M. (1982) Ethical theory and utilitarianism. In A. Sen and B. Williams (eds) *Utilitarianism and Beyond*. Cambridge: Cambridge University Press, 23–38.

Harrison, A. J. and Quarmby, D. A. (1970) The value of time in transport planning: a review. London: Department of the Environment, Mathematical Advisory Unit Note 154.

Harrison, A. J. and Quarmby, D. A. (1972) The value of time. In R. Layard (ed.) *Cost–Benefit Analysis*. Harmondsworth: Penguin.

Harsanyi, J. C. (1955) Cardinal welfare, individualistic ethics and interpersonal comparisons of utility. *Journal of Political Economy*, 83, 309–21.

Harsanyi, J. C. (1982) Morality and the theory of rational behaviour. In A. Sen and B. Williams (eds) *Utilitarianism and Beyond*. Cambridge: Cambridge University Press, 39–62.

Health & Safety Executive (1987) *The Tolerability of Risk from Nuclear Power Stations*. London: HMSO.

Heckman, J. J. (1979) Sample selection bias as a specification error. *Econometrica*, 47, 153–61.

Hicky, J. L. S. and Kearney, J. J. (1977) Engineering control research and development plan for carcinogenic materials. Report to National Institute for Occupational Safety and Health under Contract No 210-76-0147.

Hills, P. J. and Jones-Lee, M. W. (1983) The role of safety in highway investment appraisal for developing countries. *Accident Analysis and Prevention*, 15, 355–69.

Hirshleifer, J., Bergstrom, T. and Rappaport, E. (1974) *Applying Cost–Benefit Concepts to Projects which Alter Human Mortality*. UCLA-ENG-7478. Los Angeles: School of Engineering and Applied Sciences, University of California.

Hockley, G. C. (1983) Letter to the Editor. *The Financial Times*, 2 September.

International Commission on Radiological Protection (1977) *Recommendations of the International Commission on Radiological Protection*. ICRP Publication 26, *Annals of the ICRP*, Vol. 1, No. 3. Oxford: Pergamon Press.

International Commission on Radiological Protection (1983) *Cost–Benefit Analysis in the Optimisation of Radiation Protection*. ICRP Publication 37. Oxford: Pergamon Press.

Ippolito, P. M. and Ippolito, R. A. (1984) Measuring the value of life saving from consumer reactions to new information. *Journal of Public Economics*, 25, 53–81.

Jacobs, J. D. and Sayer, I. (1983) Road accidents in developing countries. *Accident Analysis and Prevention*, 15, 337–53.

Johnson, N. and Kotz, S. (1972) *Distribution in Statistics: Continuous Multivariate Distributions*. New York: Wiley.

Jones, G. H. (1946) *Road Accidents*. Report submitted to the Minister of Transport. London: HMSO.

Jones-Lee, M. W. (1969) Valuation of reduction in probability of death by road accident. *Journal of Transport Economics and Policy*, 3, 37–47.

Jones-Lee, M. W. (1974) The value of changes in the probability of death or injury. *Journal of Political Economy*, 82, 835–49.

Jones-Lee, M. W. (1975) Optimal life insurance: comment. *Journal of Finance*, 30, 902–3.

Jones-Lee, M. W. (1976) *The Value of Life: An Economic Analysis*. London: Martin Robertson; Chicago: University of Chicago Press.

Jones-Lee, M. W. (1977) Some empirical rigor mortis: an empirical procedure for estimating the value of life from tyre replacement data. Paper presented at the *SSRC Health Economists' Study Group, University of Newcastle upon Tyne*, July.

Jones-Lee, M. W. (1978) The value of human life in the demand for safety: comment. *Amercian Economic Review*, 68, 712–16.

Jones-Lee, M. W. (1979) Trying to value a life: why Broome does not sweep clean. *Journal of Public Economics*, 12, 249–56.

Jones-Lee, M. W. (1980a) Human capital, risk aversion and the value of life. In D. A. Currie and W. Peters (eds) *Contemporary Economic Analysis*, Vol. 2. London: Croom Helm, 285–321.

Jones-Lee, M. W. (1980b) Maximum acceptable physical risk and a new measure of financial risk aversion. *Economic Journal*, 90, 550–68.

Jones-Lee, M. W. (1981) The value of non-marginal changes in physical risk. In D. A. Currie, D. Peel and W. Peters (eds) *Microeconomics Analysis*. London: Croom Helm, 233–68.

Jones-Lee, M. W. (ed.) (1982) *The Value of Life and Safety: Proceedings of a Conference held by the Geneva Association*. Amsterdam: North Holland.

Jones-Lee, M. W. (1983) Letter to the Editor. *The Financial Times*, 22 August.

Jones-Lee, M. W. (1984a) Natural disasters: a comparison of alternative methods for evaluating preventive measures. *The Geneva Papers on Risk and Insurance*, 9, 188–205.

Jones-Lee, M. W. (1984b) The valuation of transport safety. In *Proceedings of the Annual Transportation Convention, Pretoria, 1984*, Vol. G. Pretoria: National Institute for Transport and Road Research, 1–14.

Jones-Lee, M. W. (1987a) The political economy of physical risk. *Journal of the Society for Radiological Protection*, 7, 33–44.

Jones-Lee, M. W. (1987b) The economic value of life: a comment. *Economica*, 54, 397–400.

Jones-Lee, M. W. (1987c) Valuation of safety. *Public Money*, 7, 14.

Jones-Lee, M. W. (1987d) Evaluating Safety Benefits. In A. Harrison and J. Gretton (eds) *Transport UK 1987*. Newbury: Policy Journals, 87–92.

Jones-Lee, M. W. and Poncelet, A. M. (1982) The value of marginal and non-marginal multiperiod variations in physical risk. In M. W. Jones-Lee (ed.) *The Value of Life and Safety: Proceedings of a Conference held by the Geneva Association*. Amsterdam: North Holland, 67–80.

Jones-Lee, M. W., Hammerton, M. and Abbott, V. (1983) *The Value of Transport Safety: Results of a National Sample Survey*. Report to the UK Department of Transport.

Jones-Lee, M. W, Hammerton, M. and Abbott, V. (1987) *The Value of Transport Safety: Results of a National Sample Survey*. Newbury: Policy Journals.

Jones-Lee, M. W., Hammerton, M. and Philips, P. R. (1985) The value of safety:

results of a national sample survey. *Economic Journal*, 95, 49–72.

Kahneman, D. and Tversky, A. (1979) Prospect theory: an analysis of decision under risk. *Econometrica*, 47, 263–91.

Kahneman, D., Slovic, P. and Tversky, A. (eds) (1982) *Judgement under Uncertainty: Heuristics and Biases* Cambridge: Cambridge University Press.

Keeney, R. L. (1980a) Evaluating alternatives involving potential fatalities. *Operations Research*, 28, 188–205.

Keeney, R. L. (1980b) Equity and public risk. *Operations Research*, 28, 527–34.

Keeney, R. L. (1980c) Utility functions for equity and public risk. *Management Science*, 26, 345–53.

Keeney, R. L. (1982) Evaluating mortality risks from an organisational perspective. In M. W. Jones-Lee (ed.) *The Value of Life and Safety: Proceedings of a Conference held by the Geneva Association*. Amsterdam: North Holland, 217–27.

Keeney, R. L. and Raiffa, H. (1976) *Decisions with Multiple Objectives*. New York: Wiley.

Kind, P., Rosser, R. and Williams, A. (1982) Valuation of quality of life: some psychometric evidence. In M. W. Jones-Lee (ed.) *The Value of Life and Safety: Proceedings of a Conference held by the Geneva Association*. Amsterdam: North Holland, 159–70.

Klarman, H.E., Francis, J. O.'S. and Rosenthal, G. D. (1973) Efficient treatment of patients with kidney failure. In M. H. Cooper and A. J. Culyer (eds) *Health Economics*. Harmondsworth: Penguin, 230–40.

Knetsch, J. L. and Sinden, J. A. (1984) Willingness to pay and compensation demanded: experimental evidence of an unexpected disparity in measures of value. *Quarterly Journal of Economics*, 98, 507–21.

Krantz, D. H., Luce, R. D., Suppes, P. and Tversky, A. (1971) *Foundations of Measurement, Additive Polynominal Representation*, Vol. 1. New York: Academic Press.

Krutilla, J. V. and Eckstein, O. (1958) *Multiple Purpose River Development*. Baltimore: Johns Hopkins University Press.

Landefeld, J. S. (1979) *Control of New Materials with Carcinogenic Potential*. PhD Dissertation, University of Maryland.

Landefeld, J. S. and Seskin, E. P. (1982) The economic value of life: linking theory to practice. *American Journal of Public Health*, 72, 555–66.

Layard, R. (1972) (ed.) *Cost-Benefit Analysis*. Harmondsworth, Penguin.

Layfield, F. (1987) *Sizewell B Public Inquiry*. London: HMSO.

Lee, T. R. (1981) The public's perception of risk and the question of irrationality. In F. Warner (ed.) *The Assessment and Perception of Risk*, Proceedings of the Royal Society, 376. London: Royal Society, 5–16.

Le Grand, J. (1984) Optimal taxation, the compensation principle and the measurement of changes in economic welfare. *Journal of Public Economics*, 24, 241–7.

Leitch, G. (1977) *Report of the Advisory Committee on Trunk Road Assessment*. London: HMSO.

Le Net, M (1978) *Le Prix de la Vie Humaine*. Paris: la Documentation Française.

Lesourd, D. A., Fogel, M. E. and Johnston, D. R. (1968) *Benefit/Cost Analysis of Kidney Disease Programs*. Washington, DC: Department of Health Education and Welfare, US Public Health Service, Publication No. 1941.

Levine, D. M. and Campbell, B. J. (1971) *Effectiveness of Lap Seat Belts and the Energy Absorbing Steering System in the Reduction of Injuries*. Chapel Hill, NC: Highway Safety Research Center.

Lichtenstein, S. and Slovic, P. (1971) Reversals of preferences between bids and choices in gambling decisions. *Journal of Experimental Psychology*, 89, 46–55.
Lichtenstein, S. and Slovic, P. (1973) Response-induced reversals of preferences in gambling: an extended replication in Las Vegas. *Journal of Experimental Psychology*, 101, 16–20.
Lichtenstein, S, Slovic, P, Fischoff, B, Layman, M. and Combs, B. (1978) Judged frequency of lethal events. *Journal of Experimental Psychology: Human Learning and Memory*, 4, 551–78.
Linnerooth, J. (1976) Methods for evaluating mortality risk. *Futures*, 8, 293–304.
Linnerooth, J. (1979) the value of human life: a review of the models. *Economic Inquiry*, 17, 52–74.
Linnerooth, J. (1982) Murdering statistical lives . . .? In M. W. Jones-Lee (ed.) *The Value of Life and Safety: Proceedings of a Conference held by the Geneva Association*. Amsterdam: North Holland, 229–61.
Lipsey, R. E. (1976) Comments on the value of saving a life: evidence from the labor market. In N. E. Terleckyj (ed.) *Household Production and Consumption*. New York: National Bureau of Economic Research, 301–2.
Loomes, G. and Sugden, R. (1982) Regret theory: an alternative theory of rational choice under uncertainty. *The Economic Journal*, 92, 805–24.
Lowne, R. W. (1972) *The Condition of Tyres in Use on Cars*. TRRL Report LR449. Crowthorne: Transport and Road Research Laboratory.
Lüdtke, R. (1873) Contribution to *Deutsche Versicherungs-Zeitung*.
Machina, M. J. (1983) *The Economic Theory of Individual Behavior toward Risk*: *Theory, Evidence and New Directions*. Technical Report 433. Stanford: Center for Research on Organisational Efficiency.
Maclean, A. D. (1979) *The Value of Public Safety: Results of a Pilot-scale Survey*. London: Home Office Scientific Advisory Branch.
Marglin, S. A. (1963) The social rate of discount and the optimal rate of investment. *Quarterly Journal of Economics*, 77, 95–111.
Marin, A. (1983a) Your money or your life. *The Three Banks Review*, 138, 2–37.
Marin, A. (1983b) Letter to the Editor. *The Financial Times*, 23 August.
Marin, A. (1988) The Cost of Avoiding Death – Nuclear Power, Regulation and Spending on Safety. *The Royal Bank of Scotland Review*, 157, 20–36.
Marin, A. and Psacharopoulos, G. (1982) The reward for risk in the labor market: evidence from the United Kingdom and a reconciliation with other studies. *Journal of Political Economy*, 90, 827–53.
Marshall, J. M. (1984) Gambles and the shadow price of death. *American Economic Review*, 74, 73–86.
Mavromaros, K. (1979) Insurance and protection of irreplaceable commodities: the case of one's own life. *Economics Letters*, 3, 9–13.
Melinek, S. J. (1974) A method of evaluating human life for economic purposes. *Accident Analysis and Prevention*, 6, 103–14.
Melinek, S. J., Woolley, S. K. D. and Baldwin, R. (1973) *Analysis of a Questionnaire on Attitudes to Risk*: Fire Research Note 962. Borehamwood: Joint Fire Research Organisation.
Miller, G. A. (1956) The magical number seven plus or minus two: some limits on our capacity to process information. *Psychological Review*, 63, 81–97.
Miller, T. R., Reinert, K. A. and Whiting, B. E. (1984) *Alternative Approaches to Accident Cost Concepts: State of the Art*. Report prepared for the Federal Highway Administration, US Department of Commerce, Washington DC: Granville Corp.
Ministry of Transport (1966) *Roads in Urban Areas*. London: HMSO.

Mirrlees, J. A. (1982) The economic uses of utilitarianism. In A Sen and B Williams (eds) *Utilitarianism and Beyond*. Cambridge: Cambridge University Press, 63–84.

Mishan, E. J. (1969) *Welfare Economics: An Assessment*. Amsterdam: North Holland.

Mishan, E. J. (1971) Evaluation of life and limb: a theoretical approach. *Journal of Political Economy*, 79, 687–705.

Mishan, E. J. (1981) The value of trying to value a life. *Journal of Public Economics*, 15, 133–7.

Mishan, E. J. (1982) Recent contributions to the literature of life valuation: a critical assessment. In M. W. Jones-Lee (ed.) *The Value of Life and Safety: Proceedings of a Conference held by the Geneva Association*. Amsterdam: North Holland, 81–92.

Mitchell, R. C. and Carson, R. T. (1986) Some comments on the state of the arts assessment of the contingent valuation method draft report. In R. G. Cummings, D. S. Brookshire, W. D. Schulze (eds) *Valuing Environmental Goods: An Assessment of the Contingent Valuation Method*. Totowa, N.J.: Rowman and Allanheld.

Mooney, G. (1977) *The Valuation of Human Life*. New York: Macmillan.

Moser, C. A. and Kalton, G. (1971) *Survey Methods in Social Research*. London: Heinemann.

Mulligan, P. J. (1977) Willingness to pay for decreased risk from nuclear plant accidents. Working Paper No. 3: Energy Extension Programs, Pennsylvania State University.

Mushkin, S. J. and Dunlop, D. W. (eds) (1979) *Health: What is it Worth?* Elmsford, NY: Pergamon Press.

National Institute of Allergy and Infectious Diseases: Transplantation and Immunology Branch (1972) *US Kidney Transplant Fact Book*. Bethesda, MD: National Institutes of Health.

National Radiological Protection Board (1980) *The Application of Cost Benefit Analysis to the Radiological Protection of the Public: A Consultative Document*. Chilton: HMSO.

National Radiological Protection Board (1981) *Living with Radiation*, 2nd edn. Chilton: National Radiological Protection Board.

National Radiological Protection Board (1982) *Cost Benefit Analysis in the Optimisation of Protection of Radiation Workers: A Consultative Document*. Chilton: HMSO.

National Radiological Protection Board (1986) *Cost Benefit Analysis in the Optimisation of Radiological Protection*. ASP9. Chilton: HMSO.

Needleman, L. (1976) Valuing other people's lives. *Manchester School*, 44, 309–42.

Needleman, L. (1980) The valuation of changes in the risk of death by those at risk. *Manchester School*, 48, 229–54.

Needleman, L. (1982) Survival discount rates. Mimeo: University of Waterloo.

Neilson, A. M. (1983) *Methods of Valuing Human Life*. Wellington: National Roads Board.

O'Brien, B. (1986) *What are my Chances Doctor? A Review of Clinical Risks*. London: Office of Health Economics.

OECD (1981) *Methods of Evaluating Road Safety Measures*. Paris: OECD.

Office of the United Nations Disaster Relief Coordinator (UNDRO) (1980) *Natural Disasters and Vulnerability Analysis*. Report of Expert Group Meeting. Geneva: UNDRO.

304 Bibliography and References

Olson, C. (1978) *Trade Unions, Wages, Occupational Injuries and Public Policy*. PhD Dissertation, University of Wisconsin.

Olson, C. (1981) An analysis of wage differentials received by workers on dangerous jobs. *Journal of Human Resources*, 16, 167–85.

Parfit, D. (1984) *Reasons and Persons*. Oxford: Oxford University Press.

Peltzman, S. (1975) The effects of automobile safety regulation. *Journal of Political Economy*, 83, 677–723.

Petty, W. (1699) *Political Arithmetick, or a Discourse Concerning the Extent and Value of Lands, People, Buildings etc*. London: Robert Clavel.

van der Pligt, J., Eiser, J. R. and Spears, R. (1986) Construction of a nuclear power station in one's locality: attitudes and salience. *Basic and Applied Social Psychology*, 7, 1–5.

Pliskin, J. S, Shepard, D. S. and Weinstein, M. C. (1980) Utility functions for life years and health status. *Operations Research*, 28, 206–24.

Pochin, E. (1983) *Nuclear Radiation: Risks and Benefits*. Oxford: Clarendon Press.

Portney, P. R. (1981) Housing prices, health effects and valuing reductions in risk of death. *Journal of Environmental Economics and Management*, 8, 72–8.

Poulton, E. C. (1975) Range effects in experiments on people. *American Journal of Psychology*, 88, 3–32.

Prescott-Clarke, P. (1982) *Public Attitudes Towards Industrial, Work-related and Other Risks*. London: Social and Community Planning Research.

Prescott-Clarke, P. and Mostyn, B. J. (1982) *Public Attitudes Towards the Acceptability of Risks*. London: Social and Community Planning Research.

Raiffa, H. (1969) *Preferences for Multi-attributed Alternatives*. Research Memorandum 5858M. Washington: Department of Transportation.

Rapaport, F. T. (1973) 'Foreword' to Organ transplantation: a human document. *Transplantation Proceedings*, 5, 1025–9.

Rawlins, M. D. (1984) Postmarketing surveillance of adverse reactions to drugs. *British Medical Journal*, 288, 879–80.

Reynolds, D. J. (1956) The cost of road accidents. *Journal of the Royal Statistical Society*, 119, 398–408.

Rice, D. P. and Hodgson, T. A. (1982) The value of human life revisited. *American Journal of Public Health*, 72, 536–8.

Road Research Laboratory (1963) *Research on Road Safety*. London: HMSO.

Rosen, S. (1981) Valuing health risk. *American Economic Review*, 71, 241–5.

Rothman, M. A. (1980) Death risk. *Analog*, 100, 40–53.

Rothschild, N. M. V. (1978) *Risk*. The Richard Dimbleby Lecture, November. London: BBC.

Rowe, R. D., d'Arge, R. C. and Brookshire, D. S. (1980) An experiment on the economic value of visibility. *Journal of Enviornmental Economics and Management*, 8, 1–19.

Royal Society (1983) *Risk Assessment: A Study Group Report*. London: Royal Society.

Russell, J. G. B. (1985) Cost and effectiveness of methods of radiation protection in X-ray diagnosis. *Clinical Radiology*, 36, 37–40.

Samuelson, P. A. (1947) *Foundations of Economic Analysis*. Cambridge, MA: Harvard University Press.

Savage, L. J. (1954) *The Foundations of Statistics*. New York: Wiley.

Schelling, T. C. (1968) The life you save may be your own. In S. B. Chase (ed.) *Problems in Public Expenditure Analysis*. Washington: Brookings, 127–76.

Sen, A. and Williams, B. (1982) *Utilitarianism and Beyond*. Cambridge: Cambridge University Press.

Shepard, D. S. and Zeckhauser, R. (1982) Life-cycle consumption and willingness to pay for increased survival. In M. W. Jones-Lee (ed.) *The Value of Life and Safety: Proceedings of a Conference held by the Geneva Association*. Amsterdam: North Holland, 95–141.

Shepard, D. S., Pliskin, J. S. and Weinstein, M. C. (1975) The non-existence of reduced form utility functions: problems in valuing lotteries on length of life. Mimeo: Center for the Analysis of Health Practices, Harvard School of Public Health, Boston.

Silcock, D. T. (1982) Traffic accidents: procedures adopted in various countries for estimating their costs or valuing their prevention. *Transport Reviews*, 2, 79–106.

Slovic, P., Fischoff, B. and Lichtenstein, S. (1981) Perceived risk: psychological factors and social implications. In F. Warner (ed.) *The Assessment and Perception of Risk*, Proceedings of the Royal Society, 376. London: Royal Society, 17–34.

Smith, R. S. (1973) Compensating wage differentials and hazardous work. Technical Paper No. 5: Office of Policy Evaluation and Research, Department of Labor.

Smith, R. S. (1976) *The Occupational Safety and Health Act: Its Goals and Its Achievements*. Washington: American Enterpise Institute.

Smith, R. S. (1979) Compensating wage differentials and public policy: a review. *Industrial and Labor Relations Review*, 32, 339–52.

Smith, V. K. (1983) The role of site and job characteristics in hedonic wage models. *Journal of Urban Economics*, 13, 296–321.

Smith, V. K. and Desvousges, W. H. (1987) An empirical analysis of the economic value of risk changes. *Journal of Political Economy*, 95, 89–114.

Spore, R. (1972) *Property Value Differentials as a Measure of the Economic Costs of Air Pollution*. PhD Dissertation, Pennsylvania State University.

Starr, C. (1969) Social benefit versus technological risk: what is our society willing to pay for safety? *Science*, 165, 1232–8.

Sugden, R. (1981) *The Political Economy of Public Choice*. Oxford: Martin Robertson.

Sugden, R. (1986) New developments in the theory of choice under uncertainty. *Bulletin of Economic Research*, 38, 1–24.

Sugden, R. and Williams, A. (1978) *The Principles of Practical Cost–Benefit Analysis*. Oxford: Oxford University Press.

Survey Research Center (1972, 1973, 1974) *A Panel Study of Income Dynamics, 1968–1974*. Ann Arbor: University of Michigan, Institute of Social Research.

Sussman, F. G. (1984) A note on the willingness to pay approach to the valuation of longevity. *Journal of Environmental Economics and Management*, 11, 84–9.

Sutcliffe, C. (1987) *The Dangers of Low Level Radiation*. Aldershot: Avebury.

Terleckyj, N. E. (ed.) (1976) *Household Production and Consumption*. New York: National Bureau of Economic Research.

Thaler, R. (1982) Precommitment and the value of life. In M. W. Jones-Lee, (ed.) *The Value of Life and Safety: Proceedings of a Conference held by the Geneva Association*. Amsterdam: North Holland, 171–83.

Thaler, R. and Rosen, S. (1973) The value of saving a life: evidence from the labor market. University of Rochester Graduate School of Management Working Paper No 7401. Also in N. E. Terleckyj (ed.) *Household Production and*

Consumption. New York: National Bureau of Economic Research, 265–301.

Thomas, K. (1981) Comparative risk perception: how the public perceives the risks and benefits of energy systems. In F. Warner (ed.) *The Assessment and Perception of Risk,* Proceedings of the Royal Society, 376. London: Royal Society, 35–50.

Thomas, K., Swaton, E., Fishbein, M. and Otway, M. J. (1980) Nuclear energy: the accuracy of policy makers perceptions of public beliefs. *Behavioural Science,* 25, 332–44.

Tobin, J. (1958) Liquidity preference as behavior towards risk. *Review of Economic Studies,* 25, 65–86.

Troy, P. N. and Butlin, N. G. (1971) *The Cost of Collisions.* Melbourne: F. W. Cheshire.

Tversky, A. and Kahneman, D. (1981) The framing of decisions and the psychology of choice. *Science,* 211, 453–8.

Ulph, A. (1982) The role of ex ante and ex post decisions in the valuation of life. *Journal of Public Economics,* 18, 265–76.

Usher, D. (1973) An imputation to the measure of economic growth for changes in life expectancy. In M. Moss (ed.) *The Measurement of Economic and Social Performance.* Studies in Income and Wealth, 38. New York: National Bureau of Economic Research, 193–232.

Vaupel, J. W. (1976) Early death: an American tragedy. *Law and Contemporary Problems,* 40, 73–121.

Veljanovski, C. (1978) The economics of job safety regulation: theory and evidence: part I – the market and common law. Mimeo: Centre for Socio-Legal Studies, University of Oxford.

Vesey, G. (1978) *Human Values.* Brighton: Harvester Press.

Violette, D. M. and Chestnut, L. G. (1983) *Valuing Reductions in Risk: A Review of the Empirical Estimates.* Report to the Economic Analysis Division, US Environmental Protection Agency. Boulder, CO: Energy and Resource Consultants Inc.

Viscusi, W. K. (1978a) Labor market valuations of life and limb: empirical evidence and policy implications. *Public Policy,* 26, 359–86.

Viscusi, W. K. (1978b) Health effects and earnings premiums for job hazards. *Review of Economics and Statistics,* 60, 408–16.

Viscusi, W. K. (1980) Imperfect job risk information and optimal workmen's compensation benefits. *Journal of Public Economics,* 14, 319–37.

Von Neumann, J. and Morgenstern, O. (1947) *Theory of Games and Economic Behavior.* Princeton: Princeton University Press.

Warner, F. (ed.) (1981) *The Assessment and Perception of Risk,* Proceedings of the Royal Society, 376. London: Royal Society.

Weinstein, M. C., Shepard, D. S. and Pliskin, J. S. (1980) The economic value of changing mortality probabilities: a decision theoretic approach. *Quarterly Journal of Economics,* 94, 373–96.

Weiss, P., Maier, G. and Gerking, S. (1986) The economic evaluation of job safety: a methodological survey and some estimates for Austria. *Empirica-Austrian Economic Papers,* 13, 53–67.

Williams, A. (1979) A note on trying to value a life. *Journal of Public Economics,* 12, 257–8.

Williamson, J. G. (1982) British mortality and the value of life 1781–1931. Mimeo: University of Wisconsin.

Woodruff, M. F. A. (1966) Transplantation: the clinical problem. In G. E. W.

Wolstenholme and M. O'Connor (eds) *Ethics in Medical Progress: With Special Reference to Transplantation*. London: Churchill, 6–23.
Woods, E. A. and Metzger, C. B. (1927) *America's Human Wealth: The Money Value of a Human Life*. New York: Kelly.
Yaari, M. E. (1965) Uncertain lifetime, life insurance and the theory of the consumer. *Review of Economic Studies*, 32, 137–50.
Zeckhauser, R. (1975) Procedures for valuing lives. *Public Policy*, 23, 419–64.
Zeckhauser, R. and Shepard, D. (1976) Where now for saving lives? *Law and Contemporary Problems*, 40, 5–45.

Index

Index by Ann Hall